# Japanese–Soviet/Russian Relations since 1945

# The Nissan Institute/Routledge Japanese Studies Series
## Editorial Board

## Other titles in the series:

# Japanese–Soviet/Russian Relations since 1945

A difficult peace

**Kimie Hara**

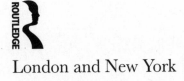

London and New York

First published 1998
by Routledge
11 New Fetter Lane, London EC4P 4EE

Simultaneously published in the USA and Canada
by Routledge
29 West 35th Street, New York, NY 10001

Typeset in Baskerville by RefineCatch Limited, Bungay, Suffolk
Printed and bound in Great Britain by
TJ International Ltd, Padstow, Cornwall

*British Library Cataloguing in Publication Data*
A catalogue record for this book is available from the British Library

*Library of Congress Cataloging in Publication Data*
Hara, Kimie.
    Japanese–Soviet/Russian relations since 1945: a difficult peace/
Kimie Hara.
        p.   cm.–(Nissan Institute/Routledge Japanese studies series)
    Includes bibliographical references and index.
    (alk. paper)
        1. Soviet Union–Foreign relations–Japan.   2. Japan–Foreign
    relations–Soviet Union.   3. Russia (Federation)–Foreign relations–
    Japan.   4. Japan–Foreign relations–Russia (Federation).   5. Soviet
    Union–Foreign relations–1945–1991.   6. Japan–Foreign relations–
    1945–1989.   7. Japan–Foreign relations–1989–
    I. Title. II. Series.
    DK68.7.J3H368   1998
    327.52047′09′045–dc21                          98–34178

ISBN 0–415–19499–7

# Contents

**PART II**
**Efforts for a peace treaty: summit meetings after diplomatic restoration**

# Series editor's preface

As the new century approaches, Japan is going through a turbulent period in which some of her most entrenched political and economic institutions and practices are increasingly being questioned. The financial crisis which began in the latter half of 1997 affected most of the so-called 'tiger economies' of East and Southeast Asia, and did not spare Japan. The collapse of several important Japanese financial institutions signalled both that the system was in crisis but also that the Government was no longer willing or able to rescue ailing institutions. The sense of crisis quickly dulled the lustre of the 'Asian model' in the eyes of the world's media, but it also concentrated minds within Japan on the task of reforming the system. The extent to which the system needed reforming remained a matter of sharp dispute, but a consensus was emerging that many entrenched practices deriving from the immediate post-war period of the 'economic miracle' needed to be radically rethought. As of July 1998, the extent and timescale of the desired revolution remains in doubt. Defeat of his party in the Upper House on 12th July forced the resignation of the Prime Minister, but whether this would accelerate or retard reform remained in doubt. Elements of the old regime seemed to be falling apart, but the shape of the new was still but dimly discernable.

Reading the world's press in the aftermath of the financial crisis, one could well have formed the impression that East Asia (including Japan) was heading for collapse and that the world could safely direct its attention elsewhere, notably to the dynamic and successful market economies of North America and Europe. Such an impression, however, would have been greatly exaggerated. Japan and its surrounding region remained a zone of intense economic production and interaction, resourceful and dynamic. Though there was a financial crisis, the economy remained massive in size and diversity, retaining great economic power both regionally and globally. Radical reform was needed, but historical experience suggested that the capacity of Japan to reform itself – even though it might take some while –

ought not to be underestimated. If the world thought that the East Asian region could safely be ignored, it was likely to be in for a rude shock in a short span of years.

The Nissan Institute/Routledge Japanese Studies series seeks to foster an informed and balanced, but not uncritical, understanding of Japan. One aim of the series is to show the depth and variety of Japanese institutions, practices and ideas. Another is to see, by using comparisons, what lessons, positive or negative, can be drawn for other countries. The tendency in commentary on Japan to resort to outdated, ill-informed or sensational stereotypes still remains, and needs to be combated. This volume explores from a fresh perspective the territorial dispute between Japan and the Soviet Union/Russia.

A British observer at a conference in Hokkaido in the summer of 1990 remarked that if he had been asked five years earlier which would happen first – the reunification of Germany or a solution to the territorial dispute over the 'Northern Territories' between Japan and the Soviet Union – he would have unhesitatingly replied: 'The latter.' Even though the Soviet Union is no more, and despite signs towards the end of the 1990s of somewhat greater flexibility in the handling of this territorial dispute by both sides, it is indeed remarkable that this dispute about several cold, barren and sparsely populated islands off the north-east coast of Hokkaido remains one of the great unsolved territorial disputes inherited from the Second World War. Both in the Soviet and post-Soviet periods, the dispute has greatly inhibited the establishment of normal relations between the two countries.

The author of this book, Kimie Hara, does an excellent job of telling us why this should be the case. She expertly takes the reader through the course of the dispute in its various phases, and has discovered extraordinarily important new documentary evidence about official Japanese positions in the early post-war period. This is an important study which throws new light on one of the most intractable of international disputes.

J.A.A. Stockwin
Oxford, July 1998

# List of figures and maps

## Figures

## Maps

# Acknowledgements

This book, which is based on my Ph.D. thesis submitted to the Australian National University (ANU), could not have come to what it is without the generous support of many individuals and organisations. My deepest gratitude is to Geoffrey Jukes, for his invaluable guidance and support throughout my Ph.D. programme at ANU. I am also deeply indebted to Jim Richardson and Gavan McCormack for their conscientious supervision and constant encouragement throughout the project. Harry Rigby and Tessa Morris-Suzuki also read the manuscript and gave me scrupulous advice and suggestions. I am also thankful to John Welfield of International University of Japan and Shugo Minagawa of Hokkaido University for examining my study carefully and constructively. Special thanks are due to Arthur Stockwin of Oxford University, who also examined the thesis, for his conscientious advice and decision to publish this work as part of the Nissan Institute/Routledge Series.

The study is based on extensive field research conducted in the USA, Russia, UK, Japan and Australia. I am particularly thankful to those current and former Japanese and Russian government officials who provided precious information for this study. In the United States, special thanks are due to Charles Morrison at the East–West Center, Masato Matsui, East Asia Collection of the Hamilton Library at University of Hawaii, and Fumiko Mori Halloran, for their kind assistance, which facilitated my study and research in the United States in many ways. I am also thankful to Yoichi Funabashi, Washington Bureau Chief of *Asahi Shimbun*, for sharing his stimulating insights on the subject from global perspective.

In Russia, at my host institution, the Institute of Oriental Studies, the Russian Academy of Sciences, special thanks to Valery P. Nikolaev and Natasha Skorobogatykh, the Department for South Pacific Studies, for their warm hospitality and assistance to facilitate my research in Moscow. Many individuals of the Russian Academy of Sciences kindly shared their experience and views on the topic. Though it is simply impossible to list all the names here, I would like to thank all of them.

In Japan, I am indebted to Haruki Wada of Tokyo University and Hiroshi Kimura of the International Research Centre for Japanese Studies for valuable guidance and comments on specific aspects of my topic and research findings, also to Teruyuki Hara of the Slavic Research Centre, Hokkaido University, for his help with material access at the Centre. Ichiro Suetsugu of the Suetsugu Jimusho was kind enough to grant me interviews and provided me with materials which otherwise I should not have been able to obtain. I also would like to express my gratitude to officials of several organisations, including the League of Diet Representatives for Japan–Russia Friendship, International Institute for Global Peace, and Japan Centre for International Exchange for their cooperation to my research.

Last, but not to the least, my sincere thanks to my parents for their understanding and encouragement.

Calgary, Canada
January 1998

# Abbreviations

| | |
|---|---|
| APEC | Asia-Pacific Economic Cooperation |
| ASEAN | Association of Southeast Asian Nations |
| ASPAC | Asian and Pacific Council |
| CBM | Confidence Building Measures |
| CFE | Conventional Forces in Europe |
| CIS | Commonwealth of Independent States |
| CNSP | Council on National Security Problems |
| COCOM | Coordinating Committee for Export Controls |
| CPSU | Communist Party of the Soviet Union |
| CSCE | Conference on Security and Cooperation in Europe (now OSCE) |
| EU | European Union |
| *FRUS* | *Foreign Relations of the United States* |
| GNP | Gross National Product |
| G-7 | The major industrialised powers. Canada, France, Germany, Italy, Japan, United Kingdom, USA |
| G-8 | G-7 countries plus Russia |
| ICBM | Intercontinental Ballistic Missile |
| IMEMO | Institute of World Economy and International Relations |
| IMF | International Monetary Fund |
| INF | Intermediate Nuclear Forces |
| ISKAN | Institute of USA and Canada |
| JCP | Japan Communist Party |
| JSP | Japan Socialist Party |
| KGB | Committee of State Security |
| LDP | Liberal Democratic Party |
| MID | Ministry of Foreign Affairs, USSR/Russia |
| MITI | Ministry of Trade and Industry |
| N.A. | National Archives, Washington D.C. |
| NATO | North Atlantic Treaty Organisation |

| | |
|---|---|
| NIE | Newly Industrialising Economy |
| NSC | National Security Council |
| OSCE | Organisation for Security and Cooperation in Europe (former CSCE) |
| PECC | Pacific Economic Cooperation Conference |
| P.R.O. | Public Record Office, Kew, London |
| SDI | Strategic Defence Initiative |
| SLBM | Submarine-Launched Ballistic Missile |
| SNC | Supreme National Council |
| SOP | Standard Operating Procedure |
| SS | Surface-to-Surface (Soviet missile) |
| SSBM | Submarine-Launched Ballistic Missile Submarine |
| START | Strategic Arms Reduction Talks |
| TBS | Tokyo Broadcasting Service |
| UN | United Nations |
| USA | United States of America |
| USSR | Union of Soviet Socialist Republics |

# Introduction

This is a study of post-war Soviet–Japanese and Russo-Japanese relations in terms of foreign-policy decision making. The objective of this book is to examine key decisions associated with the Soviet/Russo-Japanese summit meetings held in Moscow and Tokyo during the post-war era. Having the issues of political *rapprochement* and the territorial problem at the centre of the analysis, the study attempts to delineate the crucial features of post-war relations between the two countries.

Several years have passed since the so-called 'end of the Cold War' began to be proclaimed. The Soviet Union collapsed, the long-term LDP dominance of the post-war Japanese political system ended, and accordingly, after the end of Soviet–Japanese relations, their relations are now called Russo-Japanese once again. Frameworks for their new relations in this period seem to have been formulated in both a domestic and a global sense. However, their relations have not yet broken through the impasse of the 'Cold War' era. To this day, no peace treaty has yet been signed between them. The territorial dispute known as the 'Northern Territories' problem is the major obstacle preventing their signing a peace treaty and improving their cold relations. The 'Northern Territories' problem is the issue which probably best symbolises post-war relations between the two countries. It was closely associated with the political, economic and security factors that drove overall relations between Japan and the USSR during the post-war era, and it remains so in many ways today. This study, therefore, examines the bilateral relations, focusing on the issue of political *rapprochement*, with the biggest impediment being the territorial dispute, and considers the very basic questions 'why has it been so difficult to make peace between the two countries?' and 'how can they fully normalise their relations?'

The study takes a foreign-policy decision-making approach. It examines the policy decision making of and between the two countries during the post-war era, through which changes, patterns or tendencies in elements comprising their bilateral relations are considered. For this purpose, from nearly a half-century of the post-war period, the four occasions of bilateral summits are chosen for close examination. They are: (1) Japanese Prime Minister Ichirō Hatoyama's visit to Moscow in 1956, (2) Japanese Prime Minister Kakuei Tanaka's visit to Moscow in 1973, (3) Soviet President Mikhail Gorbachev's visit to Tokyo in 1991 and (4) Russian President Boris Yeltsin's visit to Tokyo in 1993. The study is conducted not only in the domestic and bilateral framework, but also in the broader context of international relations.

The book is divided into two parts. Part I concerns the genesis of the 'Northern Territories' problem, that, after all, largely determined the nature of the post-war bilateral relations. Chapter 1 delineates the background of the 'Northern Territories'. Beginning with brief explanations of their geography, economy and strategic importance, the disputed islands are reviewed mainly historically until the San Francisco Peace Treaty (1951). Beginning in Chapter 2, foreign-policy decision making is examined in association with the summit visits. The first occasion, leading up to Hatoyama's visit to Moscow, is dealt with in Part I, as it deeply concerned the origin of the 'Northern Territories' problem. The examination of foreign-policy decision making continues in Part II, focusing on the bilateral summits held after restoration of diplomatic relations in 1956, i.e., Tanaka's visit to Moscow in 1973 (Chapter 3), Gorbachev's visit to Tokyo in 1991 (Chapter 4) and Yeltsin's visit to Tokyo in 1993 (Chapter 5). Summarisation and deliberation on the overall study results follow in the Conclusion, which also includes a discussion of recent developments and future prospects.

## Conceptual framework for analysis: four occasions and three levels of analysis

Though this is a case study of foreign-policy decision making, the primary objective of the book is not to establish a new theory, nor to examine various contending theories, but to examine Soviet/Russo-Japanese relations. However, in order for the study to proceed in a systematic manner to allow comparative analysis, it is important first to clarify the conceptual framework. My rationale for focusing on those occasions and framework for the analysis is as follows.

### *Bilateral summits*

(1) Hatoyama's visit to Moscow in 1956, (2) Tanaka's visit to Moscow in 1973, (3) Gorbachev's visit to Tokyo in 1991 and (4) Boris Yeltsin's visit to Tokyo in 1993 – these are the four occasions in focus. These historic visits were potential watershed events for several reasons. For one, in the history

of relations between Japan and the USSR/Russia, these events were the only occasions of this kind, that is, an incumbent national leader's official visit to the counterpart country for a bilateral summit meeting. In this sense, the visits themselves had a significant historical meaning.[1] Especially during the first three summits in the Soviet–Japanese period, in contrast to the generally cold history of post-war relations between Japan and the USSR, relations were comparatively warm. The national leaders' visits and the summit meetings in Moscow and Tokyo can be placed as events highlighting those periods during which expectation for *rapprochement* was also growing. The summit meetings provided a forum for direct discussion at the highest level. Consequently, the potential existed for the two countries to accomplish a breakthrough or settlement in their bilateral relations, namely, towards solving the territorial problem and signing a peace treaty. The first three occasions are especially convenient for my comparative analysis because of their chronological spacing. The summit meetings fall into three time frames of 'early', 'mid' and 'late' periods, dividing post-war Japanese–Soviet relations into three segments. The interval between Hatoyama's visit and Tanaka's is 17 years, and that between Tanaka's visit and Gorbachev's is 18 years. Thus, the three visits are almost evenly spaced over a 35-year period. With the collapse of the Soviet Union, a new period in Russo-Japanese relations began. Compared to the Soviet–Japanese era, the history of the new Russo-Japanese relations is still brief. Though Boris Yeltsin carried out and also cancelled visits to Tokyo a couple of times respectively, special meaning was attached to his October 1993 visit in that it was the first bilateral summit in the history of the new Russo-Japanese relations.

### *Three levels*

If we call foreign-policy decisions dependent variables and factors affecting the decisions independent variables, there are major dependent variables to be clarified first. There are two interrelating dependent variables for the study. These are (1) decisions to seek political *rapprochement* and (2) decisions on the territorial problem; and these key decisions are associated with the national leaders' visits to the counterpart countries. As for *rapprochement*, the visits of the national leaders were something to highlight decisions of and between Japan and the USSR to improve their relations. The summit meetings of each visit also provided the final stage, where foreign policies of both nations were confronted and settled. As for the territorial problem, the official statements released at each visit can be considered as the final decisions on each occasion, though, needless to say, they were not decisions for the final solution of the issue.[2]

My focus here is to examine how those key decisions were made or reached, in terms of factors and process. That is, how the foreign policies of Japan and the USSR/Russia were made on each occasion: what made the USSR and Japan move towards improved relations, realise their summit meetings in their capitals and reach a compromise formula on the territorial issue as described in those official statements?

There are several kinds of independent variable affecting the decisions. We can classify these independent variables into several levels of analysis to allow a systematic approach. In this study, three levels are used as the conceptual framework for the analysis. They are: (1) global international relations, (2) nation state and (3) bilateral interaction.

The reason for employing these three levels here is primarily for 'methodological or conceptual convenience' in relation to this particular topic.[3] Since I am dealing with four different time periods even in the same area of decisions, a simple framework is preferable. If we try to use many levels, the relations between different factors become too intricate to grasp, considering their number. Also, the benefit of using an analytical framework with these three levels will be that the decision-making processes of these four occasions can be compared in a systematic and methodical manner. As the decisions that I deal with in the study are made not only within each nation, but also reached between the two nations, I leave the 'interaction' level, which plays an important role (especially in the form of bilateral negotiations), to be dealt with separately, in addition to the two broad levels of global international relations and nation state.[4]

Figure 1 illustrates the conceptual framework of the analysis, including these three levels that I will use. The rectangle at the bottom indicates Level 1, 'global international relations'. At this level, I examine foreign policy in terms of international or global factors. The international standing of the two nations and their changes are also examined as these affect the foreign policy at each time. I pay special attention to the international relations of the Asia-Pacific region, where both Japan and the USSR/Russia are situated.

The Asia-Pacific region has invited growing interest throughout the postwar years, as it goes through dynamic changes and its importance increases. The region is, however, also a place of complexity and instability. The geographical, ethnic, cultural, religious, historical, political and/or ideological diversity of the region produces complicated alliances and conflicts. Even for the so-called 'Cold War' era, the international system of the region cannot necessarily be explained by a simple concept such as East–West confrontation or bipolarity. Not much attention has been paid to Soviet/ Russo-Japanese relations in this context in the past. It is worth reviewing the relations between the two nations in the context of the regional international relations, as well as global international relations, as they have

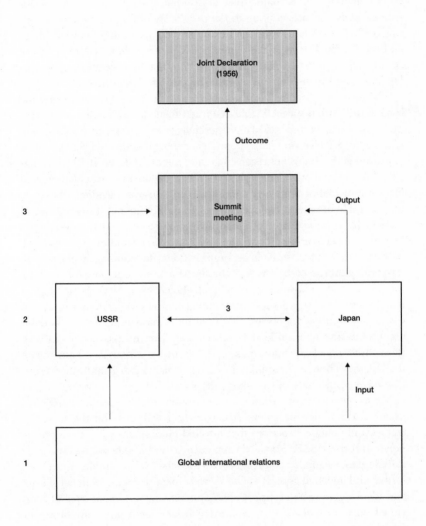

Level 1: Global international relations
Level 2: Nation state
Level 3: Bilateral interaction

*Figure 1* Three levels of analysis

great potential to play major roles in deciding the future direction of this region. Thus, paying attention to the peculiarity of the region and its contrast with Euro-Atlantic region, I examine policies of and between Japan and the USSR/Russia in the context of the international relations of the Asia-Pacific region. In this way, I will attempt to redefine the Soviet–Japanese and Russo-Japanese relations on the Asia-Pacific map.

The next level, Level 2, is illustrated with two boxes. They indicate the level of the 'nation states'. While one traditional view of foreign policy was that national governments act purposefully and respond in a calculating manner to perceive problems, approaches that provided alternative views appeared in the 1960s but received greater attention in the 1970s. Alternative views were thought to explain the place of foreign-policy decisions in the domestic political process. Graham T. Allison was a leading scholar of this kind. He presented two alternatives to the traditional 'Rational Actor' model. In his second, or 'Organisation Process' model, government behaviour is seen less as a matter of deliberate choice and more as a sort of routine output of several large organisations 'functioning according to standard patterns of behaviour'. In the third, or 'Bureaucratic Politics' model, instead of assuming a rational choice by leaders at the top, it hypothesises intensive competition among the players in the government. Consequently, foreign policies are the result of bargaining among bureaucratic units and political leaders.[5] Stretching from his pioneer works with these three models, decision-making theory made various developments in the 1970s. Though examination of particular models and theories is beyond the objectives of this study, the views they present, seeing foreign policy as an output of various domestic political processes, are valid and useful in examining decisions. Accordingly, I will focus on the domestic factors and political processes that affected the foreign-policy decisions of Japan and the USSR/Russia during each period. Domestic factors, their causal relations and/or political process are selectively examined from both formal and informal aspects, such as government structure, political culture and ideology, interest groups, public opinion, role and character of individual decision makers, etc., where I consider them to be important or relevant.

As for foreign-policy decision making in modern Japan, it is widely understood that there are closely tied and mutually dependent relations among three elite groups that play major roles in national policy making. These are the bureaucracy, the ruling party/parties and big business groups. Among many works on Japanese decision making, there are views, for example those of Chalmers Johnson, that emphasise the long-time leadership of the bureaucrats.[6] The dominant view among scholars regarding the power balance in this trilateral relationship is, however, that there was a gradual shift in policy-making initiative from the bureaucrats, who prevailed until around the 1970s, to the ruling party (Liberal Democratic Party). In particular, those LDP expert groups called '*zoku-gün*', specialising in certain fields of policies, are considered to have played an important role in gaining influence. Scholars such as T. Inoguchi, J. Zhao, T.J. Pempel, K. Calder, G. Curtis and many others support such a view, but their arguments are mainly based on their case studies focusing on Japanese foreign economic policies.[7] This LDP-led policy-making style continued until 1993 when the LDP ceased to be the ruling party. However, this view does not seem to fit well to the policy making of Japan towards the USSR, though there is little difference in the broader sense that major influence on policy decisions rested within the trilateral relations.

My study presents an example which suggests such a power balance varies depending on the subject area. A tendency seen in many past studies was that of excessive generalisation. Such balance of power or influence varies depending on the issue areas or counterpart countries. Therefore, in viewing the domestic factors, theoretical generalisations are not attempted by this case study alone. Instead, together with the concrete results observed in each occasion, the peculiarities of the issue area and nature of Japanese policy making towards the USSR/Russia are considered.

There is an extensive literature on Soviet politics, including foreign policy. Prominent works have been written about politics 'behind the curtain' by Western scholars, including A. Dallin, A.B. Ulan, D. Lane, and Z. Brzezinski.[8] In these studies, generalisation or theorisation were attempted, centring the analysis on ideology, history or geographical considerations, for example, on Marxist political philosophy, Great-Russian imperialism, Byzantine traditions, national defence, Eurasian environmental characteristics, the urge towards the sea, and so on. The principal critique of these was that there was little empirical evidence to support their sweeping generalisations. There is no comprehensive study of post-war Soviet/Russian decision making towards Japan; only fragmented studies on particular years and/or specific topics exist.[9] In addition to the low interest directed to the subject itself, this is attributable to problems of availability and accessibility of Russian sources in the past.

However, the situation has changed since the late 1980s. As the *Glasnost* policy began to prevail, it also allowed me to conduct interviews with several key people in Soviet/Russian decision making. Those individuals included current and former senior officials in Russian and Soviet government organisations, such as the Ministry of Foreign Affairs, the Central Committee of CPSU and the KGB. They candidly provided fascinating details at the interviews, conducted from July to August 1994. In addition, most of them allowed me to tape-record the interviews. This would have been unimaginable to any scholar (not only western but also Russian) a decade ago. Though there were still strict restrictions on accessing certain archival documents while I was conducting this research, the Russian government later began to open some of them.[10]

The third level of the analysis is the level of 'bilateral interaction'. At this level, I examine the foreign policies of the two countries from the viewpoint of how they interact with each other and how the interaction is reflected by the resulting decisions. Interaction level is especially important in dealing with bilateral relations. The negotiation channel provides a significant impact on foreign-policy decisions, in particular on those final decisions reached at the summit meetings in this case.

In my study, interactions through direct official channels are the central focus. Informal channels are also dealt with where they are considered important. Attention is paid to such points as bargaining strategies and their effects on interaction, and also to whether any patterns or changes were observed in their ways of interaction over the years.

In Figure 1 (p. 5), the arrow between the two 'nation-boxes' on level 2 denotes interaction in general before the summit meetings. The rectangular box above this is where final interaction takes place, at summit meetings (1956, 1973, 1991 and 1993). Since this is also a part of the issue area of the decisions, or dependent variables (the decisions for *rapprochement*), the rectangle is shaded with vertical stripes. The rectangular box on the top indicates the final product or final outcome of Japanese–Soviet (Russian) negotiations on each occasion. These are promulgated in the forms of official documentation, i.e., the Joint Declaration of 1956 used as an example here, the Joint Communiqué of 1973, the Joint Statement of 1991 and the Tokyo Declaration of 1993. Since this contains their decisions on the key issue area – the territorial problem – for these times (but not a decision for final solution of the issue), it is also shaded with vertical stripes.

### The lost chance

As I indicated earlier (p. 3), there were chances for Japan and the USSR/ Russia to accomplish a breakthrough or settlement in their bilateral relations during the periods leading up to and including those four summit meetings, though the extent of these opportunities varied depending on the period. However, no solution to the territorial issue or signing of a peace treaty took place. And the relations between the two nations are still at an impasse. At the ends of Chapters 2–4 I will consider the reasons why those chances were lost.

## Methodology and related studies (Japan–USSR/ Russia relations)

As my study covers a relatively wide range of areas and time frames, one limitation is the variation in the depth and symmetry of the analysis. The weight of each segment is decided upon the research result, relevance to the theme, originality in related fields and so on. I have made every effort, nevertheless, to present as comprehensive a picture as possible, and to provide systematic perspectives on the bilateral relations. As for the methodology, I have reviewed existing publications and materials and supplemented them with archival documents and interviews. Those specific materials are referenced as they appear in each section.

In the general field of Russo/Soviet–Japanese relations, where numerous works are found in Japanese, Russian and English, several volumes in English are of great value, especially for early and/or mid post-war periods. Among works dealing with the bilateral relations of these periods, volumes by such scholars as John Stephan, Savitri Vishwanathan and Young C. Kim are especially notable.[11] Those works provide analyses of critical dimensions of the bilateral relations from different perspectives. As for works in Japanese and Russian, it used to be held that few comprehensive scholarly volumes on the subject had been published in either language. There is in fact a substantial body of articles and volumes, especially in Japanese, and, those covering the 'Northern Territories' issue are particularly numerous. Most of the Japanese publications till the mid- or late 1980s on the issue were, however, memoir-type, ideologically coloured or journalistic writings. Compared to the number of Japanese publications, fewer works in Russian seem to have been written on the subject during the same period, which is quite understandable considering the then Soviet political position that no territorial issue existed between the USSR and Japan.

Since the late 1980s, when the territorial dispute started receiving wider publicity, not only in Japan and Russia but also in other parts of the world, the number of publications dealing with bilateral relations, especially the territorial issue, has rapidly increased. Among them, those by two scholars in particular deserve special attention. Hiroshi Kimura's contain concise analyses of both Japanese and Soviet policy on the issue (while based on the preposition that the disputed four islands are Japanese) and Haruki Wada's are well documented, dealing with the critical dimensions of the issue from a historical perspective.[12] Also, there is an exhaustive report compiled by Japanese, Russian and US scholars.[13] This is a novel attempt to study and provide policy proposals regarding the issue from global perspective, beyond a mere bilateral framework, incorporating specifically the United States as a major mediator. Vladimir Ivanov also coordinated a similar project.[14] My project was based partially on a similar awareness of the problem to the projects of Ivanov and Kimura *et al.*, but it is not bounded solely by the trilateral framework. My study approaches the issue from a different perspective by focusing on policy decision making, and by applying the same frameworks of such phased analysis to those cases of different time periods, it attempts to delineate the post-war bilateral relations in a systematic but consistent manner. However, it shares the same eventual goal of finding some keys for peaceful settlement of these issues and for improved relations.

My study is mainly based on extensive field research conducted in the USA, Russia, UK, Japan and Australia in 1994. The results of my research have revealed interesting new insights into the nature of the territorial problem, based on newly opened archival materials that I was able to access. I attach special historical significance to the long-sealed booklet from the Japanese Foreign Ministry that I discovered in Canberra, Australia (Chapter 1). The archives in Canberra had never been searched before with regard to this subject. Many of the files were found still sealed in official envelopes even after the passage of 30 years. The Japanese Foreign Ministry has not made available to the public its primary materials on Soviet– Japanese relations.[15] Although remote from the Northern Islands, and from the two countries which still contest them, the documents sealed for half a century and then unearthed in the Canberra archives shed some new light on the genesis of the problem. Important materials were also found or revisited at the National Archives in Washington DC and the Public Record Office in London following the opening of their diplomatic documents in the last few years. Unpublished documents from US State Department files (i.e. excluded from the volumes of the *Foreign Relations of the United States*), together with documents from British Foreign Office files, clarified some of the points left ambiguous in previous research.

For the latter part of the book, dealing with developments after the restoration of diplomatic relations, records of my interviews with retired government officials of both countries will become valuable sources until such time as the related archival materials are opened to researchers.

# Part I

# Genesis of the 'Northern Territories' problem and post-war Japanese–Soviet relations

# 1 The key issue

## Background to the 'Northern Territories' problem

Questions about the sovereignty of these islands were always the major concern in the periods leading up to and during the four summit visits. What are the 'Northern Territories', anyway? Where are they? Why are they a problem? Before going on to study the foreign-policy decision making on these occasions, it may be appropriate to provide some background explanation on the disputed islands.

### GEOGRAPHY, ECONOMICS AND STRATEGIC IMPORTANCE

The 'Northern Territories (*hoppō ryōdo*)', as they are currently referred to by the Japanese government comprise three islands, Etorofu, Kunashiri, Shikotan, and the Habomais, a group of islets and rocks.[1] Beginning only 3.7 km off the tip of Cape Nosappu on Hokkaido, the territories stretch in a northeasterly direction. Their land area totals 4,996 $km^2$, with Kunashiri and Etorofu accounting for about 90 per cent of this. The Russians consider the disputed islands the southernmost islands of the Kuriles, a Russian-held archipelago that stretches for 1,000 km between Hokkaido and the Kamchatka Peninsula. The Japanese government nowadays, however, claims that these islands are distinct from the Kuriles.[2]

Despite their northern location, these islands have a relatively mild climate. The waters around them, at the confluence of warm and cold currents, abound in fish and other marine products, and make up what is considered to be one of the three best fishing grounds in the world. The main industry on the islands is fishing, as it also was under Japanese rule.

As part of the gateway of islands between the Pacific Ocean and the Sea of Okhotsk, the disputed territories have long been strategically important to both nations. Hitokappu Bay on Etorofu, for example, served as the assembly area for the task force of the Imperial Japanese Navy that attacked

Pearl Harbor in 1941. For the Russians, these islands are located so as to allow control of the sea lanes between the Sea of Okhotsk and the Pacific Ocean, and have been authoritatively described as 'vital' to the security of the Russian Far East.[3] However, the degree of their strategic importance has varied with structural changes in the international system, security arrangements and speed of technological development.[4]

Geographically, Russia is Japan's closest neighbour, and their proximity has generated many confrontations over boundaries. Russia has historically appeared as a northern 'threat' to Japan, rather than a friendly neighbour. Beginning in the eighteenth century, there has been a long history of military hostility between the two countries. Their rivalry to extend influence in northeast Asia has led to actual military clashes on several occasions in the twentieth century. However, the historical dispute over the sovereignty of the 'Northern Territories' goes back to an even earlier time.

## HISTORICAL TITLE AND BOUNDARY DEMARCATIONS BETWEEN THE TWO NATIONS

Neither the Russians nor the Japanese are indigenous to these islands. In the seventeenth and eighteenth centuries Japanese and Russians began to reach the islands stretching between Hokkaido and Kamchatka. Long before their advances, the islands were populated by a native people called Ainu. The names of the islands (Kunashiri, Shikotan, Etorofu and Habomai), derived from the Ainu language, leave no doubt that they originally belonged to neither the Japanese nor the Russians, but to the Ainu.

In 1855, a year after Japan ended her history of over 200 years' national isolation by signing the Treaty of Kanagawa with the United States, Imperial Russia and Tokugawa Japan signed the first treaty between the two countries – the Shimoda Treaty of Commerce, Navigation and Delimitation. This set the boundary between Etorofu and Uruppu, and stipulated that the Kurile islands from Uruppu northward belonged to Russia. The treaty also stipulated that the large island of Sakhalin, north of Hokkaido, would have no national boundary, but would remain open to settlement by both nations.

In 1875, by the St Petersburg Treaty for Exchange of Sakhalin for the Kurile Islands, the Meiji government abandoned all of Sakhalin in exchange for the entire Kurile chain. This was the last time the two countries set their national boundaries by peaceful negotiation. In 1904–5 Japan defeated Russia in the Russo-Japanese War, and acquired Southern Sakhalin by the Portsmouth Treaty of 1905. After that, relations between the two countries continued to deteriorate, and there followed several military clashes: the Japanese Intervention in Siberia 1918–22 and occupation of Northern Sakhalin in 1920–5, the Changkufeng Incident of 1938, the Nomonhan Incident of 1939 and the final stage of the Second World War.

## THIRD-PARTY INVOLVEMENT: THE KURILES AS A BARGAINING CHIP

### During the Second World War

In January–February 1945 the leaders of the Allied Powers – Franklin D. Roosevelt, Winston Churchill and Joseph Stalin – met at Yalta in the Crimea and agreed to 'transfer' the Kuriles and 'return' Southern Sakhalin to the Soviet Union, as conditions for Soviet participation in the war against Japan.

US involvement in the 'Northern Territories' problem is well known. Referring to US historical involvement since Yalta, some scholars even hold the USA responsible for creating the 'Northern Territories' problem.[5] As a matter of fact, US involvement in territorial demarcation between Japan and USSR/Russia goes back to earlier years. In its attempt to establish the boundary line in Sakhalin, the Japanese government asked the USA to intercede.[6] In 1905, the United States played the role of mediator of the Portsmouth Treaty following the Russo-Japanese War.

The Yalta agreement, however, was different in nature from other international agreements, in that it was a secret agreement between the USSR and third parties – the USA and UK – without participation by Japan, which was then the legal owner of those territories. The islands were nothing but a bargaining chip for the USA to secure Russian participation in the war in the Pacific. As announced later, the Yalta agreement was reached 'with full knowledge of the American military leaders'.[7] Not being certain at the time that nuclear weapons could be successfully developed, or if they were, that they would produce the desired effect, the United States and Great Britain considered Soviet participation necessary in order to win the war against Japan most rapidly and (in the Anglo-American case) with fewest casualties.

American attempts to have the Russians join the war in the Pacific had started much earlier. Averell Harriman, US Ambassador to the USSR, met Stalin during Churchill's visit to Moscow in August 1942. His major task then was to involve the USSR in the war against Japan.[8] However, Stalin showed no interest at that time. The USSR was fully occupied fighting Nazi Germany, and abiding by its neutrality pact with Japan.[9]

Once victory in Europe became certain, the USSR began to consider a move to the Far East. In February 1945 the conditions for Soviet participation in the war against Japan were decided at the Yalta Conference. Andrei Gromyko, who accompanied Stalin to the Conference, said in his memoirs:

> In the 1905 peace talks after the Russo-Japanese war the USA helped the Japanese to annex considerable Russian territory. But presumably this new US position rehabilitates them in our eyes, as it were, after the support they gave Japan then?[10]

Other war-time international agreements also related to Japanese territories. Prior to the Yalta Conference, a Joint US–UK–Chinese Cairo Declaration was released in 1943. It outlined the principle of 'no territorial expansion', stipulating that Japan would be expelled from all territories it had taken 'by violence and greed'.[11] This principle of no territorial expansion was originally stipulated in the Atlantic Charter, announced in August 1941 by the Anglo-American leaders. The Potsdam Declaration, which Japan accepted at the time of the surrender, stipulated (Article 8):

> the terms of the Cairo Declaration shall be carried out and Japanese sovereignty shall be limited to the islands of Honshu, Hokkaido, Kyushu, Shikoku and such minor islands as we determine.[12]

The US attitude changed after the successful atomic bomb test in July 1945 reduced the perceived need for Soviet participation. H. Truman and J. Byrnes, the new US President and Secretary of State, had already started to perceive Japan in the context of the US–Soviet conflict expected after the war. As Harriman stated in his memoirs, 'Byrnes . . . preferred to end the war without the Russians, if possible'.[13] Also, it was natural that the US, which had borne the brunt of the war against Japan for three and a half years, did not want the Russians to derive large benefits from showing up only at the last moment. With the concurrence of Chiang Kai-shek and Churchill, an ultimatum to Japan was issued on 26 July from the Potsdam Conference. The Russians were not consulted, even though they were pledged to declare war on Japan in less than two weeks.[14] Perceiving the Japanese reaction to the ultimatum as a flat rejection, President Truman ordered the atomic bomb to be dropped as soon after 3 August as weather conditions would permit.[15] Boris N. Slavinsky, a Russian historian, argues that 'his decision was not necessary in a strategic sense, because the American Government knew that the Japanese defeat was at the final phase and the Soviets' plunge into the war against Japan was scheduled for 8th August'.[16]

East–West confrontation over the post-war international order had already started also in Stalin's mind. On 8 August 1945, by declaring war on Japan, the Soviet Union adhered to the Potsdam Declaration. Around this time, i.e., soon after the two atomic bombs were dropped, Stalin confidentially ordered hot pursuit of the USA on atomic bomb development, such as directing the spying apparatus to strengthen its capability for information gathering.[17]

## Occupation of the Kuriles[18]

On 14 August 1945, Japan accepted the Potsdam Declaration and surrendered to the Allies. At this date Southern Sakhalin and the Kuriles had not yet been occupied. Soon after the Japanese surrender, the US government sent a draft of 'General Order No. 1' regarding the occupation of Japan to General Douglas MacArthur, Supreme Commander of the Allied Powers. The Kuriles were not mentioned in this document. Stalin, who received a copy, suggested to Washington on 16 August that, in accordance with the Yalta Conference decision, the whole Kurile chain should be included in the area of Japanese surrender to the Soviet military, and so should the northern half of Hokkaido.[19] Truman agreed on the disposition of the Kuriles, but rejected Soviet occupation of northern Hokkaido, and in his reply requested an American base on one of the Kurile Islands.[20] Furthermore, on 25 August, he wrote to Stalin as follows:

> I was not speaking about any territory of the Soviet Republic. I was speaking of the Kurile Islands, Japanese territory, disposition of which must be made at a Peace settlement. I was advised that my predecessor agreed to support in the peace settlement the Soviet acquisition of those Islands.[21]

There followed an exchange of arguments between the two leaders over the issue of a base in the Kuriles. In his letter dated 30 August Stalin agreed that US military and commercial aircraft could land at Soviet airports in case of emergency during the occupation of Japan, but at the same time requested landing rights for Soviet commercial aircraft at US airports in the Aleutian Islands.[22] The United States thereupon dropped the landing rights issue.

In the meantime, Soviet commanders were 'energetically' undertaking their strategic plan of occupying the 'Northern Territories' of Japan, without knowing Washington's intentions over the Kuriles and Hokkaido.[23]

On the very same day that Stalin wrote to Truman regarding the disposition of the Kuriles and the northern half of Hokkaido (16 August), the Chief of General Staff of the Red Army, General Antonov, gave the following explanation, in response to enquiries about the surrender of Japan,

> 1. The statement of Japan's surrender made by the Japanese Emperor on August 14 is only a general declaration about unconditional surrender. The order to cease military actions still has not been given to the armed forces and Japanese armed forces continue their resistance. Consequently, there still has not been an actual surrender by the armed forces of Japan. . . .
>
> 3. In light of the aforementioned, the armed forces of the Soviet Union in the Far East will continue their offensive operations against Japan.[24]

The Soviets began attacking Japanese positions in Sakhalin on 18 August, and the occupation of the Kuriles started on 23 August on Shumshu island.

A memorandum by the Joint Chiefs of Staff for the State-War-Navy Coordinating Committee displays a contradictory agreement made on 14 August, before the Soviet occupation of the Kuriles began. It states

> On the matter of the Kuriles, the United States and Russian Chiefs of Staff have agreed to a boundary line between areas of operations which passes through Onekotan Strait. On the basis of the situation as it appears at present, the Joint Chiefs of Staff propose to instruct Admiral Nimitz to plan on receiving the surrender of the Kurile Islands south of this line. They propose at an appropriate time to inform the Russians of this procedure and that unless the Russians request assistance, the Joint Chiefs of Staff expect the Soviets to receive the surrender and disarm the Japanese in the islands of Paramushir and Shumshu.[25]

This meant that the Soviet side had agreed to give up the major part of the Kuriles, i.e., from Onekotan southward. Considering that Stalin on 16 August expressed intent to secure the whole Kuriles chain with Soviet forces, and that Truman agreed to this, it can only be assumed that the Joint Chiefs of Staff neither consulted nor informed the leaders of either nation of this agreement. It is rather comical to imagine the fear and embarrassment of the Soviet Chief of General Staff when he learned from Stalin about his agreement with Truman regarding the disposal of the Kuriles.

On 2 September 1945 Japanese Foreign Minister Mamoru Shigemitsu signed the Instrument of Surrender in Tokyo Bay. By then, the Soviet military had occupied all the Kurile chain down to Shikotan Island. According to Slavinsky's study, however, the Soviet commander decided to occupy the Habomai islands only at this point. On 2 September the Commander of the North Pacific Flotilla issued the order, and the next day Soviet troops began landing on the Habomais, all of which were occupied by 5 September.[26] If Slavinsky is right, occupation of the Habomais took place after the official surrender of Japan.

The Japanese, however, seem to feel that 15 August is the date of the surrender, for that is the day they heard on the radio the voice of the Emperor, then believed to be a living god, and learned of Japan's defeat.[27] In addition, the Japanese at that time did not know about the secret Yalta Agreement nor the later US–USSR exchanges over disposition of the Kuriles. Therefore, there remain strong feelings of distrust against the Russians, who are seen as taking the Kuriles like looters, or '*kajiba-dorobō*', from a fatally wounded Japan.

## Post-war dealing over the Pacific

Both US and Soviet interest in the Kurile Islands at the time can be inferred from the dispute over a US base on the islands. This dispute, however, further aggravated US–USSR relations, which were already deteriorating. After the Japanese surrender, acting US Secretary of State Dean Acheson offended the Russians by saying that they could occupy but not annex the Kuriles. A Moscow Radio broadcast criticised this statement.[28]

As the above indicates, the USA was not in favour of Russian acquisition of the Kuriles during the last days of the Second World War. After the Japanese surrender, however, the United States gained a new sphere of influence in the Pacific – Micronesia – by tactically negotiating its position on the Kuriles.[29] The memoirs of James Byrnes give a lively account of how the USA acquired trusteeship of these formerly Japanese-mandated Pacific islands by behind-the-scenes negotiations with his Soviet counterpart, Molotov, at the United Nations. The US claimed that as the country in possession of the mandated islands, it was the only state 'directly concerned' with regard to the trusteeship. The Soviet Union was not necessarily against the US proposal, but Molotov asked Byrnes to agree that the five permanent members of the Security Council should be regarded as 'states directly concerned' in all cases. In response, Byrnes linked the issue with the disposition of the Kuriles. He said:

> I then added that I would bear his position in mind when considering the ultimate disposition of the Kurile Islands and the southern half of Sakhalin.

Molotov replied:

The Soviet Union . . . did not contemplate a trusteeship arrangement for the Kuriles or Sakhalin; these matters had been settled at Yalta.

Byrnes pointed out to Molotov that

Mr. Roosevelt had said repeatedly at Yalta that territory could be ceded only at the peace conference and he had agreed only to support the Soviet Union at the conference. While it could be assumed that we would stand by Mr. Roosevelt's promise, we certainly want to know, by the time of the peace conference, what the Soviet Union's attitude would be toward our proposal for placing the Japanese-mandated islands under our trusteeship.

The US trusteeship agreement was voted upon later by the Security Council. The Soviet Union did not use its veto, and the issue was resolved smoothly in accordance with US intentions. Byrnes said in his memoirs,

I was delighted, but not surprised, that the Soviet representative voted in favour of our proposal.[30]

## The Cold War and San Francisco Peace Treaty: towards 'unresolved' problems

The San Francisco Treaty was very much a 'product of the era'.[31] In August 1949 Soviet success in a nuclear weapons test demolished the US monopoly of nuclear weapons, only four years after Hiroshima. US–USSR military competition thereafter became one of the biggest factors in aggravating the Cold War. In October 1949 Communist China was established. In June 1950 the Korean War broke out. At the same time, the United States intervened in the Chinese civil war, deployed the 7th Fleet off China's coast to protect Taiwan and openly supported the nationalist government there. The San Francisco Treaty was prepared in a period when East–West confrontation was intensifying and turning towards actual 'Hot War' in Asia.

Diplomatic discussions among the members of the Far Eastern Commission were initiated in the autumn of 1950 under US leadership and continued under review. The text of the final draft was released as an American–British draft on 12 July 1951.[32] According to Gromyko, who was then heading the Soviet delegation, an active part in preparing the Treaty had been taken, 'by Dean Acheson and John Foster Dulles'.[33] Naturally, the content of the treaty fully reflected US strategic interests.

The Western Allies were not necessarily in accord over all issues before

the Peace Conference: while the USA, Australia and New Zealand supported Chiang Kai-shek's government on Taiwan, Great Britain in June
1950 and India in December 1949 had already recognised the People's
Republic of China. The USA wanted to form a united front over recognition of the new China, prior to the Peace Conference. However, Great
Britain chose to go its own way. It was retreating from its sphere of influence
in the Asia-Pacific region, but still had strong economic interests in China
and, at the same time, was concerned for its colonial territories in
Hong Kong and Malaya. As a result, neither Communist nor Nationalist
China was invited to the Conference. Commonwealth countries, including
the UK, had misgivings about US loosening of economic control over Japan.
US affinity with former Japanese conservatives especially outraged
Australia, which had actually suffered from Japanese bombing during the
war.

Except for India, which pursued its own path of neutrality, in the circumstances of the Cold War each nation refrained from carrying discord too far.
The fear of an expanding new communist movement in Asia rapidly
eroded fear of Japanese militarism. The greatest interest of those countries
was in security issues in the region, and none wished to risk its security
arrangement with the USA over the Japanese issue. Noticeably, the USA
signed a mutual defence treaty with the Philippines and a tripartite security
treaty with Australia and New Zealand on 1 September 1951, immediately
before concluding the Peace Treaty on 7 September, and on 8 September
signed a security treaty with Japan.

To Soviet eyes, the American-British draft was 'not a treaty of peace but
a treaty for preparation of a new war in the Far East'.[34] Nevertheless, the
Soviets unexpectedly attended the conference, where their delegate
(Gromyko) unsuccessfully demanded the seating of Communist China and
consideration of several Soviet amendments.[35] The conference was, after
all, nothing but a signing ceremony among the countries chosen and invited
by the USA as the host government. The choice of the USSR, which could
not agree with the content of the Treaty, was therefore not to sign it.

As for the 'Northern Territories' problem, the following expression was
inserted in Section (c) of Article 2 in Chapter II 'Territory'.

> Japan renounces all right, title and claim to the Kurile Islands, and to
> that portion of Sakhalin and the islands adjacent to it over which Japan
> acquired sovereignty as a consequence of the Treaty of Portsmouth of
> September 5, 1905.[36]

The article did not specify to which country those territories were
renounced. Similarly, sections (b) and (f) of the article stated

(b) Japan renounces all right, title and claim to Formosa and the Pescadores.

(f) Japan renounces all right, title and claim to the Spratly Islands and to the Paracel Islands.[37]

In addition, Chapter VII Article 25 of the Treaty stated, that it 'shall not confer any rights, titles or benefit' on any country which 'has not signed and ratified' it. The Soviet Union did not sign, and China was not invited. This means that they did not acquire any right to Taiwan, the Pescadores, the Spratlys, the Paracels, Kuriles or Southern Sakhalin by virtue of Japanese renunciation of these territories. The Treaty did not define the Kuriles that Japan renounced, and this left room for argument later.

However, an earlier draft of the Treaty, as late as the Joint United States – United Kingdom Draft Peace Treaty of 3 May 1951, shows that the USSR was specified as the country to which Japan was to return the southern part of Sakhalin and the islands adjacent to it, and to hand over the Kurile Islands, although there was also a condition that the treaty 'shall not confer any rights, titles or benefits' upon a country which 'has not signed and ratified' it.[38] In addition, at a press conference on 28 February, Dulles said that he had made it plain to the Japanese that the United States would not encourage any revision of the Yalta decision in order to return the Kuriles to Japan.[39]

Therefore, the US intention, as late as May was that any peace treaty validation of the Soviet Union's title to South Sakhalin and the Kurile Islands would depend on its becoming a party to the Treaty. In other words, the US had at least shown its intention to keep the promise made at Yalta. However, in the revised US-UK draft of the treaty on 14 June the name of the country (USSR) to which Japan was to renounce the Kuriles and southern Sakhalin had disappeared.[40] The June draft left room, as a formality, for the USSR to participate, but stood on the premise of Soviet absence by shelving the territorial question.

Conditions were added for future contingencies. Article 26 says:

> Japan will be prepared to conclude with any State which signed or adhered to the United Nations Declaration of January 1, 1942, and which is at war with Japan, or with any State which previously formed a part of the territory of a State named in Article 23, which is not a signatory of the present Treaty, a bilateral Treaty of Peace on the same or substantially the same terms as are provided for in the present Treaty, but this obligation on the part of Japan will expire three years after the first coming into force of the present Treaty.[41]

The same article further continues:

> Should Japan make a peace settlement or war claims settlement with any State granting that State greater advantages than those provided by the present Treaty, those same advantages shall be extended to the parties to the present Treaty.[42]

The first provision of Article 26 left room for subsequent differences of interpretation. The latter provision was eventually used by Dulles himself, when the US pressured Japan during the Japan/USSR peace negotiations in 1955–1956.[43] It is not certain whether the intentions of Great Britain and other signatories of the Treaty were similar to those of the USA. However, by signing the Treaty, they supported the US attitude and, in a sense, became parts of the 'nations concerned' with the 'Northern Territories' problems.

After all, the Kuriles had been treated as nothing more than a political tool by third parties, especially the United States. Towards the end of the war these islands were used for a deal to bring the Russians into the war in the Far East, without informing Japan, then their owner. After the war the Kuriles were taken from Japanese hands with their consent,[44] but shelved without the consent of the owner-to-be, the Soviet Union. As a result, no peace treaty was concluded between Japan and the USSR. Before a 'post-war' start to relations between Japan and the USSR, the 'Cold War' had begun between the USA and USSR. Since Japan was under predominantly American occupation, the 'Cold War' wave did not pass it by. The 'Northern Territories' problem was destined to remain unresolved as a by-product of the Cold War.

The United States' attitude became even more rigid toward the USSR after signing the Treaty. On 30 March 1952, when the United States Senate ratified the Treaty it resolved to advise and consent to its ratification. As part of such advice and consent the Senate stated:

> that nothing the Treaty contains is deemed to diminish or prejudice in favour of the Soviet Union the right title and interest of Japan or the Allied Powers as defined in said Treaty in and to South Sakhalin and its adjacent islands, the Kurile Islands, the Habomai Islands, the Island of Shikotan or any other territory rights or interests possessed by Japan on December 7, 1941, or to confer any right or benefit therein or thereto on the Soviet Union, and also that nothing in the said Treaty or the advice and consent of the Senate to the ratification thereof implies recognition on the part of the United States of the provisions in favour of the Soviet Union contained in the so called Yalta Agreement regarding Japan of February 11, 1945.[45]

## EARLY CLAIMS FOR RETURN OF THE 'NORTHERN TERRITORIES'

### 1946 *Gaimushō* pamphlet unearthed in Australia[46]

In the files of the Department of External Affairs of Australia at the Australian Archives in Canberra may be found two copies of a pamphlet whose cover is shown in Figure 2. Until 1994 the file was contained in an officially sealed and unopened envelope, and one pamphlet is stamped 'secret' in Japanese. As is obvious from the cover, the pamphlet was issued by the Foreign Office of the Japanese government in November 1946.

Shortly after the war, the *Gaimushō* (now 'Japanese Foreign Ministry') had begun preparing its position for the peace settlement. In November 1945 it established a Peace Problems Research Board (*heiwa mondai kenkyū kanjikai*), consisting mainly of members of the Treaty Bureau (*jōyaku-kyoku*) and Political Affairs Bureau (*seimu-kyoku*) of the Ministry. The materials it prepared were kept among a series of Foreign Ministry documents entitled 'Relevant to Preparatory Research Concerning the Japan Peace Treaty' (*tainichi heiwa jōyaku kankei junbi kenkyū kankei*). Most of the materials prepared by this Board have no contemporary relevance, and are available for public scrutiny. However, all 'Northern Territory'-related materials were at some stage removed from the file, and have never been open to the public or researchers.[47] According to the memoirs of Nishimura Kumao, who was head of the Treaty Bureau and actually participated in preparation of the documents, three reports existed regarding the 'Northern Territories': 'Chishima (Kuriles), Habomai, Shikotan' of November 1946; 'Karafuto (Sakhalin)' of January 1949; and 'Minami Chishima (South Kuriles), Habomai, Shikotan' of April 1949.[48] The material found in the Australian Archives seems to be the English version of the first of these reports.

According to an Australian Department of External Affairs memorandum contained in the same file, these pamphlets were handed to the Australian Mission in Tokyo around May 1947 by a person known as Asakai.[49] Considering that the Canberra Conference was due to be held in August of the same year (1947) to discuss matters relating to the peace treaty with Japan, it seems probable that the *Gaimushō* had distributed this document among the nations concerned in order to present Japanese claims. If this is so, it would mark the very first Japanese attempt to obtain international support on the 'Northern Territories' problem. One may imagine the desperate effort that Japan was then making for recovery of its former territories.

# MINOR ISLANDS
# ADJACENT TO
# JAPAN PROPER

—— ★ ——

DEPARTMENT OF
EXTERNAL AFFAIRS

## PART I. THE KURILE ISLANDS,
## THE HABOMAIS
## AND SHIKOTAN

FOREIGN OFFICE
## JAPANESE GOVERNMENT
NOVEMBER 1946.

*Figure 2  Gaimushō* pamphlet, 1946

The 1946 pamphlet consists of maps (see Maps 1 and 2), two chapters of text, and illustrations. It was designed to provide various grounds to show that the islands were Japanese territory. The Yalta Agreement was not mentioned. This pamphlet, issued not long after the end of the Second World War, contains some elements which contradict the current 'Four Islands' claim of Japan, and it is understandable that the Ministry of Foreign Affairs should have chosen not to open it to researchers or the public under the Thirty Year Rule.

In order to justify its demand for their return, the Japanese government currently takes the view that these four islands are 'distinct' from the Kuriles.[50] Many pamphlets and statements have been issued in support of this claim. Here, the pamphlet issued in 1996 is used for comparison (see Maps 3 and 4), as it is the most recent version to this date (as of January 1998).

In the 1946 pamphlet, Map 1 indicates that the 'Kurile Islands' include all the islands between Hokkaido and Kamchatka, including Kunashiri and Etorofu (Yetorofu), although (probably) not Shikotan and the Habomais, which are framed and enlarged below in such a way as to indicate that they are the focus of this pamphlet. In the second map of the 1946 pamphlet (Map 2), the Kurile Islands are divided into the Southern Kuriles of Kunashiri and Etorofu, and the Northern Kuriles, i.e., the islands north of Uruppu. In this map, Shikotan and the Habomais are shaded in the same way as the Japanese territory of Hokkaido, but differently from the Kuriles proper, and different historical backgrounds are provided for them. It seems clear from these maps that the real Japanese goal of territorial recovery was then confined not to the four islands, but to the two territories of Shikotan and the Habomais.

Recent pamphlets show on their cover the islands at the focus of the present dispute – Etorofu, Kunashiri, Shikotan and Habomais – in frame (Map 3). However, in these pamphlets, the four islands of the 'Northern Territories' are distant from the Kuriles. Their maps indicate the Kurile Islands as the islands from Uruppu northwards, and do not include those from Etorofu southwards (Map 4). In the text the Kurile Islands are defined as 'the eighteen islands north of Uruppu' and Uruppu Island is 'the southernmost point of the Kurile Islands'.[51]

Chapter 1 of the 1946 pamphlet is entitled 'The Kurile Islands [Chishima]', and the 'Kuriles' here include both the Southern Kuriles (Etorofu and Kunashiri) and the Northern Kuriles (all the islands north of Etorofu). The pamphlet argues:

THE KURILE ISLANDS

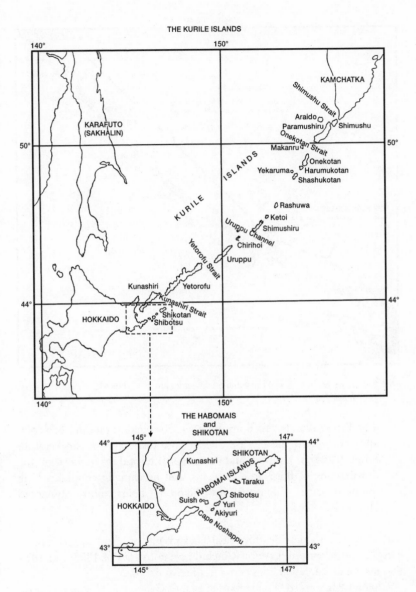

*Map 1* The Kurile Islands as illustrated in *Minor Islands Adjacent to Japan Proper*, 1946

A HISTORICAL MAP

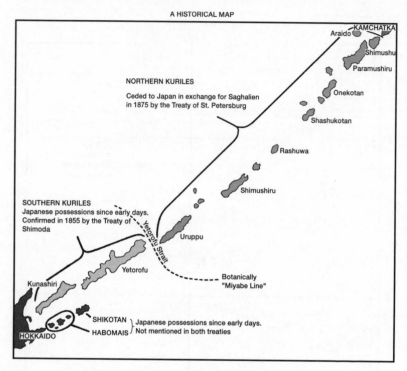

*Map 2* Historical divisions of the Kurile Islands as illustrated in *Minor Islands Adjacent to Japan Proper*, 1946

The Kurile islands which are homogeneous geotectonically, geologically and topographically are divided into two zones by the Yetorofu Strait between Uruppu and Yetorofu [Etorofu] in respect of the distributions of flora and fauna as well as climatic conditions, the southern zone (Kunashiri and Yetorofu) being more similar to Hokkaido.[52]

The chapter also provides historical background on the Kuriles from as early as the seventeenth century, including the treaties of 1855 and 1875 that set the demarcation lines between the two nations.

Chapter 2 is entitled 'The Habomai Islands Group and Shikotan Island'. By using historical materials, encyclopaedias from different countries including Russia, American sailing directories, etc., it emphasises that these islands are distinct from the Kuriles, and that they were 'topographically and geographically a part of Hokkaido', and historically 'Japanese possessions since early days'. Therefore, they were 'not mentioned in both treaties'

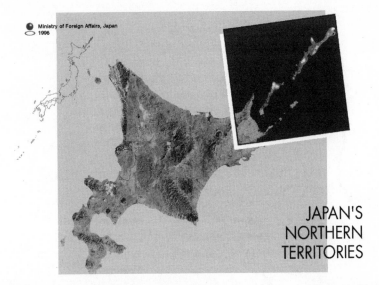

Ministry of Foreign Affairs, Japan
1996

JAPAN'S
NORTHERN
TERRITORIES

*Map 3* The 'Northern Territories' as illustrated on the cover of *Japan's Northern Territories*, 1996. © RESTEC

of 1855 and 1875. Despite this claim, however, the pamphlet also has to recognise some inconvenient facts, as in the following passage:

> In some cases the group of Habomais and Shikotan are included in the Kurile Islands (Note 1). But geologists agree that the two groups are to be distinguished geotectonically (Note 2)[53]
>     . . . More recently the North Kuriles have been administratively subdivided into two, Onekotan and the islands to the south being called the Middle Kuriles. The South Kurile group comprises Kunashiri, Yetorofu and Shikotan, but the Habomais are not included among the islands of the Kuriles.[54]

The last part of the pamphlet introduces maps of the islands at issue (Kuriles, the Habomais and Shikotan) drawn during the seventeenth and eighteenth centuries.

The 1946 pamphlet not only contradicts current Japanese arguments concerning Kunashiri and Etorofu, but also leaves some room for doubt in relation to the Habomais and Shikotan. However, it does not necessarily follow simply from this that the Japanese territorial claim is wrong. The current Japanese claim is not necessarily based on the single proposition that these four territories are distinct from the Kuriles. Though it seems

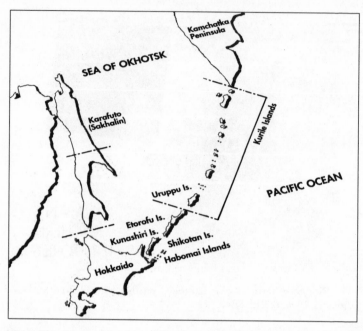

*Map 4* The Kurile Islands as illustrated in *Japan's Northern Territories*, 1996. ©
RESTEC

clear that in 1946 the Japanese goal was only the Habomais and Shikotan, it
should also be noted that Japan had already prepared bases for its current
arguments. The pamphlet does refer to all the islands as 'Kuriles' but it
already separates the Northern and the Southern groups, the latter belonging to Japan since 'early days', or 'geologically' and 'topographically' distinct from the former. In other words, Japan had then divided the territories
that it stood to lose (and it did not want to lose any of them) into three
groups according to the strength of its claims. It was trying to present the
Habomais and Shikotan as an integral part of Hokkaido, Kunashiri and
Etorofu as Japanese territory from time immemorial although part of the
Kurile chain, and the rest of the Kuriles as Japanese territory confirmed in
1875. Therefore, in order to understand the evolution of the Japanese
claims, it is important to comprehend the difference between the circumstances under which the 1946 pamphlet was prepared, and those prevailing
when the present claim was launched.

## Background to the 1946 pamphlet

Japan accepted the Potsdam Declaration and surrendered to the Allied Powers on 14 August 1945, but the terms of the Yalta Agreement were not revealed until 29 January 1946. Once it was disclosed that the Kuriles had been promised to the Russians, it became a critical matter for Japan as to whether or not the Habomais and Shikotan were part of the Kuriles. The 1946 pamphlet was a product of the *Gaimushō's* desperate efforts to maximise Japan's national interest: to regain former Japanese territories as far as possible, in the context of the time, i.e., with Japan a defeated country and the Soviet Union one of the victorious Allies.

The Canberra Conference of British Commonwealth countries was held in August 1947, and was convened to discuss a peace treaty with Japan. Before signing a peace treaty that would determine the final disposition of territories as a result of the war, Japan had to appeal to the nations concerned. It may be assumed, therefore, that the pamphlet was given to the host country, Australia, with the impending conference in mind. To Japanese eyes the rising tension of the Cold War probably looked promising in the sense that it seemed to open the possibility of exploiting differences among the victorious Allies. An Australian diplomat, W. Macmahon Ball, who represented the Commonwealth countries on the Allied Council for Japan, noted, 'In 1945 Japan was a hated and still-dangerous enemy. In 1947 it was the general belief that there was only one enemy, the Soviet Union.'[55] The *Gaimushō* probably distributed the pamphlet to the other nations concerned, including Great Britain and the United States as a matter of course. However, the pamphlet has not been found yet in the archives of these countries. This is a curious, even mysterious, matter which remains to be cleared up by future investigation.

The focus of the territorial dispute for about a decade after the Second World War was the 'Habomais' only, or the 'Habomais and Shikotan'. The first authoritative indication of US support for the Japanese claim to them came at a press conference on 28 February 1951, when John Foster Dulles, chief US negotiator for the Japanese Peace Treaty, criticised the Soviet action in occupying them under the pretext that they were part of the Kuriles awarded to Russia at the Yalta Conference.[56] In view of this US attitude, on 8 March 1951 Prime Minister Yoshida disclosed to the Upper House Budget Committee his request to the Allies for return of the Habomais. He declared that the Japanese government understood that the Habomai Islands were to be returned to Japan, since they did not belong to the so-called Kuriles group. Previous claims had been made by political leaders and minor authorities, but this was the first time that the Japanese government came out openly to request return of the Habomais.[57] Furthermore, once American support for the Japanese claim to the Habomais was announced, even a new interpretation of Shikotan as part of the Habomais appeared in Japan. The Parliamentary Vice-Minister for Foreign Affairs told the House of Representatives Foreign Affairs Committee on 7 March that the Japanese government held the view that Shikotan was included within the Habomai group.[58] At the San Francisco Conference, the Yoshida government had asked the US to take the position that Shikotan and the Habomais were not part of the Kuriles, and during the same conference Dulles reaffirmed the above view that the Habomais were not included in the Kuriles. However, Yoshida did not make a similar request in respect of Etorofu and Kunashiri.[59]

Other allies were cool towards Japan's claims in this 'Habomai-Shikotan' dispute. For example, when Dulles admitted that the Japanese had a legitimate claim at least to the Habomais, Australia expressed misgivings 'on account of the opportunity that was being left for contravention of original allied aims'.[60] Also, while admitting 'it may well be that the Japanese claim that the Habomai Islands are not part of the Kuriles is justified', it was argued that 'this point should have been made by the Allies when the Soviet Union first occupied the islands'.[61]

Various views were expressed regarding whether Habomai and Shikotan were to become Soviet territory or not, especially before and after the San Francisco Conference. However, Kunashiri and Etorofu were hardly mentioned either internationally or domestically. Only later did the argument appear that not only the Habomais and Shikotan but also Kunashiri and Etorofu were excluded from the expression 'the Kurile Islands', which Japan renounced in the San Francisco Treaty.[62]

Diverse arguments have been expressed over the years regarding the extent of the 'Kuriles', or 'Kuriles which Japan renounced at the San Francisco Treaty'. Many of them are found in Japanese literature dealing with the issue from various standpoints, such as international law, linguistics, history, geography and, of course, politics.[63] What is important is the southern end of the Kuriles, i.e., where the national border lies. It has been assumed that there are so many arguments on the question because there was no single consistent view on the definition of the term 'Kuriles'. This may be true, but the more important fact is that those arguments appeared as counter-arguments, one after another, after the Japanese government started to argue that the islands of Kunashiri and Etorofu, together with Shikotan and the Habomais, are 'distinct' from the Kuriles in order to justify its claim. The 1946 booklet, found in October 1994 in Australia during my Ph.D. research, now reveals material that undermines Japan's present position that the 'Northern Territories' are 'distinct' from the

Kuriles. Since it was issued by the *Gaimushō* itself, there may be no more room for argument on this question.

The 1946 pamphlet and pamphlets representing the current claim (of which the 1996 one has been chosen here as representative) reflect the changes in Soviet–Japanese relations over the years. The 1946 pamphlet reflects relations between the victorious Soviet Union and defeated Japan, soon after the war. The pamphlet also reveals initial Japanese thinking, and this thinking seemed to be that while Japan could not challenge the Kurile cession that the Allies had already agreed to impose on Japan, it could make a good case that the Habomais and Shikotan were not part of the Kuriles and therefore had been illegally occupied. The more recent pamphlets reflect Soviet–Japanese relations of the Cold War period, in which the Soviet Union confronted the USA, and Japan was included almost subordinately in the western military bloc. Japan then began to strengthen the case for separate treatment of Etorofu and Kunashiri, towards which it had already prepared the way in the earlier pamphlet. Because of Japan's having agreed to cede the 'Kuriles' in the 1951 San Francisco Peace Treaty, however, it had to argue that these islands were not part of them. The details of in what contexts the current four islands claim was fixed will be dealt with in the next chapter.

## The 'Northern Territories' problem is not in origin a bilateral dispute

The 'Northern Territories' problem is like an invisible wall built in the aftermath of the Second World War, and still standing, even though the 'end of the Cold War' is pronounced and the Soviet Union no longer exists. This issue was to a great extent created by third parties. It should be noted that there had been no such dispute before the war. Though the demarcation line had been changed in 1855, 1875 and 1905, this had been by mutual consent between the two nations concerned. At Yalta, however, the Kurile Islands were used as a bargaining chip by the USA and UK to bring the Russians into the war in the Far East. Japan, then the legal owner of the islands, did not even know that the agreement existed. At San Francisco, under new international conditions which came to be known as the 'Cold War', the Kuriles were again sacrificed in the power game over construction of the post-war international order. The Peace Treaty neither defines the extent of the Kuriles, nor specifies to which country Japan renounced them. The Soviet Union did not sign the Treaty, which in any case fully reflected the strategic interests of its Cold War opponent, the United States. The territorial problem was shelved at this point. Not until 1955, a decade after the war ended, were peace negotiations finally opened between Japan and the Soviet Union.

# 2   Hatoyama's visit to Moscow, 1956[1]

9. The Union of Soviet Socialist Republics and Japan agree to continue after the restoration of normal diplomatic relations between the Union of Soviet Socialist Republics and Japan, negotiations for the conclusion of a Peace Treaty.

In this connection, the Union of Soviet Socialist Republics, desiring to meet the wishes of Japan and taking into consideration of the interests of the Japanese State, agrees to transfer to Japan the Habomai Islands and the island of Shikotan, the actual transfer of these islands to Japan to take place after the conclusion of a Peace Treaty between the Union of Soviet Socialist Republics and Japan.[2]

## Restoration of diplomatic relations and 'Shikotan and the Habomais'

Prime Minister Ichirō Hatoyama paid a historic visit to Moscow from 12 to 19 October 1956, the first official visit by an incumbent Japanese premier to the Kremlin throughout the history of the bilateral Russo-Japanese and Soviet–Japanese relations. During this visit, diplomatic relations between Japan and the USSR were restored. The two countries ended the state of war, eleven years after the Second World War. However, a peace treaty was not signed. As for the territorial question, the Joint Declaration at the end of the visit contained a Russian promise to transfer the Habomai and Shikotan islands to Japan. The negotiation reached the compromise formula quickly during Hatoyama's visit. However, there was a long period of turmoil prior to this historic event. Direct contacts over peace negotiations between the two nations began in January 1955, when a letter, later to be known as the 'Domnitsky Letter', was handed to Hatoyama. It was 21 months after this first contact that Hatoyama's visit to Moscow took place and diplomatic relations were restored.

In this chapter I examine Japanese and Soviet decisions made before and during the summit visit. The chapter is structured around the three levels of analysis indicated in the Introduction (pp. 3–8). In each section the first subject covered is the improved relations between Japan and the USSR in association with Hatoyama's visit to Moscow. There had been no official contact between Japan and the Soviet Union during the first decade after the Second World War, so the relations of that period are sometimes called 'relations of no relations'.[3] So what made Japan and the USSR decide to break the silence and move to improve their relations? What factors contributed to the USSR/Japan *rapprochement* to the extent that Premier Hatoyama's historic visit to Moscow was made and diplomatic relations were restored? The second part in each section concerns their decisions on the 'Northern Territories' problem in association with the outcome of the visit, the Joint Declaration. As for the territorial problem, 'transfer' of the Habomais and Shikotan after signing a peace treaty was promised. However, to this day, no peace treaty has been signed, and no islands have been transferred. The Japanese government has consistently sought 'return' of the 'Northern Territories', including Kunashiri and Etorofu, together with Shikotan and the Habomais promised in the 1956 Joint Declaration. How did this happen? The examination in the previous chapter of the Japanese positions up to the early 1950s suggests that to extract the concession of 'the Habomais and Shikotan' from the Russians was rather a success story. Why, then, was the territorial compromise on two islands perceived as unsuccessful, and the 'four islands' claim made a national goal?

## THE 'GLOBAL INTERNATIONAL RELATIONS' PERSPECTIVE

With regard to the 1955–6 Soviet–Japanese peace negotiations, there have been detailed studies of Japanese domestic politics, but less consideration has been given to their context in global and/or regional international relations. Though American interference has sometimes been mentioned, surprisingly little study has been made from the perspective of other international factors. In global-level analysis beyond the Soviet–Japanese bilateral framework, while the movement towards an agreement is generally explained as a consequence of detente in East–West confrontation, there has been little discussion of it within the context of more diverse movement in the Asia-Pacific region where both countries are located. Post-war development of international relations in the region was exhibiting different features from East–West confrontation in Europe. The diversity of the region had become apparent in the movements for liberation from the pre-war colonial rule, and this influenced the policies of Japan and the USSR towards *rapprochement*. As for the territorial problem, the impact of American interference was so decisive that little consideration was subsequently given to expanding the analytical framework to global level. However, considering that the territorial problem, which largely determined the nature of post-war Japanese–Soviet relations, was not in origin a bilateral dispute but created by third parties without consensus between the nations concerned, i.e., Japan and the USSR, it seems worth examining the case from more diverse perspectives, beyond the bilateral and/or trilateral framework. Diplomatic documents recently opened under the Thirty Year Rule are useful for clarifying how other countries related themselves to the 1955–6 Soviet–Japanese negotiations, especially to the territorial dispute. In the following sections some consideration will be given to the 1956 Soviet–Japanese reconciliation and the territorial problem from the global perspective of the international systems level, using such primary sources as diplomatic documents and other archival materials in the USA and UK that have been opened to researchers in recent years, and also to materials from Australia, most of which were unearthed in Canberra.

## Restoration of Soviet–Japanese diplomatic relations

The Japan–USSR *rapprochement* aimed at normalisation of relations in the mid-1950s can roughly be explained by a global international systems type approach. That is, it can be understood as one of the series of movements engendered by the dynamism of global detente or 'Peaceful Coexistence', which emerged even while the Cold War structure was being established and stabilised.

### *The Cold War thaw and 'Peaceful Coexistence'*

At the end of the Second World War confrontation between the United States and the Soviet Union succeeded cooperation. Relations between them deteriorated into conflict over the spheres of power and influence that the Axis countries had lost in consequence of their defeat. As a result, two confronting blocs – the capitalist bloc and socialist bloc in economic terms, or 'Free World' and 'Communist World' in political terms – were formed, headed respectively by the United States and the Soviet Union, and countries which did not belong to either bloc began to be termed the 'Third World'.

Movement towards detente began to be observed soon after Stalin's death in March 1953, with a cease-fire in the Korean War. In the next year, the premier of Communist China, Chou En-lai, and Indian Prime Minister

Nehru confirmed the 'Five Principles of Peaceful Coexistence'. The trend towards detente was further strengthened in 1954, when an international conference that included the People's Republic of China (PRC) was held in Geneva, and the Indochina Cease-Fire Agreement was signed. In addition, the July 1955 Geneva meeting of the leaders of the United States, Great Britain, France and the USSR was a watershed event after a decade of post-war history, and raised expectations of a 'thaw' in the Cold War. Also in 1955, a Conference of 29 Afro-Asian countries was held in Bandung, Indonesia, and proclaimed anti-colonialism and peaceful coexistence. Thus, the atmosphere of detente on a global scale was the background against which Japan and the USSR made moves for *rapprochement* and restoration of diplomatic relations.

## The emerging third bloc and the independence movement in the Asia-Pacific region

While this detente wave was to prevail in Japanese–Soviet relations, special attention should be paid to the new movements in Asia, where three blocs were becoming conspicuous after Bandung. The first bloc consisted of countries having close ties with the USA, such as the Republic of Korea (South Korea), the Republic of China (Taiwan), the Republic of Vietnam (South Vietnam), Thailand, the Philippines, Pakistan and Japan. The second, Communist, bloc comprised the People's Republic of China, the Democratic People's Republic of Korea (North Korea) and the Socialist Republic of Vietnam (North Vietnam). The third, neutral, bloc comprised the countries of the Colombo group – India, Indonesia, Ceylon and Burma. Yet the relations between those three blocs exhibited fluidity and distinctions were not necessarily clear.

The Bandung Conference was of epoch-making significance in the post-war international politics of the region. The weight of Asia in the international arena and in deciding the direction of the world order increased through the gaining of UN seats by many newly independent countries in the region. A new situation arose, in which the voices of small countries, previously ignored, increased in importance in the UN, and the great powers had to reconsider their approach to them. Though Asian countries were not necessarily in accord in all aspects of their policies and there were still serious conflicts of interest among them, the participants in the Bandung Conference united in a common front against atomic and hydrogen bombs, and for peaceful coexistence.

## Changes in Soviet policy towards the region

The important point here is how such global and regional changes affected the diplomatic policies of the USSR and Japan. The USSR had to re-examine the moves by those Asian countries, which as a result became an important driving force in changing its Cold War policy, and responded to rising nationalist movements with its new diplomacy of 'Peaceful Coexistence between countries with different social systems'.[4] This did not contradict the neutrality principle of 'belonging to neither bloc'. Soviet peace diplomacy, which included development assistance to underdeveloped countries, produced results as a response to the non-aligned movement in Asia, and in expanding the communist sphere of influence against the West. Major moves were observed in that, for example, when Khrushchev and Bulganin visited India, Burma and Afghanistan from November to December 1955, they criticised western 'conditional' aid with military obligations, and offered assistance for their economic development. India, the leading country of the non-aligned movement in Asia, promoted friendly relations with the USSR and Communist China, accepted the Soviet offer of assistance in building steel mills, and proclaimed its intention to promote socialistic models in its domestic economic system. Next, countries which had shown a comparatively friendly attitude towards the West began to move towards non-alignment. The Bandaranaike government in Ceylon, which took office following nation-wide elections in spring 1956, demanded the removal of British military bases. Cambodia opened diplomatic relations with Communist China while rejecting US aid made conditional on its joining the South-East Asia Treaty Organisation (SEATO). There were also signs of vacillation in some of the countries upon which the West relied as part of its anti-communist defence group. For example, in the Philippines parliament there was an increase in expressions of discontent against US bases and the burden of military expenditures entailed by SEATO membership. A similar tendency was observed in Pakistan, where the parliament condemned US military assistance, while improving trade relations with the USSR following a visit by Anastas Mikoyan.

## Japan: towards political independence and membership of the United Nations

In contrast to the Soviet Union, which was the superpower leading the eastern bloc, Japan's international status was minimal soon after the war. During the earlier stage of its occupation period, Japan was directed by the USA to develop as a weak but peaceful nation under policies of anti-militarism and anti-fascism. However, the rising tension of East–West confrontation in East Asia lifted the geopolitical and geostrategic importance of Japan, located as it is at the eastern gateway to Asia and adjacent to the USSR, China and Korea. In accordance with changed American policy, Japan was to stand indirectly in confrontation with the Soviet Union. In 1951, Japan signed the San Francisco Peace Treaty, prepared mainly by the United States, with 48 countries, regained a kind of independence and sovereignty, and rejoined the international community, but the circumstances clearly returned it to the international community as a member of the western bloc and connected it to one pole of the Cold War structure in Asia. The US–Japan Security Treaty was an unequal and one-sided treaty, guaranteeing the US military the right to station forces in Japan under the principle of US protection of Japanese security against domestic violence and foreign enemies, and also presaging an increase in the Japanese self-defence force, but with Japan's status clearly that of a subordinate partner to the USA. Japan, as a country recently defeated in war, had no option but to place its future in the hands of the occupying nation. However, its situation changed. The US-enforced economic policy worked effectively, and Japanese recovery was further stimulated by the Korean War. Japanese diplomacy then began to seek higher international status, and was attracted by the independence movements in Asia. In other words, while US protection facilitated Japan's regaining of its national strength, it also engendered a sense that Japan's subordination was incongruent with a period when decolonialisation, a phenomenon of immense historical significance, was well under way in Asia and Africa. Also it was understandable that some conservative leaders of Japan, so recently a leading state in Asia, empathised with the nationalist movements in Asia and Africa.

Desire for United Nations membership was a factor that drove Japan towards *rapprochement* with the Soviet Union. Japan's regaining of independence in 1951 opened doors only to the western side of the world, and because of that the USSR continued using its veto to prevent Japan's obtaining a UN seat, which it needed in order to conduct diplomacy in pursuit of its national interests. The wave of detente seemed to offer a good chance for Japan to improve its relations with the Communist bloc and persuade the USSR to cease vetoing its candidature for UN membership. These considerations were reflected in the foreign policy initiated by the new Prime Minister Ichirō Hatoyama, who organised his cabinet at the end of 1954, and sought to change Japan's diplomacy towards a more independent direction than that of his predecessor, Shigeru Yoshida. Hatoyama sought revision of the unequal treaty with the USA and also to establish diplomatic relations with the USSR and China. Perceiving this Japanese move as offering an opportunity to expand its peace diplomacy in the Far East, the USSR responded with initiatives for *rapprochement*, beginning with Molotov's address in September 1954, a joint Soviet–Chinese statement released in Beijing in December 1954 and Domnitsky's letter in January 1955. Soviet–Japanese negotiations reached their apogee with Hatoyama's visit to Moscow. Japan established diplomatic relations with the Communist bloc for the first time since the war, and succeeded in joining the UN.

### Article 26 of the San Francisco Treaty

As mentioned earlier, the San Francisco Treaty was drafted in such a manner as to permit convenient interpretation in case of any future contingency. The first provision of Article 26 stated 'Japan will be prepared to conclude with any State . . . which is not a signatory of the present Treaty, a bilateral Treaty of Peace on the same or substantially the same terms as are provided for in the present Treaty, but this obligation on the part of Japan will expire three years after the first coming into force of the present Treaty'.[5] The Peace Treaty was signed on 8 September 1951 but came into force on 28 April 1952,[6] and it is probably not coincidental that the Soviets began their approach to Japan shortly before the three-year limit was due to expire. Presumably it was their interpretation that any potential nuisance to them of this clause would also lapse after three years. The San Francisco Peace Treaty had legitimised American dominance of Japan and ability to control or at least influence developments in northeast Asia, while refusal to join it had placed the Soviet Union in a relatively disadvantageous position. Restoration of diplomatic relations with Japan was therefore in Soviet interests.

### The territorial problem : 'Shikotan and the Habomais'

The history of the past half-century suggests that the territorial problem has become so programmed that it is likely to remain unresolved so long as it remains within a bilateral framework. The architects of the problem were 'third parties'. The key historical arrangement from which the problem originates was made at the Yalta Conference of 1945 and the San Francisco Peace Conference of 1951, at neither of which was there any consensus between Japan and the Soviet Union. Hence, Japan was not a party to the Yalta agreement, and the Soviet Union was not a party to that reached at San Francisco. However, the countries that did participate in these agreements became in a sense 'concerned states' with a stake in the disposal of the disputed islands. Peace negotiations between Japan and the Soviet

Union finally began ten years after the end of the war, and the real concerned states at last turned to discuss sovereignty over the former Japanese
territories.

It is evident from the fact that it took 21 months for a Soviet concession to
be arrived at, and in the event no peace treaty was signed, that it was not
easy for Japan and the USSR to reach reconciliation. During Hatoyama's
visit to Moscow, the two nations declared the end of the state of war
between them and restoration of diplomatic relations. However, this hardly
compared with Japan's signing of a peace treaty with 48 countries at San
Francisco. The promised 'transfer' of Shikotan and the Habomais to Japan
did not take place. Though the Joint Declaration at the end of the visit was
supposedly based upon agreement between the two nations, each interpreted the territorial clause differently. They agreed to continue negotiations for a peace treaty, but the Soviet attitude was that the territorial
problem had become a closed book, and there would therefore be no need
to discuss territorial demarcation. Japan, however, considered that it
reserved the right, in the course of continuing peace negotiations, to reopen
the question of the rest of the former Japanese territories occupied by the
Soviet Union. The Japanese territorial claim for the return of the four
island became established as national policy during the 1955–6 negotiations, against the background of which there was an intervention by a
third party. After 21 months of negotiations, the two nations finally reached
a compromise as shown in the Joint Declaration.

## *Global implications of the territorial expression in the Joint Declaration*

An expression of the Habomai and Shikotan transfer in the Joint Declaration; no peace treaty signed; arbitrary interpretation to continue territorial
negotiations – looking through the prism of international relations, these
were the conclusions that Japan managed to draw from the lengthy negotiations with the USSR.

As for the way other countries, or the concerned states, related themselves to the 1955–6 Soviet–Japanese negotiations, especially the territorial
negotiations, diplomatic documents released under the Thirty Year Rule
are useful for the study. In this section, I examine the Soviet–Japanese
territorial dispute and its relations to some important concerned states,
using primarily reference materials such as documents from the US State
Department and the British Foreign Office, which have gradually been
released in recent years, and also those from the files of the Australian
Department of External Affairs.

## American intervention: 'Dulles' Warning'

A vast quantity of US diplomatic documents has already been processed for release to researchers, and some of them have been published in a series *Foreign Relations of the United States (FRUS)*. Many others are accessible to researchers in microfilm. The US involvement in the Soviet–Japanese negotiations of the 1950s is best known as 'Dulles' Warning'. On 19 August 1956 during the first Moscow negotiations, more than one year after the beginning of the peace talks, the Japanese plenipotentiary, Foreign Minister Mamoru Shigemitsu, was on the verge of a compromise with the Soviet Union over their offer to transfer the Habomais and Shikotan to Japan, and to conclude a peace treaty. However, US Secretary of State John Foster Dulles put last-minute pressure on him, by warning him that Japan's residual sovereignty over Okinawa could be endangered if it were to make concessions to the USSR.[7]

During the post-war period, the primary American diplomatic objective regarding Japan was to prevent it from *rapprochement* with the Communist bloc. Conclusion of a peace treaty with the Soviet Union would put on the agenda the question of normalising relations between Japan and Communist China. Although the peace negotiations started in the 'Peaceful Coexistence' atmosphere of the mid-1950s, this temporary 'detente' was perceived by the US as working strategically to the advantage of the Soviet Union with its peace offensive, and as threatening the West through expansion of the Soviet sphere of interest by perceptions that its initiatives responded to or even stimulated nationalistic and anti-colonial movements in Asia.

At a National Security Council meeting held on 7 April 1955, before the Soviet–Japanese negotiations started, President Eisenhower expressed his concern at this phenomenon. The memorandum of the meeting states:

> The president then referred to the widespread growth of nationalism which had become obvious in the world since the end of the war. He said that it was very alarming to observe how the Communists had managed to identify themselves and their purposes with this emergent nationalism. The United States, on the other hand, had failed to utilise this new spirit of nationalism in its own interest. While this phenomenon was general, Japan was a notable illustration. Accordingly, if Japan grew more strongly nationalist, we should play up more to this development in order to bend it to our advantage.[8]

Such events as the strengthening of socialist parties and the increased activity of the post-war labour movement, which were manifest during the Soviet–Japanese talks, were viewed with profound apprehension in the

USA. A message from the US Embassy in Tokyo, informing the State Department of the result of the 1956 upper-house election, in which the Socialists made large gains to capture one-third of the seats, described it as 'a blow not only to the Japanese ruling party (the Liberal Democratic Party) domestically, but to United States policy in Japan'.[9] There were rumours that Communist money had been used to help elect Socialist candidates.[10] This was probably perceived by the US administration as indicating that its interests required a distance to be maintained between Japan and the USSR.

The 'Dulles' Warning' took place while a Foreign Ministerial Conference was being held in London to discuss the Suez Problem.[11] Both Japanese Foreign Minister Shigemitsu and Soviet Foreign Minister Shepilov flew from Moscow, temporarily suspending their peace negotiations. Shigemitsu at this time had decided, as the plenipotentiary representative, to sign a peace treaty with the Soviets on their offer of Shikotan and the Habomais. The decision had already been reported to Tokyo (which had reacted negatively) and also communicated to the Japanese journalists who had accompanied him to Moscow.[12] The Warning therefore came at the very last minute. In addition, considerable symbolic value attached to the place and occasion where 'Dulles' Warning' was delivered. The London Foreign Ministerial Conference was held *ad hoc* to discuss measures to deal with Egypt's declaration of its state ownership of the Suez Canal, one of the most significant manifestations of nationalism in the emerging Third World bloc, seen as a new threat to the capitalist powers, especially if susceptible to Soviet approaches, a development highly unwelcome to the USA and UK. Dulles' goal was probably not only to retain Okinawa, but securely to lock Japan into the 'Free World' by blocking its attempt at *rapprochement* with the Soviet Union.

Several documents recently opened in the United States have revealed interesting facts regarding the US position and its involvement in the Soviet–Japanese territorial negotiations. Prior to the Soviet–Japanese peace negotiations, the US State Department had predicted that the Russians might possibly use the Kuriles as a bargaining chip in order to put pressure on the USA to return the Ryukyus, and to increase tension between the USA and Japan. A Memorandum of the National Security Council meeting held on 10 March 1955, over 17 months before 'Dulles' Warning', states:

> Secretary Dulles observed that if it ever transpired that the Soviets gave up any significant part of the Kurile Islands archipelago, the US would at once experience heavy Japanese pressure for the return of the Ryukyu Islands to Japanese control. While it would be contrary to experience to expect the Soviets to return any of their present possessions to

Japan, they might conceivably be induced to do so precisely in order to increase tension between the United States and Japan.[13]

In the same meeting, Dulles had already implied that the Ryukyus would not be returned to Japan. He emphasised that 'the Ryukyus were more valuable to the United States than the Kuriles were to the Soviet Union'. Though he supported 'Japan's claim against the Soviet Union for sovereignty over the Habomai Islands and Shikotan', he came up with an argument that the USA should not treat 'as illegally invalid the Soviet Union's claim to sovereignty over the Kurile Islands and Southern Sakhalin'. The memorandum of the meeting records him as follows;

> If we [US] carried out this course of action he [Dulles] warned that we would be marching onto very treacherous ground. The Soviet claim to the Kuriles and Southern Sakhalin was substantially the same as our claim to be in the Ryukyus and the Bonin Islands. Accordingly, in our efforts to force the Soviets out of the Kuriles and Sakhalin, we might find ourselves forced out of the Ryukyus and the Bonins. Secretary Dulles cited the terms of the peace treaty with Japan in which the Japanese agreed to confine themselves to the four major islands of the homeland. It was this which enabled us to maintain our own positions in Japanese territories outside the four main islands. He repeated that if we succeeded in getting the Russians out of the Kuriles it is certain that we would be forced out of the Ryukyus.[14]

The memorandum continues,

> The President stated with a smile that it was also certain that we would not succeed in getting the Russians out of the Kuriles.[15]

The evidence as a whole leaves no room for doubt that the US intended to prevent any Soviet–Japanese *rapprochement* – no matter which island territories were involved. In other words, even if the Soviets had offered to return all of what is now called the 'four islands', the USA would probably have linked the Ryukyus with the rest of the territories (i.e., the Northern Kuriles and the Sakhalin). Since it could not be imagined that the USSR would return all the islands it had been promised at Yalta, the real objective of 'Dulles' Warning' was not to force the Russians to return any given number of islands to Japan, but to create unacceptable conditions in order to keep the Ryukyus under US control.

As stated earlier, Article 26 of the San Francisco Treaty contained the following 'most favoured nation' clause:

Should Japan make a peace settlement or war claims settlement with any State granting that State greater advantages than those provided by the present Treaty, those same advantages shall be extended to the parties to the present Treaty.[16]

Dulles used this clause to argue that, since transfer of territories to the USSR had not been mentioned in the San Francisco Treaty, Japanese acceptance of the Soviet proposal to return only some of them would mean Japan was granting greater advantages to the Soviet Union than to the USA, and in that case Article 26 would enable the USA to claim the territory of Okinawa.[17] At a later date, Dulles said,

That clause was put in the treaty – I wrote the treaty very largely, as you may remember – for that very purpose of trying to prevent the Soviet Union from getting more favourable treatment than the US got.[18]

Other evidence supports the view that the US did not actually believe in the principle of Japan regaining control of the islands. Thus, on 29 May 1956, Noel Hemmendinger, then Deputy Director of the Office of Northeast Asian Affairs in State Department, told A.J., de la Mare of the British Embassy in Washington that there was 'no question but that Japan must give up her aspirations to the Kurile Islands'.[19] The US *Aide-Mémoire* to Japan of September 1956 officially supporting the 'Four Islands' claim, was issued in the firm belief that Japan had no chance of regaining Kunashiri and Etorofu, so that support of a claim to them would ensure Soviet rejection.

The United States has reached the conclusion after careful examination of the historical facts that the islands of Etorofu and Kunashiri (along with the Habomai Islands and Shikotan which are a part of Hokkaido) have always been part of Japan proper and should in justice be acknowledged as under Japanese sovereignty.[20]

The US *Aide-Mémoire* did not say that Kunashiri and Etorofu should be returned to Japan because they were different from the Kuriles. A confidential 'Policy Statement' exchanged later between the USA and UK, said 'the US does not take a position on the definition of the term "Kurile Islands" renounced by Japan in Article 2 of the San Francisco Treaty. Therefore, in referring to Etorofu and Kunashiri, we should use these names and, in general, avoid identifying them either as a part of, or as distinct from the Kurile Islands'.[21] After all, the USA did not 'have basis for objection to territorial provisions identical to those in the San Francisco Treaty (i.e.

Japanese renunciation of right, title and claim to the Kuriles, without reference to Etorofu and Kunashiri or to ultimate sovereignty)', nor did it 'have
basis for objection to a simple declaration ending the state of war'. However, the US considered that Japan did 'not have the right under the San
Francisco Treaty to transfer sovereignty over territories to which it had
renounced all right, title and claim in the treaty'.[22]

This is clearly a politically inspired interpretation. US resolve to keep the
promise made to the USSR at Yalta had completely disappeared, but at
the same time, the US did not want to let Japan decide its own future.
Shigemitsu's attitude toward the territorial claim hardened when the
Moscow negotiations resumed after the London Conference and 'Dulles'
Warning', and the negotiations became deadlocked.

Before there could be any 'post-war' start to relations between Japan and
the USSR, the 'Cold War' had started and, since Japan was firmly embed-
ded in the 'Free World' bloc, its waves did not pass Japan by. The 'Northern
Territories' problem was destined to remain unresolved in consequence.
Observing Japan and the USSR preparing to open a gate in the wall that
divided them, Dulles used the threat of retention of Okinawa to lock it
firmly.

### US twofold gains from the Kuriles

The 'Dulles' Warning' was probably not a new technique of Dulles' negotiating style, nor unique to him. He probably observed and learned it well
from his predecessor. His way of dealing with Shigemitsu somewhat
resembles that of his predecessor Byrnes, when he negotiated with Soviet
Foreign Minister Molotov over the trusteeship of Micronesia.[23] Both Byrnes
and Dulles successfully threatened their counterparts by linking their
residual territorial sovereignty with US claims to other territories. The
United States was the country that benefited most among the three parties.
The Kuriles brought double gains to the USA, which did not even have
potential sovereignty, while the two real concerned states were left in a
deadlocked situation.

### Attitudes of other 'concerned' nations: United Kingdom

Though the 'Dulles' Warning' of US intervention is well known, the moves
or relations to these peace talks of other concerned states have received less
attention. United Kingdom diplomatic documents have recently been made
available to researchers, and the Tanaka study, which examines Japanese
diplomacy of the period with particular focus on Foreign Minister
Shigemitsu, refers briefly to the UK's attitude, using Foreign Office

documents preserved at the Public Record Office.[24] I have revisited the Foreign Office files and have examined them in the context of the UK's relations to the Japan–USSR territorial dispute during this period.

The United Kingdom was an important 'concerned state' that had participated in important arrangements such as the Yalta Agreement, Potsdam Declaration and San Francisco Peace Treaty. The Soviet–Japanese peace negotiations indeed started in London. The UK's reaction was, however, slightly different from that of the USA. The UK was watching the development of Soviet–Japanese negotiations carefully, and with great interest, but was trying to avoid any kind of involvement. The British Ambassador to Japan, Sir Esler Dening, in a secret memorandum to the Foreign Office of 18 August 1955, said,

> Our attitude here has been that the Russo-Japanese negotiations are primarily the concern of the two powers taking part in them, and that while we [UK] are naturally interested, we are not involved.[25]

Britain was apprehensive of the possible reopening of the San Francisco settlement, and considered it wise to avoid any kind of involvement in the Soviet–Japanese reconciliation process. The way the UK related itself to the Asia-Pacific region was a little different from that of the USA which, as the leading power of the 'Free World' bloc, was anxious about expansion of communist power and influence into this region, and was, therefore, very sensitive to the Soviet peace move towards Japan. However, the UK, in a different situation because it had already recognised Communist China before the San Francisco conference, was cautious in its own moves. The United States was backing the nationalist government in Taiwan, so China was a sensitive area between the UK and the US and both countries wanted to avoid a clash. Then, the question was what the Soviet–Japanese negotiations had to do with the UK's position on China ?

The British could foresee trouble if discussion extended to Article 2 of the territorial clause in the San Francisco Treaty, which had been drafted jointly by the USA and UK. Chapter II Article 2 of the Treaty did not specify to which country Japan renounced its former territories, and this applied not only to the Kuriles and South Sakhalin, but also to Formosa (Taiwan) and the Spratly Islands. For fear of disturbing the fragile balance of regional international relations, the UK did not want to revive the San Francisco arrangement, and admonished the USA to that effect when it escalated its anti-communist attitude after the San Francisco Conference and changed its attitude to their arrangement over the Kuriles. In 1953, not long after President Eisenhower announced that the USA would not recognise secret agreements, (in his State of the Union message of 2 February

1953), Britain announced that she would adhere to the Yalta Agreement's awarding of former Japanese territories to the Soviet Union.[26] Referring to the Yalta Agreement and the San Francisco Treaty, Foreign Under-Secretary Lord Reading told the House of Lords on 12 February 1953 that Britain would not support any attempt to repudiate international agreements governing the status of the Far Eastern islands of South Sakhalin and the Kuriles.[27]

With this background, it was natural that the UK not only did not support, but also took a conspicuously negative attitude towards Japanese moves in the territorial negotiations. Lord Reading, in reply to a House of Lords question regarding the Japanese effort to regain the former Japanese territories, pointed out that the Japanese Minister for Foreign Affairs had said in a considered statement that legally Japan had concluded a peace treaty in which she had given up her claims to the territories in question.[28] Denial of the Yalta Agreement would cause controversy in other arrangements made in the San Francisco Treaty, since the arrangement regarding the Kuriles made at San Francisco was based on the Yalta Agreement.

Also, the situation regarding China was uncertain around the time that the Soviet–Japanese negotiations started. In the same State of the Union message President Eisenhower referred to deploying the US 7th Fleet in the Formosan Channel.[29] Britain's reaction that it 'would view any naval blockade of China with concern' raised the question of the former Japanese territories.[30] In late 1954, the situation along the China coast, which had remained quiet for a while, became more volatile. Soon after Taiwan's attempt to join SEATO had been blocked by objections from the UK France, and others, Communist China proclaimed its intention to 'liberate' Taiwan, and intermittent clashes between Communist and Nationalist forces became more frequent. Against this background the US and Nationalist China, after more than a year of discussions, signed a mutual Defence Treaty on 2 December 1954, when Soviet–Japanese negotiations were just beginning.

Britain did not appear opposed to a Japanese–Soviet peace treaty, but was against the idea of re-examining the content of the San Francisco Treaty, and therefore, avoided any kind of involvement in the negotiations that might possibly lead to it. Several documents from British diplomatic files of the time reveal the UK's misgivings at a possible Japanese attempt to involve the USA and UK in the territorial negotiation as signatories of the San Francisco Treaty. In July 1955, Japanese Ambassador Haruhiko Nishi gave Denis Allen of the Foreign Office a copy of the draft treaty that the Russians had handed to Matsumoto at the beginning of the peace negotiations.[31] The British Ambassador to Japan, Sir Esler Dening, commented to Allen as follows:

I am sure you will agree that it would be very dangerous for us to become involved in expressions of opinion about the territorial clauses of the Russian draft. The Japanese can argue that since the Russians are no longer entitled to avail themselves of the option under Article 26 of the San Francisco Treaty, the Japanese themselves are not bound by Article 2(c) of that Treaty, but it is one thing to express their own view and quite another to try to involve the signatories of the San Francisco Treaty.

I hope that the United States Government are not allowing themselves to become involved in the substance of the draft presented by the Russians to the Japanese, for this might cause difficulties for the rest of us.[32]

The UK was concerned that the Japanese were taking advantage of their negotiations with the Soviets to try to re-open the whole question of their territorial cessions under Article 2 of the San Francisco Treaty.

In the meantime, a new development took place during the London negotiations. On 5 August 1955, Soviet Plenipotentiary Malik visited the Japanese Embassy and informally implied an offer of 'two islands' (Shikotan and the Habomais). At the tenth meeting of the negotiators on 9 August, this offer was officially pronounced.[33] However, on 28 August, the Japanese government gave Matsumoto new instructions to demand the 'four islands' and add a new condition for a peace settlement, that the disposition of the Northern Kuriles and South Sakhalin should be decided by an international conference.[34] On 30 August Matsumoto handed Malik a revised draft of the peace treaty, based on his new instructions.

Dening's memorandum also indicates that before the new instructions were given to Matsumoto, the Japanese had already indicated informally to the British that they rather hoped the territorial clause of the Russian draft treaty could be shelved and laid before an international forum.[35] Dening also stated:

I do not think this is only to get over an awkward hurdle but that it hoped to get some kind of reversal of Article 2(c), which might then open the way to their questioning the other clauses of this Article [of the San Francisco Treaty].[36]

As for the territorial negotiations, the British view was that the Japanese surely could not hope to persuade the Soviets either to surrender the territories or to admit that there could be any doubt about their title to them.[37] The UK's greatest concern was that by contesting Soviet sovereignty over South Sakhalin and the Kuriles the Japanese might well wish to open up the possibility of reversing Article 2 of the San Francisco Treaty.[38] Therefore it reacted apprehensively to the Japanese proposal, made after the Soviets had offered to cede the Habomais and Shikotan, that sovereignty over South Sakhalin and the Northern Kuriles should be examined by the powers concerned. Dening analysed the situation as follows,

> If we allow ourselves to become involved and the Japanese do not get what they want (which seems very probable), then they will seek to put the blame on us. If on the other hand the ultimate outcome is favourable in any degree to Japan it may create a host of trouble with the other parties involved.[39]

International relations in the Far East were probably more complicated than Japan realised as it tried to exploit the situation. The interests of different nations were interwoven even in the basic structure of the East–West confrontation. Because of its remaining colonial interests, the UK had split with the US by recognising Communist China well before the San Francisco Peace Conference, but was nevertheless fighting communist insurgency in another part of the region, Malaya. British misgivings are clear in the following extract from correspondence from Dening to the Foreign Office:

> if the Japanese can persuade other powers to reexamine the territorial clauses of Article 2 of the Peace Treaty, then it seems to me that the Far East can easily be thrown into turmoil.[40]

There was, after all, a difference in American and British attitudes towards Soviet–Japanese *rapprochement*, arising from their different interests in the Asia Pacific region. The British Foreign Office once announced that it would be unable to go along with Dulles' views on recognition of the Kuriles as Japanese territory.[41] However, the UK also wanted to avoid open discord with the USA, the leading power in the western capitalist bloc and also, as shown in the Suez Conference, an important and reliable partner in protecting British interests in other parts of the world.[42] No more obvious conflict regarding this matter surfaced thereafter. The Foreign Office and State Department arranged to coordinate their policies on this issue.[43]

The international conference feared by the UK did not take place, despite several references by the Japanese Foreign Ministry to its desirability.[44] On 19 August 1956 when Dulles was delivering his 'Warning', Foreign Minister Shigemitsu asked him whether the United States would be prepared to take the initiative to convene a conference to discuss the disposition of the Kuriles and the Ryukyus. Dulles' attitude to this was negative.[45] He was also concerned over the consequences of such a conference, i.e., the possible opening up of 'disagreeable questions' regarding Ryukyu and Taiwan.[46] In any case there was no ground for thinking the USSR would attend such a conference, if it was confined to the status of the Kuriles and Sakhalin.

A shift from the previous policy may be observed in this US attitude. In September 1955, early in the Soviet–Japanese negotiations, the US view, to be discreetly conveyed to high Japanese officials, was 'we hope Japan will do nothing implying recognition of Soviet sovereignty over the Kuriles and South Sakhalin and we believe disposition of these territories should be left for future international decision'.[47] As Dulles indicated, the US changed its stance in order to secure its position in the Ryukyus and also to avoid any conflict with Great Britain.

The memorandum of a meeting held after Hatoyama's visit to Moscow between high officials of the State Department and the British Embassy in Washington records the continuing British concern over the future of this issue while trying to coordinate its policy with the USA.

Mr. de la Mare [Counsellor, British Embassy] asked whether he was correct in supposing that the Japanese regarded the question of Kunashiri and Etorofu as still open. Mr. Sebald [Deputy Assistant Secretary for Far Eastern Affairs, State Department] replied that the Japanese had reserved their right to reopen this question but that the Soviets regarded it as a closed book. ... Mr. de la Mare thought the question of the Kuriles would make trouble at some time in the future and that some day the San Francisco Peace Treaty signatories would have to decide the fate of these islands. Mr. Sebald said that the term which Mr. Dulles had used with respect to the future settlement of these islands was 'international solvents other than the peace treaty' and he added that our legal advisers thought that Japan had a claim to the Kuriles, though admittedly it was tenuous, while the Soviet Union had no valid claim. Mr. de la Mare said that the British had expressed the same view. Mr. Sebald remarked that the Soviet nevertheless asserted claim through occupation and prescriptive right. ... Mr. Sebald said that the whole question was a little fuzzy but that we believed the islands, having belonged to Japan historically and not having been taken by force, should properly be Japan's. Unfortunately Mr. Yoshida had referred to Etorofu and Kunashiri at San Francisco as being the 'Southern Kuriles'. Mr. Sebald added that if Japan should get the Islands it would be a part of a political decision. ... Britain would prefer to see the islands go to Japan, but it would have to find an argument. ... Mr. de la Mare wondered when the question was likely to come up. Mr. Sebald thought that neither Mr. Hatoyama nor Mr. Kono was interested in raising the question in the near future because other questions such as the UN and fisheries needed settling first.[48]

The question did not arise in the way the UK feared. Hatoyama retired and Japanese politics were dominated thereafter by the pro-US Yoshida faction of the LDP. Other countries including the US and UK withdrew from the issue. Obviously they had no idea how long the Cold War and the territorial dispute would last.

### *Australian security concerns in the Asia-Pacific region*

Many of the diplomatic documents in the Australian archives have not been examined by other researchers as far as the Soviet–Japanese relations are concerned. The lack of interest with regard to this issue may be attributed to a stereotypical image that Australia's position would be identical or similar to the UK's due to its political status as a commonwealth country. But those records reveal that the reality was different. Australia's attitude merits attention in the sense that it well reflected the post-war reality of the Asia-Pacific region, with the nation making a new move to pursue its own diplomacy as an Asia-Pacific country, as well as a member of the Commonwealth.

Australia had been observing development of the Japan–USSR peace negotiations with great interest, as a participant in the war and in the post-war Occupation, and as a signatory to the San Francisco Treaty, which made it a 'nation concerned' over the unresolved problems. Australia, like the UK, avoided playing any role to affect the directions or final decisions of the Japan–USSR peace negotiations.

The East Asia Section of the Department of External Affairs prepared comments on questions put by Australian United Press on 31 August 1956. The note well reflected Australia's interests and its subtle position on Soviet–Japanese territorial questions.

As for Article 26 of the San Francisco Treaty, whose interpretation was one of the major focal points of arguments during the Soviet–Japanese negotiations, the following comments demonstrate the Australian view. As mentioned earlier, Article 26 contained two provisions. The first was that for three years after the Treaty came into force, Japan would be prepared to conclude a peace treaty with any state still at war with it on the same or substantially the same terms as the Treaty. The second provision was that 'should Japan make a peace settlement or war claims settlement with any State granting that State greater advantages than those provided by the present Treaty, those same advantages shall be extended to the parties to the present Treaty'. The note states:

> As the word 'advantages' in the latter provision is neither qualified nor defined, either in Article 26 or elsewhere in the Peace Treaty, it would appear to refer to advantages of any sort, whether financial, political, territorial, or anything else. Mr. Dulles claims that Article 26 was inserted in the Treaty 'for the very purpose of preventing the Soviet Union from getting more favourable treatment than the United States got'. Whilst this may be true as far as the United States is concerned, Australia favoured the inclusion of Article 26 to safeguard our position in the event that Japan concluded a peace settlement with one or other of the South East Asian countries, providing for the payment of cash reparations (which we had foregone under the terms of Article 14 of the Peace Treaty).
>
> We would not agree with the Japanese claim that the whole of Article 26 lapsed three years after the Peace Treaty entered into force. In our view, only the first provision lapsed on 29th April, 1955. The second provision is in no way affected by the time limit placed on the first. In fact, the second provision is designed to cover the situation when Japan is no longer bound to conclude peace settlements with non-signatory States 'on the same or substantially the same terms' as the San Francisco Treaty.
>
> Whilst Australia might, under Article 26, have a legal right to claim equal treatment with the U.S.S.R. in the event that Japan recognises Soviet sovereignty over Kunashiri and Etorofu, the following considerations would make this a purely theoretical right:
>
> (a) Australia does not occupy any former Japanese territory;
>
> (b) all former Japanese mandated islands in the Pacific are now under United States trusteeship;
>
> (c) all other former Japanese territories have been disposed of in one way or another (e.g. Korea has been granted independence, Formosa is under the *de facto* control of Nationalist China, the Ryukyus, Bonins, etc. are under US control);
>
> (d) it is difficult to see how we could claim unequal treatment if the USSR secured Kunashiri and Etorofu. Australia did not seek equality of treatment with the US in regard to the acquisition of Japanese territories, so it would be inconsistent now to seek equality with the U.S.S.R.[49]

On the question regarding the range of the Kuriles, an obvious shift is observed from the view expressed in 1951 that Australia favoured the *status quo* of Soviet occupation of these islands, including Shikotan and the Habomais. The following comments answered the question 'Does the Government interpret the Kuriles as mentioned in the Treaty (to which Japan renounced all claims) as including Etorofu and Kunashiri?'

> In accordance with normal geographical usage, the term Kurile Islands includes Kunashiri and Etorofu, and there is no doubt that we regarded these two islands as being included in the territories to which Japan renounced all right, title and claim in Article 2 of the Peace Treaty. However, it is now clear that the Japanese have considerable grounds for their claim that Kunashiri and Etorofu should be regarded as in a different category to the remaining Kurile Islands, and we would probably be prepared to concede that there is room for doubt that they should have been removed from Japanese sovereignty. Kunashiri and Etorofu are historically Japanese territory and were confirmed as such by the Russo-Japanese Treaty of Shimoda of 1855, so it would be difficult to argue that Japan acquired these islands by 'greed and violence' (Cairo declaration) or 'by the treacherous attack of Japan (on Russia) in 1904' (Yalta Agreement). We would probably agree with the United States that Japan has a case for seeking a decision from the International Court of Justice on whether Kunashiri and Etorofu are included in the term 'Kurile Islands' in Article 2 of the Japanese Peace Treaty.[50]

On the question whether the government favoured holding a conference of Second World War Allies, including Russia, to decide the sovereignty over territories that Japan had surrendered, including Manchuria, Formosa and Korea, or just including territories whose status was not made clear in the treaty, such as South Sakhalin, the Kuriles, Ryukyus and Bonins, the Australian government's position was as follows:

> The first part of this question does not for obvious reasons merit serious consideration. The answer would be a flat no. As far as the second part is concerned, even on the assumption that it might be possible to limit such a conference to a consideration of only the territories named, which would be very difficult, we would presumably not favour such a conference because of the embarrassing position in which it would place the United States. Also, a continuation of US control over the Ryukyus and Bonins is of strategic importance to Australia, and there would be the clear danger that such a conference might lead to a weakening of US control. A conference of signatories of the San Francisco Treaty to define the term 'Kurile Islands' would be another

matter, but here again, we would want a very definite limitation placed on the conference's terms of reference, and would in any case be largely guided by the attitude of the United States.[51]

Though using mild expressions, Australia basically supported US policy in the region. Its opposition to the idea of holding an international conference came from deference to the US position on the issue. The US presence in the Pacific, (Ryukyu and Bonin were referred to here) was perceived as important for Australia's security, and in the post-war era, Australia's priority as an Asia-Pacific nation was cooperation with the United States.

## Summary of the 'global international relations' perspective

The Soviet–Japanese peace negotiations started against a background of global detente. The international relations of the region are, however, difficult to explain solely in the context of easing tension in the East–West structure as in Europe. The diversity of the region brought substantial influence to the reaction of the concerned states with regard to the Soviet–Japanese negotiations. New national independence movements impacted on the foreign policies not only of Japan and the USSR, but also on those of states which were at first perceived to be merely observers; the United States emerged as the new capitalist superpower of the post-war era and its objectives included a strategic interest in confronting the expansion of Communist influence. The US not only interrupted the Soviet–Japanese *rapprochement* but also secured its own base in Okinawa. The United Kingdom, a pre-war colonial power of the region, was in a declining position after the war. It had some differences with the USA over China policy, but had to avoid open conflict, in order to protect its remaining colonial interests in the region, especially in the context of the East–West confrontation. In addition to these two nations, I also examined Australia's position as one of the Allied Powers and concerned states at San Francisco. Australia chose to place its diplomacy alongside US policy in the new post-war situation in the Asia-Pacific region, and placed its priority on finding ways to play a role in regional cooperation. The Soviet–Japanese negotiations were surrounded by the interwoven interests of several nations. The USA and UK adjusted their policies with regard to this matter, and the USA was the nation whose strategy was best reflected in the outcome of the negotiations. No Soviet–Japanese peace treaty was signed, and from the Japanese point of view the territorial problem remained unresolved.

## THE 'NATION-STATE' PERSPECTIVE: JAPAN

The Soviet–Japanese negotiations that culminated in Hatoyama's visit to Moscow deserve attention from the viewpoint of Japanese domestic politics, not only as a case study of Japanese foreign policy making, but also as the first major foreign-policy decision making exercise undertaken by Japan since it regained its independence after the war, and also because they took place during the period when the basis for the long era of LDP (Liberal Democratic Party) hegemony, the so-called '1955 system', was being established. In addition, it is especially noteworthy that domestic political moves were clearly reflected in foreign policy. The 1955–6 negotiations have therefore been discussed several times from the Japanese domestic viewpoint. Among many volumes on the subject, the memoirs of Shun'ichi Matsumoto and Ichirō Hatoyama have long been known, and are often referred to as basic primary written materials on the Japanese side.[52] As well as these books, the memoirs of Takezō Shimoda (then the head of the Treaty Bureau of the Foreign Ministry) and the diaries of Mamoru Shigemitsu later became available as important sources.[53] Other Japanese materials, such as volumes by Akira Shigemitsu, who was present at the Moscow negotiations, and by Masaaki Kubota, a journalist who was close to Matsumoto and travelled with the Japanese delegation during the negotiations, provide details of the situation of the times.[54] Works in English on the topic include those by Donald Hellmann, Savitri Vishwanathan and Young C. Kim.[55] After the Soviet introduction of *Glasnost*, the territorial dispute began to receive considerable attention again, and a great number of works have been published since then. Among those which deal with the 1955–6 negotiations from the Japanese point of view, those by Haruki Wada and Takahiko Tanaka are worthy of attention.[56] In addition to using previously available materials, Wada has made good use of primary materials recently found in Japan, conducted a detailed study and demonstrated sharp insights on the emergence of the Japanese territorial claims. Tanaka focuses on the diplomacy of Foreign Minister Shigemitsu, using diplomatic documents recently made available in the UK and US under the Thirty Year Rule, a rule which does not seem to have been adopted by Japan, as far as this particular issue is concerned. To clarify the whole picture of the negotiations, we may have to wait until the related documents are released in Japan and Russia. (For the situation in Russia, see p. 81.)

In this second part of the chapter, the basic structure and general concepts of Japanese post-war politics will be briefly explained. Then policy decision making during the 1955–6 Japanese–Soviet negotiations will be examined in terms of (a) improvement of bilateral relations and (b) the territorial question from the level of 'nation-state' Japan.[57]

### Post-war political decision making in Japan

As for political decision making in post-war Japan, there seems to be a common understanding regarding the triangular structure of the influence system, whose three sides consist of the participating groups of politics (*sei*), bureaucracy (*kan*) and business (*zai*). Though the power balance or strength of influence varies depending on the period or policy issue area, it seems there is no question about the continuing general importance of these groups in formulating national decisions.[58] A general explanation will be given on the foreign-policy decision making of post-war Japan along the lines of this tri-polar system.

*Politics (sei)*

The structure of post-war Japanese politics has at its centre the cabinet, the core unit which decides national policy. This is defined by Article 73 of the present Japanese constitution. The Japanese political party system plays an important part. Under the Constitution of 1947, the majority party (or parties in case of coalitions) in the Diet and its president, the Prime Minister, are designated the pivotal roles in decision making.[59] The majority of the cabinet are to be selected from Diet members. Since the selection of cabinet ministers is by political appointment, the cabinet consists mainly of politicians from the ruling party(ies). Thus, the cabinet's policies largely depend on those of the ruling party(ies). The minister in charge of the state's foreign relations is the Minister of Foreign Affairs. However, supreme decision-making responsibility for the state's diplomacy lies with the Prime Minister.[60] Though formally granted the highest authority, the Prime Minister is nevertheless constrained by inter-factional rivalries within the ruling party(ies). Until 1993, when the LDP government ended its long history of dominance, none of the other political parties, such as the leftist Japan Socialist Party (JSP) and Japanese Communist Party (JCP), or the middle-of-the road Clean Government Party (CGP: *Kōmeitō*) and Democratic Socialist Party (SDP), gained sufficient seats to form a government. According to the Constitution, the Diet is the supreme and only legislative organ; however, it plays only a limited role in foreign policy making. Its role remains passive, restricting the decisions of the administrative body, rather than active, taking decisions on its own initiative and having the administration carry them out. In Japan, which has a parliamentary system, it has normally been the case that the administrative body always receives support from a majority of the Diet. The Soviet–Japanese negotiations overlap the period when the bases of the politics (*sei*) part of the triangle, the so-called '1955 system' were being established. This was the period when the two conservative parties were merging and the start of the long period of LDP dominance.

## Bureaucracy (kan)

The government's decisions are carried out by the administrative organs, which are groups consisting of bureaucrats who specialise in administration.

In cases where political parties are incapable of making national policies on their own, the administrative body (such as the *Gaimushō* for foreign policy) is the biggest, or rather the only, think-tank. Information and materials necessary for formulating national policies are monopolised by these specialist groups. Those who undertake the real foreign affairs of the Japanese government work for the Ministry of Foreign Affairs (*Gaimushō* hereafter). Formally, the *Gaimushō* has been made fully subordinate to the government and is designed simply to implement the policies laid down by the ruling party. The *Gaimushō* is concerned with the technical functions of working out policy details and administering the country's international affairs. However, it is in fact those specialists who actually formulate draft policies, directly or indirectly answer questions of opposition party members at the Diet, if necessary, and administer a substantial part of the government's decisions.

When policy issues are concerned with areas other than purely political diplomacy, ministries in charge of issue areas play important roles as well as the *Gaimushō*. For example, in matters of economic relations, such as joint development, trade, etc., the Ministry of International Trade and Industry (MITI) comes to play a major role in policy making. However, as far as the post-war Japanese–Soviet/Russian relations are concerned, the diplomatic agenda has always tended to be highly political. Thus, the *Gaimushō* has mainly been in charge of policy formulation toward the USSR/Russia. Within the *Gaimushō*, where policy making towards the Soviet Union/Russia is concerned, the officials who play the most important roles are said to be the Deputy Foreign Minister, the Director-General of the Asia and European Department, the Head of the USSR (Russia) Section, and the ambassador and ministers in the Japanese Embassy in Moscow.[61] They also act as consultants to the Prime Minister and Minister of Foreign Affairs, who are normally politicians, but not necessarily specialists in foreign relations.

## Big business groups (zaikai)

The four major business groups, which emerged after the war, are well known and generally acknowledged as influential; they are the Federation of Economic Organizations (*Keidanren*), the Japan Federation of Employers' Associations (*Nikkeiren*), the Japan Chamber of Commerce and Industry (*Nihon shōkō kaigi-sho*) and the Japan Committee for Economic Development (*Keizai dōyū-kai*). The bonds binding the business community and conservative parties were established through massive amounts of financial assistance. And also through the individual relations that arise from business careers, education, etc. Not only in the political and business community, but also in the bureaucracy, leaders of these groups are members of the elitist society, which contributed to the re-establishment of Japan after the war. In the close network of personal and mutually dependent relations in such a society, the business groups demonstrate a strong influence in the making of the Japanese policies, especially on economy-oriented issues.

## Restoration of Japanese–Soviet diplomatic relations

### *Changes in leadership and political priorities*

The biggest Japanese domestic factors for reconciliation with the Soviet Union were probably the changes in political leadership and the shift in political priorities that followed. Movements for normalising relations with the USSR had existed in Japan since the signing of the San Francisco Peace Treaty. Behind such movements public opinion was strongly in favour of ending the legacy of the occupation period, reducing Japan's heavy dependency on the United States and making peace not only with the West but overall. These aspirations were promoted by advocates of 'neutrality' and 'peace', and by opposition parties. Other important issues affecting Soviet–Japanese relations were the questions of repatriation of prisoners of war from Siberia, the security of fishing in the seas north of Japan, and regaining Soviet-occupied territories. However, no substantial movement took place during the early years of conservative rule, as diplomatic priority focused on cooperation with and dependency upon the United States. Governmental attitudes towards improving relations with the USSR were therefore negative.

Many of the pre-war conservative political leaders were purged during the occupation period. After the San Francisco Treaty, some of the major ones, including Ichirō Hatoyama, returned to the political arena. Movement towards practical negotiations with the Soviet Union became conspicuous after Hatoyama replaced Yoshida as Prime Minister and formed a new cabinet in December 1954. Hatoyama received strong support from the public, who preferred his public, diplomatic and defence policies that emphasised Japanese independence and self-reliance.[62] Establishment of diplomatic relations with the Soviet Union became one of the major goals of the new cabinet's 'independent diplomacy' and practical steps began to be taken to achieve it.

## Dual diplomacy: the active informal channel

One substantial move for settlement of the Soviet–Japanese negotiations was made through informal channels used by Hatoyama and people close to him. Discord over policies toward the USSR between *Gaimushō* and the Prime Minister's office has often been described as dual diplomacy. The attitude of *Gaimushō*, the formal diplomatic channel, towards the USSR was negative and filled with distrust from past experience, while Prime Minister Hatoyama and those close to him were positive and aggressive about *rapprochement* with the Russians, and the differences in attitude were frequently manifested during the negotiations. A typical example was seen in the reaction to a letter from the Soviet government calling for normalisation of relations, later known as the 'Domnitsky Letter'. This letter, which had a direct effect in initiating the peace negotiations, was handed to Hatoyama on 25 January 1955, the day after the dissolution of the Lower House. The Soviet representative Andrei Ivanovich Domnitsky had approached the *Gaimushō* before to deliver a note to the Japanese government, but the *Gaimushō*'s attitude was negative, and so was that of Foreign Minister Shigemitsu. Since the letter was not accepted by the formal route, Domnitsky took it to Hatoyama's private residence, at the instigation of Kōta Sugihara, who was a member of the House of Councillors and a close friend of Hatoyama, Fusanosuke Kuhara, president of the National Council of Associations for Normalisation of Relations with the Soviet Union and China (*Nicchū nisso kokkō kaifuku kaigi*), and others.[63] According to Hatoyama's memoirs,

> Even before that, I had heard through someone like Mr. Sugihara that Mr. Domnitsky had contacted Mr. Shigemitsu's place several times, but Mr. Shigemitsu would not deal with him, saying 'I cannot accept unless it comes via an official route.'. . . I remember that I asked him to come through to our kitchen, since Japanese journalists might make a great fuss, if they found out, though I myself thought it would be alright to see him if he wanted to see me to hand me the letter.[64]

Since Japan and the Soviet Union did not yet have diplomatic relations, the *Gaimushō* did not consider the Soviet mission in Tokyo to be an official diplomatic post. Hatoyama met Domnitsky and received the letter anyway, and then sought and obtained confirmation that it was an official communication from the Soviet government. On 4 February 1955, the cabinet resolved to initiate negotiations for normalising relations with the Soviet Union. Thus, the negotiations with the Russians were initiated by ignoring the Foreign Office, which was supposed to be the official channel.

## Hatoyama and his entourage

During the 20 months from the first contact until the settlement, the negotiations became deadlocked and close to failure many times. Nevertheless, the summit visit took place, and diplomatic relations were restored. In achieving this several individuals, especially Hatoyama himself and those close to him such as Shun'ichi Matsumoto and Ichirō Kōno, played important roles.

Matsumoto was a former diplomat, who had held high-ranking positions in the *Gaimushō* during and after the Second World War, including Deputy Secretary-General and Ambassador to the United Kingdom. He had just entered politics, elected as a Democratic Party representative in February 1955, soon before the peace negotiations began. He participated in all the negotiations, both in London (1 June to 23 September 1955 and 17 January to 20 March 1956) and in Moscow (31 July to 14 August 1956 and 15–19 October 1956), including Hatoyama's visit to Moscow. He regarded the negotiations 'largely in relation to domestic Japanese political factors, including his own political future'. According to a Japanese diplomat of the time, he supported the proposal for early agreement on a peace treaty with the Soviets, since he felt he had 'the inside track to become Foreign Minister in the next cabinet, and a record for dealing successfully with the Soviet Government would be part of that picture'.[65]

Ichirō Kōno, Minister for Agriculture in the Hatoyama cabinet, probably played the most vital role in ensuring that the negotiations were not shelved and reached some kind of settlement in the shape of restoration of diplomatic relations. He had been a close associate of Hatoyama, and, like him, was purged during the occupation. In 1952 he was re-elected to the Diet, subsequently joining Hatoyama's group and eventually his cabinet. Some scholars observe that Hatoyama's illness and Kōno's own domineering personality made him virtual Prime Minister during this period. Kōno had strong views on foreign policy.[66] Though not neglectful of the importance of friendly relations with the United States, he was unenthusiastic about the US alliance. Japan's future, he considered, lay not with the United States but with an independent pan-Asianist community, incorporating the developing non-Communist nations to the south.[67]

It was Kōno who several times unblocked the negotiations and played a leading role in normalising ties with Moscow. On 21 March 1956, the day after the second round of the London negotiations was suspended in deadlock, the Soviet government announced restrictions on fishing in the north Pacific. This hit the Japanese fishing industry hard, because the northern sea salmon and trout fishing season was about to begin, and the Soviets played the fishery card in order to make the Japanese reopen the negotiations.[68] Though he had not been authorised to discuss peace with the Soviets at this time, Kōno made a breakthrough on this occasion and the negotiations were reopened. On 29 April 1956, the Kōno mission was sent to Moscow to solve the fishery problem, and on 14 May the USSR signed a Fishery Convention on the express condition that the negotiations for normalisation of relations be resumed not later than 31 July 1956. The formal diplomatic channel of *Gaimushō* was again ignored. On the day that the fishery talks reached a settlement, Kōno met Soviet Prime Minister Bulganin. He distrusted the *Gaimushō* as not only generally negative towards reconciliation with the Soviets, but also in close contact with the US State Department, so he refused the services of Kinya Niizeki (later Ambassador to the USSR), who had been designated to accompany him as interpreter. As Kōno had thought likely, Niizeki later contacted the American diplomatic mission. A State Department document records,

> Although Mr. Niizeki says that he speaks quite good Russian, he told me that when the chief Japanese delegate, Minister of Agriculture Kono, had a private meeting with Mr. Bulganin, Russian interpreters were employed and that no Japanese nationals were present. He added that he has never been told what was discussed during the meeting between minister Kono and Mr. Bulganin. Apparently Mr. Niizeki was trying to suggest that some undisclosed agreement could have and indeed might have been entered at that time.[69]

Kōno promised to continue the peace negotiations, despite opposition from the *Gaimushō* and the Yoshida faction in the ruling party. According to press reports of this period, it was the Soviet side that claimed the fishery agreement could be put into effect only after diplomatic relations were restored, and attached the condition that the peace negotiations reopen by the end of July.[70] However, according to the confession later made by Nikolai Adyrkhaev, the Russian interpreter at the Kōno–Bulganin meeting, Kōno himself suggested the linkage, but asked the Soviets to make it appear they had forced him to accept it, explaining that 'without such a condition it would be difficult to resume the negotiation, because some forces in Japan opposed *rapprochement* with the Soviet Union.'[71] Of the three Plenipotentiaries at the time of Prime Minister Hatoyama's visit – Matsumoto, Kōno and Hatoyama – it was chiefly Kōno who had the key meetings with Khrushchev and reached a compromise.

Besides his political beliefs and enthusiasm, another factor drove Kōno to promote Soviet–Japanese negotiations. He had close relations with a particular business interest group, the fishery industry, which was distinct from the four major business groups, but strongly concerned with protection and promotion of Japanese fishing rights in the north Pacific. He had been connected with the fishery industry since his time as a journalist on the *Asahi Shimbun*, one of Japan's major newspapers, and it had been a major financial supporter of him since he entered politics. The relationship was strengthened during his term as Minister of Agriculture and Fisheries. Defeat in the war and the consequent loss of the northern territories had had a severe impact on the Japanese fishing industry, which therefore became one of the most enthusiastic groups to promote post-war diplomatic normalisation with the USSR, since it regarded friendly relations with the Soviets as essential for securing safe operation and development of fishing. In pursuit of this objective, several fishing industry leaders, such as Tsuneji Hiratsuka of the Greater Japan Fisheries Society (*Dai Nippon Suisankai*) and Kensaku Ōnishi of the Hokuyō Suisan Company had participated in the National Convention for normalisation of relations with China and the Soviet Union (*Nicchū–nisso kokkō kaifuku kokumin kaigi*) together with leftist leaders. The Domnitsky letter was handed to Hatoyama by an assistant of Hiratsuka. Incidentally, when the Soviets placed restrictions on Japanese northern Pacific fishing, pressure from the fishery industry for a breakthrough in the peace negotiations increased. Thus, this may be considered as a case where a domestic pressure group had a direct and indirect impact on Japanese foreign-policy formulation.[72]

## Hatoyama's visit to Moscow

The 1955–6 Japanese–Soviet negotiations for normalising relations concluded with a visit by the Japanese Prime Minister to the Soviet Union. After Kōno had promised continuation of the peace negotiations at the fishery negotiations, the first Moscow negotiations (31 July to 12 August 1956) began with Foreign Minister Mamoru Shigemitsu as the plenipotentiary, but stalled again. Hatoyama then made a resolute decision to go to Moscow himself, despite strong domestic opposition to his doing so. He was old and unwell, and wished to crown his political career by carrying out his initial pledges to the nation during a prime ministership which could not be of long duration. The most tangible sign of success would be to secure the repatriation of the Japanese prisoners of war; the issue of the territories could be raised later. In his memoirs he said:

At the time when Mr. Shigemitsu's negotiations faced deadlock, I gradually made up my mind that 'after all, I myself would have to visit Moscow and engage in the final discussions'.[73]

Hatoyama also decided to resign the leadership of the party. At the LDP leaders' meeting in Karuisawa on 10 August, he stated:

I don't intend to stick to political power. I would like my successor to be decided amicably soon.[74]

He officially announced his intention to resign at a press conference held before his departure for Moscow in October. The opposition within the ruling party seemed softened to some extent, because the focus of interest shifted onto the question of the next LDP president. Kōno was considering adorning Hatoyama's departure from the stage with a settlement in the Japanese–Soviet negotiations.[75]

## *Two* shinchō-ha *groups*

In hindsight, though Hatoyama was appointed Prime Minister with substantial public support, his campaign pledges were not easily carried out. There existed roughly two major groups of *shinchō-ha* (literally cautious faction), which preferred prolonged negotiations, as opposed to Hatoyama's *sōki daketsu-ha* (quick settlement faction), which sought an early solution in the negotiations. The first group of *shinchō-ha* was that of the *Gaimushō* and Minister Shigemitsu. Another *shinchō-ha* was found within the conservative parties, led by former Prime Minister Yoshida, consisted of those leaders who had formerly belonged to the 'US–UK faction' in the *Gaimushō* and had played leading roles during the period of turmoil and transition after the war. These two groups were connected via the *Gaimushō*, and found common ground in that their policy priority was cooperation with, including dependence on, the United States, while their attitude towards the USSR was cautious and generally negative. They exerted a restraining influence upon the Hatoyama government's policy toward the Soviet Union – the first in dual diplomacy, and the second in the merger of the conservative parties. This was most clearly reflected in policies towards the territorial negotiations.

## The territorial problem: 'Shikotan and the Habomais'

In the Joint Declaration, which was the final outcome of the 1955–6 negotiations, the transfer of Shikotan and the Habomais was specified. Japan's current territorial claim for 'four islands return' involves interpreting the Joint Declaration in combination with the 'Matsumoto–Gromyko Letters', exchanged before Hatoyama's visit to Moscow and announced together with the Declaration. These letters confirmed the two nations' intention to continue 'negotiations on the signing of a peace treaty', which would include 'the territorial issue' even 'after the re-establishment of diplomatic relations'.[76] In short, the Japanese interpretation is that the return of Shikotan and the Habomais was promised, and negotiations over Kunashiri and Etorofu were to be continued as part of the peace treaty negotiations. Through the prism of Japanese domestic politics, it can be shown that this interpretation of the territorial clause emerged unilaterally and quite politically as a last resort, from a complicated mixture of factors such as discord between the premier's office and the *Gaimushō*, or political bargaining within the conservative parties at the time of establishment of the '1955 system'.

## Initial policy of negotiation

At the beginning of the Soviet–Japanese negotiations, the Japanese had a flexible view of potential territorial claim. At the cabinet meeting in February 1955, the Hatoyama government resolved to start peace negotiations with the Soviet Union. It is said that after this cabinet meeting Masayuki Tani the Councillor of the *Gaimushō* (*komon*) and Kōta Sugihara of Hatoyama's policy advisory staff sat down to draft specific policies, and the draft they formulated was approved at a later cabinet meeting.[77] Though the original copy of this draft policy has not yet been released, there are published materials which provide information about its content. They are mentioned in volumes by Hellmann and Kubota, and in the memoirs of Matsumoto and Shimoda. Wada has recently introduced documents sent by Sugihara to Hatoyama containing the basic guidelines for the Japanese–Soviet negotiations. These materials do not necessarily agree at all points, but, at least the following can be summarised as far as the territorial claim is concerned. First, the instruction indicated that the return of all former Japanese territories occupied by the Soviets, i.e., the Habomais, Shikotan, the whole of the Kuriles and South Sakhalin, was to be requested. The most notable point is that the return of Shikotan and the Habomais was considered as the minimum condition satisfactory to the Japanese government.[78]

Based on these minimum and maximum goals, the *Gaimushō* prepared more specific strategic scenarios for the territorial negotiations. According to Shimoda, who was then Head of the *Gaimushō's* Treaty Bureau, the *Gaimushō* constructed a strategic negotiation policy comprising three stages of conditions for peace with the USSR, and gave it to Matsumoto before he left for London. According to this strategic policy, Japan was first to request South Sakhalin, the entire Kuriles chain, Shikotan and the Habomais. Second, it was to drop its request for South Sakhalin and the Northern Kuriles. Then, if there was no concession from the Soviet side, Japan was to insist only on the return of Shikotan and the Habomais. Thus, once the Japanese delegation had tabled its maximal position, it was to wait and see how its negotiating partner responded, keeping return of Shikotan and the Habomais as the minimal goal.[79]

As noted in the previous chapter, Japan had already prepared the bases for such arguments, by dividing the territories into three groups according to the strength of its claims, as early as November 1946. At this point, they became a specific negotiation policy. Considering the course of the territorial dispute from 1946 until around the San Francisco Conference of 1951, it seems natural that Japan set the return of Shikotan and the Habomais as a realistic minimum condition of compromise, and it does not seem to be the case that Japan expected more. Whether they belonged to the Shigemitsu- *Gaimushō* group or the Hatoyama group, all considered that even regaining those two island groups would be extremely difficult. Wada analyses this point as follows:

> Thus, Hatoyama's side ... considered that a peace treaty would be concluded if Japan could achieve return of two islands, while the former Premier Yoshida's faction, including part of the *Gaimushō*, who were cautious about the rapid establishment of diplomatic relations with the USSR, thought peace could be prevented by fixing this condition, since the USSR would not agree to return the two islands.[80]

In any case, as far as the territorial claim was concerned, it seems that there was outwardly a consensus of opinion to pursue the claim for return of two islands.

### Instructions to Matsumoto during the London negotiations

Even after it was decided to open peace negotiations with the Soviets, Shigemitsu and the *Gaimushō* maintained a negative attitude and appeared to be hindering the negotiations. For example, while Hatoyama was flexible about their location, Shigemitsu insisted on New York; and during the London negotiations which began in June, Shigemitsu responded to Matsumoto's suggestion of holding meetings with his Russian counterpart Malik twice a week in order to achieve a quick solution, by instructing him to limit the meetings to once a week.

The first chance for *rapprochement*, nevertheless, came during the first London negotiations. In August 1955, two months after the negotiations began, the Soviet offer of the 'Small Kuriles' (the Habomais and Shikotan), was implied by Malik. Considering the history of the disputes over these territories, the offer was far more generous than the Japanese had anticipated. Matsumoto said he could hardly believe his ears.[81] When Matsumoto reported this to the Japanese government, however, it stiffened its original position and sent him a new set of instructions to suggest that (a) Kunashiri and Etorofu should also be unconditionally returned to Japan, and (b) the future of the Northern Kuriles and South Sakhalin should be decided by an international conference.[82]

Considering the time of these instructions, still before the merger of the conservative parties (November), it seems curious that the Japanese government took this position when Prime Minister Hatoyama favoured a quick *rapprochement*. There may be two possible explanations: (a) behind-the-scenes negotiations with regard to the LDP merger were under way, and a compromise had already been reached on policy toward the territorial negotiations; or (b) the *Gaimushō* sent the instruction without consulting or informing Hatoyama. The following description of events by Akira Shigemitsu,[83] where he describes the domestic situation of Japan before the negotiations started in June 1955, has some bearing on (a):

> In Japan, some kind of chaotic situation was emerging within the political arena, to be specific, within the conservative bloc forming the government ruling party. After all, the Yoshida cabinet was taken over by the Hatoyama cabinet. But the tug of war continued among several factions among the conservatives preceding the LDP merger. The important diplomatic matter of normalising Japanese–Soviet relations was incorporated into this tug of war.[84]

Thus, it may be argued that Hatoyama had already made a political compromise with the Yoshida faction and abandoned his position of *rapprochement* with the Russians. However, this line of argument does not explain the behaviour of Hatoyama's faction during the Japanese–Soviet negotiations, for example their efforts to promote the talks even through informal channels.

The second explanation, (b), that Hatoyama was not kept informed on details of the negotiations, is based on what Matsumoto and Hatoyama wrote in their memoirs. For example, Hatoyama states:

> I suppose that the details of the negotiations were reported to *Gaimushō* but they didn't give me the information, though I often asked them.

What I received was nothing but general telegrams. . . . They were after all not brought before my eyes.[85]

If this is true, it follows that the nation's foreign policy was out of the hands of the nation's formal top decision maker, the Prime Minister. The *Gaimushō* from past experience did not trust the Soviets, and recognised a need for hard bargaining to extract any concessions. The initial principle of the Foreign Office's diplomatic philosophy can be observed from Shigemitsu's comments on 13 August during the London negotiations. He said 'if negotiations do not produce agreements satisfactory to Japan, we have to be ready even to terminate them'. In his speech at the National Press Club at the end of August, during his meetings with US government leaders such as Secretary of States Dulles, Shigemitsu also stated, 'the Japanese–Soviet negotiations are not meant to seek friendly relations with the Soviet Union'.[86] The discrepancies between the attitudes of the premier's office and the Foreign Ministry resulted in inconsistencies in Japanese foreign policy, that bewildered the Soviet Union and other nations. Akira Shigemitsu, who attended the negotiations, stated that suspension of them was 'the only bargaining power Japan held'.[87] In short, the *Gaimushō* regarded the reopening of diplomatic relations as a bargaining card or 'concession' from the Japanese side, and considered that it could postpone the negotiations if the situation became inconvenient to Japan. (This point will be further discussed on pp. 100–2). None the less, the Matsumoto–Malik meetings proceeded as a form of 'dual diplomacy' reached deadlock, and fell into an *impasse* with no prospect of solving the territorial problem. The negotiations were suspended this time on 23 September, and Matsumoto flew back to Japan.[88]

## Merger of the conservative parties and the territorial claim

During the period before the interrupted London negotiations reopened in January 1956, the merger of the conservative parties took place and the Liberal Democratic Party (LDP) was established on 15 November. This was a most important event, and greatly affected the future directions of the Soviet–Japanese negotiations. The merger formed the basis for the long period of LDP hegemony in post-war Japanese politics, but the strongest driving force for effecting the merger was the remarkable growth of the socialist parties and their internal merger. The most striking political phenomenon of the 1950s in Japan was the expansion of the socialist movement.[89] The recovery policy and the development of industrialisation were brought to Japan by the USA, and external situations such as the Korean

War contributed to growth. But this also produced increased numbers of manual workers, and spontaneous growth in the labour movement. The growth of the socialist parties was supported by strong labour unions. On 13 October 1955, before the LDP merger, the socialist parties, which had for four years been divided into right and left factions by disagreements over foreign policy, succeeded in reaching a political compromise and were reunited. The Hatoyama cabinet had been formed on the weak foundation of the small Democratic Party. Its merger with the Liberal Party was undertaken in order to form a large ruling party to oppose the then strengthening Socialist Party, and did not result from a policy accord. Japanese politics here entered a new era of confrontation between two major parties (and the ruling LDP predominance) – the so-called '1955 System', which was nothing but a reflection of Cold War politics in the domestic arena. And, as far as the Japanese–Soviet negotiations were concerned, the policies to be followed in them became political bargaining tools at the time of the LDP merger. Even during the period of the solely Democrat cabinet, negative moves by Shigemitsu and the *Gaimushō* hindered the efforts of Prime Minister Hatoyama's office to promote peace talks with the USSR. As a result of the merger, the strong faction hostile to Soviet–Japanese *rapprochement* led by Yoshida became part of the new ruling party and this increased the proportion within the party of opponents of Japanese–Soviet *rapprochement*. Upon establishment of the LDP, the leaders of the Democratic and Liberal parties negotiated to coordinate their policies on normalisation of relations with the Soviet Union. The outcome was announced in the form of a policy document called 'rational adjustment for Japanese–Soviet negotiations' (*Nisso kōshō no gōriteki chōsei*) and announced on 12 November. The new LDP policy for the Japanese–Soviet negotiations was specified in the document, where return of the Southern Kuriles (Kunashiri and Etorofu), together with Shikotan and the Habomais was demanded, and the future of the other territories should be decided by an international conference.[90] This was the result of a major political concession that Hatoyama's group made to the Liberals, in order to bring about the merger. Needless to say, the content of the new policy was the same as that of the government instruction sent to Matsumoto at the end of August. Once the ruling party (LDP) dominance system was established LDP policy equalled government policy. At this point, the present 'four islands return' claim was settled, establishing its position as national policy by escalation from one of the *Gaimushō* policy options.[91]

The solid position of the 'four islands return', established as a result of the LDP merger, was nothing but a political compromise that Hatoyama made with the Yoshida faction from the Liberals. Those in charge of the negotiations, such as Plenipotentiary Matsumoto and the *Gaimushō*, well understood that the Soviets would not agree with this 'four islands return'. A memorandum kept in a file of the US State Department recorded a *Gaimushō* senior official's remarks endorsing the fact that Matsumoto was negotiating along the line of Japanese government policy, though sensing that the Soviet government would never agree to the return of the Southern Kuriles.[92] Knowing it to be impossible, Matsumoto had to pronounce the party policy, i.e., the government policy. The *Gaimushō*'s role was to work out the negotiating strategy in accordance with the same policy.

The reopened London negotiations (17 January to 20 March 1956) again became deadlocked on the territorial problem, and were suspended.

## The Adenauer Formula

Prior to the LDP merger in Japan, the Soviet Union reached an agreement to restore diplomatic relations with West Germany on 13 September 1955, the same day that Soviet–Japanese negotiations were suspended in London. In the Soviet–German peace negotiations, territorial problems were not discussed. West German Chancellor Adenauer held a press conference on 14 September and stated his view that decisions on demarcation lines should be postponed until a peace treaty was signed.[93] When it became clear that a compromise between Japan and the USSR on the territorial issue would be very difficult to attain, a great deal of attention was directed to this so called 'Adenauer Formula', as a possible solution.

## The Moscow negotiations: Shigemitsu's decision

Shigemitsu became the plenipotentiary representative at the Moscow negotiations that started on 31 July 1956. During these negotiations he made a complete personal volte-face and, at his discretion, tried to make a settlement with the two islands transfer.[94] However, Tokyo and Washington stopped him.

As mentioned earlier, Shigemitsu was circumspect at the beginning of the peace negotiations, probably because of his severe perception of the Soviet Union fostered in his years as a diplomat, and also by his sensitivity to US misgivings over Japan's possible reconciliation with the Communist bloc. However, by the time of Moscow negotiations, more than a year had passed since the peace talks began. As for the territorial negotiations, it is not likely that Shigemitsu expected more than Shikotan and the Habomais. He had been Foreign Minister when the war ended, and it was he who had signed the instrument of surrender on board the USS *Missouri*. Although purged and imprisoned, given his career connection with the *Gaimushō*, Shigemitsu was probably still among those most familiar with the post-war development of the territorial problem: announcement of the Yalta Agreement; *Gaimushō's* efforts to regain the Habomais and Shikotan, such as producing the pamphlets; and striving for international support before signing the San Francisco Treaty.

Tanaka, who noted the Japanese three-stage negotiation strategy of the 1955–6 negotiations, analyses Shigemitsu's negotiating policy toward Russia as follows:

> The claim for the Southern Kuriles was originally proposed by Shige-mitsu from his strategic thinking as one of the transitional points in the three-stage negotiation policy, and was to be dropped when a certain concession was made by the Soviet Union. In other words, Shigemitsu thought it possible to control the substance of the territorial claim of Japan, depending on the progress of the negotiations.[95]

There is room for doubt in Tanaka's analysis in respect to whether this three-stage negotiation policy was Shigemitsu's or not, especially taking into consideration that he was in prison when the basis of this strategy was formed. However, it seems certain that, given his global perspectives, he assiduously pursued Japan's best interests depending on the given circum-stances. This attitude came from his sense of reason as a diplomat, and differentiated him in nature both from the Yoshida faction, which persisted in its US dependency policy and rigidity towards the USSR, and from the Hatoyama faction, which compromised on its territorial policy in the domestic political struggle. As his country was locked into the Western bloc, Shigemitsu attempted to draw support from the former Allies in that bloc and waited to see how it would work. It seems that this strategic thinking of Shigemitsu and the *Gaimushō* was well reflected in the new set of instructions given to Matsumoto during the London negotiation: the Habomais, Shiko-tan, Kunashiri and Etorofu to be returned, and the future of the rest of the Kurile Islands to be decided by a future international conference. In sum, this thinking did not aim at a quick solution, but sought for as many conces-sions from the Soviets as possible. The suggestion of an international con-ference was a part of the strategy aimed at attracting support from the other concerned nations, while delaying the settlement with the Soviets.

The fact that Shigemitsu became the plenipotentiary surprised people around him, including Hatoyama. But, having tried all conceivable meas-ures and fully understanding the situation, Shigemitsu probably made a final judgement that Japan had no alternative but to make a settlement by accepting the Soviet terms with the two islands concession, as he wired Tokyo on 12 August.[96] Over one year of negotiations was long enough to learn the Soviet's bargaining cards and intentions, and also the limit of their concessions. Shigemitsu and the *Gaimushō* made every possible effort to attract international support for the Japanese claims, but failed. Moscow was chosen as the place for the negotiations, because Shigemitsu wanted to finalise them by direct discussion with the Soviet leaders and top decision makers. A telegram from the American Ambassador to Japan, Allison, to US Secretary of States Dulles reports that Shigemitsu told him

> Moscow chosen because as Foreign Minister he thought he could nego-
> tiate better there with access to Soviet leaders than by dealing with
> Soviet ambassador London.[97]

However, the new LDP policy of 'rational adjustment for Japanese–Soviet negotiations', which was decided at the time of the merger, was nothing but a fetter for Shigemitsu. The claim for the Southern Kuriles, created as a negotiating technique from the *Gaimushō*'s strategic thinking, escaped the hands of its designers, and found its niche as a national policy. It was impossible for Foreign Minister Shigemitsu, whose domestic political influence was not strong, to shift the political situation back to one more convenient for him to negotiate with the Soviets.[98] As Tanaka noted, when created, the territorial claims had been intended to be controllable according to the circumstances of the negotiations.[99] However, the change in the Japanese domestic climate gave them a certain position, and they ceased to be controllable by their creators. Shigemitsu was against the Adenauer Formula, and wished to conclude a peace treaty only after resolving all the disputes between the two nations. In February 1955, even at the stage before the peace negotiations stated, Shigemitsu was reported as stating that once the termination of war with Russia was formally accomplished Japan would lose forever its claims for return of the Kuriles and Southern Sakhalin: therefore, the Soviet attitude towards territorial questions should first be clarified before the termination of war.[100] If Japan accepted the Adenauer Formula, Shigemitsu saw a danger that it would give up even the two islands return in the future.[101]

On 31 July at the first meeting of the reopened negotiations, Shigemitsu made a long statement of a modified version of the Japanese claim. The statement was the 'four islands' claim and logically well organised 'integral territory theory' (*koyū-no-ryōdo-ron*) as supporting argument for it. It admitted that Japan had renounced South Sakhalin and the Kurile Islands in the San Francisco Peace Treaty, and though the Soviet Union did not sign, it had indicated that the future of the renounced territories could be decided between Japan and the Soviet Union. After stating these points, Shigemitsu claimed the return of the four islands, arguing that Kunashiri and Etorofu were an integral part of Japan, were not included in the Kuriles that Japan renounced, and should be returned in the spirit of 'no territorial aggrandizement' enunciated in the Atlantic Charter of 1941. Shigemitsu stated a further developed and detailed version of the 'integral territory theory' at a later meeting as a counter-argument to the Soviet's rejection.[102] The international conference proposed in the London negotiations had disappeared here. Furthermore, renunciation of South Sakhalin and the Kuriles was not consistent with LDP policy.[103]

Negotiations between Shigemitsu and the Soviet Foreign Minister and Plenipotentiary Dimitri Shepilov deadlocked over the islands of Kunashiri and Etorofu. Facing a consistently rigid Soviet attitude on this matter, Shigemitsu gave up the 'four islands return', decided on his authority as plenipotentiary to conclude the negotiations by accepting the Soviet offer of two islands, and reported his decision not only to the Tokyo government, but also to the press.[104] But capitulation to this degree exceeded what conservatives leader considered 'discretion', and the cabinet refused to sign a peace treaty under such conditions.[105] Meanwhile, both Shigemitsu and Shepilov temporarily suspended the negotiations, and flew to London to attend the Foreign Ministers' Conference. The decisive blow was the 'Dulles' Warning' delivered in London. As a result, the conclusion of a peace treaty on the basis of a 'two islands' return became impossible, and the negotiations finally failed.

### Change in the nature of negotiation

Since Foreign Minister Shigemitsu was still in Moscow, Matsumoto, who accompanied him there, received an indication from the Soviet side that there would be some room left for settlement if Hatoyama visited Moscow. Receiving this information by an informal route, Hatoyama agreed to visit Moscow on 19 August.[106] The political crisis centring around policy in negotiations with the Soviets and specifically the question of Hatoyama's proposed mission to Moscow became more acute after Shigemitsu's return to Japan. Hatoyama's proposed mission continued to be strongly opposed by a powerful segment of the LDP, spearheaded by the ex-Yoshida faction, but including the bulk of ex-liberals and possibly a majority of the 'neutral' rank and file. This opposition was based in part on a domestic political consideration, namely the desire to push Hatoyama out of office. Some opponents considered the mission was merely a device to prolong the life of Hatoyama's regime; others were convinced that there was no possibility of a satisfactory settlement. After his return Shigemitsu, while proceeding cautiously in view of the delicacy of his political position, generally aligned himself with the opposition to Hatoyama's trip. In public statements he consistently took the line that all means of negotiation with the Soviets (including the Adenauer Formula) had been exhausted, and that there was no possibility of reaching a satisfactory settlement, no matter who went to Moscow. At the same time he stressed that there was 'no hurry' about resuming the talks, and reiterated this view in his report to the LDP Executive and party members in 5 September.[107]

Hatoyama, Kōno and the mainstream faction continued vigorously to advocate that Hatoyama go to Moscow to make a final attempt at a settlement. They expressed the hope that there was still room for agreement using the Adenauer Formula, with the territorial issue (possibly including the Habomais and Shikotan) shelved,[108] a view based on the wishful thinking of Matsumoto, who had returned from Moscow. In this situation, the Hatoyama–Bulganin and Matsumoto–Gromyko letters were exchanged for the purpose of confirming the negotiating conditions. The cabinet approved Hatoyama's visit to Moscow on 2 October, but strong opposition continued.

One important point has tended to be ignored in past studies, namely that the nature of the negotiations changed at this point. They had begun as negotiations for a peace treaty, but since the prospect of reaching a consensus on the territorial solution had disappeared, they were changed, by shelving the territorial issue, to negotiations for restoration of diplomatic relations. Hatoyama's letter to Bulganin of 11 September stated:

> Taking into consideration the particulars of the negotiations between the two nations to date, on this occasion making it a condition to continue negotiations regarding the territorial issue at a later date, I, the Prime Minister, notify that the government of Japan is ready to enter negotiations to effect the normalisation of our diplomatic relations, if the Soviet Union agrees beforehand on the following points (1) ending of the state of war between the two nations, (2) mutual establishment of embassies, (3) instant repatriation of the Japanese detainees, (4) effectuation of the fishery treaty, and (5) the support of the Soviet Union for Japan's joining the United Nations.[109]

Bulganin replied on 13 September, accepting the conditions mentioned in Hatoyama's letter, so both sides here clearly promised to make it a 'condition to continue negotiations regarding the territorial issue at a later date'. In the subsequent Matsumoto–Gromyko letters of 29 September, both sides agreed 'to enter negotiations in Moscow on the normalisation of Soviet–Japanese relations without the signing of a peace treaty at this time', and also agreed 'to continue negotiations on the signing of a peace treaty which would also include the territorial issue, after the re-establishment of normal diplomatic relations'.[110] However, the Japanese domestic, specifically the party, situation pulled the position of the delegations further apart. On 20 September, after the Hatoyama–Bulganin letters had been exchanged, the LDP held an *ad hoc* general meeting and decided to make the previous policy on the Japanese–Soviet negotiations the party platform. In addition to demanding the unconditional and immediate repatriation of the Japanese POWs, the main points regarding the territories were as follows: (1) immediate return of Shikotan and the Habomais, (2) continued negotiation over Kunashiri and Etorofu after effectuation of the treaty, (3) observance of the sense of the San Francisco Treaty for the rest of the territories.[111] This platform contradicted the agreement to postpone the territorial negotiations. It should be noted that the official diplomatic agreement made under the name of the Prime Minister, who is supposed to be the top decision maker of a nation, was perverted here, not by Diet nor cabinet decision, but a party decision.

According to Matsumoto, the government prepared three draft negotiation policies based on this party platform. With respect to the peace treaty and the territorial problem, the first draft policy was aimed at normalisation of Japanese–Soviet relations, again, on the basis of a formal peace treaty by resolving the territorial problem. The territorial claims were prepared as follows:

(A) the Soviet Union
   1. immediately to return the Habomais and Shikotan.
   2. to return Kunashiri and Etorofu after the USA returned Okinawa.
(B) Japan to renounce South Sakhalin and the Kurile Islands north of the above-named.

The second and the third draft policies were aimed to end the state of war, reopen diplomatic relations and solve other pending problems, by securing a reservation to sign a peace treaty at a later date, and settlement was to be made by signing each basic agreement or exchanging official documents (i.e. shelving the territorial negotiations and not signing a peace treaty at that time).[112] These policies were truly the products of deliberate effort, taking all conditions into consideration: Japanese domestic politics, US restrictions and the history of the negotiations with the Soviets.

### *Hatoyama's visit to Moscow and the Japanese–Soviet Joint Declaration*

Hatoyama arrived in Moscow and negotiations began on 15 October. As prepared in the draft policy for negotiation, the territorial issue, which was not supposed to be raised, was brought up, and this offended Khrushchev. At the first meeting between Kōno and Khrushchev on 16 October, Kōno said:

> though we were willing to conclude the negotiations while shelving the territories, we had to put the party platform of transferring the Habomais and Shikotan and postponing the others because of opposition within the party. Thus, I am very sorry for having changed our proposal, but I would like you to understand our domestic situation and cooperate with Premier Hatoyama's and my wishes.[113]

Khrushchev's response was:

> The Japanese side was not to mention the territorial question. We agreed to this and clarified it in Gromyko's letter to Plenipotentiary Representative Matsumoto. Since the transfer of Habomai and Shikotan is a territorial problem, it is also involved with the peace treaty. If the Japanese side wishes to conclude a peace treaty, why don't we prescribe this in it?[114]

Kōno was a party politician. He could not go back to Japan without raising the territorial issue as required by the new party platform. However, it was already clear from the past negotiations that the Soviets would not accept the first draft policy. After various discussions, the long period of negotiations between the two countries finally ended with the territorial clause cited at the beginning of this chapter (p. 34). The USSR and Japan indeed ended the state of war and restored diplomatic relations. However, the result was neither a complete *rapprochement* by signing a peace treaty, nor the shelving of the territories question according to the Adenauer Formula – it may be that the Japanese consequently steamrollered the negotiations at the end.

At the drafting stage of the Joint Declaration, the Japanese side tried to include a passage 'including territorial negotiations' after (*in front* in the original of the Japanese language) 'negotiations for the conclusion of a Peace Treaty', but the Soviet side refused.

Though consensus was reached on the terms of the Joint Declaration, it had to be interpreted in such a manner as to preserve the plenipotentiaries' face at home. So it came to be interpreted in conjunction with the Matsumoto–Gromyko letters, which they announced together with the Joint Declaration. That is, the Habomais and Shikotan were promised in the Joint Declaration, and the question of Kunashiri and Etorofu was to be settled during negotiations for a peace treaty.

The Hatoyama delegation visited the US on the way back from Moscow. There is an interesting memorandum of conversation of this time kept in a record of the US State Department file:

> When Mr. Robertson asked about the situation with respect to Etorofu and Kunashiri, Mr. Hatoyama said that Japan had forfeited Etorofu and Kunashiri in the San Francisco Peace Treaty, and could neither ask for them back nor give them to the USSR. Mr. Kono said the real reason for the present territorial arrangement was that fundamentally the Japanese had no desire to disturb the San Francisco Peace Treaty. There was no chance for the present to regain Etorofu and Kunashiri but Japan would have to wait for a crack to appear in the Soviet position.[115]

As I mentioned earlier, it was during the London negotiation and after the LDP merger, when Matsumoto was negotiating for the 'four islands return' knowing it impossible, that the negotiation deadlocked. Even at this point, after the Moscow summit meetings, the Japanese government evidently acknowledged that Etorofu and Kunashiri were included in the Kuriles that Japan gave up at San Francisco and that they could get no more than the Habomais and Shikotan. However, in not making a perfect peace by signing a peace treaty, some room for future negotiation was retained in their 'four islands' claim.[116]

In the end, the Soviet–Japanese negotiations concluded with results favoured by Yoshida in the domestic sense and by the USA in a global sense, and also symbolised the future direction of Japan. Hatoyama retired soon after returning to Japan, and the foci of the domestic politics were shifted to other issues such as the selection of the next prime minister and revision of the security treaty with the US.

### *Japanese policy making in the 1955–6 Soviet–Japanese negotiations*

The Japanese–Soviet peace movement in the mid-1950s consisted of various factions with complex interactions. In addition to the global factors and situations, a key to understanding the important policy decisions is the domestic political situation of the time, when Japan was undergoing fundamental changes in its political system. I have been describing how decisions on Japanese–Soviet reconciliation and the territorial problem (expression of the territorial clause) were considered at the nation-state level from the Japanese point of view. It may be appropriate now to provide a brief summary of Japanese policy decision making *vis-à-vis* the Soviet

Union in the period before and during Hatoyama's visit to Moscow, in the contexts of the business (*zai*), bureaucratic (*kan*) and political (*sei*) relationships mentioned on pp. 57–9.

In the *Zaikai* (big business groups), the fishing industry brought important pressure to bear through its connections with particular political factions or individuals during a critical period of the negotiations, eventually contributing to an important shift of the government's policy direction. Thus, a domestic interest group became an important driving force to promote diplomatic objectives, and this could not have been achieved through formal government channels alone. The *Zaikai* as a whole did not have strong motives to promote economic relations with the USSR; their primary concern was to stabilise conservative goverment[117] and avoid the negative effects on their trade relations with the USA and the possible increase in the domestic communist movement that they expected would result from opening doors to the USSR. Some groups of the *Zaikai* even threatened to cease political funding if the split and conflict among the conservatives continued.[118] Thus, during the 1955–6 Japanese–Soviet negotiations, little importance was attached to economic or trade issues, and the main focus in policy making was on purely political considerations. Therefore, apart from the fishing industry, whose future could depend heavily on the result of the peace negotiations, the *Zaikai* as a whole had little interest in promoting them, or becoming involved in specific policy making by using their personal or financial ties with the conservative parties.[119] As a whole, the role of the *Zaikai* in decision making regarding the Japanese–Soviet negotiations was therefore minimal compared to those of bureaucracy and politics.

The bureaucracy (*kan*) played a central role in foreign policy making during the early period of post-war Japan, when 'politics' was absent under the American occupation. While the 'politics' part was not functioning, the bureaucracy part was fully in charge of the national administration under US guidance. As seen in Chapter 1, the 1946 pamphlet was drafted by *Gaimushō*. Making the best use of their intelligence on history, geography and other facts, the pamphlet was presumably written with the potential negotiation strategies of the future in mind. The foundation of the Japanese claim was there, dividing the territories into three groups according to the strength of its claims. The realistic goal for territorial return was the islands of Shikotan and the Habomais.

Over the following decade after regaining national independence, the 'politics' (*sei*) part resumed their influence. During the negotiations with the USSR, legal roles and the history of the actual initiative between the politics and the bureaucracy began to form a complex and ironic mixture in national policy making. 'Politicians' and 'bureaucrats' were not necessarily divided in policy towards the USSR. It was the conservative party(ies) which was/were divided. Two conservative parties with different foreign policies merged, as they came into accord domestically to confront the socialists. During this process of political struggle, the negotiation policy with the USSR, which had been made with the bureaucracy leadership, was disordered. Constitutionally, the right of decision making is placed in the cabinet and its constituent ruling party(ies). The lead in policy making had been taken by the bureaucracy, and this had worked well with previous regimes. However, under the constitution, the *Gaimushō* is made fully subordinate to the government and is designed simply to implement the policies set down by the party. Thus, it holds no decision-making authority. The policy for the territorial negotiation with the USSR was absorbed in the political struggle within the ruling party upon the establishment of the '1955 system'. Departing from the three-stage territorial policy made by the *Gaimushō*, the 'four islands' claim was made into national policy. Control over negotiation manoeuvring was then taken from the bureaucracy.

Foreign Minister Shigemitsu stood distinct in the cabinet. He consistently played a role of diplomat rather than a politician, probably from his former experience as a career diplomat. While the *Gaimushō*'s policy was becoming more and more difficult to carry out, as it differed from that of the Prime Minister's office and the LDP merger became involved in the process, he tried to restrain different movements. However, he did not have the power as a politician to repeal the LDP policy. It is assumed that he became the plenipotentiary so as to seek decisions based on national interest, rather than the party interest. Thus, an interesting point about the bureaucracy in this case of foreign policy making is the relationship between the Ministry of Foreign Affairs and the Foreign Minister. Cabinet ministers are chosen by political appointment, and consequently gaps are usually observed within ministries between the bureaucrats, who are technical and administrative specialists, and the ministers, who are usually party politicians. In this particular case, however they worked in harmony. In negotiations with the Soviet Union thereafter, the general pattern was that ministers, not necessarily specialists in foreign affairs, carried out or followed the foreign policy manuals prepared under the leadership of the Ministry of Foreign Affairs. But the situation was different in this case. Shigemitsu was a politician with a long previous career as a diplomat, and was probably a thorough diplomat in his thinking till the end. He performed literally as the head of the Ministry of Foreign Affairs.

As for the domestic structure of policy making in the 1955–6 Japanese–Soviet negotiations, the following picture may be drawn. At the beginning of the Japanese–Soviet negotiations, three major groups existed to decide the future direction of the Japanese foreign policy. The first was the mainstream Democrats, Prime Minister Hatoyama and people close to him; the second was the Yoshida faction of the Liberals; and the third was the Ministry of Foreign Affairs (*Gaimushō*) with Shigemitsu as its head. The Hatoyama group was making a strong push for a quick settlement with the Russians. It was confronted by the Yoshida and *Gaimushō* groups, exhibiting clear contrasts in foreign policy making. Especially when the group in the Prime Minister's office and the *Gaimushō* group proceeded with their policies without reaching consensus within the domestic decisional unit, they often leaked information to the media to create situations advantageous to themselves. For example, Shigemitsu 'knifed' Matsumoto by leaking the Soviet proposal during the London negotiations. This offended the Soviet leaders. Matsumoto returned the compliment by leaking the news of 'Dulles' Warning', thus offending the US State Department.[120]

A change occurred in the political (*sei*) arena in the middle of the Japanese–Soviet negotiations: the conservative parties merged and the political compromise made at that time came to be reflected in the ruling party's negotiation policy. The structure of conflict then became separated roughly into two: 'politics' (*sei*) versus 'bureaucracy' (*kan*). Despite the LDP's policy decision on the territorial issue, Foreign Minister Shigemitsu, recognising it as unrealistic and impossible to pursue it, decided to settle by accepting the Soviet 'two islands' offer and concluding the peace treaty. But his decision was aborted by US pressure rather than by disapproval from the Tokyo government.

At the time of Hatoyama's visit at the final stage, it is arguable that the three groups presented a similar structure of conflicting positions to that in the early stages of the negotiations, in the sense that both the Yoshida and the *Gaimushō* groups were against Hatoyama's visit to Moscow. But it seems more appropriate to view Hatoyama's group as steamrollering the situation, instead of grasping the power balance between the conflicting groups. The skid device set in 'politics' at the time of the LDP merger, i.e., the 'party platform', worked effectively and complete *rapprochement* was not achieved.

As for the power balance in Japanese policy decision making towards the USSR/Russia in general, it is commonly understood that the bureaucracy normally enjoys a dominant position compared to the ruling party(ies) or business groups. However, the case of the 1955–6 negotiations seems to be an exception. Judging from the result, it was a case of party political dominance.

Tossed about by the waves of political battle within the conservative parties (or later the ruling party), policy towards the USSR lost direction and consistency even without a change of the premiership. In the end, the summit meetings took place with Prime Minister Hatoyama, and the long period of negotiations finally concluded with the Joint Declaration.

# THE 'NATION-STATE' PERSPECTIVE: THE SOVIET UNION

No detailed research work on the 1955–6 Soviet–Japanese negotiations has been done from the Soviet point of view comparable to that for Japan. Even in the works of Professor Hiroshi Kimura, a leading Japanese scholar who has published a great number of publications on the subject of post-war Japanese–USSR/Russian relations, only a few sentences have been devoted to it.[121] It was taboo for Soviet academics to analyse actual Soviet political decision making, so the lack of Soviet work on the subject is understandable. The obligatory Soviet academic approach to Soviet foreign policy in general was mainly focused on its structural and ideological aspects, primarily because the availability of sources was limited due to governmental control of expression, and most publications were ideologically coloured to serve propaganda purposes. Since initiation of the *Glasnost* policy in the late 1980s, Soviet-period diplomatic documents have been gradually released, and new facts are being revealed with regard to policies towards, for example, Eastern Europe or the Korean War. However, probably for the same reasons as have prompted Japanese non-disclosure of relevant documents, namely that the still unresolved territorial dispute might be affected, materials regarding Soviet policy towards Japan seem to be beyond the range of the *Glasnost* policy, at least to this date. In 1994 my request for access to materials on the subject more than 30 years old, received after two weeks a polite refusal from the Russian Foreign Ministry Archives. The Archives of the Central Committee of the Communist Party allowed me access to some documents on the subject, including records of the late 1980s, but they were not of significant substance. The most important primary written material currently available for studying the perceptions of the then Soviet top decision maker is probably Nikita Khrushchev's own memoirs, *Khrushchev Remembers: The Glasnost Tapes*, published in 1990.[122] The volume includes his recollection of the Soviet–Japanese peace negotiations, including the territorial negotiations. Although, like all memoirs, these present the author's role in the most favourable possible light, they offer insights into Soviet perceptions of Japan in this period. Khrushchev and most of the other key figures who participated in making the crucial decisions during the 1955–6 negotiations with Japan are now dead. It was, therefore, especially gratifying that some former senior officials from the Soviet Ministry of Foreign Affairs (MID) and from the International Department of the Central Committee, who were in some way engaged in policy formulation towards Japan as Asian specialists at the time, kindly gave of their time and shared their experiences in interviews for this particular study.

## Soviet foreign-policy decision making

Unlike that of Japan, the Soviet political system did not change as a result of the Second World War. Naturally, the Soviet system cannot be explained by the same triangular framework as the Japanese political influence system. Nevertheless, it is appropriate to provide some general explanation of Soviet foreign-policy decision making before going into specific issues.

The most important decision-making unit in the Soviet Union was the Politburo of the Communist Party. As the sole party in the Soviet state, relations between the Communist Party and the government were those of two sides of a coin. The Party was granted legal authority as the leading body of the nation by Article 126 of the Soviet Constitution of 1936.[123] According to its rules, its highest policy-making body was the Party Congress, which was supposed to be held every four or five years (though Stalin did not convene a Party Congress between 1939 and 1952), but for most of Soviet history the Congress was manipulated by the party leadership and it adopted policies essentially determined before it began. The Central Committee was nominally the body directing party policy between Congresses; its members held leading offices in party and state organisations, including central and regional party organisations, editorships of the main newspapers and journals, or were leading scientists, academicians, and top personnel of the armed forces, police, trade unions, etc. About two dozen functionaries from the Ministry of Foreign Affairs, including the ambassadors to the Soviet bloc countries, were those who represented the government's foreign affairs apparatus.[124] The most powerful individual post not only within the Communist Party but within the Soviet Union was for nearly all of Soviet history the General Secretaryship of the Central Committee (called First Secretaryship of the Central Committee between 1953 and 1966). The highest collective policy-making organ was the Politburo (renamed Presidium of the Central Committee, 1953–66), headed by the General Secretary. Under Stalin, it came first to dominate the Central Committee and the Party Congress, and then to be ruled by Stalin himself. For over a quarter of a century, Stalin exercised real dictatorship in the Soviet Union, personally making all important decisions, including foreign policies.[125]

The government apparatus of the USSR played a responsible role in conducting or formulating Soviet foreign policy, but major decisions were taken by the Politburo. The Council of Ministers was the body formally responsible to the Supreme Soviet for the administration of State affairs. The Ministry of Foreign Trade, Committee for Foreign Economic Relations, the State Committee for Cultural Relations with Foreign Countries and TASS (the Telegraph Agency for the Soviet Union) were also involved to greater or lesser extents in Soviet foreign affairs. The Committee for State Security (KGB), whose first main administration had primary responsibility for espionage, was believed to be more important. The military did much more than implement defence policy. It also contributed significantly to the formulation of a broad range of decisions affecting national security. It had close contact with the Politburo, through the State Defence Committee in the Second World War, and the Supreme Defence Council after it, both bodies chaired ex officio by the General Secretary. The Ministry of Foreign Affairs was the primary agency for implementing foreign policy. Its minister was assisted by the Collegium of his deputies and various department heads named by the Council of Ministers. Formally there was a check and balance relationship between minister and Collegium, i.e., if disagreements arose the matters were to be brought to the Council of Ministers or the Central Committee of the Party. However, in reality, there was no such check on official actions once approved by the highest party leaders.[126]

## Restoration of Japanese–Soviet diplomatic relations

### *Change of leadership and foreign policy*

From the nation-state perspective, the Soviet–Japanese reconciliation can be explained as a series of changes in both countries brought about by a new political leadership and the new foreign policies that it initiated. However there was a big difference between Japan and the USSR in these similar moves, a difference in the impact of national-level changes on the global system of international relations.

When considering the relationships of the two units, the global international system and nation states, two major flows of influence are noticeable: one from the international system to the nation states and the other from the states to the system. Japan in the mid-1950s, integrated almost subordinately into the US-led Western bloc and its Asian sub-system, had almost no influence on the international system, but that system and changes in it greatly affected the Japanese foreign policy. In contrast, the Soviet Union, the global superpower leading the Eastern bloc in the Cold War world, had tremendous influence on the global international system. In the previous section, I discussed the policies of Japan and the USSR towards each other from the global international relations perspective. The major global factor in the Soviet–Japanese reconciliation process, the change in the international system, was largely a result of the tremendous influence of foreign-policy inputs in the name of detente and/or peaceful coexistence, from the nation-state level unit of the USSR. Changes in the general movement in the Soviet Union at nation-state level therefore also warrant considerable attention.

In 1953 Stalin died. After his death, the direction of the Soviet diplomacy underwent fundamental changes towards 'Peaceful Coexistence'. The period of the Soviet–Japanese peace negotiations in 1955–6 was also the period when Nikita Khrushchev was gradually strengthening his position to become virtual supreme leader of the USSR. The first few years after Stalin's death were years of collective leadership and struggle for power. Khrushchev, who was initially ranked behind Malenkov, Molotov, Beria and Kaganovich, had become acting First Secretary of the Party within few weeks of Stalin's death. In September 1953 he was confirmed in that post, but Malenkov, whose name preceded that of Khruschev's as Prime Minister, continued to be seen as the top leader both within and outside the Soviet Union. Khrushchev fortified his status as supreme Soviet leader, as distinct from party First Secretary, when Malenkov was overthrown from Chairmanship of the Council of Ministers and replaced by Bulganin, who was under Khrushchev's control, in February 1955.[127] The short period of collective leadership headed by Malenkov ended at this point, and through the Bulganin–Khrushchev period, his one-man politics flourished for several years.

Though the Twentieth Congress of the CPSU in February 1956 is best-known for Khrushchev's 'de-Stalinisation' speech, it was also significant in the sense that the new direction of Soviet diplomacy was clearly indicated both to the country and to the outside world. Khrushchev advocated 'Peaceful Coexistence' between the communist and capitalist countries. Until then, the Soviet view of the world had long stood on Stalin's dogmatic understanding and interpretation of Marxism-Leninsm. According to his 'two camps theory', the world was divided into the two camps of communism and capitalism. The two camps stood on mutually incompatible principles and no permanent compromise could be made between them. They would eventually fight each other, and communism would prevail world-wide.

Nikita Khrushchev recognised that nuclear weapons had fundamentally altered the character of international politics. Perceiving the danger of a nuclear war with the United States, he needed to found an ideological ground for the durability of a relationship between communism and capitalism that would not lead to war.[128] Although the atomic bomb came into existence while Stalin was in power, he died without modifying his two camps theory. In his report to the Twentieth Party Congress, Khrushchev remarked,

There is, of course, a Marxist-Lenist prescript that wars are inevitable as long as imperialism exists. This precept was evolved at a time when

(1) imperialism was an all-embracing world system, and (2) the social and political forces which did not want war were weak, poorly organised, and hence unable to compel the imperialists to renounce war. . . . In that period this precept was absolutely correct. At the present time, however, the situation has changed radically. Now there is a world camp of socialism, which has become a mighty force. In this camp the peace forces find not only the moral, but also the material means to prevent aggression. . . . As long as capitalism survives in the world, the reactionary forces representing the interests of the capitalist monopolies will continue their drive towards military gambles and aggression, and may try to unleash war. But war is not fatalistically inevitable.[129]

Khrushchev's modification included recognition of another category, the Third World, of developing countries. These countries mostly in Asia and Africa, belonged to neither the communist nor capitalist blocs but aimed to liberate themselves from colonial control by imperialistic capitalist countries, in a process conceived as a struggle for both political and economic freedom, in which the grant of political independence would mark only an intermediate stage.[130] Their driving force could be transformed into a revolutionary movement, and they would possibly choose a course towards communism, should indoctrination and assistance be provided by the leading communist countries. In fact, Lenin had prepared the ideological foundations for a communist alliance with the 'forces of national liberation', but it did not become practicable until the late 1950s.[131] In its early years the besieged Soviet state had lacked the resources for operational commitment, and though Stalin had more resources at his command, his preoccupation with events elsewhere and consequent lack of interest nullified the Leninist perception of strategic opportunities in the 'imperialist reserve'.[132] Reflecting on the distorted policies of the Stalin era, Khrushchev pointed to the developing nations of Asia, Africa and the Middle East. Concurring with their moves against imperialistic control by the UK, France, the USA and others, the Soviets provided economic and military assistance. The growth of the Soviet domestic economy at the time provided resources, as did new Soviet economic and resource policies.[133]

## The approach to Japan

This shift in Soviet foreign policy derived from analysis of the reality by the new Soviet leadership after Stalin's death. Moves for *rapprochement* with Japan, an initiative taken by the Soviet side, can be understood in the context of this new foreign policy, which aimed to abandon the deadlock diplomacy of Stalinism, adjust relations with the outside world, including former enemies, and expand the Soviet sphere of influence in circumstances where the victory of a communist revolution in the developed western countries was unlikely in the foreseeable future. This ushered in a thaw in international relations, including Soviet relations with Japan.

In a speech before the Presidium in August 1953, Premier Malenkov declared that with the attainment of a truce in Korea, the time had come to normalise relations with various countries in the Far East, especially Japan.[134] In accordance with the general improvement of East–West relations in 1954, the Soviet Union continued to send indications of its wish to normalise relations with Japan. The joint Sino-Soviet communiqué issued in October 1954 during Khrushchev's visit to Peking expressed their readiness to normalise relations with Japan.[135] On 17 December, following the formation of the Hatoyama Cabinet in Japan and Foreign Minister Shigemitsu's announcement of Japan's inclination to normalise relations with the USSR and China, Molotov replied in a Moscow broadcast that the USSR was ready for normalisation if Japan truly desired it.[136] However, no further diplomatic move followed from the Japanese government. Then, in a dramatic move, the Soviet Unions's representative in Japan, Andrei Ivanovich Domnitsky, delivered a letter directly to Hatoyama early the next year.

Soviet policy decision making appeared far more monolithic than that of Japan at the time of their negotiations and, as I have already said, has been studied far less. Nevertheless, in dealing with the bilateral relations and decisions made between the two nations, it is still essential to study the decision makers' perceptions and the processes and factors involved in policy formulations. Khrushchev's memoirs are revealing, for, as on other issues, he criticised Stalin, calling his failure to sign the San Francisco Peace Treaty 'a blunder'. The memoirs record:

> However, we have to give the Americans some credit. When the protocol of the peace treaty with Japan was drafted, there was a place reserved for our signature. Our interests were totally taken care of there. All we had to do was sign, and everything would have fallen into place; we would have gotten everything we were promised. We would also have restored peaceful relations with Japan and been able to send representatives of our diplomatic service to Tokyo.[137]

> We should have signed. I don't know why we didn't. Perhaps it was vanity or pride. But primarily it was that Stalin had an exaggerated idea of what he could do and what his influence was on the United States. He took the bit in his mouth and refused to sign the treaty. I

think his logic worked like this: If we signed the treaty, we would be recognising the fact – perfectly obvious to any thinking man – that the United States had suffered the main losses from Japanese treachery and borne the principal burden in crushing Japan (although the interests of England, Holland, and other European colonial countries were also affected). Stalin didn't want to do that. There was no question that the Americans gave us the back of their hand, refusing to recognise our contribution to the extent that they should have. Still, we should have taken a sober view of events. If we compare what we contributed with what the United States contributed to the defeat of Japan, then we have to recognise that we did even less in the war against Japan than the Americans and British did to defeat Hitler's Germany.[138]

He candidly acknowledged that Stalin had fallen into a trap set by US strategy, left Japan under monopolistic US control, and thereby deprived the Soviet Union of any opportunity to expand its sphere of influence or develop economic relations with Japan:

when we refused to sign the Japanese surrender, forces in the West probably thought it was to their advantage. And it later turned out they were right. Just look at who benefited from the situation. It was our own fault, because if we had signed we would have had an embassy there. We would have had access to Japanese public opinion and influential circles. We would have established trade relations with Japanese firms.

We missed all that. That's just what the Americans wanted; it was in their interest. They didn't want our representatives to be in other countries. In general, they wanted to isolate us. That is the policy they carried out from the first day of the Soviet state: encirclement, nonrecognition, and intervention. Now we ourselves swallowed this very bait and ended up pleasing aggressive, anti-Soviet forces in the United States, all because of our shortsightedness.

Since we had absolutely no contacts with Japan, our economy and our policy suffered. The Americans, meanwhile, not only had an embassy in Tokyo, they were masters there. They behaved brazenly. They built bases. They waged an anti-Soviet policy. They incited the Japanese. They did what the most frenzied monopolists and militarists wanted them to do. They seethed with hatred against the socialist camp, primarily against the country that first raised the Marxist-Leninist banner of the working class and achieved great successes.[139]

The answer to the question 'what urged the Soviet Union to improve its relations with Japan' is already clear. As in other parts of the world, the

Soviet goal was to weaken US ties with Japan, and expand Soviet control and interests. In order for this strategy to succeed, an initial foothold was needed. Khrushchev stated,

> Who benefits from our absence in Tokyo? The Americans, that's who! The United States is in control of Japan. Our return to Tokyo would benefit the Japanese, especially the progressive people there. As soon as our embassy reopens in Tokyo, it will act like a magnet, attracting all those who are dissatisfied with Japan's current policies. These elements will begin to establish ties to our embassy, and we will begin to exert some influence on Japanese politics.[140]

Khrushchev claimed that there were good grounds in Japan for sweeping the US away and promoting the Soviet advance.

> There was, naturally, great dissatisfaction in Japan, first because of Hiroshima and Nagasaki. It was the United States more than any other country that destroyed Japan. Truman's use of the atomic bomb against Japanese cities was the first atrocity of this kind in history committed against humanity. Of course, the dead can't register their dissatisfaction, but the wounded, their relatives, and the politicians – they were of a single strong mind on this issue. But they were unable to take any action because they had been weakened, and the United States had behaved quite arrogantly. American soldiers were rude and committed acts of violence against the populace. Also, the Japanese lost Okinawa to American occupation – a fact that could have been a major impetus for friendship with the Soviet Union, and for mobilising forces against the occupiers.[141]

Khrushchev was probably right. In fact, given the casualties and territorial losses that Japan had suffered from its war against the USA, the USSR might have gained more. Post-war Japan, as a matter of fact, presented fertile ground for the communist-socialist movement to revive. A large number of intellectuals had been drawn to Marxism since the early twentieth century. To such 'dangerous thoughts', which had been persecuted for decades, the freedom of expression was brought by the US Occupation reforms. Furthermore, the Occupation shift 'from reform to rehabilitation' accompanied the advent of the Japanese socialists to high office.[142]

Incidentally, Soviet overtures to Japan began before Khrushchev gained the top position. He mentioned in his memoirs that there was a consensus within the collective leadership on the need to terminate the state of war

and sign a peace treaty with Japan, though not all members of the decisional unit were in complete accord.

> After Stalin's death I spoke to Mikoyan, Bulganin, and Malenkov about
> it. We all agreed that we needed to find a way to sign a treaty and end
> the state of war with Japan. That way we could send an ambassador to
> Japan who would carry our proper work. But Molotov showed the
> same fierce stubbornness, the same obtuseness, that he did when the
> question of concluding a peace treaty with Austria was discussed. 'We
> can't do it', he said. 'They haven't done this, and they haven't done
> that. There is no way we can sign the agreement'. In short, he repeated
> all the same arguments that Stalin had used to refuse signing the treaty
> the first time around.[143]

Molotov was consistent in playing his role of the faithful and cool execu-
tant of Stalin's diplomacy. For those who directly participated in negotiations over the post-war treatment of Japan and its former territories, it was
hard to shift their perceptions. Molotov considered that the USSR had
secured the future of the Kuriles, promised at Yalta, in negotiations with US
Secretary of State Byrnes at the high cost of conceding US trusteeship of
Micronesia, then had been betrayed at the San Francisco Conference. It
can be assumed that he had no wish to give up even a small part of those
territories. Khrushchev, who criticised Stalin's policy and sought a new
direction, obviously had different perceptions towards Japan.

> I told Molotov, 'The biggest favour we could do for the Americans
> would be stubbornly to reject contacts with Japan. That would give
> them a chance to exercise absolute power there and to turn Japan
> steadily more against the Soviet Union. We'll be making it easy for the
> Americans to claim that the Soviet Union illegally seized this or that
> piece of territory and that the Soviet Union still has some hidden
> intentions'. Of course, not even Stalin had any such thing in mind. [144]

Since he had not been involved in diplomacy, Khrushchev was not influenced by negative experiences or memories of past negotiations and therefore he could accept the reality of the international relations that the USSR
was facing, and come up with more realistic measures and strategies.

> We told him: 'Comrade Molotov, you must look at what we are able to
> accomplish here, exactly what kind of influence we have. What's done
> is done; it's water under the bridge. The only thing we can do is try to
> fix the situation. If we can get them to let us sign the treaty, it will set
> things right.[145]

Khrushchev's analysis was correct, but it was probably too late to put it into practice. The USA had had ten years of control of Japan, and had convinced conservative Japanese power holders of the importance of relations and alliance. As mentioned earlier, when the San Francisco Peace Treaty was ratified on 30 March 1952, the US Senate resolved to advise and consent that the treaty was not intended to give rights or benefits to the Soviets over Soviet-occupied former Japanese territories, including the Habomais and Shikotan. From the Soviet angle, leaving Japan under US occupation was a blunder; not signing at San Francisco was also a blunder, perhaps a fatal one.

At the initial stage of contact with Japan, the new Soviet leadership (Khrushchev, Bulganin, etc.) was enthusiastic about normalising relations, but Foreign Minister Molotov in charge of diplomacy was not. This somewhat resembles the situation in Japan in the same period where Prime Minister Hatoyama and his supporters were seeking a quick *rapprochement*, but Foreign Minister Shigemitsu's attitude was negative. However, the situations differed thereafter. In Japan, Hatoyama, who had become Prime Minister with extremely strong public support, lost his authority in the domestic political turmoil, while Shigemitsu continued as Foreign Minister throughout the negotiation period. In the Soviet Union, Molotov was dismissed from the post of Foreign Minister; Khrushchev also removed the other members of the 'Anti-Party' group in June 1957, and strengthened his authority by adding headship of the government to that of the Party.

To the Soviet leaders, the attitude of Japan's then new Prime Minister, Hatoyama, looked 'promising'.[146] Khrushchev recalled 'he was very attentive to what we had to say and made efforts to normalise relations with the USSR',[147] though 'in the end he was blocked by internal political forces in Japan, but the main obstacle was the influence of the United States'.[148] This is correct, but it seems that Khrushchev thought relations with Japan would have improved if Hatoyama's regime had lasted longer.

> Perhaps if that man had lived longer and increased his power, public opinion would have changed, but he was elderly when he visited [in October 1956], and very ill. Soon after returning to Japan, he died.[149]

Did Khrushchev notice that it was to oppose growing socialist power and to protect the conservative regime in domestic politics that Hatoyama made concessions on territorial policy to the other conservative group at the time of the LDP merger? The situation Khrushchev assumed likely could have occurred only if the initial Hatoyama Democratic Party Cabinet had strengthened its power and concurrently the socialist parties *had not*. Hatoyama's emergence and promotion of his independent policy, growth in the labour movement and in socialist power may have given the Soviet leadership impressions of Japan similar to those they had formed of the Third World, and looked 'promising' for a Soviet advance, but though Hatoyama sought independence for Japan, he was a conservative politician, never a communist or socialist. Since growth of socialist power in Japan was what the Soviet Union sought, it was ironic that a positive cause produced a negative effect. It is certain that the chance for Soviet–Japanese *rapprochement* was lost when the Hatoyama regime became controlled by the pro-US factions.

## Policy making towards Japan

Alexander Nikolaevich Panov, a Russian elite diplomat with long experience of dealing with Japanese affairs, has commented:

> In the Soviet state, participants in foreign policy decision making – diplomats, military officers, party officials, staff of the intelligence service and the committee of State Security – are traditionally allotted the role of implementing the decisions of the highest leadership, and they could not make any substantial alteration to dogmatically decided policies, nor they did not even think of making alterations, not wanting to upset the top leaders. In addition, these political activists and bureaucrats were brought up in the spirit of worshipping formal doctrine and hardly doubted its credibility.[150]

On pp. 82–3 I gave a brief explanation of Soviet foreign-policy decision making in general. How was specific policy making towards Japan conducted? Khrushchev was not a Japan specialist, so who formulated specific policies regarding Japan?

Within the Ministry of Foreign Affairs, the Far Eastern Department was technically responsible for the specifics of policy regarding Japan. At the initial stage of the peace negotiations, Ivan Fedorovich Kurdiukov was its head. According to Mikhail Kapitsa, who was then number two in the department and later succeeded Kurdiukov, the department covered the whole of the Far East including Japan, China, Mongolia and the Koreas. Molotov was replaced as Foreign Minister by Dmitri T. Shepilov, the chief editor of *Pravda*, before the formal negotiations started. Since he held the position only for a couple of years, Shepilov has left a negligible impression compared to his predecessor, or to his successor, Gromyko. However, Kapitsa commented he was a Secretary of the Central Committee when he was appointed Minister of Foreign Affairs. He was a very strong minister. He was so strong that he even joined the group of Molotov and Kaganovich, to kick out Khrushchev. After that he was dismissed too [in June 1957, for having attached himself to the so-called Anti-party Group].[151]

The importance of the International Department of the Central Committee has often been pointed out for its influence on Soviet policy towards Japan. According to a former senior official of the International Department, who was at that time working for the State Committee for Cultural Relations with Foreign Countries as a Japan specialist under E.M. Zhukov and later rose to become a Deputy-Director of the International Department of the Central Committee, the documents needed for the negotiations were prepared jointly by the Foreign Ministry and the International Department.[152] It may be true to a certain extent. But the MID's perception of the situation was that it had taken the major initiative in policy formulation and not been influenced much by the Central Committee. Kapitsa pointed out:

> We were closer much later. The Central Committee was behind the scenes. It was the Far Eastern Department (that played a major role in formulating policies).[153]

In respect of influence on policies, since final authority to make decisions did not rest with these organs, the influence of area specialists on decision making was marginal. The Politburo was above the International Department in the policy-making hierarchy, and the final decision was made by Khrushchev himself. As he participated in the negotiations directly with the Japanese representatives, Khrushchev was interested in relations with Japan. The Japanese Diet delegation visited the USSR and met with Bulganin and Khrushchev on 22 September 1955. A member of the delegation recalled the visit and stated at a Diet Foreign Affairs Committee:

> In fact, as for Khrushchev's remarks to us, as Bulganin who was staying by him said that he wanted us to perceive Mr. Khruschev's remarks as the opinion of the government as a whole, we may probably consider them as their government announcement . . .[154]

Both these former senior officials clearly pointed out that Khrushchev gave firm leadership as First Secretary in policy decision making towards Japan.

## The territorial problem: 'Shikotan and the Habomais'

The Joint Declaration stated 'The USSR agrees to transfer to Japan the Habomais and Shikotan . . . desiring to meet the wishes of Japan and taking into consideration the interests of the Japanese State'. Then how about 'the wishes of the USSR' and 'interest of the Soviet State'? Three questions arise when the territorial expression in the Joint Declaration is considered. First, what was the reason for returning any territories to Japan? Second, why did they decide to return Shikotan and the Habomais? Third, did they have any intention to return the 'four islands' which Japan has been claiming for the last several decades? I will now consider the answers to these questions.

At the initial stage of the formal negotiations with Japan, the Soviet position on the territorial question was that it considered it 'had been settled by the Potsdam Declaration, the Yalta Agreement and SCAP Instructions No. 667',[155] and it requested specification in the future peace treaty that

> Japan recognises the complete sovereignty of the Soviet Union in South Sakhalin, including the adjacent islands and the Kuriles, and renounces all her rights and claims in the above territories. The Boundary between the Soviet Union and Japan will lie in the middle of Nemuro Strait, Notsuke Strait and Goyomai Strait.[156]

However, during the negotiations in August 1955, the Soviet negotiator Malik indicated an offer of Shikotan and the Habomais to Japan. Malik did not have the authority to offer this on his own initiative. The decision of course came from the Kremlin. Khrushchev in his memoirs answered his own question on this decision.

> Why were we willing to yield on the issue of the islands? We felt that this concession really meant very little to the Soviet Union. . . . On the other side of the equation, the friendship that we would have gained with the Japanese people would have had colossal importance.[157]

The primary Soviet goal at that stage was to normalise diplomatic relations with Japan. But:

> There was another consideration, too. We wanted to strengthen the influence of that particular prime minister both at home and abroad, so that Japanese policy might develop in the direction of strengthened friendly relations with the USSR.[158]

It was an opportunity never before available. On the Soviet side, the Stalin period had ended, and the policy of peaceful coexistence was flourishing. On the Japanese side, the pro-US and anti-Soviet Yoshida cabinet had collapsed and the Hatoyama regime had emerged under the slogans of an overall peace (as opposed to a one-sided peace) and independent diplomacy. The Soviet leaders wanted to seize the opportunity to improve relations with Japan. Thus, as Kapitsa commented, 'we decided to sacrifice something to encourage improved relations with Japan'.[159]

### Why were Shikotan and the Habomais offered?

Did the Soviets consider it legitimate that Shikotan and the Habomais should be transferred to Japan? If they did, there could be two kinds of arguments to justify doing so. The first takes account of the time they occupied those islands. That is, recognising that occupation occurred after the official surrender of Japan on 2 September 1945, they decided to return them as 'illegally occupied'. Second is that they concluded that although the extent of the Kuriles was not specified in any of the relevant international agreements, such as Yalta, San Francisco, Cairo or Potsdam, Shikotan and the Habomais were not part of them, i.e., they accepted the contention advanced by the Japanese government in the 1946 pamphlet. However, in the absence of documentary evidence, these arguments can be only speculative, and since the Soviets call these small islands the 'Little Kuriles' it is difficult to assume that they accepted the second argument. However, although these arguments do not necessarily justify the return of Shikotan and the Habomais, they do throw some doubt on the Soviet concept of the legitimacy of their possession of them.

Khrushchev left at least one clear answer to the question of cession:

> The islands were deserted; they were used only by fishermen and also by our defence forces. In these days of modern military technology, the islands really have very little value for defence. With missiles that can attack at distances of a thousand kilometres, the islands have lost the significance they had in the days when shore-based artillery was the main defence. Nor have the islands ever had any economic value. As far as I know there has never been any mineral wealth discovered on them.[160]

Among the great number of arguments and discussions over the territorial dispute, or the 'Northern Territories' problem, the strategic importance of the islands had often been pointed out. However, it should be noted that the top leader of the Soviet Union had recognised that developments in science and military technology had contributed to reduce the importance of these islands. It was in 1945 that the US nuclear development programme succeeded and created the tragedy of Hiroshima and Nagasaki. According to Jukes's study:

> the first Soviet nuclear weapons test took place in 1949, but not till almost six years later, two years after Stalin's death, was the military permitted to initiate a discussion in its professional journals about the effects of nuclear weapons on strategy and tactics.[161]

Thus, the Soviets were certainly in possession of nuclear weapons by 1955, which coincided with the year when the Shikotan/Habomai offer to Japan was brought up. It is probably fair to assume that the development of other conventional weapons was in progress along with nuclear weapons, as a matter of course. It is conceivable enough that against the background of the Soviet leader's perception that modern military technology decreased the strategic importance of the islands there was the fact of certainty of their nuclear possession.[162]

To add one more point concerning the strategic importance of the islands: it should be remembered that Dulles acknowledged that the importance of Okinawa to the US was much higher than that of the Kuriles to the Soviet Union.

### Did the Soviets have any intention to return the 'four islands'?

Was the Soviet Union prepared to offer the 'four islands' that Japan currently claims? Even if the above arguments regarding the legitimacy of the return of Shikotan and the Habomais are applicable, it seems difficult to expand its interpretation to cover Kunashiri and Etorofu. It is still possible to argue that Soviet occupation of the Kuriles took place after Japan accepted the Potsdam Declaration, though before the instrument of Japanese surrender was signed. But in that case, the question becomes more a matter of the whole Kuriles, not just the four islands. While the thesis of integral territories, that 'these four islands were never territories of another nation', can be sustained, the thesis of legitimacy, that 'they are not the Kuriles', is not applicable to Kunashiri and Etorofu. Considering that this thesis was then not yet established even in Japan, it was probably out of the question in the Soviet Union.

To give up all the islands promised at Yalta must have been unimaginable for those Soviets who witnessed the arrangement, such as Molotov and Gromyko, but the new political leaders admitted the blunder of Stalin's diplomacy in failing to sign at San Francisco. Along this line of extended interpretation, had those leaders thought about making some concession over Southern Sakhalin and the Kuriles as well? The Japanese did (and still do) have a sentimental wish to recover those islands. Furthermore, in respect of technology development and strategic importance, though there may be differences in degree, the argument could at the time also be applied to the other islands. Would they have been prepared to grant more than two islands, if they could obtain larger concessions from Japan in exchange?

There were some signs that before the San Francisco Conference the Soviets had made approaches to Japan using the Kuriles. In March 1950 Agence France Presse reported from London that the Japanese Foreign Office was considering a Soviet proposal to return the Kurile Islands in exchange for an agreement for extensive commercial relations with Communist China.[163] Similar reports appeared in London in the *Sunday Times* and *Chronicle*,[164] but were flatly denied by a Japanese government spokesman.[165] Considering the Japanese situation of the time, under US occupation and with the pro-US Yoshida government in power, the reaction of the Japanese spokesman would probably have been the same wherever the truth lay. Recalling the Foreign Ministry's rejection of the Domnitsky letter, which initiated the peace talks after it was handed to Hatoyama, it is also possible that the denial was a way of rejecting a Soviet trial balloon initiated in the same manner.

Not long before the news report, on 2 February 1950, Professor Leontiev, an authoritative writer and lecturer on international affairs (who authored an article in *Pravda* 'On the Peaceful Co-Existence of the Two Systems' even during the Stalin era) gave a public lecture entitled 'International Survey', in the course of which he stated: 'Japan wants the Kurile Islands back but the Soviet Union will not agree'.[166] An Australian diplomat, viewing these two sets of contradictory information, wrote:

> If these later reports are true it may be that Soviet policy in regard to the Kurile Islands has undergone a change since the beginning of February when Leontiev gave his lecture. On the other hand, it is conceivable that the Soviet authorities do not as yet want their own people to know that she is prepared to make any territorial concessions to Japan.[167]

When the Soviet offer of the two islands was made in 1955, the situation of Japan was different from that of March 1950, when conservative politicians such as Hatoyama and Kōno, later to return to office and react to nationalism in Asia and Africa by espousing Japan's political independence, were still in Sugamo prison.

Khrushchev did not seem to be familiar with the historical background of the islands:

> There was no historical basis at all for Japan to claim that territory, since Japanese imperialists had seized the islands by force at a time when Russia was weak and unable to defend its own territory.[168]

Some scholars have pointed out that President Roosevelt was also under the misapprehension that Japan had seized the Kurile Islands from Russia together with South Sakhalin in 1905.[169]

Khrushchev continued:

> Nonetheless, we discussed their demand at length within the Soviet leadership and came to the conclusion that we should meet the Japanese halfway and agree to give the two small islands to Japan – but only on the condition that we sign the peace treaty and that US troops no longer be stationed in Japan. Otherwise, it would have been sheer folly to relinquish the islands to Japan when the country was essentially under American occupation.[170]

This condition of withdrawal of US troops from Japan was specified in the draft peace treaty presented by the Soviet side during the first London negotiations. The Soviet Union requested Japan to promise 'not to enter into any coalition or military alliances directed against any Power which took part in the war against Japan'.[171] The Japanese response was 'we cannot make such a promise'.[172] The promise of the return of two islands was nevertheless made. So could the Soviets be flexible about the number of islands, depending on the conditions and the negotiations? During the first half of the entire negotiation period, the domestic situation in Japan seemed favourable to the Soviet Union, with a great growth in the socialist parties and the apparent prospect of their triumph in the national election. If the possibility of making the initial wishes come true, for example removing US forces, had materialised, would the Soviet leaders have agreed to increase the number of islands?

An article in the *New York Times* of May 1955 reported:

> These circles, including the most influential members of the conservative parties, fully expect the Soviet Union to use the conferences as a vehicle for expanding its 'neutral belt' policy and weakening the position of the free world. When the question arose in Japan's House of Representatives today, premier Ichiro Hatoyama said his Government was not contemplating a policy of neutrality 'at present' . . . *Premier*

> *Hatoyama was reliably reported to have suggested in a private talk with opposition leaders that the Russians, in exchange for the same pledge, might even offer to return to Japan the Kurile Islands and southern Sakhalin,* to which Japan renounced title in the San Francisco peace treaty with the Western powers. . . .[173]

During the period of the Soviet–Japanese negotiations, the Soviet leadership was comparatively stable as Khrushchev strengthened his power. Unlike Hatoyama, he could make decisions, sometimes flexibly, without being bound by other political restrictions. Therefore, as the article indicated, it can be assumed that the possibility of 'four islands' return was not necessarily nil on the Soviet side. However, even if Khrushchev was in a position to be flexible, Hatoyama was not. He was after all not a socialist, but a conservative (Democrat) politician, and when the LDP merger took place, he had to compromise with the pro-US Yoshida faction over negotiation policy toward the Soviet Union, so the prospect receded. After his visit to Moscow, Hatoyama the Kremlin's favourite retired, and direction of the Japanese foreign policy shifted back to its conservative inclination of placing the top priority on its pro-US policy. There was no more room for the Soviets to use concessions to exploit the differences within the ruling party.

## THE 'BILATERAL-INTERACTION' PERSPECTIVE

The final decisions of the negotiations for normalising relations were taken at the summit meeting in Moscow between the leaders of Japan and the Soviet Union. The final decisions in this particular study mean dependent variables seen in the outcome of the Soviet–Japanese negotiations. In other words, the expressions with regard to (1) USSR–Japan *rapprochement* and (2) the territorial issue specified in the Joint Declaration. As for (1), restoration of diplomatic relations was achieved but no peace treaty was signed. As for (2), 'transfer' of Shikotan and the Habomai islands was pledged, but the two nations had differing interpretations. In reaching these settlements, two types of negotiation channels were used, respectively within and outside formal diplomatic channels. The formal negotiations to normalise relations spread over four periods in two years, the first London negotiations (1 June to 23 September 1955), second London negotiations (17 January to 20 March 1956), first Moscow negotiations (31 July to 14 August 1956) and second Moscow negotiations at the time of Hatoyama's visit (15–19 October 1956). The Moscow fishery negotiations (29 April to 15 May 1956) were supposed to be irrelevant to the peace talks, but this channel played a breakthrough role for progress of the peace negotiations. I now review the 1955–6 Soviet–Japanese negotiations from the bilateral-interaction perspective.

## *Japanese goals and Soviet goals*

While the Joint Declaration contains the final outcomes of the 1955–6 negotiations, the original goal aimed at by both Khrushchev and Hatoyama was *rapprochement* by signing a peace treaty. However, the nature of the negotiations had been changed from negotiations for signing a peace treaty to those of diplomatic restoration. Thus, the original goal was not achieved at that time and has not been achieved yet. However, there were also other goals that each country sought to achieve through the negotiations.

Before the peace talks began, Japan listed several issues that it wanted to settle in the negotiations.[174] Among them, the highest priorities attached to such issues as (1) the territorial problem, (2) the repatriation of Japanese POWs from the Soviet Union, (3) membership of the United Nations and (4) the fisheries problem. Compared to these issues, the restoration of diplomatic relations itself meant less to Japan.

With regard to the territorial problem, Japan did not have a single solid claim demanding fixed areas of island territories, but the realistic goal seemed to be Shikotan and the Habomai islands. As for the issue of the Japanese POWs, there were still over a thousand of them detained on Soviet territory, out of more than 600,000 who had surrendered in 1945 in Manchuria, North Korea, Northern China, Sakhalin and the Kuriles and had been taken to prison camps in the Soviet Union[175]. Most of them had been repatriated by April 1950, but some who had been sentenced under Soviet law were still detained. The number still alive and imprisoned at the end of 1954 was 1,425 according to the Japanese Government, or 1,031 according to the Soviet Red Cross.[176] Their repatriation was not only the wish of their families and relatives but also of the whole nation. Japan had regained its sovereign independence at San Francisco in 1951, but had been unable to join the UN because of the Soviet veto. To overcome this and gain UN membership was one of Japan's major diplomatic objectives. The fisheries problem, as I mentioned earlier (pp. 62–3), was also of great concern. It was important for Japan to secure safe fisheries in the North Pacific.

The Soviet side's primary or immediate goal of the negotiations was, as I have said, restoration of diplomatic relations itself. The longer-term aims of weakening US–Japanese relations and expanding Soviet influence over Japan did not directly affect the negotiations. The difference in goals produced a clear contrast between the Japanese and Soviet negotiating positions. While the Soviets sought *rapprochement* with Japan as part of their global strategy, the Japanese motivation for *rapprochement* was to solve immediate and pressing problems.

The Soviet wants-list was formulated and presented in the draft treaty handed to Matsumoto at the beginning of the first London negotiations. Its immediate goal is found in the opening section of the draft.

> The Union of Soviet Socialist Republics on one hand and Japan on the other . . . have resolved to declare the termination of the state of war and to reestablish official relations, and with this aim to conclude the present peace treaty, which, in accordance with the principles of justice, will form a basis for good-neighbourly and friendly relations between the Soviet Union and Japan . . .[177]

The second goal was conveyed in Article 2.

> Japan binds herself not to enter into any coalitions or military alliances directed against any Power which took part in the war against Japan.[178]

After all, for the Soviet Union, the primary goal for the peace negotiation was to found a base for future policy by reopening its diplomatic relations with Japan, and there were no concrete problems to be solved except clarifying the border demarcation lines. However, on the territorial problem, since it was the Soviet Union who occupied all the disputed territories, its position for the negotiations was thereby stronger.

### Soviet and Japanese bargaining cards

In bilateral negotiations, the goals of one side become bargaining cards for the other. For the Soviet Union these cards were such issues as the territorial issue, repatriation of POWs, UN membership and fisheries problems.

Did Japan have any bargaining cards? When the notion 'Soviet goals are Japanese cards' is applied, the first bargaining card is the primary Soviet goal, *rapprochement* with Japan. This may sound strange, since Japan also sought *rapprochement*, and that is why negotiations began, but examination of the attitude taken by the *Gaimushō* suggests that this thinking was actually applied in Japanese negotiation strategy to extract concessions from the Soviets. In other words, the Japanese bargaining card was suspension of the negotiations. According to Akira Shigemitsu:

> For Japan, which returned to international society only three years ago, and whose recovery from the war was not yet complete, the only card it could use to have its claims accepted by the Soviet Union, which is a commonly acknowledged super-power, is simply to say 'Then, unfortunately, we have to postpone our restoration of diplomatic relations with the USSR'.[179]

Once diplomatic relations were restored, Japan would have no cards left to use to extract further concessions. This provides an apparent rationale for the stand taken throughout by Foreign Minister Mamoru Shigemitsu and the *Gaimushō*, that a peace treaty could be signed only after all the problems had been solved. It is assumed that the Japanese aimed at achieving their objectives one after another, while showing off its card, but not using it up. In fact they achieved most of their goals during the first London negotiations.

The negotiations over the territorial problem were expected to be very difficult. The Japanese supplemented the 'suspend negotiations' card with another, by dividing the territorial demand into three. The basis for this was already prepared as early as the *Gaimushō*'s 1946 pamphlet. Depending on the climate of the negotiations, the territorial demand was to be softened according to the strength of the claim, to create an impression that the Japanese were making concessions. In this sense two sets of demands – (1) the maximum demand, for South Sakhalin and the entire Kurile chain and (2) the mid-range demand for the Southern Kuriles – could be used as bargaining cards to achieve the minimal Japanese objective. The card of maximum demand was very effective domestically to control public perception.[180] It was also useful to create the impression that 'the four islands (Kunashiri, Etorofu, Shikotan and the Habomais) were inalienable territories of Japan, even if South Sakhalin and the Northern Kuriles could be conceded. However, one miscalculation of the *Gaimushō* was that the 'four island claim' lost flexibility as a bargaining card and become the fixed national claim, due to the domestic political turmoil and also pressure from the USA.

Diplomatic documents made available in the US archives suggest that this thinking was working in the strategic mind of the Japanese delegation throughout the negotiation period with the USSR, i.e., even after the 'four islands' claim became LDP policy following the merger. Though he felt that the Soviet government would never agree to return the South Kuriles, Plenipotentiary Matsumoto had to demand them during the second London negotiations. It is certain that Matsumoto was constrained by the new LDP policy, but he was also instructed by the *Gaimushō* to use the above-mentioned bargaining cards. According to a record of conversation between Shigenobu Shima, Minister at the Japanese Embassy in Washington, and Robert O. Blake of the State Department, Shima

> shared Matsumoto's feeling that the Soviet Government would never agree to the return of the Southern Kuriles. However, he felt that the Japanese would gain stature by breaking off negotiations with the Soviet Government, and then reopening them only when the Soviets

had something to offer. He felt that Japan had nothing to lose by this step, although it might be politically difficult. He had so advised the Japanese Government, and this had also been the opinion of the Japanese experts on Soviet affairs.[181]

The same thinking seems to have been working even at the time of the summit meeting, the final stage of the negotiations. The State Department's memorandum of conversation at the time of the Hatoyama mission's visit to Washington DC, on the way back from Moscow was referred to on p. 77. While knowing that it was impossible for Japan to regain more than Shikotan and the Habomais, Japan raised its demand for other territories. Kōno said that 'There was no chance for the present to regain Etorofu and Kunashiri but Japan would have to wait for a crack to appear in the Soviet position'.[182] After all, by not signing a peace treaty and having the peace negotiations to be continued, Japan in a sense, according to the strategic mind of the *Gaimushō*, managed to keep in its hands its bargaining positions for regaining more than the promised islands of the Habomais and Shikotan.

Another Soviet goal was the weakening of US–Japanese relations. However, the *Gaimushō* did not dare to create any strategy using this as a bargaining card, as relations with the USA were (and had been) given highest priority in Japanese diplomacy. It rather took the opposite step. According to information that Minister Shima provided to Robertson of State Department at the beginning of the first London negotiations, the Japanese position, as approved by the cabinet, was that

> Ambassador Matsumoto is instructed to open the negotiations by stating that Japan is tied to the free world by the San Francisco Peace Treaty and to the United States by the Security Treaty, and that it does not propose to break or alter those ties. If the Soviet Union is going insist upon some modification in these relationships, there is no point in further negotiations.[183]

### The Japanese and Soviet ways of negotiating

The Japanese–Soviet negotiations were between a winner and a loser of the war, and were thus different in nature from negotiations between equals. Some specific features are noted in negotiations between such asymmetrical counterparts.

The Japanese way of negotiating featured 'dual diplomacy' and moves called in Japanese *nemawashi*, *gaiatsu*, and *gorioshi*. Dual diplomacy was referred to in a previous section (pp. 56–80). Not only were different policies released before a domestic consensus had been reached but the Prime Minister's Office and Foreign Ministry sometimes knifed each other in order to create a situation convenient for their own policy objectives. The content of the peace negotiations and moves by different factions and intentions of the government were released through the media, perplexing not only the Soviet Union, but also other nations.[184] For example, the 'Dulles' Warning' was leaked to the Japanese press. According to a record in the UK diplomatic documents,

> The State Department are of course exceedingly angry that a private conversation between Mr. Dulles and Mr. Shigemitsu in London should have leaked to the press and they are convinced that this was done deliberately by a member of Shigemitsu's entourage with the intention of embarrassing not so much the Americans as Shigemitsu himself. They comment that ' . . . it is hard to do business with these fellows they are all knifing each other to beat the band'.[185]

Another document followed this and said:

> the person who had been 'knifing' Shigemitsu (my letter 10638/2/43/56 of September 7) was Matsumoto himself. It was he who had leaked the conversation between Mr. Dulles and Mr. Shigemitsu in London and he had sent private reports to Kono in Tokyo that Shigemitsu was botching the negotiations.[186]

*Nemawashi* and *gaiatsu* are terms sometimes used to describe Japanese negotiating style. *Nemawashi* describes a certain behaviour, translated as 'laying the ground work for attaining one's objective', or 'manoeuvring behind the scenes'. A typical example of *nemawashi* was seen in the Japanese attempt to attract support from other Western Allies by exploiting Cold War tensions. It seems likely that *nemawashi* before the San Francisco Treaty contributed to the announcement of US support for the return of Shikotan and the Habomais to Japan. However, the Japanese approaches to the USA and the UK did not produce as much support as the Japanese negotiators hoped to receive.

*Gaiatsu* means 'foreign pressure'. Two kinds of *gaiatsu*, (1) induced foreign pressure and (2) genuine foreign pressure, were employed during the negotiations. A good example of induced *gaiatsu* was Kōno's secret agreement, reached during the fishery negotiations. It has often been pointed out that the Japanese prefer not to clarify where responsibilities lie. In Japan it is often convenient and safe for politicians to attribute responsibility for policy decisions to *gaiatsu* rather than to themselves. At the fishery negotiations, it was Kōno himself who suggested that the Soviets link normalisation of relations with effectuation of the fisheries treaty. In order to avoid domestic criticism, it was convenient for him to make it appear that he had been obliged to promise the one in order to achieve the other.

Towards the end of the long period of negotiations, US support for the Japanese 'four islands' claim was declared. However, it resulted neither from the *Gaimushō's nemawashi* nor from Kōno's attempt at induced *gaiatsu*. 'Dulles' Warning' was rather a genuine *gaiatsu*, prompted by US strategic interest in holding Okinawa and blocking Japanese–Soviet *rapprochement*.

*Gorioshi* (steamrolling) and arbitrary interpretation were the last measures that the Japanese mission resorted to. The 'Hatoyama–Bulganin letters' and 'Matsumoto–Gromyko letters' were exchanged before Hatoyama's visit to Moscow in order to confirm the conditions for the Moscow negotiation under the so-called 'Adenauer Formula', in which diplomatic relations were to be restored without signing a peace treaty and the territorial problem was to be shelved for future negotiation. However, the Hatoyama mission found itself fettered with the LDP-determined territorial claim, had to prepare its negotiating strategy in accordance with party policy, and negotiate on the territorial issue in spite of preliminary agreement with the Soviets to shelve it. At the meeting with Khrushchev on 16 October, Kōno asked for his understanding of the Japanese domestic situation, and raised the territorial question. Khrushchev responded that it had been the Japanese side which had not wanted to deal with the territorial issue at that time, and that that was why Gromyko had sent a letter of agreement to Matsumoto. He went on to say that they could either adopt this measure and merely restore diplomatic relations, or demarcate their boundary lines and sign a peace treaty right away. The result turned out to be neither of these things: two islands were promised in the Joint Declaration, and diplomatic relations were restored. Turning Khrushchev's flexibility to good account, the Japanese side steamrollered the Japanese claims through against the background of domestic political turmoil. Not only that: an arbitrary interpretation was added to the declaration for the purpose of domestic politics. When final agreement had been reached on the terms of the Joint Declaration, the Japanese delegation decided to interpret it as including discussion of the territorial problem in the future peace negotiations.

'If the front door is closed, open other doors to enter' was a feature observed in the Soviet way of promoting the negotiations. The peace talks began in a sense at the kitchen door, Hatoyama's residence, to which Domnitsky brought the Soviet letter after having it had been rejected at the front door, the official diplomatic channel of the *Gaimushō*. The same attitude was seen in its linkage of the fisheries card to resumption of the peace talks, at the time when the London negotiations were suspended. To reopen the talks, the Soviet Union used the door of the Ministry of Fisheries and Agriculture avoiding the closed door of the *Gaimushō*. It seems that the Soviets learned from Domnitsky's experience to move things forward by shunning the formal diplomatic channel when it did not work.

The second case of the fishery linkage may also be interpreted as an expression of discontent rather than as use of other channels. On 21 September Khrushchev complained about the Japanese negotiating attitude to the Japanese Diet delegation, which visited Moscow during the intermission in the London negotiations. He said 'the Japanese side is cool toward normalising Soviet–Japanese relations, and I have the impression that they are prolonging the negotiations on purpose'.[187] The Soviets sometimes went beyond words, and expressed their discontent by actual and unilateral actions against Japan, for example by unilaterally restricting fishing rights in the North Pacific, unilaterally conditioning the return of the promised islands in 1961 against revision of the US–Japan Security Treaty, and later by deploying an army division on the disputed islands in 1978, following the Sino-Japanese *rapprochement*.

One further observation I have to make on the Soviet way of negotiating is that they used up their strong cards early in the negotiations, before achieving their primary goal. The Soviet leaders expected an early settlement, and granted solutions to most of the issues, including UN membership and repatriation of Japanese POWs, in accordance with Japanese wishes. Even the territorial concession, the offer of Shikotan and the Habomais, came during the first London negotiations. However, though Hatoyama and the mainstream Democrats sought an early settlement, other groups of Japanese policy makers had no such intention. The negotiations were after all prolonged, and the only card the Soviets managed to use later was the fisheries card. Japan in a sense retained its bargaining card by not signing a peace treaty. In addition to their other original goals, the Japanese succeeded in having the Soviets promise the two islands without concluding a peace treaty. On the contrary, the Soviet Union could not completely achieve even its initial goal in the peace negotiations. Though the Soviet negotiators had several strong cards, they did not make efficient use of them, their major miscalculation perhaps being to overestimate Japanese eagerness for a quick settlement and not to realise the constraints of pluralist politics placed on the leaders.

Judging from the initial goals and final results, it seems clear which side gained more from the negotiations. Khrushchev, who had criticised Stalin's 'blunder' for not signing the peace treaty at San Francisco, ended up making the same mistake five years later in Moscow. Khrushchev regretted this later. He said:

We were reminded of what a grave error we made in not signing the Japanese peace treaty later, when our relations with China had utterly deteriorated. [In July 1964] Mao Zedong received a delegation of Japanese industrialists – bourgeois figures of some kind. . . . During their discussions, the Japanese raised the issue of their claims against the Soviet Union, including southern Sakhalin and the Kuril Islands. And what happened? Mao Zedong supported their claims![188]

Where the 1955–6 Soviet–Japanese negotiations are concerned, the smaller gained more than the larger. The two islands were promised to Japan, and bilateral diplomatic relations were restored, but without a peace treaty, thus giving Japan room for further territorial claims. Since the Japanese inputs were often not backed by a domestic consensus, they may not necessarily be called a strategy in a genuine sense. However, from the point of interaction between the two states, the inconsistent outputs worked rather like a strategy and brought more to the Japanese side, which had begun the negotiations from a position far less advantageous than that of the Soviet Union.

## LOST OPPORTUNITIES

At least two good opportunities were missed during the negotiation period. The first came during the first London negotiations, when Malik floated the Soviet 'two islands' offer, but disappeared when the Japanese government advanced new territorial claims. The second was during the first Moscow negotiations, and disappeared when Shigemitsu's decision to settle was blocked by US pressure. The atmosphere conducive to Soviet–Japanese *rapprochement* that arose in the mid-1950s gradually disappeared after Hatoyama's visit to Moscow. While economic relations developed, political relations between Japan and the USSR cooled towards the 1960s. The transfer of the promised islands did not take place, the peace treaty was never signed and the different interpretations of the territorial issue were not reconciled. By the early 1960s all prospects for early *rapprochement* had faded.

### US–Soviet conflict

At the global level, East–West relations deteriorated again towards the 1960s. Tensions in US–Soviet relations increased and reached a low point in the Cuban missile crisis of 1962. As for the territorial problem between Japan and the USSR, the USA reconfirmed its position of support for the Japanese 'four islands' claim in a note of 23 May 1957, regarding the Soviet shooting down of a US aircraft three years earlier (1954). It stated,

> The United States Government . . . reiterates . . . that . . . neither the Yalta Agreement regarding Japan nor the Treaty of Peace with Japan, signed in San Francisco on September 8, 1951, conveyed any title in the Habomai Islands to the Soviet Union or diminished the title of Japan in those islands, and the phrase 'Kurile Islands' in those documents does not and was not intended to include the Habomai Islands, or Shikotan, or the islands of Kunashiri and Etorofu which have always been part of Japan proper and should, therefore, in justice be acknowledged as under Japanese sovereignty.[189]

### Change in political leadership in Japan

Domestically, Prime Minister Hatoyama gradually lost political power for various reasons, such as a lost general election and the LDP merger, during the course of the 1955–6 negotiations. After his retirement, his successors did not have a strong interest in improving political relations with the USSR. In the meantime, the 'four islands' claim was settling well in the consciousness of the Japanese public with government endorsement.

### Soviet preparation of the 'two islands' transfer

The Soviets were preparing to transfer the islands of Shikotan and the Habomais after Hatoyama's visit and ratification of the Joint Declaration. In July 1958, the Kyodo News Agency reported that Soviet coastguard personnel and civilians on the Habomais had almost all been evacuated. The crew of a Japanese fishing boat, *Yusei Maru No. 1*, which was captured by a Soviet patrol while operating off Nemuro on 31 May 1957 and detained on Shibotsu island, one of the Habomais, testified after being repatriated that 'all but a handful of Russians living on the islands, including coastguard servicemen and civilians, left for Shikotan island on June 25', and that 'Before the released Japanese fishermen left Shibotsu island, a dilapidated detention camp on the islands had already been pulled down and only a few Russians remained'.[190] Recent 'news' of testimony by a Japanese man, who used to work for the Far Eastern Fishery Cooperative appears to endorse this old news item. Hiroshi Satō, who lives in Vladivostok and interpreted for the Russians at the Soviet–Japanese fishery negotiations, visited Shikotan and the Habomais in 1959. According to him, ordinary civilians had already left the islands and only coastguards remained when he landed on Shikotan. On the Habomais he saw the few remaining Russian residents packing up to leave. Since the coastguards could pull out within a day, the islands were ready for transfer any time. But in June 1960, Russians started coming back to the islands, and their numbers gradually increased thereafter.[191]

### Revision of the US–Japanese Security Treaty

Japan and the United States revised and renewed their security arrangements in January 1960. This greatly offended the Soviets and swept away their intention to transfer Shikotan and the Habomais. On 27 January 1960 a memorandum was handed from Soviet Foreign Minister Gromyko to Japanese Ambassador Kadowaki in Moscow. It stated:

> since the new military treaty signed by the Japanese Government is directed against the Soviet Union as well as against the People's Republic of China, the Soviet Government cannot contribute to extending the territory available to foreign troops by transferring the islands to Japan. Thus, the Soviet Government finds it necessary to declare that Habomai and Shikotan will be transferred to Japan only if all foreign troops are withdrawn from Japan and a Soviet–Japanese peace treaty is signed – as was stated in the Joint Soviet–Japanese Declaration of October 19 1956.[192]

Relevant comments are found in Khrushchev's memoirs,

> to give the two small islands to Japan – but only on the condition that we sign the peace treaty and that US troops no longer be stationed in Japan. Otherwise, it would have been sheer folly to relinquish the islands to Japan when the country was essentially under American occupation. We figured that the minute we gave Japan the two islands, the United States would turn them into military bases. We would have been trying to obtain one thing and would have ended up with quite another. Therefore, as we told the Japanese, any discussion about transferring the islands to Japan could only take place when the Japanese-US military alliance aimed against the Soviet Union was no longer in force.[193]

Mr Satō's testimony about the return of the Russian residents to the two islands also matches the timing of revision of the US–Japanese Security Treaty and this memorandum of the Soviet government. The Soviet attitude became more rigid thereafter and they started to claim that the territorial problem had already been solved in a series of international agreements.

The big wave of opportunities for *rapprochement*, which emerged in the mid-1950s, thus was lost completely and the two nations had to wait until another wave appeared in the early 1970s.

# Part II

# Efforts for a peace treaty

Summit meetings after diplomatic restoration

# 3   Tanaka's visit to Moscow, 1973

> The two sides recognised that to conclude a peace treaty by resolving the yet unresolved problems remaining since Second World War could contribute to the establishment of truly good-neighbourly relations between the two countries and conducted negotiations of matters concerning the content of such a peace treaty.[1]

The second chance for Soviet–Japanese *rapprochement* during the post-war period came in early 1970. In January 1972, Soviet Foreign Minister Andrei Gromyko visited Japan. In October of the same year, Japanese Foreign Minister Masayoshi Ōhira visited Moscow. This meeting marked the First Peace Treaty Negotiation to be held after the diplomatic restoration of 1956. In March 1973, the top leaders of the two countries, Kakuei Tanaka and Leonid Brezhnev, exchanged letters and confirmed the necessity to have a dialogue at the highest level. The event that highlighted their *rapprochement* movement was Tanaka's visit to Moscow, which took place at Soviet invitation from 7 to 10 October 1973, 17 years after Hatoyama's visit to Moscow. The summit meetings were also regarded as the Second Peace Treaty Negotiation, following the first negotiation held in the previous year upon Ōhira's visit to Moscow. As is well known, no peace treaty was signed, and as far as the territorial problem is concerned, only a vague expression about 'yet unresolved problems remaining since Second World War' appeared in the Joint Communiqué.

For the Soviet–Japanese negotiations and the summit meeting in the 1950s that were dealt with in the previous chapter, archival documents recently opened in some countries proved very useful. However, as far as the summit meetings of 1973 and later are concerned, such documents are not at present available. Nevertheless, using currently available sources, the following sections are devoted to analysis of Japanese and Soviet decisions in terms of improved relations and the territorial problem during the period leading up to and including Tanaka's visit to Moscow, which highlighted the chance to normalise relations between Japan and the USSR in the 1970s. Though top decision makers who attended the summit meetings, such as Prime Minister Kakuei Tanaka and Foreign Minister Masayoshi Ōhira of Japan, General Secretary Leonid Brezhnev and Foreign Minister Andrei Gromyko, are already dead, volumes of memoirs written by them or by those who were close to them provide helpful sources on the foreign-policy decision making of the time. In addition, other materials such as newspapers, almanacs, government publications, existing research and volumes on the subject are supplemented by my individual interviews conducted both in Japan and Moscow. Some officials involved since the summit meetings of 1956 and occupying much higher positions at the 1973 summit, are still alive. In addition to them, some other officials then in office, especially those who have since left the Japanese or Soviet Foreign Ministries, kindly shared candid and valuable accounts with me, on condition of anonymity.

## THE 'GLOBAL INTERNATIONAL RELATIONS' PERSPECTIVE

### USSR and Japan: The second *rapprochement* wave

Looked at from the perspective of global international relations, the period of the late 1960s to early 1970s, during which Japan–USSR relations were again warming and the two countries held peace talks, was the period when the world was greeting the second *détente* after a quarter-century of Cold War. The Japan–USSR *rapprochement* aiming at normalisation of relations in this period can also be explained as one of a series of movements generated by this second *détente* of the post-war era.

### Détente *in the 1970s and Japan–USSR* rapprochement *moves*

The warming of East–West relations or '*détente*' of the early 1970s presented common features with that of the 1950s in that (1) peace was not necessarily achieved in an ideological sense and (2) the relative influence of the USA was declining. However, the biggest difference at this time was that the initiative for *détente* moves was taken by the USA.

The USA contributed most to the structural change of the international system of the period. The Nixon regime inaugurated in January 1969 entered upon improvement of East–West relations, campaigning 'to dialogue from conflict'. The US adopted a policy of accommodation with

China and the USSR, as the Vietnam War moved toward a settlement. In Europe, the East–West dialogue made progress toward resolution of the Cold War conflict. This change of American policy broke the Cold War framework that the USA itself had taken a leading role in creating. This was because America's absolute military preponderance was broken by the Soviet military build-up after the Cuban Missile Crisis, the situation in Vietnam did not eventuate favourably for the USA and accordingly it had lost some of its global influence. Each country in the international community had to find its own interest in the flow of such a global structural change.

In Europe *détente* was further developing, taking the form of recognition and stabilisation of the political *status quo*. In September 1971, the USA, UK, France and the USSR initialled an agreement to recognise the status of Berlin. This was truly a recognition of the Yalta System and its post-war results in Europe, a long-time goal of Soviet policy. Additionally, it paved the way for opening the Conference on Security and Cooperation in Europe (CSCE).[2] Thereafter, three interrelated negotiations, CSCE, the Strategic Arms Limitation Talks (SALT-1), and the Anti-Ballistic Missile (ABM) limitation treaty, were initiated and signed. Also Germany, divided as a result of the Second World War and the ensuing Cold War, was admitted to the UN and returned to the international community as two Germanys. Thus, *détente* between the US–USSR bipolar systems proceeded in Europe, covering everything from nuclear weapons to Berlin and the two Germanys, a recognition of the status quo, or in other words, a *de facto* legitimisation of Europe's new post-war balance of power.

### Détente *in the Asia-Pacific region*

Change in US foreign policy brought the Asia-Pacific region a different kind of development of *détente* from the European type of *de facto* legitimisation, and led to formation of a new power structure in the region. Failure of its Vietnam intervention forced the US itself to modify its Asia-Pacific strategy. The diplomatic strategy that the US then adopted was to approach China and the USSR, exploiting their conflict, and to extract some concessions from each so as to succeed in its own peace move. While one reason for the active US approach to China was to influence the course of the Vietnam war, balance-of-power considerations were also clearly in the United States' thinking.[3]

Since Khrushchev's 'deStalinisation' speech at the Twentieth Congress of the CPSU in 1956, relations between China and the USSR had been deteriorating, with repeated, mainly ideological, debates over the course of socialism. Yet until the late 1960s, the conflict remained at the level of oral or written disputation. However, it escalated to a military clash in 1969 over the ownership of Damansky Island in the Ussuri River on the Sino-Soviet border. The 'opening' to China was also a means of exerting leverage upon the Soviet Union to mitigate tensions between Washington and Moscow in *détente* diplomacy. In July 1971, Henry Kissinger, then President Nixon's National Security Adviser, visited China from Pakistan and, met Chou En-lai and it was announced that President Nixon would visit China. In October 1971 Taiwan was ousted from the Chinese seat at the United Nations, and the Chinese People's Republic (PRC) was admitted to membership. In February 1972 Nixon visited China, and a Sino-American Joint Statement was released, which constituted virtual US recognition of the PRC. America's success in improving relations with China also advanced its policy of isolating North Vietnam. This in turn created leverage upon the USSR to cooperate in ending the Vietnam war.

One of the symbolic phenomena of structural change in the Asia-Pacific region in accordance with the US–China *rapprochement* may be seen in the dissolution of the Asia and Pacific Council (ASPAC). ASPAC was established in 1966 on the proposal of South Korean President Park Chung Hee as a forum aimed at strengthening ties among countries in the Asia-Pacific region. Participant countries were Japan, South Korea, Australia, Taiwan, Malaysia, New Zealand, the Philippines, Thailand, South Vietnam and Laos (observer). Its formation on South Korean initiative, and Taiwan's enrolment in it, indicated that in substance it was an organisation intended politically to unify anti-communist countries. This anti-communist alliance lost its rationale after Nixon's visit to China in 1972 signified a Sino-US *rapprochement*. In 1972 Japan normalised its relations with China, and the Labor governments in Australia and New Zealand followed suit. The countries that recognised the PRC and stood on a position of 'one China' naturally cooled toward ASPAC, of which Taiwan was a member.[4]

Thus, along with the US–China and the US–USSR *rapprochement* moves, a new regional power equilibrium emerged with the USA, USSR and China as its three major poles. Henry Kissinger, the brain behind the shift in US foreign policy, perceived the world of the 1970s as multipolar, with the two post-war superpowers having lost their absolute dominance, and saw world peace as achievable when the balances of the multipolar powers were in equilibrium. Multipolarity did not necessarily mean that all poles were equal. Militarily, US–Soviet bipolarity remained; politically, China became a third pole; and economically Japan and the European Community brought the number of poles up to five. The most important equilibrium for world peace was that between the USA and USSR. Japan and Western Europe were poles cooperative to the USA, and the United States, as the centre of this tripolarity, attempted to utilise it in seeking equilibrium with the USSR. This thinking was reflected in the concept of the New Atlantic Charter announced in April 1973. China was a political pole, also to be 'utilised' in adjusting US–USSR relations, because of its conflict with the USSR. Thus US intention was to create a 'peace configuration' where a power equilibrium existed among the multipolars, and it was to be aimed at a so-called 'US–USSR lead type' peace.[5]

## Resource nationalism

Another important movement in this period was increasing resource nationalism centred in the Middle East. In fact this had started in the 1950s with oil policy. Iran attempted to nationalise the Anglo-Iranian Oil Company in 1951, but had failed to withstand US and multinational counteraction. The Organisation of Petroleum Exporting Countries (OPEC) had been formed in 1960 to promote cooperation among oil-producing countries against pressure from international capital, and pressed in international forums, including the UN, for the right of producing countries to control their natural resources. In the 1970s this resource nationalism entered a new stage against the background of an internationally anticipated energy crisis. The nationalisation of foreign oil companies' assets by the Qaddafi regime in Libya in September 1970 set a precedent for producing countries to play the 'oil card' in the international arena. Libya's successful raising of crude oil price encouraged other OPEC members to stand against foreign capital and claim participation in management or nationalisation of the oil companies. Such resource nationalism was also accelerating in resources other than oil, as former colonies strove to add economic to political independence by sweeping away the residual privileges of former colonial powers or international capital. On the other hand, for those countries which depended on Middle East oil, coping with this nationalism became another important new issue.

## The Soviet approach to Japan

The drastic changes in international relations from the late 1960s to early 1970s brought a change of attitude in Soviet policy toward Japan. The US–China *rapprochement* against the background of China–USSR conflict and China's joining the UN changed the political landscape of East Asia and motivated the Soviet Union to open more frequent dialogue and to improve political relations with countries including Japan, which it had tended to neglect in the past. In addition to its geographical importance, with its advanced economy and technology Japan had developed to such an extent that it could be said 'Japan has emerged as a major power centre'.[6] Japan presented attractions for the USSR, worth an effort to improve ties. Especially in a period when resource nationalism was prevailing in the Middle East, there is no doubt that the Soviet Union wanted Japanese involvement in developing Siberia, which presented the potential for a vast energy supply.

Though successfully improving its relations and promoting political and strategic arrangements quite favourable to itself with the USA on the European continent, the Soviet Union was not necessarily handling the situation as well in the Asia-Pacific region. While, finally, 18 years after the Soviet Union proposed its conception of a European security arrangement in 1954,[7] the CSCE had began to move towards its aim of stability and cooperation in Europe, Soviet diplomacy was facing a much more difficult reality in its Asian policy. The USSR was energetically campaigning for its Asian Collective Security Arrangement proposal, claiming itself qualified to make it because two-thirds of Soviet territory lay in Asia. However, this proposal did not receive a positive response from nations in the region, because they perceived it as designed for containment of China, and viewed support of it as detrimental to their relations with that country.

Nevertheless, the USSR had an underlying expectation that improved ties with Japan would meet its own national interest. By expanding its economic relations, which had recently shown smooth growth, to its political relations (I will deal with these in later sections), the Soviet Union wanted to reduce Japanese reliance on the United States or, for that matter, US reliance on Japan, particularly as a logistical base for the war in Vietnam, thereby weakening the 'aggressive character' of the Japanese–US Security Treaty and its potential threat to the Soviet Union.[8]

## Japan's approach to the USSR

The biggest difference between Hatoyama's and Tanaka's prime ministerships was Japan's vastly increased economic power, and accordingly its increased importance in global economics. Hatoyama's Japan, a decade after the end of the war, was still economically weak in a global sense, though the Korean War had brought considerable economic recovery. However, 17 years after Hatoyama's visit to Moscow, Japan had established itself as the third-largest economic power, after the USA and USSR (and second in the 'free world').

Japan's diplomacy was standing at the crossroads in the early 1970s. It had found it most beneficial to maintain an entirely pro-US diplomatic posture, and enjoyed rapid economic growth by locating itself under the US military umbrella with the bilateral security arrangement. However, the two 'Nixon Shocks' made Japan rethink the direction of its diplomacy. On 17 July 1971 President Nixon's decision to visit China was announced, and the

US State Department notified the Japanese government of the decision only three minutes before the announcement. Japan was mortified not to have been consulted regarding this critical step.[9] The next shock was conveyed to Japan on 16 August, when the USA gave it only ten minutes' notice of its announcement of a dollar protection policy, including suspension of dollar–gold convertibility and the imposition of surcharges on US imports.[10] In September tension arose over the Japanese export of textiles to the USA. These 'shocks', accompanying the US approach both to China and the USSR, showed international relations from the end of 1971 through the beginning of 1972 going into flux and starting to show multipolarised aspects.

The change of US foreign policy and the fundamental developments in the general structure of the international system made Japan fully aware of the need to adapt its diplomacy to the era of multipolarity. Change was observed in its recognition of Bangladesh in February 1972 at the time of Nixon's visit to China, announcement of contact with North Vietnam and establishment of diplomatic relations with Mongolia.

In July 1972, Kakuei Tanaka became Prime Minister, replacing Eisaku Satō, who had contributed a great deal to the return of Okinawa and later received the Nobel Peace Price for this. Tanaka reacted quickly to the changes in the international configuration. On 29 September negotiations for normalising relations with China concluded successfully, and a Joint Statement was signed. For Tanaka the USSR was next. As with China and other countries, it looked beneficial for Japan to broaden the channels of dialogue and give itself more room to manoeuvre.

Another global move in resource nationalism also affected Japan's diplomacy toward the USSR. Japan depended totally on imported oil, importing more than 99 per cent of its consumption, of which oil from the Middle East constituted nearly 90 per cent.[11] Given the uncertain situation in the Middle East and the oil transport route therefrom, this skewed dependence appeared too risky. In order to secure a stable supply of necessary resources, Japan needed to diversify its energy sources away from dependence on the US-based major petroleum companies (US Majors). Cooperation for Siberian development seemed to promise Japan certain benefits in natural resources supply, and geographical proximity was an additional favourable factor.[12] Also, Siberia, and the Soviet Far East as a whole, presented themselves as potential markets for Japanese industrial and consumer products. Despite its poor political relations, Japan had developed relatively amicable economic ties with the USSR through bilateral trade over the previous decade, and thus it was natural at this time for the Japanese to envisage larger-scale cooperation by bringing governmental-level support, for which improved political relations were a prerequisite.

## 'Unresolved problems'?: The territorial problem

Like the territorial clause of the Joint Declaration of 1956, the Joint Communiqué of 1973 was interpreted differently by Japan and the Soviet Union. The split was over the expression 'unresolved problems'. The Japanese government saw the 'yet unresolved problems remaining since World War II' as including the 'Northern Territories' problem, and claimed that this was confirmed between the two leaders.[13] However, the Soviet side then denied that they had agreed to this.[14] As the different interpretations of the 'unresolved problems' expression will be dealt with in the following sections, the rest of this section will be devoted to considering such international factors as moves by other countries, the influence of changes in the international system, etc.

### 1970s détente *and the disputed islands*

The global *détente* of the early 1970s, which drastically changed the Cold War structure of international relations, also affected Japanese–USSR relations, which developed to the extent that another summit meeting took place between them. However, the territorial problem received little or no attention from or involvement by nations that had contributed greatly to creating the problem. Furthermore, leaving the issue unresolved for so long made it difficult for Japan and the USSR to reconcile their respective positions. The change of the international configuration brought new support for Japan from China, but this only offended the Russians. Japan in reality secured neither constructive nor favourable involvement from the international community for solution or reconciliation of the territorial dispute.

In the Japan–USSR *rapprochement* movement driven by global *détente*, the trend in international relations in fact appeared to be moving in favour of the Soviet side. European *détente* took the form of legitimatising the status quo, and the German Federal Republic accepted the post-Second World War boundaries in a treaty signed on 12 August 1970. This seemed to give the Soviets confidence that their peace diplomacy could achieve a similar outcome in the territorial dispute with Japan.

As for the US, Richard Nixon was President during the period in which Japanese–USSR relations were developing towards realisation of Tanaka's visit to Moscow in 1973, and it was under his presidency that the United States had promoted the *détente* that eventually led to improved USSR–Japanese relations. It was not that he had had no connection with this territorial dispute. At the time of the 1955–6 Japanese–Soviet negotiations, he had been Vice-President.[15] Okinawa, which the United States had linked with the Kuriles during the 1956 negotiations, was returned to Japan in

1972. This turned Japanese public concern to the remaining territorial issue in the north. However, the reversion of Okinawa did not give any substantial impetus towards mobilising international support for Japan's territorial claim against the USSR. After the agreement, but before Okinawa's return, Prime Minister Eisaku Satō appealed to the international community for the return of the disputed islands in a speech given on 21 October 1970, commemorating the UN's 26th anniversary, and officially the US continued to endorse the Japanese government's position. However, at this time when the crucial objective of its own diplomacy was *détente* with the Soviets, US support for Japan's claim to the northern islands was unlikely to be substantial. On the other side of the globe, in exchange for Soviet concessions over Vietnam, the USA, France and Britain signed an arrangement with the Soviet Union in September 1971 to recognise the status quo of the Yalta System in Europe. US policy over the Kuriles was originally motivated by its own global strategic interests, and it changed its position depending on its policy goals at the time. Since 1956, when the USA had officially supported the Japanese claim to the 'four islands', it had perceptibly withdrawn from active involvement in the issue, and its indifference at times appeared inconsistent with its official position. In 1957 when the US Arctic disarmament plan was introduced, it inadvertently included the Kuriles in Soviet territory, thereby offending the Japanese government and media.[16] In 1968 a Vietnam-bound Seaboard World Airways jet carrying US military personnel was forced to land on Etorofu after intruding into Kuriles air space.[17] To secure the release of the aircraft and its passengers, the State Department rushed to apologise to Moscow for trespassing on Soviet territory.[18] This again offended the Japanese, and Japan had to remind the US that the airspace violated was not recognised as Soviet, so that the USA then had to apologise to Japan for apologising to Moscow.[19] Regardless of its official position, it was unthinkable in this particular period that the US would take a radical step to reverse the status of the post-war international boundaries. It was also probably convenient for the USA that the territorial dispute remain unsettled to maintain tension and distance between Japan and the USSR, since the fundamental framework of the Cold War had not yet disappeared.

Another third party was interested in maintaining these tensions and preventing a settlement. The country most vociferously supportive at this time of Japan's claim to the disputed islands was China. Its position on the 'Northern Territories' problem reflected changes in its political relations with the USSR, Japan and the United States. It supported the Soviet position during the 1950s and the early 1960s when it had an alliance relationship with the USSR. On 4 December 1950, when Chinese 'volunteers' were about to join in the Korean War, Chou En-lai expressed support for the

Soviet occupation of the islands.[20] China ordinarily entertained no sympathy for Japanese irredentism, and also had a territorial dispute with Japan over the Senkaku Islands (Diaoyū in Chinese).[21] But the Sino-Soviet dispute became so intensified as to change China's views on the 'Northern Territories' issue. On 10 July 1964 Mao Tse-tung, at a meeting with a Japan Socialist Party delegation led by Kōzō Sasaki, endorsed the Japanese claim, reportedly saying 'I approve of the Kuriles being returned to Japan. Russia already has taken too much land'. He went on to enumerate the Amur region, Outer Mongolia, Sinkiang, Poland, Rumania, Czechoslovakia and the Baltic States to draw his point, and implied that the Kurile issue was inseparable from China's own 'account' to be settled with Moscow.[22] Furthermore, as the conflict escalated to military clashes in 1969, China further raised its voice to support Japan's claim for the Kuriles. In the early 1970s, China repeatedly pronounced its strong support on various occasions, which coincided with the timing of Soviet–Japanese *rapprochement* moves – for example Chou En-lai's interview with Japanese journalists on the eve of Gromyko's visit to Japan in January 1972, or Chinese Deputy Foreign Minister (Chiao Kuan-hua)'s pronouncement at the United Nations General Assembly on 3 October 1993, four days before the Japanese Prime Minister Tanaka's visit to Moscow.[23]

China's support for Japan achieved no more than offending the Soviet Union, and it was not to be expected that other Asian nations which had suffered from Japanese expansionism would support Japan's claim for return of territory as a victim of Soviet expansionism.[24]

## THE 'NATION-STATE' PERSPECTIVE: JAPAN

### USSR and Japan: the second *rapprochement* wave

After diplomatic relations were restored in 1956, the USSR and Japan showed favourable developments in economic relations, but politically relations were stagnant for a long time, until in the early 1970s Japan took steps to improve them. The Japanese cabinet at that time was headed by Kakuei Tanaka, who replaced the former Prime Minister Eisaku Sato in October 1972 and appointed Masayoshi Ōhira as Foreign Minister. As a matter of fact, both Tanaka and Ōhira had been in the Yoshida faction during the 1955–6 political turmoil, and were among the 71 Deputies who absented themselves from the Diet to demonstrate their opposition to the Soviet–Japanese Joint Declaration when it was ratified by 356 votes to nil, but it was this Tanaka–Ōhira combination that took the initiative to improve Japanese–Soviet political relations 17 years later.

Behind this, strong domestic and international economic factors were at work.

## LDP politics in transition: Tanaka and independent diplomacy

Like Hatoyama, who had restored diplomatic relations with the USSR, Tanaka was a very popular politician.[25] In Japanese political society, with its strong tendency to bureaucratic predominance, Tanaka, as someone who basically had started from nothing (he was from a poor family in a remote rural area, and lacked higher education), enjoyed great support and popularity among the Japanese public. Tanaka greatly differed from Hatoyama in his absolute political power and influence. LDP internal politics, which had dominated the position of the ruling party and stabilised its political foundations, reached their apogee when the 'Tanaka faction' was established to support Kakuei Tanaka's bid to succeed Satō as party president. This changed the nature of LDP factional politics from policy-oriented groups to money power, and Tanaka, even after ceasing to be Prime Minister, would continue to influence his successors (Ōhira, Suzuki and Nakasone) and their cabinets as leader of the LDP's largest faction. Tanaka became Prime Minister through attracting Japanese business attention with his 'thesis of reconstructing the Japanese Archipelago' (*Nihon retto kaizō-ron*), and making good use of his natural talent to acquire money. His strong ties to business society (*zaikai*), dating from his time as Minister for International Trade and Industry (MITI), largely determined his policy priorities.

Tanaka's diplomacy also recalls Hatoyama's in that it was, in a sense, groping for a new independent direction. The two 'Nixon Shocks' prompted Japan to reconsider its previous pro-US or US-dependent way of diplomacy. The particular necessity to re-evaluate Japan's direction of resource diplomacy drove Tanaka to make significant changes from the diplomacy of Hatoyama's era.

The independent and multidirectional diplomacy to which Tanaka devoted himself was actually all resource diplomacy, including normalising relations with the PRC.[26] Tanaka strongly understood the necessity to reform Japan's resource policy in medium- and long-term perspectives, because he was familiar with Japan's energy situation from his experience as minister in charge of MITI.[27] The rapidly developing economy of resource-poor Japan, with GNP growing by 10 per cent per annum throughout the 1960s, depended entirely on stability in supply and cost of resources such as oil. Tanaka aimed at securing stable energy sources to realise his long-cherished thesis 'reconstruction of the Japanese archipelago', and especially sought diversified sources. By participating and cooperating in resource development in several countries, and opening up new ways for development and import of natural resource,[28] Tanaka's choice appeared to aim at relative independence from the American oil Majors. Thus, some political analysts later commented that by 'attempting to leave the American Majors' umbrella over the resource issue, Tanaka ended up by "stepping on a tiger's tail".'[29]

## Zaikai *and Siberian development*

The amicable development of Japanese–Soviet economic relations, despite the poor political relations, was facilitated by the Japanese–Soviet Joint Economic Committee, established during Mikoyan's visit to Japan in 1964 on a Soviet proposal, and the concurrence of the Federation of Economic Organisations and the Japan Chamber of Commerce. This committee provided a framework for project planning between the Japanese private-sector participants and the governmental agencies which made up the Soviet side, the Japanese government opting only for indirect participation.[30]

With resource nationalism creating global uncertainties, this was a propitious time for proposals for more active Japanese participation in Siberian development to figure in Japanese–Soviet economic relations. Among them were three large-scale development projects – the Tyumen oil field, Yakut natural gas, and Sakhalin continental shelf oil and natural gas. But for such large-scale projects Japanese government financial participation was desirable, for example in trade insurance, export credit guarantees and endorsing (low-cost) export–import bank financing. The business community thus became more vocal in soliciting governmental financial support for their projects.

## The approach to the USSR

In Japan's move towards *rapprochement* with the USSR, the influence of the business community (*zaikai*) was very different from that of the 1950s. In the mid-1950s Soviet–Japanese thaw, *zaikai* had little interest or involvement, except for the fishing industry. However, development of Japanese–Soviet economic relations, and trends in the world economy thereafter changed the *zaikai's* attitude to government policy toward the USSR, and as an interest group it greatly influenced Tanaka's policy decisions.

The post-war Japanese bureaucracy generally had a strong influence on industrialisation policy until the 1960s, but as the industries developed and private business became stronger, it lost much of its influence to the private sector. In consequence, as in the United States, business lobbying of government increased, and was inevitably focused less on the bureaucracy and more on politicians and political parties, seen as the more important makers of policy, including economic policy toward the USSR.[31] It should also be noted that the warming bilateral relations leading up to the summit meetings were mainly due to economic factors. From the late 1960s MITI was concerned about Japan's capacity to supply its rapidly expanding, heavy-industry-based economy with the energy sources and raw materials it needed, and as the agency charged with economic 'parameter maintenance', or assurance of an international environment favourable to Japanese economic activity,[32] it also took a positive attitude towards further development of relations with the USSR.

## The policy of separating politics and economics: seikei bunri seisaku

When Gromyko visited Japan in January 1972, both nations agreed to begin negotiations for signing a peace treaty by the end of the year. From the Japanese government's viewpoint, the only reason why no treaty had been signed in 1956 was the territorial problem, and it had become characteristic of Japanese–Soviet political relations during the 1960s that they did not improve because this problem was always put forward. In the early 1970s when both nations were in the mood for improving their political as well as their economic relations, it was not convenient to Tanaka or *zaikai* if linkage to the territorial dispute should impede the three large joint projects in Siberia. In their annual speeches to the Diet on 27 January 1973, both Tanaka and Foreign Minister Ōhira brought up the importance of cooperation in Siberian development, and expressed Japanese willingness to cooperate,[33] and, significantly, Tanaka's speech contained no reference to the territorial problem. Both men's speeches sounded as if the Siberian project was top of their political agenda, and as if economic cooperation could proceed independently of political issues. Japanese newspapers reported that the Japanese government was about to take a line of separating politics and economics (*seikei bunri rosen*), since the USSR had not officially changed its traditional rigid attitude of refusing to alter national boundaries established after Second World War, and if Japan linked the issue of the three joint projects to Soviet return of the disputed territories, there was a risk that the Russians would be offended and neither issue would be resolved.[34] Furthermore, on 7 March 1973 Foreign Minister Ōhira told the Foreign Affairs Committee of the House of Representatives:

> we consider that the economic cooperation and the territorial problem are not issues to be linked, and not issues that should be linked . . .[35]

On the previous day the Japanese Ambassador to the USSR, Kinya Niizeki, had given Brezhnev a letter from Tanaka, expressing the necessity of holding peace negotiations by the end of that year and the importance of a dialogue between the top leaders.[36] On 28 March Soviet Ambassador Troyanovsky delivered Brezhnev's reply, officially inviting Tanaka to Moscow. Tanaka visited Moscow from 7 to 10 October, after visiting France, UK and West Germany. This was the second negotiation for a peace treaty.

## 'Unresolved problems'?: The territorial problem

The expression in the declaration at the end of the summit meetings was 'unresolved problems', inserted as a last resort, since the Soviet side refused to have the territories specifically mentioned. The Japanese interpretation was that Brezhnev agreed that the expression included the territorial problem, that the Soviet stance had therefore changed from claiming that the territorial issue had been solved to recognising that a territorial problem existed, and that the Japanese government could therefore give itself a positive evaluation.[37]

### The Japanese claim to the disputed territories

The Japanese position on the territorial problem at the time of Tanaka's visit to Moscow was that all four territories must be returned together. The thesis of 'four islands return' (*yontō henkan-ron*), which emerged at the time of the LDP's formation as the policy of the ruling party, and therefore of the government, was by now of long standing. In March 1957, for example, the Japanese government went through the formality of publishing educational maps that showed Etorofu, Kunashiri, Shikotan and the Habomais as Japanese.[38]

The bases for both nations' claims were clearly stated in the early 1960s in a series of letters exchanged between Khrushchev and the Japanese Prime Minister Hayato Ikeda.[39] The Japanese arguments for the 'four islands' demand may be summarised in the following five points.

1 The final disposition of territories as a result of war is essentially to be made by a peace treaty. In the case of Japan and the USSR, a joint declaration, not a peace treaty, was taken to end the status of war, since they could not reach agreement on the territorial problem except for the Habomais and Shikotan. Thus, the territorial problem has not yet been resolved.

2 The Yalta Agreement, according to the US explanation, was simply 'a statement of common purposes by the then heads of the participating

powers, and not a final determination by those powers or of any legal effect in transferring territories'.[40] Japan was not a party to the Agreement nor was it mentioned in the Potsdam Declaration which Japan accepted. Therefore, Japan is not legally bound by it.

3  The Potsdam Declaration states that the terms of the Cairo Declaration shall be carried out. The Cairo Declaration reconfirmed the principle of no territorial expansion by means of war, as set forth in the Atlantic Charter of 14 August 1941. It also declared that Japan was to be expelled from territories which it had taken by 'violence and greed'. Thus the Soviet claim is contradictory to the Cairo Declaration, in respect not only to the Kuriles, which Japan never took by 'violence and greed', but also to the islands of Kunashiri and Etorofu, which have traditionally been Japan's inherent territory, and have never belonged to any other country but Japan.

4  Japan renounced Southern Sakhalin and the Kurile Islands by the San Francisco Peace Treaty. The treaty, however, contained no provision indicating to which country these areas should finally belong. Thus, the Soviet argument that the territorial problem is resolved lacks grounds. Moscow is anyway not entitled to pursue claims under the San Francisco Treaty since it was not a party to it.

5  Kunashiri and Etorofu have internationally been recognised as Japanese territory since the mid-nineteenth century. Russia in 1855 recognised them as Japanese territories by the Treaty of Commerce, Navigation and Delimitation with Japan. Furthermore, the Treaty for Exchange of Sakhalin for the Kurile Islands signed between Japan and Russia in 1875 lists the names of 18 islands of the Kuriles from Shimushu to Uruppu to be handed over by Russia to Japan, in return for Japan's relinquishing all claim to Sakhalin Island. Therefore the historical facts confirm that the Kurile Islands which Japan renounced at the San Francisco Peace Treaty are the islands from Urup northwards, and Japan has never renounced any rights or claims for its inherent territory of Kunashiri, Etorofu, Shikotan and the Habomais.[41]

Once the goal was fixed to the four islands, Japan began to strengthen the case for separate treatment of Etorofu and Kunashiri, for which it had already prepared the way in the earlier pamphlet.[42] Because Japan had agreed to cede the 'Kuriles' in the 1951 San Francisco Peace Treaty, it had to argue that these islands were not part of the Kuriles. This argument was not made in 1946; the Japanese government then described Kunashiri and Etorofu as the Southern Kuriles (at that time the realistic goal for regaining territory was presumably only Shikotan and the Habomais).[43]

## Formulation of Japanese policy towards the USSR

The territorial issue replaced Siberian development and became the top policy priority at the time of Tanaka's visit to Moscow. This change of priorities may reflect a change in the parties taking policy initiatives towards the USSR. This Moscow summit also marked the Second Peace Treaty Negotiation after the diplomatic restoration of 1956.[44] When it came to the peace treaty, the ministry fully in charge of preparation was the Ministry of Foreign Affairs (*Gaimushō*). From its perspective, the peace treaty and the territorial problem were inseparable issues. One year prior to Tanaka's visit, the First Peace Treaty Negotiation was held when Foreign Minister Ōhira visited Moscow in October 1972. Ōhira at that time was given the duty of reminding the Soviets of the connection between the two issues, and did so remind them.[45] Though the Tanaka regime in general seemed to place priority more on economics, and thereafter to tone down the territorial issue, the focus shifted back to the territories when it came to the summit meeting and peace negotiations. In his luncheon speech on the summit meeting's first day, 8 October 1973, Tanaka pronounced that a peace treaty had to be concluded to establish a long-term friendly relationship, by resolving the problems left over from the Second World War, as Brezhnev had remarked in his speech at the commemorative session of the 50th anniversary of the USSR.[46]

In the later session of the talks on the same day, while Brezhnev concentrated most of his long speech on the development of Siberia and the importance of economic cooperation with Japan, Tanaka plainly asserted that the primary objective of the summit was to conclude a peace treaty, and that resolution of the territorial issue was a prerequisite for it. The economic cooperation stressed by Brezhnev was relegated there to a secondary role, and he urged Brezhnev seriously to work on the main issue of the summit.[47] This, from a Prime Minister whose policy priorities were generally economic, clearly indicates how strongly the *Gaimushō*'s influence was reflected in policy making towards the USSR.

Compared to the so-called 'dual diplomacy' of the 1956 summit meeting, Japanese policy making for the 1973 summit was relatively monolithic. Tanaka's diplomacy as a whole was concordant with that of Foreign Minister Ōhira, in distinct contrast to that of Hatoyama with Shigemitsu during the 1955–6 negotiations, which was portrayed also as Prime Minister's Office versus *Gaimushō*. Shigemitsu was a Foreign Minister who had been a diplomat, and was in fact as well as in name the head of the *Gaimushō*. Ōhira, though in his second term as Foreign Minister (a post he had previously held in 1962–4), was a dedicated LDP party politician like Tanaka, and had no objection to the Japanese territorial claim that had already been fixed under preceding LDP regimes since 1955. Once the national goal was set by the ruling party, the administrative body *Gaimushō* was solely in charge of making concrete policy to achieve the goal.

In preparation for the summit meetings, the *Gaimushō* took the initiative in formulating the negotiating strategy, and the political leaders obediently followed the manual prepared by the bureaucrats. The Prime Minister has regular contact with senior *Gaimushō* officials, normally the Deputy Foreign Minister once a week for a foreign policy briefing. When the situation becomes special, such as before a trip abroad, intensive study meetings are held. It is said that before leaving Japan, Tanaka received from the *Gaimushō* a preparatory text for the meetings with Brezhnev more than 15 cm thick. It was a collection of detailed assumptions of negotiating exchanges, including how to bring up the territorial issue, what wording to use in the opening remarks, etc. Special study sessions based on this text were held between Tanaka and the *Gaimushō* from August onwards, and Tanaka performed at the meetings just as he had been taught.[48]

As far as the content of the territorial claim, Tanaka could have no objection to the well-established claim for 'four islands return' (*yontō henkan*) or 'integral territories' (*koyū no ryōdo*), since the bases were set 17 years previously, when the LDP was formed. At the 17 September press conference referred to earlier, Ōhira also said,

> Thanks to Prime Minister Hatoyama's visit to the USSR, the basic path was at least made. Therefore we only have to drive on what the concerned authority has prepared.[49]

The 'concerned authority' is of course the *Gaimushō*. The pivotal strategic centre for the relevant policies is the Soviet office in the Asia and European Department. Though legal-policy decision making lay with cabinet, Ōhira's remark suggests that no objection was raised against the strategy prepared by the *Gaimushō*. In post-war policy making towards the USSR, especially in negotiations for a peace treaty and on the territorial problem, the *Gaimushō*, specifically the Soviet office, which monopolised secret and important information, dominated the role of think-tank, and there was no room for alternative policy.

In contrast to countries like the USA, where prominent academics are often appointed to senior positions in, for example, State Department, the Department of Defence or the National Security Council, and directly participate in national policy making, it is rare for Japanese academics to have direct influence on government policy making. In their political culture, connection of academics with politics has generally been perceived as unprincipled, and scholars who have strong ties with politics are often disparagingly called '*goyō-gakusha*' (government-patronised scholars). In making Japanese policy towards the USSR and Russia, the *Gaimushō* has enjoyed unchallenged dominance, and the influence of scholars has been almost nil. In addition to the convention of academic non-involvement in politics, Soviet studies in Japan were not highly developed at the time.[50] It is said that there was a virtual vacuum in specialised study of the Soviet Union from the mid-1930s to the late 1970s. Soviet studies in Japan had not established a stable infrastructure, due to inability to secure adequate funding. Instead of depending on Japanese academics, the *Gaimushō* trained its staff by sending them to prestigious institutions in the USA or UK. Except for those few who had close ties and/or shared views with the *Gaimushō*, Japanese academics did not reach a large audience, and played only minor, if any, roles in discussions of the Soviet Union.[51]

Among organisations of the Northern irredentist movement is the 'Council on National Security Problems' (*Anzenhoshō mondai kenkyū-kai*). This non-governmental organisation is headed by a private individual, Mr Ichirō Suetsugu, and has been widely supported by individuals or companies. The Council was inaugurated in February 1968 under the title 'Research Council for the Issue of Bases in Okinawa' (*Okinawa kichi mondai kenkyū-kai*). The principle of 'no nuclear weapons, as in the main islands, reversion in 1972' (*kaku-nuki, hondo-nami, 72-nen henkan*) proposed in the Council's report was adopted by the government for its negotiations with the USA, and became the basis of the Sato–Nixon agreement of 1969. Noting the deep involvement of American academics in policy making, Mr Suetsugu met Edwin Reischauer, obtained a list of such American scholars, and selected panels to be invited for the Council's meetings. Since then, the Council has been interacting with prominent scholars from various countries, while maintaining close contact with prime ministers, foreign ministers, other governmental figures, leaders of political parties and Japanese academics.[52] The Council was renamed 'The Council on National Security Problems' in 1970. Its contacts with the Soviet Academy of Sciences began just before Tanaka's visit to Moscow. The Japan–Soviet Experts' Conference (*Nisso senmonka kaigi*) that started in May 1973 continues to function as the Japan–Russia Experts' Conference (*Nichiro senmonka kaigi*). As the absolute initiative in policy formulation lies in the *Gaimushō*, however, the Council's role may be mainly in its cooperation in publicising government policy output rather than providing input.

The *Gaimushō's* work at times was not only dealing with negotiation policies, but also extended to controlling expression in the domestic press. Professor John Stephan, a leading American scholar in Russian-Japanese history, has mentioned that plans to publish his book *The Kuril Islands* in

Japanese were terminated due to indirect intervention by the *Gaimushō*. The volume, based on detailed historical research, contains a critical analysis of the territorial dispute, and he refused to alter the text to accommodate the *Gaimushō*'s interest.[53]

Among Diet members, the League of Diet Representatives for Japan–Soviet Friendship was established in February 1973, headed by Hakuei Ishida (LDP), and sent a delegation to the USSR from 27 August to 6 September, shortly before Tanaka's visit. The League was non-partisan, including members from different political parties with differing views on the ways to resolve the dispute.[54] The Democratic Socialists (DSP) and Kōmeitō members essentially supported the LDP's position, while the Socialists (JSP) and Communists (JCP) demanded the return of the entire Kuriles chain.[55]

The Diet has passed a number of resolutions on the 'Northern Territories' issue. Starting with 'the resolution regarding the entreaty for return of the Habomai islands' (*Habomai shotō henkan konsei ni kansuru ketsugi*) of March 1951, they include: 'resolution regarding the territorial problem' (June 1951); 'resolution regarding the territories' (July 1952 and July 1953); 'resolution regarding recovery of Japan's inherent Northern Territories' (March 1962); 'resolution regarding return of the Northern Territories' (April 1965 and September 1973).[56] The 1973 resolution names the 'Northern Territories' that Japan should attempt to regain as 'the Habomais, Shikotan, Kunashiri, Etorofu *and so on (tō)*'. When the resolution was put, the LDP, JSP, DSP, JCP and Kōmeitō reportedly judged it as covering all their differing claims, and so all voted for it.[57]

Not only were the negotiating priorities changed, but technological and economical assistance for Siberian development became a bargaining counter for regaining the territories. According to a newspaper report from the then West German capital, Bonn, which Tanaka was visiting before going to Moscow, 'Siberian development will in principle be treated together with the Northern Territories'.[58] Thus, in the *Gaimushō's* strategy for the summit, Japanese policy toward the USSR changed from *seikei bunri* (separation of politics and economics) to *seikei fukabun* (no separation of politics and economics).

The government's persistent policy of refusing a peace treaty without return of the 'Northern Territories', and its new linking of politics with economics prompted some groups to put forward an alternative, pragmatic, solution: namely, buying back the 'Northern Territories'. The big business community *zaikai* desired improved, and stable political relations with the USSR, and at an LDP National Land Development Research Council (*Kokudo kaihatsu kenkyū-kai*) meeting the head of the Japan Chamber of Commerce and Industry, Shigeo Nagano, suggested 'buying up the

Northern Territories' from the USSR, using Japan's increasing accumulation of foreign currency.[59] Obviously, this was not accepted.

### The 'four islands' territorial claim and the Japanese incentive for a peace treaty.

It is open to question whether the Japanese government or *Gaimushō* policy makers really were interested at the time in making progress on the issue of political *rapprochement*. According to the head of the Soviet office of *Gaimushō*, the peace treaty could have been concluded if the USSR had returned the islands, and Japan would have gone ahead whether or not the USA objected.[60]

However, there was no possibility of the USSR ceding all four territories. Throughout the contacts preceding the summit meeting, it became clear enough that the two sides' positions on the territorial problem were very far apart. In contrast to the Japanese package claim for all four islands, the official Soviet position, that 'the territorial problem is solved', denied even the existence of a dispute. Therefore, optimism about the prospects for a peace treaty had already faded by the summit. On 17 September Foreign Minister Ōhira told journalists that 'if we cannot achieve anything by the visit this time, it will be none the worse for that'. With so obviously large a gap between the positions of the two sides, their negotiating practices should have suggested a search for a middle course. However, negotiating policy, as publicised at the beginning of the Summit was:

> The Northern Territories: If the Soviets rigidly refuse the return of Habomai, Shikotan, Kunashiri and Etorofu, have them make a definite promise to continue peace treaty negotiations in the future. At the same time, try to work for solution of other important issues for Japan,such as safe fishery operations etc. (2) If continued discussion is realised, have the Soviet Union promise to return the islands in question, Kunashiri and Etorofu, with reimbursement by us for their investment on those islands. Then confirm that Japan will not make other territorial demands than the four islands including Shikotan and the Habomais.(3) In order to achieve the above demands, our country will not accept any terms of compromise.[61]

During the course of the Summit, *Nihon Keizai Shimbun* reported that Tanaka suggested to his Russian counterparts:

> If Japanese sovereignty over the four islands is recognized, the timing of returning the Habomais and Shikotan, as agreed to be returned

upon signing of the peace treaty, and the remaining islands of Kunashiri and Etorofu could be differenciated.[62]

As the Japanese territorial claim had been for the four islands to be returned altogether, it was probably a 'kind' of flexibility shown by the Japanese government. However, their principal attitude towards the negotiation was that solution of the 'Northern Territories' problem, i.e., the return of the all four islands, was prerequisite to develop relations with the USSR, including economic cooperation.[63] Although Brezhnev in return proposed the conclusion of a peace treaty first and then settlement of other issues in the framework of friendship and cooperation, this 'shelving' of the territorial issue was totally unacceptable to Japan.[64] Thus, there was little flexibility in pursuit of a mutually acceptable concession scheme, and the gap between the two positions did not narrow.

It is true that the demand for 'four island return' was already settled national policy. However, the inflexible Japanese posture seemed to be based on an assumption of less incentive than before for a political *rapprochement*. When in 1956 diplomatic relations were reopened without a peace treaty, there were pressing humanitarian problems over Japanese prisoners of war held in the USSR, but they had since been repatriated. Another reason may be found in the *Gaimushō's* traditional distrust of and animosity against the Russians. Furthermore, despite East–West *détente*, the fundamental structures of ideological conflict were still in place, and there was also a concern with China, with which Japan was also attempting to improve its relations. In such circumstances there was no great need to sign a peace treaty with the USSR unless for an exceptionally good deal, i.e, the return of the four islands (or more?). The return of Okinawa by the USA at this time shifted the attention of irredentists from south to north, but the campaign did not acquire the intensity of that which had preceded the reversion of Okinawa.[65] While nearly a million Japanese lived on Okinawa, none resided in the disputed islands.

### Brezhnev's 'Da'

The Joint Communiqué issued on 10 October at the conclusion of the talks made no direct reference to the territorial problem, but instead referred only to 'unresolved problems left over from the World War II'. As mentioned earlier, Japan came to assert its interpretation that the expression included the 'Northern Territories' problem. The Japanese side indeed wanted to include the word 'territory' in the communiqué, but the Soviet side firmly refused to do so. The original Japanese draft contained the singular form 'problem', since the territorial issue was the single impediment to a peace treaty between the two nations, but it was changed to 'problems' at Soviet request.[66] The Japanese endorsed their interpretation from their record of the summit meeting. It notes that when Tanaka asked if they could interpret the expression 'unresolved problems' (plural) as including the territorial question, Brezhnev said '*Ya znayu*' (I know). Then when Tanaka asked again for confirmation, Brezhnev answered '*Da*' (yes). The record of conversation is said to be preserved in the *Gaimushō*.[67]

The Japanese recorded the entire meeting, at which the *Gaimushō* had skilled recorders. This came from the experience of the Kōno–Bulganin meeting during the 1956 Moscow fishery negotiations, when, in what *Gaimushō* professionals call 'the biggest stain on Japanese diplomacy', a secret agreement was reached with no *Gaimushō* official present. Since then 'never let anyone go alone to meetings with the Russians' has been an iron rule of the Ministry.[68] Incidentally, Mr Kinya Niizeki, who was supposed to accompany Kono in 1956, but was left behind, was Japanese Ambassador to the Soviet Union at the time of the 1973 summit. On Brezhnev's '*Da*' there is a variety of views, such as that he was merely clearing his throat. However that may be, in the ears of the Japanese side, the 'Northern Territories' problem was included among the 'unresolved problems'.

## THE 'NATION-STATE' PERSPECTIVE: THE SOVIET UNION

### USSR and Japan: The second *rapprochement* wave

#### *The 1970s détente and the USSR's domestic situation*

The domestic factors that drove the Soviet Union towards *détente* and hence towards *rapprochement* with Japan in the early 1970s could be found mainly in its economic situation. The Soviet economy was already beginning to stagnate. The growth rate per annum of gross national product (GNP), which had been 6.4 per cent between 1950 and 1958, dropped to 5.4 per cent from 1958 to 1967, and to 3.7 per cent in the period 1967–73.[69] The series of economic reforms introduced in the mid-1960s appeared clear failures by 1970, the end of the eighth five-year plan. This was also the time when Siberia loomed large as a new source of natural resource supply, which would certainly boost the entire economy. Large-scale economic cooperation for Siberian development started to be discussed from the mid-1960s. However, the Soviet Union lacked capital, technology, manpower and consumer goods, and the infrastructure in Siberia was inadequate.[70] Thus, the

Soviets had strong incentives to improve their relations with the non-Communist industrialised countries.

## Approach to Japan: Change in perception of Japan among the Soviet leaders

In the past, the Soviet perception of Japan was negative, or Japan was viewed as a country of secondary importance. However, Japan's rapid economic growth in the two post-war decades, especially from the devastation of a lost war, gradually changed the Soviet leaders' perception.

A notable change of Soviet policy towards Japan was observed in May 1964, when First Deputy Prime Minister Anastas I. Mikoyan visited Japan. Mikoyan praised Japan as a great country for its economic power, and for not pursuing military power, and expressed wishes that the two nations would expand their economic and cultural exchanges, and that Japan would cease following US policy and adopt its own independent diplomacy. In the subsequent growth of bilateral economic relations, Soviet trade with Japan had risen to the billion dollar level by 1972, Japan had become the Soviet Union's largest trading partner among the capitalist countries, and the two nations had begun to discuss several large economic cooperation projects centring on development of Siberia.[71]

The Soviet leadership placed its hopes on Japan's new Prime Minister, Kakuei Tanaka. Knowing Tanaka as conservative and not very sympathetic to the Soviet Union, they at the same time knew that he was strong and very influential, and were interested in making contact with him,[72] especially as Japan in the early 1970s, under the impact of the series of 'Nixon Shocks', appeared to be reviewing its US-dependent policy and seeking a direction for its own independent diplomacy. Incidentally, it seemed to the Soviets that the USA did not like this new Japanese premier.[73] Both in the international background and incentives for the two nations, the time appeared ripe for them to sign a peace treaty and improve their political relations.

## Decision making in the Brezhnev period

Soviet policy decision making in the Brezhnev period was not so monolithic as under his predecessor. Politicians often learn from a predecessor's failure. Khrushchev gradually increased his political power after the death of Stalin, enjoyed his one-man politics, and because of that was expelled from power. The survival strategy that Brezhnev learned from Khrushchev was therefore reinforcement of the collective leadership system, and good treatment of the elites. Brezhnev was a very prudent politician, who never ignored the Politburo or took important decisions by himself. In his attitude to policy and to personnel changes, Brezhnev was said to have displayed 'caution and patience' where Khrushchev had been 'bold and impulsive'.[74] Though very cautious, as he avoided premature personnel shake-ups that might lead to dangerous confrontations, Brezhnev nevertheless succeeded in gradually removing his former and potential rivals and replacing them by people whom he could trust or had close ties with.[75]

In April of 1973, the year the Soviet–Japanese summit was held, Defence Minister Andrei A. Grechko, KGB director Yurii V. Andropov and Foreign Minister Andrei A. Gromyko were appointed to the Politburo. Among the government apparatus, the Ministry of Defence influence in policy decision making is often pointed out. In this case the international situation the USSR was facing at that time, especially its military security factors, more specifically the USSR's increased military strength and its strategy towards China seem relevant. 'Peaceful coexistence' in the Brezhnev period differed somewhat from that of Khrushchev's time. By the early 1970s, the Soviet Union had achieved approximate parity in nuclear weapons with the United States for the first time. The Strategic Arms Limitation Talks (SALT-1) agreement and the signing of the 'Basic Principles of Relations between the USA and the USSR' in 1972 were the most obvious examples of US acknowledgment of Soviet strategic power. Thus, against the background of increased military force, the military held a strong influence in policy decision making in Brezhnev's regime. Brezhnev's susceptibility to military flattery was so obvious that he later (1976) had himself given the highest military rank of Marshal of the Soviet Union, and awarded the Order of Victory, a decoration created and previously conferred only in 1945 and awarded only to the very highest Soviet and Allied Second World War commanders.[76] The increase of the military's voice in decision making also seemed to be concerned with worsening relations with China to the extent that it led to a military clash. Perceiving the emerging tripolarity of the new international political configuration, the USSR campaigned widely in Asia for its Asian Collective Security Arrangement proposal. When Brezhnev announced this proposal in June 1969, he devoted much of his speech to criticising China, and it therefore came to be perceived as an anti-Chinese measure.[77]

As for the influence of academics on Soviet decision making, several institutions of the Soviet Academy of Sciences came to be known as influential in the policy making of the Gorbachev period, such as the Institute of World Economies and International Relations (IMEMO), the Institute of the USA and Canada (ISKAN), the Institute of Oriental Studies (IVAN) and the Institute of the Far East (IDV). However, the influence of those institutions on the Kremlin's policy decision making was minimal before this. Successive Directors of IMEMO or ISKAN were indeed members of the Central Committee of the Communist Party, and therefore said to have had close relations with its International Department.[78] Their relations were nevertheless subordinate to the Ministry of Foreign Affairs (MID) or the Central Committee, and their public roles more of propagandising government policy. Arkady N. Shevchenko, who defected to the USA from the post of Deputy Secretary-General of the UN – the highest position ever achieved by a Soviet citizen in an international organisation – admonished the West for tending to overestimate the influence of those institutions on Soviet foreign policy. For instance, while many American observers thought Georgy Arbatov of ISKAN played an important role behind the scenes in preparation of policy toward the SALT treaty, Shevchenko pointed out that ISKAN did not participate in the key part of the policy formulation process toward the USA. No one in ISKAN was consulted by the MID or given access to its proposals to the Politburo. Essentially the important decisions, he wrote, were all made by the Politburo 'on the basis of recommendations by Gromyko, Ustinov, and Grechko, with the aid of their top professional assistants'.[79]

## Policy making towards Japan

As for policy towards Japan, except for replacement at the top, almost the same people as in 1956 were in charge at the MID. At the time of Hatoyama's visit, the Far Eastern Department of MID was responsible for all of the Far East including Korea, China, Mongolia and Japan, but it had later been divided into two, First Far Eastern Department headed by Mikhail Kapitsa, to concentrate on Sino-Soviet relations, and Second Far Eastern Department headed by Ivan Fadeevich Shped'ko, to handle the rest of the Far East, including Japan.

Policy details regarding Japan, such as Gromyko's visit to Tokyo and Tanaka's visit to Moscow, were all handled in the MID, with the Second Far Eastern Department taking the central role, and inputs from other concerned agencies including the International Department of the Party's Central Committee, Military, KGB, and Ministries of Finance or Trade.[80] In this period it was notable that Brezhnev did not take decisions by himself, and that MID influence in the supreme decision-making Politburo increased, especially after Gromyko's ascent to it.[81]

In the International Department of the Central Committee, Ivan Kovalenko, a Japan specialist and the chief of the Far Eastern Section was marked as a symbolic figure,[82] and later became a Deputy-Director of the Department. Though he was perceived outside the USSR rather negatively as a wire-puller,[83] he had little influence or decision-making power, according to former government officials, including himself, except on small matters. On important decisions concerning national security, such as the territorial question, he simply followed decisions from above, i.e., the Politburo, and did as he was told.[84]

Soviet Japanologists were no exception. Dmitri Petrov was a research fellow at IMEMO, one of the most prestigious institutions of the Soviet Academy of Sciences referred to above. In the early 1970s he argued in an article that the USSR should pursue improvement of its relations with Japan, despite Japan's close relationship with the United States.[85] His argument turned out to be unacceptable to Politburo member Mikhail Suslov, who opposed the existence of the US–Japan military alliance, and aimed at breaking the basic strategic ties of those two nations. Petrov is said to have been transferred as a result from IMEMO to the Institute of the Far East (IDV).[86]

## Gromyko's 'smiling diplomacy' in 1972

Gromyko's January 1972 visit to Japan was an obvious sign of Soviet seriousness in pursuing a drastic move to improve relations with Japan. Gromyko was the longest-serving Foreign Minister in Soviet and Russian History (1957–85), becoming a member of the Central Committee in 1956 and of the Politburo in April 1973. He was long described as a technician – a product of the career foreign-affairs bureaucracy. Though Khrushchev treated him as a low-level functionary and even made a joke against him to the effect that Gromyko would lower his trousers and sit on a block of ice if ordered to do so by the First Secretary,[87] he later gained influence and played a more prominent role in policy making, especially after his elevation to the Politburo.[88] His perception of Japan was far from positive; he retained a traditional Russian view, and later was to say in his memoirs,

> History has taught us to be cautious when Japanese statesmen express their good intentions. In 1904 the Japanese broke an agreement and attacked Port Arthur – which led to the outbreak of the Russo-Japanese war. Then there were the events of 1937 at Lake Khasan and 1939 at the Khalkin-Gol river, when the Japanese militarists suddenly undertook to test the defences of the Soviet frontier. There was also the unexpected attack on the US naval base at Pearl Harbor. Finally, we have also been put on our guard by the American military bases the Japanese have over the last few decades permitted on their territory.[89]

Gromyko, directly and indirectly was one of those most familiar with the path of Soviet diplomacy during and after the Second World War. He participated in the 1945 Yalta and Potsdam Conferences. From 1946 to 1948 he was Permanent Soviet Representative at the UN Security Council. At the San Francisco conference in 1951 he headed the Soviet delegation. He also witnessed the 1955–6 negotiations as First Deputy Foreign Minister. With regard to the negative relations with Japan, he concluded,

> This has been far from our fault. The unevenness in our relations derives from the zigzag nature of Japanese politics. Tokyo's policy in the past has alternated between reason and hypocrisy, with a growing tendency towards the latter.[90]

Gromyko was not one to change his views on anything. He was very strict and serious,[91] and was therefore nicknamed *Grom* (thunder) by his colleagues or Mr *Nyet* (No) by his foreign counterparts. In January 1972, this Mr *Nyet* visited Japan and performed 'smiling diplomacy', indicating that the Soviet leaders were serious about political *rapprochement* with Japan.[92] At that time, the Prime Minister was still Eisaku Satō and Foreign Minister Takeo Fukuda. As discussed below, Gromyko indicated that the Soviet Union intended to conclude a peace treaty with the transfer of Shikotan and the Habomais. Incidentally, when Gromyko visited Japan in 1972, the director of both First and Second Far Eastern Departments, M. Kapitsa, accompanied him. The presence of Kapitsa, a China expert, seems to indicate how much the Soviet overture to Japan was driven by the awareness of China.

The Soviet Asian Collective Security proposal was raised as a matter of course, but no positive response was received from the Japanese side. The Soviet desire seriously to improve political relations with Japan was expressed further. In his speech on the 50th anniversary of the USSR on 21 December, referring to the forthcoming negotiations, Brezhnev indicated the Soviet intention to improve relations with Japan:

> in the next year important Soviet–Japanese negotiations are to be held. Their purpose is to resolve problems left over from the Second World War, and to establish a treaty as the basis for relations between our countries.[93]

The Japanese grasped the implications of this periphrasis, and Tanaka's letter was sent to Moscow. It was March when an official invitation to visit Moscow was delivered to Tanaka.

## 'Unresolved problems'?: The territorial problem

### *The Soviet claim to the disputed territories*

Soviet officials denied the Japanese claim that Brezhnev had affirmed that the territorial problem was included in the expression 'unresolved problems' in the Joint Communiqué. By the early 1970s, when peace moves resumed, the Soviet official view was that 'no territorial problem exists with Japan'. During the 1960s, in the politically cold period of their relations, as the Japanese arguments for its 'four islands' claim had appeared complete, the Soviet basis for refutation had been fully articulated.

The Soviet counter-arguments may be summarised as follows.

1  The Japanese government signed the instrument of surrender and pledged itself to carry out the terms of the Potsdam Declaration. The Declaration limited Japanese sovereignty to the islands of Honshu, Hokkaido, Kyushu, Shikoku and minor islands.
2  Since Japan had renounced its right, title and claim to the Kuriles Islands in the San Francisco Treaty, Japan could in no way lay claim to any part of them.
3  The Yalta Agreement clearly specified to which country the Kuriles and Southern Sakhalin would belong. The Allies' terms which Japan accepted originated from several agreements among the Allies, including the Yalta agreement.
4  The claim that Kunashiri and Etorofu are not included in the Kuriles is not sustainable. The fact is that Japanese historical and geographical materials admit that these islands are part of the Kuriles.
5  The treaties of 1855 and 1875 are not relevant to this issue. Japan had already lost its right to refer to the previous treaties by its seizure of Southern Sakhalin as a result of the Russo-Japanese War (1904) and the Portsmouth Treaty (1905). Furthermore, in the early 1920s, Japan again invaded Russia breaking this Portsmouth Treaty, and occupied the northern part of Sakhalin and the Soviet Far East.[94]
6  The territorial problem between Japan and the USSR is already solved.[95]

### *Gromyko's visit to Japan and the 'two islands' offer*

After the *Glasnost* policy was introduced, it was revealed that the 'two islands' offer had again been made to Japan during Gromyko's visit to Japan in 1972, the year before Tanaka's visit to Moscow. Mikhail Kapitsa, who was then heading the First Far Eastern Department and had accompanied

Gromyko to Japan, disclosed this in an interview he gave to a *Jijitsūshin* Moscow correspondent, and this became news. Kapitsa's claim was denied by Takeo Fukuda, Japanese Foreign Minister at the time of Gromyko's visit, and also by Kyōji Komachi, Head of the Russian Department of the *Gaimushō* when the news came out. But no comment on this came from Lyudvig A. Chizhov (then Russian Ambassador to Japan) who was an interpreter on that occasion, and the credibility of Kapitsa's account was also questioned by a Japanese scholar.[96] However, there are also several signs that such an offer was actually made. On the Russian side, it is referred to by Panov:

> During Gromyko's visit to Japan in 1972, at a meeting between him and concerned people in the Japanese government the Soviet side indicated preparedness to deal with the solution of the territorial problem on the basis of the 1956 Declaration.[97]

In addition, during interviews with the author, the account of this 'two islands' offer was confirmed by former Russian officials, including the then section head in charge of relations with Japan, and Kapitsa himself. It turned out that this 'two islands' offer was not a spontaneous proposal by Gromyko, but a decision discussed and resolved by the Politburo.[98] In other words, there was a firm consensus on this offer among the Soviet leaders. Also, on the Japanese side, there is a record of a statement by Foreign Minister Masayoshi Ōhira to the Foreign Affairs Committee of the House of Councillors held on 17 July, 1973, to the effect that

> the other party [the USSR], as I understood, seems to wish to solve the territorial problem by dealing with the islands up to Shikotan and the Habomais.[99]

If this account of the 'two islands' proposal is true, why was it decided to make the offer? First, the sensible answer would be the fact that the offer to transfer those two territories had previously been made in 1956, and almost all those responsible for preparing the policy protocol then were still in office in 1972. However, there must have been something more to trigger the positional shift from 'no territorial problem' to the 'two islands' offer. The reversion of Okinawa to Japan in 1972 may be one reason. In connection with the Soviet–Japanese territorial dispute, its impact on US policy and/or international opinion was minor, but it may be relevant to the Soviet attitude. As Khrushchev had said, the Soviet leaders were against US retention of Okinawa. The linkage between the 'two islands' transfer and treatment of Okinawa was a point on which the USSR insisted until the very last moment at the 1956 summit. Also, at a meeting during the visit of a Japanese parliamentary delegation to the Soviet Union in September 1964, Khrushchev remarked that the Habomais and Shikotan would be returned if the United States returned Okinawa to Japan.[100] Thus, Gromyko's 'two islands' overture and the reversion of Okinawa may not necessarily be unconnected.

According to a former Soviet official, the Soviet side was at that time seriously considering *rapprochement* with Japan by means of a peace treaty. As bilateral relations were improving in the early 1970s, those in charge of policy making on the Soviet side thought the time had come to seek a breakthrough with the two islands concession. They were indeed making minute preparations. For example, concrete calculations were made on the Soviet side such as how much Japan should pay for facilities, etc. if Shikotan and the Habomais were transferred. In addition, consultations went on not only within the MID, but also with the KGB, the Central Committee, the Navy, the Agriculture and Forestry Ministry, and the Fisheries Ministry.[101] Whatever may have been happening behind the scenes of the policy formulation process, the publicly stated Soviet official view remained that no territorial problem existed with Japan.

Lack of Soviet academic writings on the subject, as I mentioned earlier, derived from the nature of the Soviet political system. For academics to doubt the government's views or make counter-proposals meant they risked the loss of their positions. Mentioning the territorial problem was taboo.[102] After *Perestroika*, one scholar described his experiences from this period, recalling them as 'extreme unpleasantness'. When he was Deputy Chief Academic Secretary of the Presidium of the Far Eastern Sciences Center, he publicly stated at a youth conference in Nakhodka. 'The USSR once promised Japan in 1956 to return Shikotan and Habomai upon conclusion of Peace Treaty, and so-called *pacta servanda sunt*'.[103] The Japanese consulate in Nakhodka, Japanese press and Japanese participants in the conference publicised his remark. As a result, the Primorski Krai party organisation severely reprimanded him.[104] Later, he participated in the preparation of a collective work entitled 'Foreign Policy of the USSR in the Far East: 1945–86 (*Vneshnyaya politika SSSR na Dal'nem Vostoke, 1945–1986* gg., M., 1988). During editing of this publication, all references to the 'Northern Territories' or Soviet–Japanese relations were deleted.[105]

### The Soviet 'nyet' to the 'unsolved problems'

When the Japanese side claimed that Brezhnev had confirmed inclusion of the 'Northern Territories problem' among the 'unsolved problems' mentioned in the Joint Communiqué, the Soviet representative adamantly denied it. Wherever the truth lay, the fact is that the Soviet position had returned to the former rigid one that no territorial problem existed between the two countries. Why did flexibility disappear from the Soviet position? Panov suggests that the Moscow summit failed despite Soviet readiness to confirm the transfer of Shikotan and the Habomais, because of strong military opposition. He said that, just before the summit, Defence Minister Grechko reversed his attitude, and opposed the islands' transfer to Japan on strategic grounds. Khrushchev had regarded these islands as strategically unimportant in the nuclear age. However, the strategic environment around the Kuriles changed in the 1970s.[106] Especially considering the strong influence of the military of that time, this view of the military opposition to the islands' transfer seems to be valid.

Panov describes another view, perhaps more reliable, as the source attended the Moscow summit. According to this account, Brezhnev became very angry at Tanaka's attitude when he stated the Japanese position, as Tanaka curtly told Brezhnev to take notes of what he would state about the Japanese position and understand the reasons for Japan's not giving up the 'four islands' demand. The meeting having started in such an undiplomatic manner, Brezhnev was said to have decided not to discuss any possibility of returning to the position of the 1956 Joint Declaration.[107] If this account is true, it was probably either one of the exceptional cases where Brezhnev took a decision by himself, or Tanaka's attitude produced an immediate consensus among the top leaders. Whatever the truth of either explanation, the Japanese side, however, still asserts that Brezhnev in fact recognised the existence of the territorial problem. According to a former MID senior official who attended the meeting,

> Tanaka all the time demanded that Brezhnev recognise that there was a territorial problem between Japan and the Soviet Union. Though Brezhnev refused, Tanaka today, tomorrow, and the day after tomorrow all the time said 'Well, you tell there is [*sic*]'. After all, he [Brezhnev] once unofficially said 'All right, I know!'. But afterwards we confirmed that it was not written in any document.[108]

With regard to the last point, another former MID official who was in the secretariat told me it was his personal view that when Brezhnev met Tanaka, no member of the secretariat such as himself attended the meeting. As a result, there was no record left with the Soviet side. The other individuals who attended the meeting were all in senior positions; they did nothing but listen, and took no notes. There is consequently no way to confirm whether or not Brezhnev said '*Da*'.[109]

## THE 'BILATERAL-INTERACTION' PERSPECTIVE

The Joint Declaration of 1956 issued during Hatoyama's visit to the Soviet Union was the final product of over 21 months' negotiation. By contrast, the Joint Communiqué of 1973 on Tanaka's visit was dashed off in a short time, and prepared just before Tanaka's departure from Tokyo, leaving the final decisions to be made at the summit.[110] As for the negotiation channels, in contrast to the complicated interactions of 1955–6 through formal and informal channels that were therefore called dual diplomacy, it appeared that the major action was taken by the formal channel in the peace negotiations of the early 1970s.

### Japanese goals and Soviet goals

Tanaka's visit to Moscow in October 1973 was also the Second Peace Treaty Negotiation, following the first negotiation held upon the Foreign Minister Ōhira's visit to Moscow in October 1972. In this sense, the mutual and primary goal of the summit was to be the peace treaty. As is known, however, no such treaty was signed. By the time of Tanaka's visit expectations were already fading, for, as mentioned before, the discrepancy between the two countries' positions over the territorial issue had become apparent.

The biggest difference between Hatoyama's and Tanaka's visits to Moscow is that in 1973 the relations of the two countries were no longer those of winner and loser of the war. Issues such as UN membership and repatriation of Japanese POWs, the major Japanese goals of the 1955–6 negotiations, had already been resolved. Japan's primary goal at the 1973 summit was resolution of the territorial issue, the 'problem (singular) left over from Second World War' and also the only problem left over from the 1956 summit. Solution of the territorial problem was therefore a prerequisite for Japan to sign a peace treaty. Japan did not have a solid claim demanding fixed areas of island territories in the peace negotiations of the 1950s; however, from the beginning of the peace negotiations in the 1970s, the Japanese government put forward the 'four islands' claim that had become fixed under the stabilised LDP regime. While the Japanese side maintained this stance throughout the negotiations, it became clear at the preliminary drafting stage that the Soviets would not agree to it. Thus, the key to the Moscow negotiations became how to achieve a 'positive' Soviet attitude for the Joint Communiqué in this matter.[111] Securing sites for stable resource supply and expanding economic cooperation were also what Tanaka and the business community wanted. However, when it came to the peace treaty, they were given only secondary priority, and rather were treated as a bargaining counter.

The Soviet primary goal was complete political *rapprochement* with Japan, specifically the signing of a peace treaty, an issue left over from 1956. Political *rapprochement* with Japan would also fit into Soviet global strategy. Having been hit twice by the 'Nixon Shocks', Japan at that time was searching for a new direction for its diplomacy, and in addition, the favourable development of Japanese–Soviet economic relations was perceived as providing a greater opportunity for political *rapprochement*. The Sino-US *rapprochement* against the background of the Sino-Soviet conflict further motivated the Soviet leaders in their peace overture to Japan. The ideal goal for the Soviets in this move was probably to integrate Japan into its Asian Collective Security Plan. However, this plan in general was not making favourable progress, and there was little prospect that such a collective system could be organised instantly, if at all. Yet, there was still another possibility of proposing an arrangement similar to the Soviet–Indian Treaty of Friendship and Cooperation of 1971, which specified mutual cooperation.

The realistic goal of the summit was indeed something more practical and pragmatic, meeting the need of the time, i.e., to obtain the Japanese government's endorsement of economic and technological cooperation. For economic reconstruction of the country and for Siberian development, Japan, whose economy was growing at an unprecedented pace at that time, seemed an ideal partner for the USSR, since it was poor in natural resources and needed ever-increasing imports of those resources to sustain its economic growth. Thus, the complementary nature of the two economies appeared to be providing a reasonable ground for cooperation and mutual benefit. At the second meeting of the summit, on 20 October, Brezhnev, in a speech lasting over two hours, stated that the important issue was economic cooperation, not the peace treaty, spoke of the abundance of Soviet natural resources and emphasised the significance of economic cooperation, repeatedly referring to a map of the whole Soviet land spread out on a table.[112]

## *Bargaining cards and negotiating strategies*

One of the bargaining tactics that Japan had used to achieve its goals during the 1955–6 negotiations was suspension of the negotiations. This 'then, unfortunately . . .' card had been used to achieve Japanese goals one after another, tactically exploiting the primary Soviet goal of a peace treaty. This was, however, no longer so effective in 1973, apparently because the expectation that a peace treaty could be achieved was low on both sides. The Soviet side perceived little flexibility in the fixed and rigid Japanese attitude toward the peace negotiations. Yet, it seems certain that similar thinking existed on the Japanese side, specifically in the *Gaimushō*. In other words, it seems that they thought it was the Soviet side which would be in trouble if the negotiation was unsuccessful. It had in fact been the Soviet Union which had made overtures to Japan and taken the initiative in movement towards a peace treaty. For Japan recovery of the 'Northern Territories' was far weightier than signing a peace treaty with the USSR. In addition, while the Japanese primary goal of regaining the territories, which they had already pursued for a long time, would not disappear if not immediately attained, the Soviets' primary goal was more urgent, deeply related to the international situation and their domestic economy, and Japan was equipped with the necessities, or new bargaining card, on which its attainment could depend. The new card was that of their advanced economy and technology, needed for the development of Siberia. Though it was originally meant to be separated from the territorial issue (*seikei bunri*) and dealt with on its own, as Foreign Minister Ōhira remarked at the Diet, the position changed when it came to the peace negotiations.

The *Gaimushō*'s strategy was to make the best use of the Soviets' immediate goal of economic cooperation as a bargaining card, and to try to induce as positive an attitude as possible over the territorial question from the Soviet side. Prior to the summit, Tanaka was told by Mr Arai (head of the Soviet Section of the *Gaimushō*) that

> When the Soviet Union tosses in various proposals for economic cooperation, we should not at once throw in the card of our intention to cooperate. If we throw the card in, they would take only the card and shelve the territorial problem.[113]

It is thus assumed that the Japanese government linked its decision regarding economic cooperation to a Soviet concession over the territorial problem.

The Japanese Government came to need a bargaining counter for regaining the territories, so it relinked economics and politics (*seikei fukabun*). This inconsistency in negotiation policies or principles is not necessarily unique to the Japanese, but reminds us of the 1956 summit, at which territorial negotiations were supposed to be shelved, but were taken down from the shelf and discussed.

There was another version of the three-stage demand over the former Japanese territories during the 1955–6 negotiations. This was no longer the same, since the Japanese government had already set the four islands as 'Japan's Northern Territories' to be returned from the USSR. The return of only Shikotan and the Habomais, which was the most realistic goal of 1956, was no longer available as a minimum claim. Differences among the different political parties nevertheless seemed to leave room for three levels of demands, (1) 'four islands', (2) the entire Kuriles chain and (3) all former Japanese territories, including Southern Sakhalin. Some opposition parties laid claim to a greater area of the 'Northern Territories' than the ruling party and the government. In the draft resolution introduced jointly in the House of Representatives by the LDP, the DSP, the JSP, the JCP and Kōmeitō and passed on 20 September 1973, the 'Northern Territories' to be returned were the four islands 'and so on (*tō*)'. Also, as reported in the *Asahi Shimbun* of 8 October 'have the Soviet side promise the return of those islands [Kunashiri and Etorofu]. Then corroborate that Japan will not make any other territorial demand than the four islands including Shikotan and the Habomais', as Japan had not officially withdrawn its claim for areas other than the four islands. Thus, it can be assumed that there was a small possibility of using the rest of the Kuriles and Southern Sakhalin as a card, to create an impression that they were making a concession over these areas which they could also claim. The USSR was already familiar with this strategy. Kudryavtsev's article in *Izvestia* on 13 November 1970 pointed out that the return of the disputed territory would not wholly satisfy the Japanese, who would then demand the northern part of the Kuriles and, eventually southern Sakhalin as well.[114]

A new bargaining card, an application of this strategy, was noted this time, i.e., differentiating the timing of the islands' return. By sifting its position from demanding the four islands to be returned altogether to offering an option to return Kunashiri and Etorofu at a later date, the *Gaimushō* probably tried to create an impression that Japan was ready to make another concession over the timing of the islands' return, as long as the Soviet Union acknowledged Japanese sovereignty over those islands. However, this card did not attract the Soviet leaders at all.

The Soviet Asian Collective Security proposal was perceived as aiming to weaken the US–Japanese alliance and treated by the Japanese in a similar manner as the case of the 1955–6 negotiations.[115] That is, Japan did not even dare to use it. When the notion 'Soviet cards are Japanese goals' is applied, the Soviets' first bargaining card was the disputed islands. In fact the Soviets held the major advantage on the territorial issue. If Japan thought that its strongest card was economic and technological cooperation, and that the Soviet side would lose the most if the negotiations failed, it miscalculated badly. It was the Soviet Union which actually occupied and controlled the disputed islands. Japan did not have alternatives for negotiating the territorial dispute. In contrast, against the background of the international situation of this period, i.e., becoming multipolar, transitional and/ or in flux, the Soviets had other options for economic and technological cooperation in Siberian development: they could get effective assistance from the USA and Western Europe. Furthermore, as the world energy problem became exacerbated, Japan's bargaining advantages of capital and technology were to wane. Before leaving Japan, Tanaka affirmed that the territorial settlement was the prerequisite for economic cooperation in Siberia. However, the global political and economic reality of the time subsequently made Japan more pragmatic in its attitude.[116] Thus, various joint projects with the USSR proceeded year after year based on purely economic considerations.[117]

The Soviets' attitude towards the territorial problem had changed and they had abandoned their position of the 1956 Joint Declaration, where they had agreed to transfer Shikotan and the Habomais. No transfer took place, and the position changed to 'the territorial problem does not exist'. This change may be associated with assertion of the Japanese 'four islands' claim. As mentioned earlier, the revision of the US–Japanese Security Treaty in January 1960 led to a change in the Soviet attitude towards the territorial problem. It should be noted that it was around the same time that the 'four islands' claim and its bases were consolidated in Japan. As also mentioned earlier, there are records indicating Soviet withdrawals from Shikotan and the Habomais apparently in preparation for their transfer. In other words, since Japan added a claim to two more islands to the promised Shikotan and the Habomais, the Soviets in the same manner stepped back from promising two islands to promising none. Considering that the MID personnel concerned were almost unchanged from the 1955–6 negotiations, and that the MID was said to have strong influence on decision making in this period, it may not be too extreme to assume that the USSR changed their attitude based on their bitter experience in the past – during the 1955–6 negotiations the Soviets had used up their cards too early before achieving any of their goals, while the Japanese achieved their goals one after another by making best use of their very limited cards.

Agreement to include the expression 'unresolved problems' in the Joint Communiqué was reached only a few hours before Tanaka's departure from Moscow. Neither side made any concession on its basic attitude until the end. Then the last resort was this expression, inspired by Brezhnev's speech of the previous year (at the 50th anniversary of the USSR on 21 December 1972). In the original draft proposed by the Japanese side, 'problem' was written in the singular in order to indicate that the territorial issue was the only problem, but Soviet agreement was given only to the plural 'problems'. As with the 1956 Joint Declaration, different interpretations were to be made later.

Though derived from the economic aspect of their relations, the Soviet–Japanese moves towards political *rapprochement* at this time resulted in no concrete achievement with regard to a peace treaty or the territorial issue.

## LOST OPPORTUNITIES

The second chance for normalising Soviet–Japanese relations, which had emerged after a long spell since the 1956 summit, gradually disappeared after Tanaka's visit to Moscow. Upon the outbreak of the Middle East War on 6 October 1973 (coincidentally during Tanaka's visit to Moscow), the Arab countries attempted to use oil as a strategic weapon, and initiated oil-supply restrictions. Japan was directly hit by the oil shock and experienced an unprecedented economic crisis. Japanese failure to regulate the excessive amount of capital transactions driven by the 'archipelago reconstruction boom', combined with the direct hit of the oil shock, brought a sudden rise in land and consumer prices, and in the turmoil of high inflation the Tanaka regime rapidly lost popularity and political power.[118] With the lethal blow of the revelations about his financial dealings which appeared in the *Bungei Shunjū* in October 1974, Tanaka was forced into resigning in December.

The Soviets did not give up their political *rapprochement* with Japan even after the summit. They proposed a Treaty of Friendship as a intermediate step before a peace treaty in a personal letter from Brezhnev to the next Japanese Prime Minister, Miki Takeo, in February 1975, but this received only a negative reaction from Japan. The MiG-25 incident occurred in September 1976, when a defecting Soviet pilot landed his MiG-25 at Hakodate. Japan angered the USSR when its Defence Agency invited the USA to join in examining the aircraft and permitted the pilot to leave for the USA. The USSR nevertheless proposed a Treaty of Friendship again in January 1978, when Foreign Minister Sonoda Sunao was in Moscow. The offer could not wreck or postpone a peace treaty between Japan and China, but inclusion at Chinese request of an 'anti-hegemony' clause aimed at the USSR in the Japan–China Treaty of Peace and Friendship signed in September brought an immediate Soviet reaction. The Soviets began a build-up of forces in the Far East, including the deployment of 40 MiG-23 fighter-planes and one division of troops and the construction of new military facilities on Etorofu and Kunashiri. Relations deteriorated further in 1979 when Japan joined the United States in sanctions against the Soviet Union over the latter's invasion of Afghanistan, and regular foreign ministerial contact between the two countries was suspended.

At the time of the Soviet invasion of Afghanistan, Japan for the first time specified the USSR as a potential threat in a White Paper prepared by the Defence Agency. Furthermore, as I have already said, the strategic import-ance of the Kuriles increased in the 1970s. Since a key element of Soviet strategy was to defend the USSR's Pacific bases and maintain access to the Pacific, the USSR rapidly increased its Pacific fleet, air-force and navy, in addition to deployment in the disputed islands.

The relations between the two nations went into a glacial period thereafter. The annual foreign ministerial meetings, supposed to be held once a year, were postponed until January 1986.[119] Meanwhile the Japanese government designated a 'Northern Territories Day' in 1981, and promoted a campaign to make the return of the 'Northern Territories' 'the unanimous wish of the entire nation'.[120]

# 4 Gorbachev's visit to Tokyo, 1991

4. Prime Minister Toshiki Kaifu of Japan and President M.S. Gorbachev of the Union of Soviet Socialist Republics held in-depth and thorough negotiations on a whole range of issues pertaining to the preparation and conclusion of a peace treaty between Japan and the Union of Soviet Socialist Republics, including the problem of territorial demarcation, taking into consideration the positions of both sides on the ownership of the Islands of Habomai, Shikotan, Kunashiri, and Etorofu.

The joint work done previously – particularly the talks at summit level – have made it possible to state a number of conceptual provisions: that the peace treaty should be the document making the final resolution of war-related issues, including the territorial problem, that it should open the way for long-term Japan–USSR relations on the basis of friendship, and that it should not infringe upon either side's security.

. . .

As well as emphasising the primary importance of accelerating work to conclude the preparations for the peace treaty, the Prime Minister and the President expressed their firm resolve to make constructive and vigorous efforts to this end, taking advantage of all positive elements that have been developed in bilateral negotiations in the years since Japan and the Union of Soviet Socialist Republics jointly proclaimed an end to the state of war and the restoration of diplomatic relations in 1956.[1]

## Gorbachev's visit to Tokyo and the Joint Statement

Soviet President Mikhail S. Gorbachev visited Japan from 16 to 19 April 1991, 18 years after Tanaka's visit to Moscow. The third big wave of Soviet–Japanese *rapprochement* came when the Cold War of the post-war era was coming close to its end. The opportunity at this time was created by the then Foreign Minister Shevardnadze's visit to Japan in January 1986. The visit reopened the Foreign Ministerial talks after an eight-year interval, and reopened the Peace Treaty Negotiations after a ten-year interval since 1976.

After more than five years of vicissitudes, a Soviet–Japanese Summit finally took place for the first time on Japanese soil. President Gorbachev became the first incumbent leader to visit Japan throughout the history of Russia and the USSR (and thus he turned out to be the first and the last Soviet leader ever to do so). With regard to a peace treaty and the territorial issue, the Joint Statement (quoted at the beginning of this chapter) was announced as the outcome of the summit.

Since the late 1980s, a large number of publications on Soviet–Japanese relations and the territorial dispute have emerged, not only in Japan and the Soviet Union, but also in other parts of the world. The *Glasnost* policy permitted public discussion within the USSR, which resulted in raising international public attention and interest in solution of the territorial dispute. Soviet–Japanese relations and/or the territorial issue became a popular topic, and opinions were publicly exchanged not only among academics and journalists, but also among politicians and bureaucrats in both countries. Among those publications, the volumes by Russian and Japanese foreign service officials deserve special attention as they constitute the primary written materials for considering their policy decision making.[2] In this chapter I will examine policy decision making in association with the 1991 summit, and on the Japanese–Soviet *rapprochement* move and the territorial issue, using existing literature, other materials and my interviews with several people, including the authors of those volumes, and other officials involved in the negotiations.

## THE 'GLOBAL INTERNATIONAL RELATIONS' PERSPECTIVE

### Japan/USSR: the third *rapprochement* wave

#### The 'closing days' of the Cold War

Gorbachev's visit to Japan took place against the global background of the 'closing days' of the Cold War. In the late 1980s East–West relations entered into an era of dramatic relaxation in tensions that was considered to mark the 'end of the Cold War'. In December 1989, the 'end of the Cold War' was proclaimed by George Bush and Mikhail Gorbachev at the US–USSR Malta Summit. With this declaration by the leaders of the two superpowers that had originally headed the East–West confrontation, it may indeed be possible to state 'against the background of the "end of the Cold War"'. However, considering that events such as the disintegration of the Soviet Union, the collapse of LDP dominance of the Japanese domestic political system (the so-called '1955 system') and other changes took place after Gorbachev's visit to Japan, it seems more appropriate to say that the warming period of Japan–Soviet relations up until Gorbachev's visit in April 1991 were the 'closing days' of the Cold War.

## The end of the Cold War in Europe

The global factors facilitating Japanese–Soviet *rapprochement* moves were always East–West *détentes*, started by Soviet initiative in the 1950s and by US initiative in the 1970s. The *détente* of the late 1980s apparently started with the Soviet initiative of Gorbachev's *New Thinking* diplomacy.

The major factor for this new *détente* was a series of disarmament proposals courageously made by Gorbachev after his appointment as General Secretary of the Soviet Communist Party in March 1985. Gorbachev unilaterally suspended nuclear testing from summer 1985, proposed total abolition of nuclear weapons by the year 2000, and began concrete strategic arms reduction talks with the United States at Reykjavik in 1986. Though the Reykjavik Summit did not reach any settlement, the series of moves eventually led to the signing of the INF total abolition treaty in December 1987. The arms control and disarmament negotiations, which had started in the early 1970s against the background of US–Soviet nuclear parity, thus made unexpected progress, and this trend further developed with the opening of the US–Soviet Strategic Arms Reduction Talks (START).[3] The Malta Declaration of December 1989 by the US and Soviet leaders marked the end of post-war US–Soviet confrontation characteristic of the Cold War.

The relaxation of the East–West tensions became conspicuous and showed dramatic development in Europe after 1989. The Conventional Forces in Europe (CFE) treaty among NATO and Warsaw Pact nations, negotiation of which began in March 1989, was signed in November 1990. After a series of symbolic events, such as revolutions in Eastern European countries, the collapse of the Berlin Wall and the reunification of Germany, the 'end of the Cold War' was proclaimed also at the Paris summit of the Conference on Security and Cooperation in Europe (CSCE) in November 1990. This meant the collapse of the East–West confrontation structure of the Cold War, which had formed the core of international politics of the post-war era in Europe, i.e., the so-called 'Yalta System'.

The arms reduction initiative taken by the USA and USSR was largely motivated by the common factor of economics. While both countries were suffering (though to different degrees) from comparative economic decline, new economic centres were emerging, with the NIE countries following Japan and/or moves to create a united/common market in Western Europe by the European Community. Both the polar powers of the Eastern and Western blocs had realised that while they had been spending their money arming against each other, other countries and regions had advanced their economic power by gaining capital and competitiveness. As for the USA, the waning of former economic advantages in energy, technology and agriculture had decreased its capacity to finance its hegemony,[4] and its economic problems were becoming symbolised by deficits in both trade and finance. It had thus become important for the USA to reduce the military burden imposed by confronting the USSR. Under the concept of 'burden sharing', an attempt to have Japan and other US partners share the security burden had already started. However, the Soviet proposal of overall military reduction fundamentally addressed the core of the problem and provided an opportunity for reduced US military spending. Furthermore, since the Soviet domestic reforms conducted under *Perestroika* and *Glasnost* began to change western perceptions of the Soviet Union, Soviet proposals for military reductions could no longer be simply ignored as mere propaganda.

### Détente in Asia

The advance of the Soviet *New Thinking* diplomacy also created various movements towards *détente* in Asia. In his famous speeches in the Far East, at Vladivostok (1985) and Krasnoyarsk (1988), Gorbachev declared Soviet intent to play a broader and more active role in the Asia and Pacific. As specific actions, withdrawal of Soviet forces from Mongolia, Camranh Bay in Vietnam and Afghanistan became important initiatives towards *détente* in this region. The Soviet Union and South Korea established diplomatic relations in 1990. As for Sino-Soviet relations, through a series of exchanges of VIP visits (Gorbachev's visit to China in 1989, and visits to the USSR by Chinese Prime Minister Li Peng in 1990 and Communist Party General Secretary Jiang Zemin in 1991) relations were fully normalised.[5] Easing of tensions was also observed in relations between countries other than the USSR. South Korea and China agreed to open trade representation missions in October 1990, and established diplomatic relations in August 1992. In 1990, China normalised diplomatic relations with Indonesia in August, and in October established diplomatic relations with Singapore. In the Korean Peninsula, a summit meeting was held in Seoul in September 1990, for the first time since the country was divided into North and South, and in September 1991 both Koreas joined the UN simultaneously. In Cambodia, following the complete withdrawal of Vietnamese forces there since 1987, significant progress was observed in their peace moves especially after the Supreme National Council (SNC) started to function in 1990. Though neither so drastically nor so fundamentally as in Europe, the tension of confrontation was gradually easing in this region too.

## *Japanese–Soviet* **rapprochement** *moves*

Gorbachev's regime made an early approach to Japan. In January 1986, a half year after his appointment as Foreign Minister, Eduard Shevardnadze visited Japan. Four months later Japanese Foreign Minister Shintarō Abe visited Moscow in return. Expectations were raised of an early visit by Gorbachev to Japan, and of Japanese–Soviet political *rapprochement*. The Soviet overture to Japan can be easily explained either in the context of the Asian *détente* or as part of Gorbachev's Asia-Pacific policy.

The Asia-Pacific region in the 1980s became the most dynamic economic region of the globe. Its exports doubled as a proportion of world exports between 1960 and 1982, and the most notable development was that trade within the region grew faster than trade with the rest of the world.[6] Leading the NIE countries, Japan presented itself as the central player in this new locus of global economic activities. The oil shock and the end of the Vietnam War provided stepping-stones for Japan further to promote economic development towards rationalising its non-military industry. Overcoming the economic crisis by structural transformation towards computerisation and microelectronics, the Japanese capitalist economy experienced further rapid development. In 1985 the Japanese economy outstripped that of the USSR to become the world's second largest (next to the USA) in terms of GNP. Both in name and substance, Japan had become an important player in international economics, and Soviet attention was directed towards it as Gorbachev began to search for a new economic model. Furthermore, Japan's growing military strength, commitment to protect sea-lanes and capability of blocking the straits in the event of war further prompted the Soviet Union to rethink its attitude. In his 1986 Vladivostok speech, Gorbachev acknowledged 'Japan has turned into a power of front-rank importance'.[7]

In hindsight it is evident that the Soviet approach to the region and to Japan gradually changed its nature from ideologically coloured or politically motivated to more pragmatic and economically inspired. In previous periods of the Cold War 'Thaw' or *détente*, against the different political landscapes of liberation movements from western colonialism and/or rising neutralism of the region in the 1950s and of the Sino-Soviet dispute of the 1970s, there was always strong political motivation for the USSR to expand its power and influence in the region against the background of Cold War confrontations. However, reflecting the change in the international situation called 'resource nationalism', economic factors such as Siberian development emerged in the Soviet approach during the 1970s. Soviet overtures from the late 1980s showed increased economic motivation prompted by the contrast between the severely deteriorated Soviet domestic economic situation and the remarkable economic development and increased importance of the Pacific Basin. It was characteristic of the last years of Soviet diplomacy that the approach became more pragmatic and less ideological.

Though they did not develop so smoothly, the Japan–USSR *rapprochement* moves of this period were supported by another underlying motive: the easing of tension in East Asia was providing a new possibility for regional cooperation in the Far East. Unlike at the time of the *détente* of the 1970s, the Sino-Soviet conflict in the background was now being resolved. In addition, Soviet reforms provided growing opportunities for integrating the geographically vast Soviet territory in East Asia into the mainstream of economic and political life in the North Pacific. This area was rich in resources for potential development but sparsely populated. As a distinguished American scholar has pointed out, 'a center–periphery relationship once accepted as immutable has suddenly appeared inequitable and expendable'.[8] Furthermore, the Gulf War, which broke out after the disappearance of the balance of tensions between the USA and USSR, imparted a certain increased momentum or urgency to these moves.

The Soviets' comprehensive approach to Japan in the context of regional cooperation was also seen in their attitude towards regional organisations. The Pacific Economic Cooperation Conference (PECC) was established with the leadership of Japan and Australia, aimed at promoting regional cooperation through economic, cultural and personnel exchanges. On July 30 1986, Evgenii Primakov, then director of IMEMO, expressed the Soviet wish to participate in the fifth general assembly of PECC scheduled for November in Vancouver.

Though initiated early under Soviet *New Thinking* diplomatic moves, Japan–Soviet relations did not improve as rapidly as Soviet relations with other countries. It was five years after Shevardnadze's first visit to Japan that Gorbachev's visit finally took place. Even compared to former Japan–USSR *rapprochement* moves and summit visits, whose timing did not lag so far behind the pace of global *détente*, movement in Japanese–Soviet relations this time appeared very slow. This may be explained comparatively easily from a global perspective, in terms of the traditional correlation of intensity and intimacy among US–USSR, US–Japan and Japan–USSR relations. Considered from this perspective, the early approach of Gorbachev's regime can also be viewed as motivated by the intensification of US–Japan friction centring on economic issues, and aimed at using the differences to appeal to Japanese nationalism.[9] Then the temporary cooling of Japan–Soviet relations after Japanese Foreign Minister Abe's visit to Moscow in

1986 can be attributed to the climate of US–USSR relations and the US–Japanese alliance. For example, the atmosphere in bilateral relations fluctuated when US–USSR relations at one point appeared opaque with the breaking-off of the Reykjavik Summit in autumn 1986, when Japan announced its intention to join the US Strategic Defence Initiative (SDI), when the Toshiba Machine Company was accused of violating restrictions imposed by the Coordinating Committee for Export Controls (COCOM) and suspected of selling classified US Air Force information to Soviet agents, and when the Japanese Ministry of Trade and Industry (MITI) toughened its export regulations (1987). Also, though the Gorbachev regime often proposed an Asian collective security system, backed up by the success of CSCE in Europe, Japan rejected it, as it had previous proposals, even at this closing stage of the Cold War. The Soviet proposal appeared to contain a possibility of undermining US strategic policy in this region, which was (and still is) based on forward deployment and bilateral or trilateral security treaties with individual countries. In addition to its general primacy in diplomacy, Japan, which enjoyed various benefits under the US military umbrella provided by the security treaty, could not go beyond the degree of US–USSR *rapprochement*, nor do anything that could ruin the US strategy.

However, the progress of US–USSR negotiations, and the overall diplomatic improvement in the region, brought the USSR a new policy to change the nature of the correlation among the US–USSR–Japan relations. At the Soviet–Japanese annual foreign ministerial meeting on 3 May 1989 in Moscow, Soviet Foreign Minister Shevardnadze stated that a peace treaty could be concluded between the Soviet Union and Japan despite the existence of the US–Japan security treaty, a clear change in the Soviet approach to the issue.[10] Though indirect, this was also an indication that the Soviets' 1960 *mémoire* to the Japanese government was retracted.

While relations with Japan were stagnating, the USSR successfully improved its relations with other nations. Concerned at potential isolation, and using its global status as a leading economic power, Japan resorted to the G-7 arena. At the Toronto G-7 meeting of June 1988, Prime Minister Takeshita stressed it was necessary for his government to give a full explanation of its policy on the 'Northern Territories' problem to the other G-7 leaders, and noted that Moscow has not yet exercised its '*Perestroika* (reform) policies in its diplomacy toward Asia'.[11] In the Houston Summit of July 1990, this became integrated into the Chairman's Statement, which said that the seven heads of government and president of the European Community agreed that the Asia-Pacific region 'has yet to see the same process of conciliation, military disengagement and reduction of tensions that has characterized East–West relations in Europe'.[12]

Using this new framework and arguing that the remaining problem in

Japan–USSR relations also affected their common interests, Japan sought unity and cooperation of the economic powers. In the meantime, the need for assistance to the USSR was arising as a new international agenda. Reflecting the drastic political changes, the end of the Cold War in the Euro-Atlantic context, and also the progress of *Perestroika* in the Soviet Union itself, the international community's view of the Soviet issue changed around the time of the July 1990 Houston Summit. Assistance to the Soviet Union to promote its democratisation and introduction of a market economy had become an important diplomatic agenda item for the western nations. Also, as the USSR's economic situation worsened, it began to be perceived that the danger of domestic turmoil could be more serious than the Soviet military threat. The G-7 countries such as France and Germany showed a positive attitude towards substantial support for the USSR, because in addition to the abstract idea of continental solidarity, they feared that domestic turmoil in the USSR could lead to a large refugee influx, and/or delay the withdrawal of the 270,000-strong Soviet force stationed in the former East Germany.[13] However, until around the July 1991 London G-7 Summit, three months after Gorbachev's visit to Japan, the UK and USA took the same cautious position as Japan, whose relations with the USSR were still stagnant, about providing large-scale financial assistance to the USSR. The US and Japan were confronting a different situation in the Asia Pacific region, which, as said in the G-7 statement, had yet to see the same drastic changes of East–West relations in Europe. Also, prudent Soviet-watchers warned that bold moves would be premature, as the Soviet Union was neither sufficiently prepared for large-scale economic reform to introduce a market economy, nor advanced enough in democratisation. So, 'A common understanding was reached among the Summit participants' not to provide large-scale financial assistance.[14]

Would Japan have stepped forward to provide large-scale assistance if economic and political changes in the USSR had been more advanced? The answer is probably 'no', because the primary objective of Japanese policy toward the USSR, namely the 'Northern Territories' issue, remained unresolved, and Japan had not changed its policy of 'no separation of politics and economics' (*seikei fukabun*).

## The territorial problem: 'ownership of the islands of Habomai, Shikotan, Kunashiri, and Etorofu'

In the Joint Statement released at the end of Gorbachev's visit, the following points were notable in comparison with former summit statements: (1) formal acknowledgment of the existence of the territorial problem for the first time; (2) the four territories 'the Habomais, Shikotan, Kunashiri and

Etorofu' were named for the first time; (3) it was confirmed that the territorial problem would be settled in the peace treaty; and (4) reference to the 1956 Joint Declaration was left vague. Though still far from reaching a territorial demarcation, the document appeared more specific than that issued by the 1973 summit. However, room was again left for different interpretations, this time over the expression 'all positive developments since the 1956 Soviet–Japanese Joint Declaration'. Whereas the Japanese interpretation of this would include the 1956 Joint Declaration where the transfer of Shikotan and the Habomais was promised, the Soviet would not.

## The 'closing days' of the Cold War and the territorial dispute

Did the global international situation of the 'closing days of the Cold War' have any implications for this territorial dispute? Fundamental changes indicating the collapse of the Yalta System were taking place in Europe. Germany was reunified, the Baltic states declared their independence (formally approved on 6 September 1991), the Eastern European countries were freed from Soviet interference and moved towards democratisation. Viewing territorial problems in the context of the Cold War, those changes seemed to be offering positive influences for resolution of the territorial problem between Japan and the USSR. If the 'Northern Territories' problem is perceived as the legacy of Stalin's expansionism, as Japan claims, what was happening in Europe could be perceived as liquidation of Stalin's expansionism. Furthermore, those changes in fact originated by Soviet initiative. However, things did not work out as well in the Asia-Pacific region. Though remarkable progress was observed in relaxation of tensions, there remain continuing conflicts over territorial sovereignty from the so-called 'Cold War' period: the Korean Peninsula remains divided, the situation between China (PRC) and Taiwan is basically the same, disputes over the sovereignty of the Spratly and Paracel islands continue, etc. The Japanese–Soviet territorial dispute is no exception. However, against the background of drastic changes in international relations, what was notable this time was Japan's new attempt to break through using this new global landscape, namely the G-7 meetings.

Japanese appeals to the international community over its territorial dispute had been observed several times in the past. Since 1980 the UN General Assembly had become a regular place for Japan to air the 'Northern Territories' problem in its foreign ministerial speeches. In the warming of the international relations of this time, prime ministers also addressed this issue in the UN arena (for example, Nakasone at the 42nd UN General Assembly in August 1987 and Takeshita at the UN arms reduction meeting in June 1988). However, Japan's attempt to 'internationalise' the territorial issue entered a new stage with the use of the G-7 summits of the leading capitalist countries. In view of Japan's principle of 'no separation of politics and economics' (*seikei fukabun*), it is understandable that it took a negative attitude towards economic assistance, an important bargaining card. By bringing this outside the bilateral framework to the arena of G-7, and involving other leading nations, Japan seemed to be aiming at magnifying the effect, 'internationalising' its 'no separation of politics and economics' (*seikei fukabun*) strategy. The Chairman's Statement at the Houston Summit of July 1990 contained the following:

> We support the early resolution of the Northern Territories issue as an essential step leading to the normalisation of Japanese–Soviet relations.[15]

Also, the following sentence was included in the economic declaration:

> We took note of the importance to the government of Japan of peaceful resolution of its dispute with the Soviet Union over the northern territories.[16]

Since the G-7, after all, did not initiate large-scale financial assistance to the USSR, Japan's 'internationalisation' approach seemed to be working, at least until the G-7 summits in London (1991) and Munich (1992).

With the end of US–Soviet confrontation, the USA no longer needed to maintain tensions in Soviet–Japanese relations, but remained consistent in its support for the Japanese position in the territorial dispute. For example, at the press conference after announcement of the Chairman's Statement at the Houston G-7 Summit, Secretary of State James Baker emphasised US support for the Japanese position on the 'Northern Territories' problem.[17] From the other side of improved East–West relations, unexpected support for the Japanese position came from North Korea which, at the Foreign Ministerial Meeting in September 1990, supported the Japanese position in protest at its own deteriorating relations with the Soviet Union.[18]

On the 'internationalisation' of the territorial problem, there was another noteworthy move, the 'LDP Map Mission'. In 1980, the *Gaimushō* conducted a world-wide survey of international maps. It found that only four countries – South Korea, China, West Germany and Panama – specified the disputed islands as Japanese territories, and only six others annotated them advantageously to Japan as 'in dispute'. The 'Northern Territories Map Mission' was dispatched by the LDP to the USA in 1984, and visited the State Department, UN Headquarters and map producers to request revisions. Upon this request, the US State Department decided 'to annotate the islands as occupied by the USSR since 1946 and with Japan claiming sovereignty over them'. LDP Map Missions were also sent to the UK, France, West Germany and Italy in 1988. At this time the British government announced its official support for the Japanese claim, based on the Allies' general principle of not seeking territorial expansion from the War, and declared its intention to urge the USSR to have serious discussions with Japan for its solution.[19] The UK statement was important because of its historical involvement with the problem. On this announcement, Professor Kimura commented, 'the significance of the British Government officially announcing a similar attitude to that of the US is immeasurably large'.[20]

How effective was Japan's 'internationalisation' of the dispute? Was the expression in the Joint Statement achieved by this strategy? What Japan's 'internationalisation' invited was Soviet rejection. Head of the MID's Information Bureau Gerasimov announced Soviet official opposition to the remarks in the G-7 Houston Summit statements, and described the issue as purely bilateral, not something in which other countries should become involved.[21]

In his volume published in 1989, reviewing Japan's attempt to 'internationalise' the territorial dispute, Professor Kimura suggested that it had achieved as much effect as could realistically be expected and should not be pursued further.[22] This evaluation proved foresighted. As the next chapter will show, the G-7's next decision did not turn out as Japan wanted.

## THE 'NATION-STATE' PERSPECTIVE: JAPAN

### USSR and Japan: The third *rapprochement* wave and Gorbachev's visit to Japan

#### *The LDP Kaifu cabinet: The last stage of the '1955 system'*

Toshiki Kaifu was Prime Minister of Japan at the time of Gorbachev's visit. His high popularity was probably the only feature he had in common with Tanaka and Hatoyama, premiers at the previous summits.[23] As the wave of radical and fundamental changes in the international political arena was slowly reaching the Japanese domestic scene, the Cold War '1955 system' of Japanese domestic politics began to be shaken. The LDP regime was entering the last stage of its 38-year dominance.

LDP factional politics had changed the nature of the Japanese party system from one of policy orientation to the logic of numbers and money, and had led to corruption involving politicians, bureaucrats and business-men. In 1987, following Yasuhiro Nakasone's five-year regime, the head of the largest LDP faction, *'Keiseikai'*, Noboru Takeshita formed a cabinet. During this Takeshita period, the 'Recruit' corruption scandal was uncovered, stalling a number of leading politicians. The next (Uno) cabinet was formed with strong support from the *Keiseikai* faction, but this puppet regime collapsed after only two months. Money politics, the forcing through of a consumption tax, and sex scandals involving Premier Uno himself increased public distrust of the LDP regime, and this was reflected in the result of the House of Counsellors election, which followed. The Japan Socialist Party led by Takako Doi made substantial gains, and the balance between the ruling and opposition parties was reversed. With this erosion of the LDP's absolute majority in the Diet, the 1955 system began to crack. Toshiki Kaifu, a popular LDP politician with a clean personal image, was made president of the party in order to improve public perception of it during its regime crisis, and was elected prime minister by the House of Representatives, where the LDP remained in the majority. Though he aimed at political reform, Kaifu came from a small and weak LDP faction and, being unable to take any strong policy initiatives against bureaucratic and factional resistance, his regime ended up as yet another puppet of the *Keiseikai* faction.

## The Soviet overture and Japanese policy towards the USSR

Concrete moves towards Japanese–Soviet *rapprochement* had resumed during Nakasone's prime ministership, when Shevardnadze had visited Japan in January 1986. While the summit visits of Hatoyama and Tanaka had gestated and come to fruition within their prime ministerships, Gorbachev's visit to Japan was a diplomatic agenda item inherited by the Kaifu cabinet from previous regimes, and therefore not embodied in their terms of reference. This is indeed partially associated with the Japanese political system whereby regimes rotate in relatively short terms, but such a situation was the same with Hatoyama and Tanaka.[24] As referred to earlier, compared to their relations with other countries, little development was made in the relations between Japan and the USSR. Viewing this domestically by considering where the leadership lay in policy making towards the USSR in Japan, it seems self-explanatory. There was no change in the *Gaimushō's* dominance in the Japanese policy-making initiative toward the USSR.

It is common for the bureaucracy to play a more influential role in policy decision making when the political regime is unstable. Japan's policy-making during this period may fall into this category. However, even on the occasion of Tanaka's visit to Moscow when 'politics', or the ruling LDP, appeared in strong control of policy-making, the *Gaimushō*'s leadership and influence in policy making towards the USSR was predominant, and it is commonly acknowledged both inside and outside the *Gaimushō* that this tendency has been consistent.

Japanese perceptions of the USSR were far more benign than in the pre-Gorbachev period, yet compared to the enthusiastic 'Gorby boom' in European or other countries, the Japanese reaction was relatively cool and cautious, including to Gorbachev's overture to Japan.[25] To Japanese policy makers' eyes, the Soviet Union had been a potential threat to Japan for a long time. Among the Japanese leaders, especially influential conservatives, there was deep distrust of the Soviet Union, dating from even before the Cold War. There is a sizeable group of hard-liners or right-wing alarmists, whom Rozman calls 'The Totalitarian Expansionist Group', which alleged a Soviet intention to invade Japan or described Gorbachev's proposals as 'lies' intended to deceive the capitalist countries. As Rozman points outs, the core of this group is found among former and current Soviet specialists in the *Gaimushō*.[26] Traditionally, many LDP conservatives also deeply distrusted the USSR and espoused a hard line against it. Japan's negative vision of the Soviet Union long constituted an important part of political life, since it discredited the principal opposition parties, the Japan Socialist Party (JSP) and the Japan Communist Party (CJP).[27]

Another tradition of importance in policy formulation by those conservatives was their consideration of its likely impact on Japan–US relations. Throughout the post-war years, the first priority of Japanese diplomacy was always the relationship with the USA. *Gaimushō* officials in charge of Soviet affairs always maintained close contact and consultation with the US State Department and National Security Council personnel, especially their Soviet specialists, in order to avoid confusion or avert negative consequences to the US–Japan relationship resulting from changes in Soviet–Japanese relations.[28] As mentioned in earlier sections, the temporary cooling of Japanese relations with the USSR after late 1986 was in part associated with the status of USA–USSR negotiations.

During this period economic assistance to the Soviet *Perestroika* had become a major concern, and began to be discussed among the leading western nations. However, Japan took a negative attitude towards giving financial assistance to the USSR, since it adhered in principle to its policy of 'no separation of politics and economics' (*seikei fukabun*) and considered return of all four islands of the 'Northern Territories' to be the 'entry point' or prerequisite for improved relations (*ryōdo iriguchi-ron*). For example, at a meeting with Shevardnadze in Paris in 1989, Japanese Foreign Minister Sōsuke Uno declared that Japan would not consider progress (economic assistance) in relations, unless the USSR intended to move forward on the territorial issue. This attitude did not please the Soviet leaders, and accordingly 'no enthusiasm to advance the summit visit emerged from the Soviet side either'.[29]

### The softened approach and Gorbachev's visit to Japan

Being aware that Soviet relations with other countries were improving faster than those with Japan, and also in response to Soviet complaints about its ultimatum-style attitude, some modification was made in Japan's attitude toward the USSR in and around 1989. A new expression, 'balanced equilibrium' (*kakudai kinkō*), came into frequent use. The softened Japanese policy was first explained by Foreign Minister Sōsuke Uno at his meeting with his Soviet counterpart Shevardnadze in May. The idea was to promote overall improvement in relations encompassing many other fields in a balanced form, though continuing to include solution of the territorial problem and signing of a peace treaty as the most important items on the agenda.[30] In the past opposing the position of *iriguchi-ron*, in which the solution of the territorial problem was defined as the 'entrance' or prerequisite, a different position, *deguchi-ron*, had been considered. It sought to define solution of the territorial issue as the outgrowth, or 'exit', of an overall improvement, but was not favoured by the government hard-liners. The concept of 'balanced equilibrium' of this time appeared slightly different, in that advances could take place in other fields, but solution of the territorial problem retained priority. In other words, this was neither the zero-sum approach defining the territorial issue as prerequisite or 'entrance', nor the outgrowth or 'exit' type approach of awaiting overall improvement in other fields, but intermediate between the two, marking government awareness that the former zero-sum approach was no longer realistic.

Japanese economic relations with the USSR were growing in the private sector, and Japanese–Soviet trade reached a record level of $6.09 billion in 1989, making Japan the USSR's fourth-largest non-communist trading partner, behind West Germany, Finland, and Italy.[31] Japanese imports of Soviet raw materials increased to record levels between 1987 and 1990, while *Perestroika* increased Soviet demand for Japanese high-technology and high-quality goods.[32] At a study meeting of the Northern Territories Problem Countermeasure Association (*Hoppō ryōdo mondai taisaku kyōkai*), held on 28 October 1989, the head of the Soviet section of the *Gaimushō* himself remarked,

There are certain [economic] issues, for which the Government can plainly give restriction or administrative guidance (*gyōsei shidō*). However, under the situation that projects can proceed even without government support such as Far Eastern/Siberian mini projects, there is a difficult aspect in considering the concept of '*seikei fukabun*' which the Japanese government has been taking.[33]

Thus, based on reality, and also probably realising that the traditional rigid negotiation attitude had become counter-productive, the Japanese government modified and softened its approach by emphasising the existing positive aspects of Japanese–Soviet relations. This resembles Japanese diplomacy before Tanaka's visit in 1973, in that the territorial issue was toned down to avoid a negative impact on economic cooperation.

### Positive 'human factors'

In his volume entitled *From Distrust to Trust*, Alexander Panov referred to some Japanese individuals in terms of human factors that contributed to the improvement of bilateral relations. Since this was written by a Russian diplomat, the individuals mentioned can be considered the main contributors to improvement of Soviet perceptions of Japan. They included at governmental level Foreign Ministers Shintarō Abe and Tarō Nakayama, and Japanese Ambassador to the USSR Sumio Edamura.

During Shintarō Abe's period as Foreign Minister, *rapprochement* with the USSR became a diplomatic goal, and his enthusiasm for and contributions to the improvement of relations were highly regarded. When he visited Moscow in May 1986, various arrangements were quickly made, such as agreements on resuming Japanese grave visitations to the disputed islands, on cultural exchanges, taxation, trade payments, and establishment of a committee on science and technology. Even after ceasing to be Foreign Minister, he headed a LDP delegation to Moscow in January 1990, met Gorbachev, expressed Japanese support for *Perestroika* as part of actualisation of the 'balanced equilibrium' policy, and made proposals for eight categories of economic and cultural exchanges, known as the 'Abe program'.[34] When Gorbachev visited Japan, Abe, though critically ill, showed his enthusiasm and sincerity by attending a reception shortly before his death.

Panov also mentioned the positive impression created by the constructive attitude of Ambassador Edamura, who had no previous experience in Soviet affairs. Without infringing diplomatic niceties he succeeded in indicating that he considered the traditional Japanese approach directed by the *Gaimushō* Soviet specialists, or, as Panov called them, the 'Russian group', created only negative impressions, for example by limiting former ambassadors' publicity and scope of activity, and rendering interaction with Soviet diplomats dry and formal. Panov said that the 'non-Russian group' Ambassador Edamura was one of the human factors that contributed to the improved atmosphere between MID and the Japanese Embassy.[35]

Panov went on to praise another Foreign Minister, Tarō Nakayama (of Kaifu's cabinet) for his frank manner, constructive attitude and contribution to mutual understanding. During the UN General Assembly meeting in mid-1990, Nakayama proposed a meeting of foreign ministers of the Asia-Pacific region. Despite the reluctance of foreign ministers of other countries and of the *Gaimushō* staff to invite the USSR, Nakayama played an important role in securing its inclusion. This is said to have contributed to strengthening trust between the foreign ministers of Japan and the USSR. However Panov noted, 'Soviet participants in the meetings at times received the impression that the traditional nature of the Japanese career diplomats in the delegation was restraining Nakayama from quickly and positively responding to the realistic proposals made by the Soviet Foreign Minister. They would try not to give any agreement without advance detailed analysis and adjustment among many Japanese policy makers'.[36]

However, Panov in general implies that positive factors for improvement of bilateral relations were increasing, though traditional forces remained influential and worked to restrain rapid improvement. These restraining factors were none other than the *Gaimushō* Soviet or Russian school and the LDP conservatives.

As mentioned in an earlier chapter, the Council on National Security Problems (CNSP), a private organisation sponsored by Mr Suetsugu's office, has been making various contributions to promoting mutual understanding in Soviet/Russo-Japanese relations, receiving a wide range of private support from individuals and enterprises, and taking almost the same line as the *Gaimushō* on the issues of the territorial problem and peace treaty.[37] There were organisations such as the Japan–Soviet Friendship Association for grassroots-level promotion of the Japan–Soviet relations. However, the CNSP is unique in the sense that, though a private organisation, it provides windows for interaction close to governmental decision making. What deserves careful attention is that participants to the Council from the Soviet side have included former Directors of the Institute of World Economy and International Relations (IMEMO) – N.N. Inozemtsev, E.I. Primakov and A. Yakovlev, Director of the Institute of USA and Canada G.A. Arbatov, and Director of the Institute of Africa, A. Gromyko – people who have played influential roles in Soviet policy making. According to Mr Suetsugu, almost all the officials who came with Gorbachev in 1991 turned out to be people he already knew.[38] His organisation, by providing over a long period places for mutual understanding and discussion to people who eventually strongly influenced the foreign-policy decision making of Gorbachev's regime, may have exerted more influence on Soviet than on Japanese foreign-policy decisions.

In other aspects of bilateral relations, a wide range of positive factors in various fields came to the foreground and attracted attention. For example, the Governor of Hokkaido, Takahiro Yokomichi, took exceptional measures to save the life of a 3-year-old boy from Sakhalin who received severe burns in an accident. He was immediately brought to Japan for treatment in 1991. Non-governmental level exchanges increased: for example a Japanese journalist from the Tokyo Broadcasting Service (TBS) joined the Soviet orbiting space station *Mir*, the first Japanese space flight. During the Soviet economic crisis, various funds raised money to send to the USSR.

In the overall improvement of perceptions of the Soviet Union, a decisive role was played by Soviet reviews of their own domestic and foreign policies, and the perceived results of democratisation and *Glasnost*. Above all, the implementation of Soviet military reductions brought a visible change even at the level of cautious Japanese government perception. In the 1990 version of the Defence White Paper, the description of the USSR as a 'potential threat to Japan', consistently used since 1980, was omitted.

## The territorial problem: 'ownership of the islands of Habomai, Shikotan, Kunashiri and Etorofu'

As I have already described, the names of the four islands, 'Habomai, Shikotan, Kunashiri and Etorofu' were specified in the Joint Statement for the first time as the object of the territorial problem to be solved in the peace treaty. In the Joint Declaration of 1956 only the Habomais and Shikotan had been mentioned, and in the Joint Communiqué of 1973 nothing had been specified.

### Japan's claim and diverse opinions

Japanese–Soviet relations steadily deteriorated from the late 1970s to the late 1980s. During that period the Japanese government enthusiastically promoted a northern irredentism campaign all over Japan. In 1981, 7 February was designated 'Northern Territories' Day' to commemorate the signing date of the 1855 'Shimoda Treaty of Commerce, Navigation and Delimitation', which set the boundary between Etorofu and Urup, the location currently claimed by Japan.[39] In 1982, the 'special establishment law for promotion of solution of the Northern Territories problem and so on' was passed and the foundation for promoting irredentist activity was said to be further 'consolidated'. In September 1981, then Prime Minister Zenkō Suzuki paid an inspection visit of the 'Northern Territories' to Hokkaido.

Similar foreign ministerial visits were carried out more often – by Miyazawa (1976), Sonoda (1979), Itō (1980), Sakurauchi (1982), Abe (1983) and Uno (1988). The Diet resolution on the 'Northern Territories' problem passed after the 1973 summit was passed seven times more at plenary sessions of both Houses between February 1979 and April 1991, the last time immediately preceding Gorbachev's visit.[40] Above all, repetition of the same claim for over 30 years greatly contributed to inculcating the doctrine of 'four islands return'.

The Japanese territorial claims had been extensively discussed in many newspapers and journals around the 1955–6 peace negotiations. Since then, however, for over 30 years up until around the late 1980s, there had been little discussion or questioning regarding the 'four islands claim' and/or its legitimacy. As a very exceptional case, in an article published in *Foreign Affairs* in September 1975, Kazushige Hirasawa, a foreign policy adviser to the late Premier Miki, proposed fulfilment of the promised two islands return, and freezing of the status of the other two.[41] This proposal, motivated by economic interest and seeking a more pragmatic approach, received no domestic support. From the late 1980s, however, almost 30 years after the peace negotiations, a wide range of public discussions began regarding Japanese–Soviet relations and the territorial problem. Diverse opinions were expressed. Among those, Haruki Wada's and Shichirō Murayama's studies regarding the range of the Kuriles became sensational, questioning the legitimacy of the government's 'four islands claim'.[42] The 'Northern Territories' had become a popular media topic for discussion, involving academics, government officials, politicians, commentators, etc. Various options were discussed, for example, in addition to the traditional 'four islands' return, 'two island' return, shelving the other two islands, joint management, demilitarisation, and/or recognition of Japanese sovereignty.

Even within the ruling LDP, some less conservative attitudes came to be observed. LDP Secretary-General Ichirō Ozawa openly noted the importance of mutual concessions for solution of the territorial problem.[43] LDP Vice-President Shin Kanemaru stated on 23 April in Fukuoka 'if the four islands are impossible, we should at least get two islands returned. I think that we may buy them.'[44]

## Manoeuvres for control

Though broad public discussion and government policy making are not necessarily unconnected, government decision making in Japan often does not reflect the result of public discussion. This tendency seems to be stronger when supremacy in policy making rests with bureaucrats, who do not have to worry about the next election. Kanemaru's above-mentioned statement was immediately rebutted by the *Gaimushō*, which adamantly emphasised the importance of retaining the claim for 'four islands' return. In consequence, Kanemaru at a general meeting of the Takeshita faction on 26 April said 'there will be no change in the posture of demanding all four islands'.[45] As mentioned earlier, and as *Gaimushō* officials themselves admit, it is well known that the *Gaimushō* had strong leadership in policy making towards the USSR. This was clearly evidenced in their ability to make even Kanemaru, who was called the 'boss' (*don*) of politics, reverse his earlier statement.

As mentioned in the next section, on 5 September, 1990 a bipartisan Diet delegation visited Moscow with Soviet official visas issued specifically to negotiate the 'Northern Territories' problem for the first time in 30 years. Tetsu Ueda, a Socialist Party member of the House of Representatives and Chairman of the Special Committee for Okinawa and Northern Issues, headed the delegation. He wrote that various attempts were made in Japan to interfere with the procedure and negotiations for this visit, and indicated that they were mainly made by the *Gaimushō*. According to him 'there was even a slander that the invitation from the Supreme Soviet is incomplete and invalid', and when nevertheless it came to the point that the visit was definitely to take place, a *Gaimushō* senior official visited him and firmly reminded him 'Please keep two points definitely. One is to persist in the four island return, not the two island return, the other is the "no separation of politics and economics"' (*seikei fukabun*).[46]

In the public debates in the various media since the late 1980s, the *Gaimushō* and LDP conservatives expressed concern at the danger of splitting Japanese public opinion regarding the territorial issue. It was impossible for them to control expression by the masses, but they could selectively punish what they considered excesses by some groups. Since obtaining a visa to visit the disputed islands could be taken to imply recognition of Soviet sovereignty over them, a cabinet meeting in autumn 1989 resolved to ask Japanese nationals not to apply for Soviet visas to enter the 'Northern Territories' until the issue was solved. However, the Japanese media TBS and *Mainichi Shimbun* sent staff to the disputed territories in April 1991, and reported news from there. As a result, the *Gaimushō* reportedly retaliated against them with 'punishments' (*seisai*) such as excluding their reporters from informal (*kondan*) or exclusive interviews with senior officials, limiting cooperation with their activities abroad, denying *Gaimushō* auspices to TBS-sponsored events, etc.[47]

In a Diet session on 19 October 1990, Prime Minister Kaifu said that solution by only 'two islands' return was unacceptable, and emphasised that the 'four islands' return would continue to be demanded. It is not certain what Kaifu's personal view was, while public opinion began to diversify.

When Tanaka visited Moscow in 1973, priority was given to the territorial issue as the *Gaimushō* intended. However, public opinion was then more unified, the LDP regime was stable, Tanaka was a politician from the Yoshida faction, and his own political base and influence were then strong and stable, so it does not seem that Tanaka as an individual had any problem in supporting the 'four islands' claim. Shortly before Gorbachev's visit to Japan a meeting was reportedly held between Kaifu and the LDP's senior politicians – including former prime ministers Takeshita, Suzuki, Nakasone and Fukuda. They reportedly re-emphasised that no concession should be made in linking economic assistance to the territorial issue, and asserted that no change was to be made in the Japanese official attitude.[48] In the last days of LDP supremacy, and with his weak political base and influence, Kaifu could in no way afford to risk changing the territorial claim, as to do so would provide a convenient tool for his political overthrow. He was also too busy with domestic policies such as political reform to restabilise the LDP regime. In that sense he resembled Hatoyama, but he was less devoted to a political breakthrough with the USSR, and apart from aspiring to a second prime ministership in the future, was not so old nor ill as to make the territorial issue an adornment to an exit from politics. Regardless of his individual opinion, Kaifu would have no choice but to follow the prepared line of the mainstream of the *Gaimushō* and LDP.

### Territorial policy making towards the Summit

Incidentally at the same time as Ambassador Edamura's appointment, a nucleus of Soviet specialists was formed in *Gaimushō* headquarters to prepare for Gorbachev's visit. Specifically, Nagao Hyōdō 'a well experienced diplomat and Soviet specialist', was appointed Director-General of the Asia and European Department, while Kazuhiko Tōgō, 'a distinct and enthusiastic representative from the Russia group' continued to serve as head of the Soviet Section.[49]

After a series of negotiations, it became clear that the distance between the two countries' positions was large, and the territorial issue would not be solved during the Soviet President's visit. As a realistic goal for the summit, the *Gaimushō* often stated that it would like to 'achieve a breakthrough upon this visit'.[50] What was notable about Japanese moves before the summit was frequent reference to recognition of the 1956 Declaration. It should be noted that the 1973 summit negotiation had gone nowhere because the Japanese side simply adhered to the 'four islands' demand, not even mentioning the 1956 agreement. The question of recognition of the 1956 declaration was raised for the first time in December 1988, when Foreign Minister Sōsuke Uno began new negotiations with the Soviets. It can be said that some flexibility was observed after a long interval in the Japanese negotiating attitude over the territorial issue.

Then, was the Japanese goal only the four islands? This is not completely clear. In the 'resolution regarding the promotion of the Northern Territories problem' passed at the plenary session of the House of Representatives in April 1991, immediately before Gorbachev's visit, the 'Northern Territories' in question were still 'Habomai, Shikotan, Kunashiri, Etorofu, *and so on* (*tō*)', and not necessarily limited to the four islands.[51] Looking back, in the 1955–6 negotiations the LDP policy became the 'four islands' return and an international conference for the rest of the 'Northern Territories', i.e., all former Japanese territories occupied by the USSR. For the 1973 summit, the former Japanese territories remained as bargaining factors for regaining the four islands, at least in Soviet eyes. Tōgō clearly said in his volume that at the time of Gorbachev's visit in 1991 they did not aim at 'solution of the territorial problem' as a realistic matter.[52] Specifically, the first goal of the negotiation was to 'confirm both islands of Kunashiri and Etorofu as the object of the negotiations, leaving no room for doubt'[53] and the second goal was to 'confirm the transfer of Shikotan and the Habomais after signing of a peace treaty, which was specified in the Japan–Soviet Joint Declaration of 1956'.[54] In addition to the fact that the territorial demand of the Japanese government (i.e. of the LDP) had consistently been for the four islands for over 35 years, the concept of the above strategy 'the two islands first and then the other two' already excluded other former territories than the four islands. Thus, it seems certain that the final goal of the Japanese 'Northern Territories' claim was then no more than the four islands.

This problem, however, could never be shelved as Japan shelved similar problems with China and South Korea upon their *rapprochement*.[55] It may be assumed that the *Gaimushō*'s traditional thinking since the 1955–6 negotiations was still working there. The reason why Shigemitsu did not favour the Adenauer formula came from his fear that Japan might lose its claim for the 'Northern Territories' forever if the territorial issue was shelved. Though there might have been differences of degree, it cannot be completely denied that the traditional feeling of distrust, based on experience of Soviet/Russian unpredictability, still existed. In addition, since the basis of the demand was set as a minimum demand of the government upon the 1955 LDP merger, the 'four islands' return had been the policy objective which those in the administrative body of the government, especially the *Gaimushō* Russian school, had sought throughout their lives. To change a policy goal is beyond the authority of an administrative body, the *Gaimushō* in this case. The role of the *Gaimushō* is to achieve the goal set by political decisions, but not to make political decisions. Then, what could it do? Though the attitude was modified, the goal and the basic strategy for achieving the goal had not been changed.

It is noted that the principle of 'no separation of politics and economics' (*seikei fukabun*) policy was not changed. As seen in the Japanese attitude at the G-7 Summits at Houston in 1990 and London in 1991, after Gorbachev's visit, Japanese remained negative or 'cautious' toward large-scale financial assistance to the USSR, and tried to have other G-7 nations take the same stance. It was argued by the government mainstreams, including the *Gaimushō* Soviet section chief Tōgō, 'the West should not bail Moscow out of its crisis, at least not until Moscow makes a much more drastic change in course'.[56] Needless to say, 'much more drastic change' meant the return of the disputed territories. Director-General of the Asia and European Department, Nagao Hyōdō, answering a question in the Diet, stated:

> in order to carry out serious and large-scale economic cooperation, that is, centring financial assistance, there has to be a stable political foundation between Japan and the USSR. Such a politically stable foundation can never be considered without signing a peace treaty, and the signing of a peace treaty can never be considered without solution of the 'Northern Territories.' We see it this way.[57]

Between Shevardnadze's first visit and Gorbachev's visit, there had been several dialogues and negotiations through diplomatic and political channels. Japan, expecting application of the Soviet *New Thinking* diplomacy to the 'Northern Territories', kept demanding a Soviet 'political decision', but received no specific answer from the Soviet side.[58] Since the *Gaimushō*'s 'no separation of politics and economics' strategy achieved no positive result, the last resort was taken by the 'politics' side attempting to buy the islands. Former Russian Foreign Minister A. Kozyrev disclosed in his recent memoirs that after diplomatic negotiations failed, a leader of the ruling Liberal Democratic Party (Ichirō Ozawa) offered $US 28 billion to buy the islands.[59] Before the 1973 summit, a proposal to buy the islands was made by an influential businessman, but it was only expressed domestically. This time, the influential politician Ozawa went to the Soviet Union to make an approach directly. However, obviously this attempt did not succeed.

Japan, expecting a word *ex cathedra*, kept requesting the Soviet leader's 'decision' until the end of the summit. In the summit meetings of Gorbachev's visit, based on its understanding that 'since transfer of the islands of Habomais and Shikotan is promised in the Japan–Soviet Joint Declaration of 1956, the main axis of the territorial issue is regarding the sovereignty of the two islands of Kunashiri and Etorofu', Japan obstinately 'urged confirmation of Japanese sovereignty over these islands'.[60]

In the Joint Statement, the names of the four islands were specified for the first time, and the expression 'the problem of territorial demarcation' was also used, which meant the USSR officially recognised the existence of the territorial problem. However, not only was the sovereignty of those disputed islands not resolved, the statement left room for different interpretations of the ambiguous expression regarding whether the 'two islands' return of the 1956 Declaration was reconfirmed or not. In its 'abstract of the Japan-Soviet Summit Meeting' issued on 23 April, the *Gaimushō* said that the expression in question 'all positive elements that have been developed. . . restoration of diplomatic relations in 1956' of course included the Joint Declaration of 1956, and that the reason why the Soviet side did not clearly confirm the 'Declaration' this time was presumably because it had to consider its domestic political situation.[61]

Because of the high media expectations before the summit, many commentators expressed disappointment at the lack of significant progress on the territorial issue. Viewing the outcome of the summit in long-term perspective, it was actually an important advance achieved by strenuous efforts of the *Gaimushō*, which had worked to achieve the LDP government's goal of 'four islands return' ever since the 1956 summit. As Tōgō later stated, from the Japanese side it was 'a significant matter, considering how much pains our predecessors (*senpai*) took in order to have the one word "territorial problem" written down in the Japanese–Soviet negotiations'.[62]

## THE 'NATION-STATE' PERSPECTIVE: THE SOVIET UNION

### USSR/Japan: the Third *rapprochement* wave and Gorbachev's visit to Japan

In Chapter 2, I commented that 'the Soviet Union, the global superpower leading the eastern bloc in the Cold War world, had tremendous influence on the global international system'; 'the major global factor in the Soviet–Japanese reconciliation process, the change in the international system, was largely a result of the tremendous influence of foreign-policy inputs in the name of *détente* and/or peaceful coexistence, from the nation-state level unit of the USSR'; and that 'Changes in the general movement of the Soviet Union at the nation-state level therefore also warrant considerable attention.'[63] The same thing can be said about the series of global movements leading up to Gorbachev's visit. Soviet inputs to the international system this time were far more significant than those of the 1950s' or 1970s' *détente*. The changes in domestic politics and accordingly in the foreign policy of the USSR were both domestically and internationally the beginning of the largest-scale transformation of the twentieth century, as they led to the collapse of the Soviet Union and the so-called 'end of the Cold War.'

## Change of leadership and foreign policy

After his elderly predecessors Brezhnev, Andropov and Chernenko died in rapid succession, a younger leader, Mikhail S. Gorbachev (1931–), became General Secretary of the Communist Party in March 1985. His politics were those of fundamental reforms. At a surprisingly fast pace, he initiated reforms in various forms and aspects of Soviet society. Gorbachev introduced key words such as *Perestroika* in political and economical reforms, *Glasnost* in social democratisation of freedom of information, or *New Thinking* in diplomacy, and appealed for domestic and foreign understanding. Against the background of the Soviet *Perestroika*, there was the reality that the contradictions and depression of Soviet society were reaching their limit. Economically, the long depression of the Brezhnev era was substantially coming close to zero growth and showing signs of crisis already at the time of Brezhnev's replacement by Andropov in December 1982.[64] The command economy management system had come to the deadlock of bureaucratism, which created distressing economic irrationalism, huge losses of productivity and consequent social disorder. The economic depression, derived from Soviet socialism itself, had further deteriorated since the invasion of Afghanistan in 1979, and through the need to provide loans and assistance to Poland after the 'Solidarity' upheaval of 1980. In addition, the economic burden inflicted by the escalated arms race with the USA drove the national economy to a crisis situation. Thus, the Soviet economy was already approaching destitution by the time Gorbachev assumed power. The gap between it and the economies of the developed non-communist industrial countries, which had already entered a new stage of development by focusing on high technology, continued to increase.

In diplomacy, Gorbachev's first major reform was a personnel shake-up in the Ministry of Foreign Affairs (MID). In July 1985 long-serving Foreign Minister Gromyko was replaced by Eduard Shevardnadze, a Georgian. He had no diplomatic experience, but together with Gorbachev and other progressives he played a central role in setting forth the *New Thinking* diplomacy, and took major steps to change the international scene from Cold War to *détente* and eventually to the so-called 'end of the Cold War'. The Gorbachev regime replaced almost a third of all Soviet ambassadors in its first eighteen months, and over half of them in its first three years.[65] Its Ambassador in Japan, Petr Abrasimov, was replaced in May 1987 by

Nikolai Soloviev who, unlike his predecessors, was a career diplomat, not a member of the CPSU Central Committee, and, having served as Head of the MID's Second Far Eastern Department for ten years, had wider knowledge of and familiarity with Japan.[66] Soloviev was later replaced by another MID Japan specialist, Lyudvig A. Chizhov. The changes in leading post in the MID demonstrated serious Soviet intent to make changes under the *New Thinking* diplomacy.

Early in his regime, Gorbachev set about reforming the Communist Party, the Soviet Union's only political party since 1918, and the core force of leadership both legally and in system terms. The International Department of the Central Committee controlled diplomacy, and had been headed by Boris Ponomarev for 31 years. He was quickly replaced, first by Anatoliy Dobrynin, who had been Soviet Ambassador to the United States for 23 years, and then by Valentin M. Falin, another former career diplomat who was president of Novosti News Agency. Other changes followed. An International Policy Committee with 22 members was established in the central committee, Gorbachev appointed as chairman Alexandr Yakovlev, who had risen rapidly from directorship of IMEMO of the Soviet Academy of Sciences in 1983 to head of the Central Committee's Propaganda Department in 1985 and to membership of the Politburo in 1987.[67] What these new leaders aimed at was to create international circumstances favourable to radical reform of Soviet society, which was becoming a critically pressing issue. Then unconventional concepts of international relations, less ideologically coloured than those based on the class concept of the past, began to be advocated under the name of *New Thinking*. Downgrading the diplomatic value of military power, this position emphasised interdependence in economics and political dialogues over such 'global issues' as nuclear weapons, the North–South divide, and ecological problems, rather than differences in economic/political systems.[68] Soviet diplomacy gradually bore fruit by, for example, displaying flexible attitudes in arms control negotiations, undertaking some unilateral disarmament, engaging in summit meetings, and reducing Soviet commitments to the Third World.

### Approach and policy making towards Japan

The Soviet Union made an early approach to Japan. At his meeting on 14 March 1985 with Prime Minister Nakasone, who was in Moscow for former General Secretary Chernenko's funeral, Gorbachev said that the Soviet Union wanted to develop amicable bilateral relations with Japan, and further indicated readiness to undertake substantial action to that end.[69] It was therefore not coincidental that, ten years after Gromyko's previous visit,

Shevardnadze went to Japan in January 1986, only six months after his appointment as Foreign Minister.[70]

The Soviet leaders' interests in Japan, especially economically motivated interests, had already been apparent for two decades, but gained a 'powerful boost' under *New Thinking*.[71] With the Soviets' policy shift towards reducing military expenditure and aiming at economic recovery, Japan's importance to them greatly increased. In his Vladivostok Speech in 1986, Gorbachev praised Japan as 'the country which became the first victim of American nuclear weapons covered a great distance within a brief period, demonstrated striking accomplishments in industry, trade, education, science and technology'.[72] As mentioned earlier, relations with Japan, however, did not improve smoothly, not necessarily solely due to Japanese reluctance. In the early period of Gorbachev's regime he had other policy priorities, such as relations with the USA and Europe, disarmament issues and withdrawal of Soviet troops from Afghanistan; nor at that time were prospects for relations with Japan well understood among the Soviet leadership, because of their association with the territorial problem. The Politburo, still overwhelmingly comprising old members, attached no high priority to improving relations with Japan.[73]

However, Gorbachev's organisational and personnel shake-ups contributed to shifting the direction of Soviet policy towards Japan, by decreasing the influence of orthodox conservatives who retained hawkish views towards Japan derived from former regimes, and increasing that of progressives and especially of Japan specialists. In the series of reforms in 1986 and 1987 the Asia-Pacific authority in the MID, Deputy Foreign Minister Mikhail Kapitsa, was replaced by Igor Rogachev, and the MID's Asian section was streamlined to reflect the reality of the importance of the Asia-Pacific region.[74] A Bureau of the Pacific Ocean and Southeast Asian Countries was created to handle policy towards Japan, Oceania and the ASEAN countries, and Alexander Panov was appointed to head it.[75] Rogachev was a rather 'old-thinking career diplomat'[76] and little attitudinal change was observed from traditional high-handedness. However, the appointment of Panov, a rather progressive Japan specialist, came to provide more constructive factors towards improved relations with Japan. Japanese diplomats perceived the Soviet attitude in bilateral dialogue as less inflexible and more constructive.[77]

The Deputy Head of the International Department of the Central Committee, Ivan Kovalenko (given to advocating a rigid, mistrustful and cautious attitude to Japan, which he alleged to have military and political expansionist ambitions[78]) was replaced by a liberal, Evgenii Bazhanov. The International Department was said to have regained its influence after Gromyko left the MID,[79] and since many Japanese Soviet-watchers considered Kovalenko the most influential person in Soviet policy making towards Japan,[80] his replacement was regarded as one of the most substantial indications of a policy shift.

Characteristic of Gorbachev's era in terms of foreign-policy decision making was the increased influence of academics. The basic concept of Gorbachev's diplomacy, downgrading the diplomatic value of military power and emphasising peaceful coexistence or interdependence, at first appeared in the approach of a group of academics called *mezhdunarodniki* (international affairs specialists) in major institutions of the Soviet Academy of Sciences, even during the late years of Brezhnev's era.[81] Gorbachev officially adopted the concept, together with its originators, bringing into key positions individuals such as Yakovlev, Shakhnazarov and Frolov (who became Assistant to the General Secretary of the CPSU Central Committee), and appointing others to important posts in various institutions. The same line of movement was observed in the narrower arena of policy towards Japan. Institutions of the Soviet Academy of Sciences such as the Institutes of World Economy and International Relations (IMEMO), of Oriental Studies (IVAN), and of the Far East (IDV), and the Moscow State Institute of International Relations (MGIMO) retained Japan specialists, and the *Glasnost* policy enabled them to express and publish opinions and policy proposals that directly or indirectly constituted policy inputs to government decisions. Diversified opinions, some of them opposed to governmental positions, began to be expressed on the territorial or economic cooperation issues with Japan. As mentioned earlier, at a Foreign Ministerial Meeting it was indicated that the USSR could sign a peace treaty with Japan without abrogation of the US–Japan security treaty. Originally suggested by D. Petrov in his IMEMO years,[82] the concept finally became policy input after many years. Participation of academics in government policy making toward Japan was noted in various other forms. For example, having worked in IVAN and IMEMO, Georgii F. Kunadze joined the Russian MID in the late period of Gorbachev's regime. Konstantin Sarkisov of IVAN became a member of the Preparatory Committee for the Soviet President's Visit to Japan, established in November 1990 with Yakovlev (later replaced by G. Yanaev who was Vice-President under Gorbachev) as Chairman.

## *Gorbachev's regime at the time of the Tokyo Summit*

Gorbachev's long-awaited visit to Japan finally took place five years after Shevardnadze's first visit. By that time Gorbachev's regime had greatly changed both in formal structure and in decisional power of the leader himself. He had become executive President as well in an amended political system.

Under Gorbachev's leadership, the most dramatic changes in the Soviet political system since the 1917 Revolution itself took place, especially in 1989–90. As his attempt at *Perestroika* within the Party was blocked by conservatives, he aimed to continue the reform by making a significant power transfer from party to state institutions. A qualitative change began in 1989 with the introduction of competitive elections for a new legislature, the Congress of People's Deputies of the USSR, which in turn elected from among its members an inner body, the Supreme Soviet. Unlike the old Supreme Soviet, which met for only a few days annually, it sat for about eight months of the year, and became a force to be taken into account within the political system.[83] Furthermore, in February 1990 Article 6, which specified 'the leading role of the Communist Party' was dropped from the Constitution of the USSR, thus abolishing the one-party dominance of the Communist Party and permitting a plural political party system. The next step was creation of an Executive Presidency, for the first time in Russian or Soviet history. Gorbachev was elected first President by the Congress of People's Deputies. Politburo meetings became less frequent than in the past and by 1990 no longer contained all the most powerful politicians.[84] The Soviet system became more pluralistic and diversified, when elections were held for the legislatures of the various Union Republics.[85] After Boris Yeltsin's election as Chairman of the Supreme Soviet of the Russian Republic in May 1990, a dual authority came into being in Moscow, with Yeltsin tending to pursue policies that conflicted with those of the All-Union Government headed by Gorbachev.[86]

While Gorbachev was struggling for power and attempting to strengthen his political base by a series of political reforms, the already problematic economic and social situations deteriorated further, and ethnic tensions intensified. In such a political, economic and social climate, the recovery of order became a higher priority for the general public than progress in reforms. Thus from around the autumn/winter of 1990, Gorbachev began cooperating with the conservatives from the Party, the military and the KGB.[87] Personnel changes that took place in the Soviet leadership clearly indicated that Gorbachev was shifting back to conservatism. For example, Vadim Bakatin was replaced as Minister of Internal Affairs by the former Chairman of the All-Union Committee of Party Control, Boris Pugo. Yakovlev was replaced as Chairman of the Commission on International Policy of the CC, CPSU by Gennadii I. Yanaev, who became Vice President.[88] Furthermore, in December 1990 at the Congress of People's Deputies, Shevardnadze announced his resignation as Foreign Minister, warning of the strengthening influence of the anti-reformist groups. The post of Foreign Minister was then taken by Aleksandr A. Bessmertnykh. (Important positions of the Soviet leadership were thus being filled by those conservatives, who were to lead, or have suspected involvement in, the 1991 August coup attempt.) In January 1991, Shevardnadze's warning became reality. The armed suppression of the capitals of Lithuania (Vilnius, 13 January) and Latvia (Riga, 20 January) exemplified the Gorbachev government's turnabout towards an authoritarian regime resorting to forced measures.

The visit to Japan took place, but there was strong opposition to it right up to the last minute. Panov has revealed that an influential group of people from the Party, military and military-industrial establishments visited Gorbachev and asked him to cancel it, on the grounds that Japanese rigidity made it unlikely that much economic assistance would be forthcoming, and the visit would therefore be fruitless.[89]

## The territorial problem: 'ownership of the islands of Habomai, Shikotan, Kunashiri, and Etorofu'

Looking at the outcomes of Gorbachev's visit from a long-term perspective, the mention of the territorial issue in the Joint Statement was a remarkable change, as it was the first official Soviet admission that the four islands were disputed territories. However, many viewed it as lack of significant progress in the short term, as the statement contained no specific agreement, and the vagueness of the sentence ending with '1956' again left room for differing interpretations. The so-called 'end of Cold War', observed in Soviet relations with other countries, had certainly not yet arrived in relations with Japan.

### Glasnost *and diversified opinions*

Though Japanese domestic opinion on the territorial issue had begun to diversify in the late 1980s, the diversity of opinion in the USSR was a further significant and epochal phenomenon. Freedom of expression was being experienced for the first time in several decades, and opinions were much more diverse than in Japan. From around 1988, journalistic and academic articles explaining the Japanese case began to appear.[90] Various proposals for solving the dispute were discussed publicly by academics, journalists and government officials – a marked change from the past, when only the traditionally hard-line voice of the Soviet government was heard. From late 1990, the number rapidly increased, and discussion intensified as Gorbachev's visit to Japan drew closer. More articles on the Kuriles and the territorial dispute were published in the USSR during the six months preceding the visit than in the previous 45 years.[91]

Public opinion was a new factor for the Soviet leadership in considering their position. To classify Soviet domestic views based on the number of the islands discussed for transfer, they may be roughly divided into three views: zero, two and four. Many of those who advocated zero transfer were naturally conservative bureaucrats and politicians, perpetuating the traditional positions of 'no territorial problem' or 'unwarranted claims'.[92] However, this zero-transfer position came to include a more flexible attitude than previously, such as retaining Soviet sovereignty but proposing options such as: renting the islands,[93] shelving the issue, as was done over the Senkaku Islands dispute when Japan–China relations were normalised – the so-called *Senkaku rettō* formula[94] – or jointly developing the disputed island together with part of Hokkaido as a Special Economic Zone.[95] The zero-transfer position was also supported by newly vocal public opinion and nationalism emerging as a result of *Glasnost* and *Perestroika*, and branding 'selling inalienable Russian territories' as corrupt.[96] At the 28th Congress of the CPSU, International Department Head Falin stated that the Party members and majority of general public were supporting the non-agression of both west and east national borders of the Soviet Union.[97]

Many of the 'two islands' transfer advocates were among the Japan specialists in the Soviet Academy of Sciences, whose discussions were supported by a 'solid basis'.[98] What they especially often argued were the illegitimacy of the Soviets' 1960 *Aide-mémoire* and the necessity of keeping the 1956 promise.[99] Some of them raised or supported the so-called 'two islands plus alpha' proposals, in which the concept of 'two islands' transfer was combined with various other concessions in respect of one or both of Kunashiri and Etorofu.[100]

Others supported 'four islands' transfer, i.e., complete acceptance of the Japanese position. These were mainly 'new politicians'[101] who had emerged in the course of *Glasnost* and democratisation, including the former Dean of the Economic Faculty of Moscow State University and then mayor of Moscow Gavriil Popov,[102] a Professor at Moscow State Institute of History and Archives (renamed the Humanities University in 1992) Yuri Afanas'ev,[103] and the Nobel Peace Prize-winning physicist Andrei Sakharov.[104] Their arguments were based on economic benefits expected from the islands' transfer to Japan.[105] Some 'two islands' advocates, for example Nodari Simoniya, Anatolii Zaitsev and Alexei Zagorsky later shifted their positions to 'four islands' transfer, reportedly because their political judgment was that Soviet–Japanese relations would never improve until all four territories were returned.[106] It was anyway not easy to find 'mutually acceptable' (*vzaimopriemlemye*) accommodations.

Special attention should be paid to Boris Yeltsin's attitude and how this changed later. In January 1990 when he visited Japan as a People's Deputy of the Soviet Union, he announced his famous 'five-stage-resolution' proposal. That was: Stage 1, the Soviet Union would officially acknowledge the existence of the territorial problem; Stage 2, the Soviets would establish a Free Economic Zone on the four disputed islands; Stage 3, they would demilitarise the islands; Stage 4, the two countries would then sign a peace treaty; and, Stage 5, after completing Stages 1 through 4 in 15–20 years, the 'next generation' would resolve the question of ownership.[107] Yeltsin's proposal was perceived as more progressive than the Gorbachev's, in the sense that it acknowledged the existence of the dispute, while the Gorbachev regime still had not officially done so.[108]

Later that year, however, Soviet official recognition of the territorial dispute was implied in the form of the issuing of visas to a Japanese Diet Delegation for the purpose of 'Northern Territories' negotiation.[109] Since the early 1960s, the Soviet government had consistently taken the position of 'no territorial problem with Japan', and despite frequent Japanese requests, no visas were issued specifically for such a purpose. For over 30 years, therefore, there were no official territorial negotiations between the two countries. This policy was hence reversed, and with visas issued for the specific purpose of 'territorial negotiations', a bipartisan delegation of Japanese Diet members visited the USSR and indeed discussed the territorial issue with the Soviet leaders, including Primakov from the Presidential Office and Yanaev and Frolov from the Party in September 1990.[110]

Meanwhile, *Perestroika* hit deadlock. Combined with economic deterioration and the intensification of ethnic conflicts, the basis of Gorbachev's regime was shaken by increased criticism and denunciation of his policies. When the political base is unstable, especially as in the USSR of this time where the domestic situation was extremely complex, policy change, especially over a territorial issue, can easily be used as a weapon in the political battle. One good example is Yeltsin's change of attitude on the territorial dispute with Japan. At first, when he made the 'five-stage-resolution' proposal, he said:

> If the transfer of the all four islands, as suggested by some people, were decided, our people would immediately dismiss such leaders. Therefore, while making the Japanese people bear consciousness of trust and credibility that the problem is not standing still but progressing, we, on the other hand, should try gradually to form our public opinions along this line.[111]

After election as Chairman of the Supreme Soviet of the Russian Republic, Yeltsin appeared to resile from his 'five-stage-resolution' proposal. The revised Constitution of the Russian Republic indeed stipulated that its territories or boundaries could not be altered without a national referendum. When he visited Kunashiri during his trip to the Far East in August 1990, he said 'this land is too good to transfer to another nation'.[112] As his relations with Gorbachev later drastically deteriorated, towards the end of 1990, it seems Yeltsin himself used the disputed islands as a strategy for political survival against the background of the rising nationalism in Russia, his constituency.

Many Soviet leaders were concerned that relinquishing the disputed islands could create a dangerous precedent. Apart from the three Baltic states seized by the Soviet Union in 1940 and reoccupied in 1944–5, Finland, Germany, Poland, Czechoslovakia, Hungary and Romania had all been made to cede territory to the Soviet Union between 1940 and 1945, and there was the possibility that ceding territory to Japan would result not only in risking the political disintegration of the USSR, but also in inviting similar claims from other countries.

The strategic importance of the islands was argued to justify opposition by the military. The islands were militarised from the late 1970s, initially in reaction to the China–Japan *rapprochement*. More importantly, after new developments in strategic deterrence, the Sea of Okhotsk became a 'bastion' for Soviet SLBM submarines based at Petropavlovsk-Kamchatskii, with associated air, naval and army facilities established along the Kuril-Kamchatka line. Russian military writers have put forward several arguments on the need to retain these facilities and accordingly those islands.[113]

As Gorbachev's scheduled visit was approaching, the MID had to consider the domestic situation in official-level preparation of the Soviet positions on a peace treaty and the territorial problem. It was quite obvious that territorial concessions to Japan would become another source of conflict in the domestic situation. According to Panov, the Bureau of Pacific Ocean and Southeast Asian Countries in MID drafted two positions in the late 1990.[114] The first position was aimed at exploring concessions for settling the problem based on the 1956 Joint Declaration. This plan implying the 'two islands' (the Habomais and Shikotan) cession to Japan was not adopted. The second position did not contain specific accommodation of the territorial dispute, but included some new content related to it, for example, acknowledging the names of the four islands for the first time as the islands in dispute, together with promising demilitarisation of the Southern Kuriles, resumption of visa-free mutual visits to and from those islands, and proposals for joint industrial activities.[115] In an effort to obtain a domestic consensus over these two plans, several high-level meetings were held, including of Gorbachev with Yeltsin, and of the Preparatory Committee for the Presidential Visit to Japan. The second plan was adopted at a meeting summoned by Gorbachev himself with representatives from various fields. In the International Committee of the USSR Supreme

Soviet, however, strong opposition was expressed upon its introduction by Foreign Minister Bessmertnykh.[116] Not until the day before Gorbachev's departure for Japan did the Committee finally approve the second plan.[117] There is little doubt that Gorbachev would have had fewer domestic problems in gaining a settlement with Tokyo had he sought it in 1986 or 1987 – before democracy and *Glasnost* had begun to take hold in the USSR – rather than in 1991 when his political freedom of manoeuvre was already sharply constrained. The instability of Gorbachev's political base towards the end of his regime was clearly indicated by the rejection of the specific plan for settlement of the territorial issue on the 1956 basis. The conflict within the USSR on the territorial issue was also reflected in the political composition of the delegation Gorbachev took with him – a mixture of conservatives, reformists and representatives from the Union Republics (but no Japan specialist).

The summit negotiations turned out much longer than scheduled. The point pressed by Prime Minister Kaifu and rejected by Gorbachev until the end of the summit was recognition of the 1956 Declaration. The outcome of the summit, the Joint Statement, made no reference to the 'Soviet–Japanese Joint Declaration.' At the press conference on 19 April, Gorbachev equivocated on this point as 'those, which were not actually carried out, whose chances were lost, or which history prepared different options for, were not recuperated'.[118] On his return to Moscow, he had to report to the public that he had made no concession on the territorial dispute. In his speech at the Supreme Soviet on 26 April, he clearly denied the recognition of the 'two islands return' provision, stating: 'though Prime Minister Kaifu insisted on specifying the Declaration in the Statement, I did not agree to it'.[119]

During Gorbachev's regime, the *Glasnost* policy generated a wide range of discussions on the territorial issue, which, as well as excessively raising observers' expectations, gave too many options for the decision maker to choose. The domestic political situation in the late years of his and also the Soviet regime, however, drove Gorbachev into a position where he could no longer take decisions on his own.

## THE 'BILATERAL-INTERACTION' PERSPECTIVE

During Gorbachev's visit, six meetings took place, totalling over twelve hours, far more than originally scheduled.[120] This seemed to symbolise the longer path to the summit than in 1956 and 1973. Since the (fifth) peace negotiation was held upon Shevardnadze's visit to Japan in 1986, five years had passed until the realisation of Gorbachev's visit to Japan. During that time there were many contacts and discussions at different levels: seven official (foreign ministerial) peace negotiations,[121] seven deputy foreign ministerial level meetings of the Peace Treaty Working Group, which was established under the agreement of December 1988,[122] and many other official level meetings. While domestic opinions were becoming diversified, negotiation channels seemed to be mainly through official levels centred on the two Ministries of Foreign Affairs. Under the leadership of the *Gaimushō*, Cabinet members and LDP leaders participated in the discussions or negotiations. Following domestic political changes, however, not only the Soviet government, but also the Russian government and even regional government came to take part in the negotiations on the Soviet side. This presented a kind of dual or multiplex diplomacy and, since it took place in a period of political instability, diplomacy to some extent resembling the Japanese side of the 1955–6 negotiations.

## Japanese goals and Soviet goals

The ultimate goal of the bilateral negotiations was, needless to say, political *rapprochement* for the two countries. In order to sign a peace treaty, however, there remained almost insuperable hurdles to overcome. The Japanese side had the resolution of the 'Northern Territories' issue as its primary goal and as the prerequisite for signing a peace treaty. As mentioned earlier, the final goal was with almost no doubt return of the 'four islands'. The dialogues for *rapprochement* started again with the Soviet overture. It was a part of their *New Thinking* diplomacy, which aimed at overall improvement of their diplomatic relations. Specifically with Japan, it was for the most part driven by economic motives. By the time of Gorbachev's visit to Japan, the Soviet economy was on the verge of collapse. The failure of the economic reforms appeared to be giving more reasons for the Soviets to pursue Japanese economic and technological assistance. However, in the process of negotiations leading up to the summit, it became clear that not much assistance could be expected from Japan. Though raised on the bilateral diplomatic agenda several times, the summit did not take place for five years due to the distance between the two countries' positions. Thus, the reality itself of Gorbachev's visit appeared to become the goal. On the Japanese side, the traditional rigid attitude toward the USSR was persistently maintained at first, but success of the Soviet diplomatic *rapprochement* with other countries in the meantime made Japan feel that it was being left out of the global mainstream. Therefore, as seen in the emergence of a new slogan 'balanced equilibrium' (*kakudai kinkō*), Japan began to aim at a realistic objective of overall improvement in relations, while keeping the territorial issue as the prerequisite for signing a peace treaty. Against this background, the notable feature of this summit was that the two countries came closer to each other in their realistic goal settings.

In Japanese Ministry of Foreign Affairs documentation, Gorbachev's visit to Japan in April 1991 is listed only as 'Japan–Soviet Summit', not as 'Peace Negotiation'. Because of the distances between their positions, neither side expected a complete *rapprochement*. The concrete goals of the summit are described in books by Panov and Tōgō, the Soviet and Japanese senior officials directly in charge. Comparing those two volumes, it can easily be discerned that by the time of the summit the two Foreign Ministries well understood each others' situations, and had prepared almost identical frameworks for compromise. Though the Japanese ultimate goal of 'four islands return' had not been changed, according to Tōgō, Japan's specific goals at the summit were (1) to ensure that the islands of Kunashiri, Etorofu, Shikotan and the Habomais were the objects of the negotiations, and (2) to confirm the (transfer of Shikotan and the Habomais in the) 1956 Joint Declaration. According to Panov, what the MID prepared for the summit was (1) a plan based on the 1956 Joint Declaration, and (2) another plan with no concrete territorial accommodation, but naming the four islands for the first time as the islands in dispute. However, as Panov revealed, the first plan was rejected domestically in the USSR before the summit, and Gorbachev had no choice but to carry out the second plan.

The long summit talks were after all negotiations between Kaifu, who was instructed to confirm the two islands return of the 1956 Joint Declaration, and Gorbachev, who was unable to make any concession beyond naming the four islands. The outcome of the summit was almost foreordained.

## Japanese and Soviet bargaining cards and negotiating strategies

The two countries' positions at the Tokyo summit presented an interesting contrast to the former two summits. In 1956, it was a summit between a winner and a loser in the War. In 1973, their relations had already moved beyond that stage and presented a different kind of asymmetry. In 1991 their positions seemed in a sense reversed from 1956 and clearly contrasted from the standpoint of the Cold War. The Soviet Union was the ex-leader of a collapsed bloc, and even its status as a unified sovereign state was on the verge of disintegration. On the other hand, Japan was a member of the confronting Western bloc and a strong ally of the USA. Economically the difference in status was even clearer; the USSR was painfully experiencing a collapsing socialist economy, while Japan had grown into a capitalist economic superpower.

In the previous chapter I pointed out that the Japanese side tended to take the attitude that it would be the USSR rather than Japan which would be in trouble if the negotiations failed. This tendency was also observed, especially in their early moves this time. In 1955–6 there were several pressing issues after the War. In 1973 when the oil crisis begun to be rumoured and Japanese business was urging the government to promote resource diplomacy, economic and technological assistance did not become a strong card. In 1991, however, after overcoming the difficulties of the oil shock by industrial structural change, and having continued its development as an economic power, Japan in the bilateral framework did not have such pressing incentives as in the past for improving relations with the USSR. The overture for diplomatic *rapprochement* this time came indeed from the Soviet side again. For Japan, the 'Northern Territories' had consistently been the priority. Long years had already passed while repeating the same demand and the issue did not disappear because it was not immediately resolved. Japanese leaders calculated that the logic of *Perestroika* sooner or later would bring *New Thinking* diplomacy towards Japan.[123] Japan's attitude was also based on its judgement that the Soviet economic reforms could not succeed without Japanese assistance, and the risk was too high to invest in politically unstable countries. The Japanese attitude was therefore arrogant and no change was made in its traditional zero-sum attitude of 'no separation of politics and economics' in the 'Northern Territories' strategy. On 8 January 1989 in Paris, at an international conference on banning chemical weapons, Foreign Minister Uno told Shevardnadze that if the Soviet Union had no intention to progress on the territorial problem, Japan did not intend to discuss substantial issues when the Soviet President visited Japan, i.e., they were not enthusiastic about dealing with signing or arranging various economic agreement positively.[124] Such statements naturally offended the Soviet Union.

During Uno's visit to the USSR from 30 April to 5 May 1989, Shevardnadze asked him to pay attention to the importance of 'expanding areas of agreement, deepening mutual understanding and not bringing up any prerequisite' in Soviet–Japanese relations.[125] At a press conference about Uno's visit, Soviet Deputy Foreign Minister I. Rogachev more clearly stated that in preparing for Gorbachev's visit to Japan neither side should stipulate any prerequisite or preconditions.[126] Gorbachev indicated to Uno that in such circumstances the time would not be right for a summit visit. Judging from the announced official reports about the meeting, the Soviet Union was clearly unhappy with the Japanese attitude. Gorbachev called for getting rid of the idea that the Soviet Union desired improved relations more than Japan. He also requested avoidance of ultimatum-type proposals on any issues.[127]

The different positions of the two nations well reflected the closing days of the Cold War. Japan had for the time being succeeded in involving other developed western capitalist countries in its 'no separation of politics and economics' strategy in the G-7 arena. The Chairman's Statement at the G-7 Summit meeting had made special reference to the 'Northern Territories Issue' and large-scale economic assistance had not been given to the USSR. In July 1990, addressing business representatives in Nagoya Uno's successor as Foreign Minister, Tarō Nakayama, defended the Japanese position on the grounds that 'Giving financial assistance to the Soviet Union now is just like throwing money into a ditch.'[128]

Did the Soviet side have any bargaining cards? It was indeed the Soviet Union that continued to occupy the disputed territories. It can be assumed that the bargaining point for the Soviet Union this time was probably to what extent they could make concessions in the expression regarding these islands in the official statement (Joint Statement). That is, since 'no territorial problem existed' in the last bilateral summit of 1973, if the four islands were to be the maximum concession, there must have been various mid-way compromise options in between. In the discussion facilitated by *Glasnost* policy, there were several proposals for settlement of the issue. Expectations for political *rapprochement* were heightened especially over the 'two islands' return, supported by solid historical arguments by academics. However, using the sovereignty of these islands as bargaining cards to induce Japanese economic assistance was impossible for Gorbachev to risk at the time of his visit, even if it had been possible earlier. In addition to the low prospect of economic assistance from Japan, deepening political turmoil and increased influence of the conservatives, who were against the summit visit itself, cornered Gorbachev. Gorbachev then no longer had power to make drastic decisions on the issue, as Panov revealed in his volume. In the end, admitting the 'existence of the problem' but not conceding on sovereignty, was the maximum concession possible from the Soviet side. However, as mentioned earlier, viewing the result in a long-term perspective, this shift of the Soviet position from 'no territorial problem exists' to admitting that one existed can be considered a big concession.

However, using the concept of bargaining cards on the changes of Soviet attitude, or applying the same old framework of considering negotiations as gain or loss, may not be valid. Abandoning the zero-sum approach that had caused the impasse, a new 'positive-sum' approach began to appear in their relations. The Joint Statement included one clause stating that the former enemy country clause of Japan had lost meaning in the United Nations' Charter. This inclusion was proposed by the USSR, making it the first nation in the UN Security Council specifying this point in an official document.[129] Another example was the expression of Soviet concern over the issue of the Japanese prisoners of war, who were detained and/or died in Siberia during and after the Second World War. On his way to Tokyo, Gorbachev visited a Japanese POWs' cemetery in Khabarovsk on 15 April. In his speech at a banquet in the imperial palace on the 16th, he expressed 'condolence' (*soboleznovanie*) to their bereaved families.[130] This attitude of being conciliatory to the other side or trying to find common grounds for development in relations was also observed in the Japanese attitude towards various actions performed under its new 'balanced equilibrium' (*kakudai kinkō*) concept.

Those different aspects of both nations' attitudes may be explained in terms of both continuity and discontinuity. On the Soviet side, discontinuity appeared with *Perestroika*, was apparent in flexibility of policies and became the driving force for improving relations with Japan. Continuity was represented by the remaining conservatives and their influence, that worked as constraints on the progressives. This may be easier to understand if considered in comparison with the earlier summit meetings. The 1973 summit contained stronger continuity from that of 1956. Experience from the 1955–6 negotiations appeared to affect behaviour at the 1973 summit, probably because almost all the same people were still in charge of policy making towards Japan. In 1955 they had used up all their cards without achieving their own goals, and had allowed the Japanese to take what they aimed at one after another. That experience had made their negotiating attitudes toward Japan fairly rigid, and the official position ('no territorial problem exists') did not change, just as if they were confronting a Japanese fixed demand for the four islands with no sign of concession. But at the 1991 summit, a stronger discontinuity was brought into the policy-making approaches by *Glasnost* and *Perestroika*, as well as by changes in personnel.

In contrast, continuity appeared stronger in Japanese policy making towards the USSR, specifically on the territorial problem. In the short term, the Japanese attitude appeared to have become more flexible or to have changed by introducing the 'balanced equilibrium' policy, but in the long term their policy seemed to retain more factors of continuity from the earlier period. Though the phrase itself had not been invented in 1973, at the time of Tanaka's visit to Moscow bilateral relations were exhibiting 'balanced equilibrium' type development, centring on economic relations. However, the same 'no separation of politics and economics' (*seikei fukabun*) strategy was also retained at that time. Thus it seems that the same pattern was simply repeated, with addition of some new terminology. The negotiating style also appeared to display continuity from the old days, i.e., an ultimatum-style approach with no sign of concessions, such as 'Yes or no', 'Return or not', 'Admit the existence of the territorial problem', or zero-sum type thinking that 'negotiation is a contest'. Though this once appeared to have toned down, when the 'balanced equilibrium' policy began to be proclaimed, Japan after all reverted to it and urged Gorbachev to make his ultimate 'decision' or 'resolution' at the summit. Though softened from the extreme of calling the territorial return an 'entrance' (*iriguchi-ron*), i.e., a prerequisite, the Japanese policy of 'no separation of politics and economics' was nevertheless essentially a continuation from the previous period.

The Japanese side persistently urged decisions on the Soviet leader until the last moment. In addition to maintaining a traditional attitude of being rigid towards the USSR, the Japanese leadership probably kept a slight hope alive for Gorbachev's decisional power, that created several 'end of the Cold War' stories. Its expectations were probably supported by such things as the concessions Gorbachev had made in order to improve the USSR's relations with many other countries under the *New Thinking* diplomacy, and also the newly emerged wide-ranging discussions over the territorial problems under the Glasnost policy in the USSR. The biggest Japanese miscalculation was failure to realise that Gorbachev no longer had decisional power.

Though the Japanese domestic Cold War '1955 system' was on the verge of collapse, policy making towards the USSR was bureaucratically stable. In contrast, in the USSR both the domestic political base and the foreign-policy decision-making system, including that towards Japan, were very unstable. With the two countries' international standing in a sense reversed from the 1950s, the Soviet domestic political situation to some extent resembled that of Hatoyama's Japan.

## MISSED, CONTINUING AND NEWLY EMERGED OPPORTUNITIES

The former *rapprochement* opportunities in the 1950s and 1970s were 'lost' due to changes in the international and domestic circumstances surrounding the Soviet Union and Japan, such as reintensification of the Cold War and replacement of political leadership. With regard to Gorbachev's visit to Japan, however, considering the time intervals between the past bilateral summits (17 and 18 years), it may still be too early to judge whether or not the *rapprochement* opportunity created at this time was 'lost.' A Russo-Japanese bilateral summit was in fact held two and a half years later in 1993, when Russian President Yeltsin visited Japan. In the meantime, bilateral relations experienced further changes both internationally and domestically. These significant changes potentially could fundamentally influence the issues of peace and the territorial problem between the two nations.

## The collapse of the USSR and '1955 system' and the end of the Cold War

The major changes occurred first in the Soviet Union. In August 1991, four months after Gorbachev's visit to Japan, a coup was attempted by Soviet conservatives. It failed in short order, but sealed the fate of Gorbachev's regime, which had been locked in tension between conservatives and reformists. Even after the breakdown of communist rule, Gorbachev strove for the survival of both his regime and the disintegrating Union by forming a loose federation of Soviet republics. This came to nothing; instead, with the formation of the CIS in December 1991, the USSR came to the end of its 69-year history. Ironically, Gorbachev became the first and last Soviet leader ever to visit Japan. With the collapse of the Soviet Union, the chance for 'Soviet'–Japanese *rapprochement* indeed disappeared. However, the chance he created for a new era in bilateral relations had not necessarily disappeared along with the USSR. Soviet diplomacy was to be succeeded by Russian.

A large transitional period also arrived in Japanese politics. Supported by Kaifu's personal popularity, his cabinet was about to implement political reforms aimed at cleansing Japanese politics, when Kaifu was deposed by *Keiseikai*, the largest LDP faction, ironically the same faction that had backed him for the leadership. Reversion to the old system appeared to be occurring with a series of movements in the LDP leadership, These included the designation of Kiichi Miyazawa, whose involvement in the 'recruit scandals' was known, as LDP president, or in other words the next prime minister, and also appointment of former prime ministers Nakasone and Takeshita as the LDP's supreme advisers. However, disclosure of the *Sagawa kyūbin* political corruption scandal stopped this trend. The arrest and forced resignation from the diet of the *Keiseikai* leader and Deputy Prime Minister Shin Kanemaru for association with the scandal weakened the centripetal forces among the LDP factions which had sustained LDP domination in the Diet. New parties began to be established or to break off from the LDP, and this ended the period in which the LDP president automatically became prime minister. In August 1993, with the establishment of the non-LDP Hosokawa cabinet, the '1955 system' of LDP factional politics ended its 38 years of history.

The purpose of Gorbachev's visit to Japan in 1991 was to conduct summit negotiations between Japan and the USSR at national level and between Kaifu and Gorbachev at personal level. It was a summit between two countries with totally different political systems, and can be depicted as one between leaders of totally different levels, as Gorbachev was a prominent figure internationally and historically, while Kaifu was rather weak and negligible even among the many post-war Japanese prime ministers. However, between these nations and individuals, we can somehow find common features of the 'closing days of the Cold War', as well as the grand and global flow of this major period and its dynamism.

## Missed, continuing and newly emergent opportunities

The collapse of the Soviet Union and of the Japanese '1955 system' marked the end of the Cold War in both countries. What those changes brought to their bilateral relations were the continuation or creation of chances, rather than losses. Legacies of Gorbachev's visit such as various positive arrangements were achieved between Russia and Japan. In the short term, chances were certainly lost a couple of times after the collapse of the Soviet Union. In particular the last-minute cancellation of Russian President Yeltsin's visit in September 1992 severely offended the Japanese. Yet, both the cancelled visit and the actual 1993 visit were laid on the same continuum as the chances created in the Gorbachev's era. The series of historic political changes that took place after Gorbachev's visit, both internationally and domestically, will probably serve as positive influences on negotiations for a peace treaty and the territorial issue in the long term. Considering that the territorial problem was created largely as a by-product of the Cold War, the foundation of post-war impediments to bilateral talks were removed both domestically and in a global sense. On the former Soviet side, the independence of the Baltic republics has already created precedents.

Though the Cold War was considered 'ended' both in the domestic levels of Japan, the USSR and the global level of international relations, there was no clear picture of what kind of era would come next. In the meantime, there were many hurdles to overcome in the short run. Yeltsin's visit to Japan took place in such a transitional period.

# 5 Yeltsin's visit to Tokyo, 1993

2. The Prime Minister of Japan and the President of the Russian Federation, sharing the recognition that the difficult legacies of the past in the relations between the two countries must be overcome, have undertaken serious negotiations on the issue of where Etorofu, Kunashiri, Shikotan and the Habomai Islands belong. They agree that negotiations towards an early conclusion of a peace treaty through the solution of this issue on the basis of historical and legal facts and based on the documents produced with the two countries' agreement as well as on the principles of law and justice should continue, and that the relations between the two countries should thus be fully normalised. In this regard, the Government of Japan and the Government of the Russian Federation confirm that the Russian Federation is the State retaining continuing identity with the Soviet Union and that all treaties and other international agreements between Japan and the Soviet Union continue to apply between Japan and the Russian Federation.[1]

## Yeltsin's visit to Japan and the Tokyo Declaration

Boris Yeltsin visited Japan from 11 to 13 October 1993. The purpose of his visit was to accomplish the first bilateral summit in the Russo-Japanese era after the end of the Soviet–Japanese era. From a long-term perspective, we can probably consider it to have been accompanied by the fundamental changes brought by the collapse of the Cold War structure, both globally and domestically. In that sense, it should be seen as the starting point of a new period. However, as I mentioned at the end of the last chapter, it had a strong sense of continuity from the previous period. The initial opportunity was created during the Gorbachev's time in office. The visit had originally been scheduled for an earlier date, but was cancelled – twice. There was, after all, a two-and-a-half-year interval between Gorbachev's and Yeltsin's bilateral summit meetings with the Japanese.

# THE 'GLOBAL INTERNATIONAL RELATIONS' PERSPECTIVE

## Yeltsin's visit to Japan

### *The 'end of the Cold War' and the collapse of the Soviet Union*

Several years have passed since the 'end of the Cold War' began to be proclaimed. By the time of Yeltsin's visit to Japan in October 1993, and also to this day, the concept of the 'end of the Cold War' had been well inculcated into people's belief/understanding, and has been taken for granted as a precondition for the present international relations. Consequently, academics, journalists and politicians have been searching for a new international order, paradigm or framework.

However, Yeltsin's visit to Japan was in its nature not something newly created by the new international environment brought about by the 'end of the Cold War'. It is more appropriate to see it as a continuation of the opportunity created in Gorbachev's era, and different from the three previous summit visits, whose chances were created in the context of the new thawing in global relations. Yeltsin's Tokyo visit was originally scheduled for September 1992, but was cancelled at the last minute and another visit scheduled for the next May was also not carried out. These cancellations caused a deterioration in relations between Japan and Russia. Viewing this visit in the global context, upon the political changes that had taken place in Russia right before his visit, there was a strong element of 'performance' by Yeltsin to demonstrate his power of control and also to obtain international support for his regime.

### *The 'End of the Cold War' in the Euro-Atlantic and détente in the Asia-Pacific?*

After the collapse of the Soviet Union, relations between Russia and the West in the Euro-Atlantic region, i.e., the US and Europe, further shifted direction and nature from those of former enemies to new allies. Russia signed the START-II agreement with the United States.[2] Efforts were also made to strengthen relations with the European Union, aiming at future free trade, a European security regime, etc.[3] The 'post-Cold War' era had certainly started in this part of the globe.

Incidentally, in this book, I have placed the 'end of the Cold War' in 'parenthesis', or limited it to the Euro-Atlantic regional context. This is because, reviewing the present status, including the point of the Yeltsin's

Tokyo visit, the question arises whether the Cold War has really ended in the Asia-Pacific region. I will consider this point below.

In retrospect, when and how did the Cold War end in the Asia-Pacific region? The 'end of the Cold War' declarations made at the US–USSR Summit in Malta (1989) and at the CSCE Summit Meeting in Paris (1990) were based on such clear facts in the Euro-Atlantic region as, for instance, remarkable progress in US–USSR arms reduction talks, democratisation of the Soviet Union and the Eastern European countries, the collapse of the Berlin Wall and reunification of Germany. However, on what basis did the Cold War end in the Asia-Pacific? Indeed, with the collapse of the Soviet Union (1991), it may be possible to say that the Cold War has fundamentally vanished, both in ideology and in political forms. Yet, it does not seem to provide enough ground for ending the Cold War in the Asia-Pacific region, whose situation is much more complex than that of Europe.

The post-war international situation of the Cold War was often called the 'Yalta System' in Europe. It originated from the war-time agreement made at Yalta in February 1945 by the leaders of the US, UK and the USSR over the construction of the post-war international order. In contrast, the Cold War system in the Asia-Pacific was often referred to as the 'San Francisco System' and this is certainly more appropriate than calling it the 'Yalta System'. The secret agreements regarding Japan were indeed made at Yalta in the context of bringing the Soviets into the war in the Pacific, but after the surrender of the Axis countries the East–West confrontation intensified and the Cold War turned towards actual 'Hot War' in Asia. By the time the Peace Treaty with Japan was signed in San Francisco in 1951, the Yalta Agreement was bent or made equivocal by US–UK hands. The USSR did not sign the treaty, nor did the other communist states, and the governments of the PRC and Taiwan were not invited to sign. In the Asia-Pacific region, the international situation was already complex and the San Francisco Treaty overlaid the foundation of the principal and basic structure of Cold War confrontation. Before ending the war with a clear settlement, the region became involved in the new war called the 'Cold War', and absorbed in the new regional international 'San Francisco system'.

It should also be noted that the Cold War in Asia was different from that of Europe in the latter stages, in that it developed into a tripolar US–USSR–China system, against the background of the Sino-Soviet conflict. In the series of movements from the late 1980s, Sino-Soviet and US–USSR *rapprochement* were indeed achieved, and the Soviet Union collapsed. However, China still clearly exists as a communist pole in the region. Not only China, the existence of communist states such as North Korea and Vietnam indicates the existence of tangible structures of ideological conflict. Additionally, not only the Russo-Japanese dispute, but also other unresolved problems over territorial sovereignty and border demarcation, specifically over Taiwan, the Spratlys and Paracels and the Korean Peninsula, are clear evidence for continuation of the San Francisco System. These issues have tended to be treated as separate, but tracing back to their origins, they all derive from the San Francisco Peace Treaty of 1951. The sources for future dispute were left in the Kuriles, Taiwan and the Spratlys, because the treaty did not specify to which country Japan renounced those territories. Though the Korean Peninsular was ceded to 'Korea', and its independence was recognised in the treaty, no reference was made to the two governments of the divided peninsula. Certainly, dramatic relaxation in tensions has occurred among many nations and the overall international relations have drastically improved in the region. However, rather than the 'end of the Cold War' this appears similar to the detente that occurred in Europe in the 1970s in that there has been no renunciation or collapse of communism. Just as the *détente* in the 1970s was in part sustained by Soviet attainment of military parity against the US, China's potential aggressiveness in its ambition for military expansion should not be ignored, nor should issues of democratisation and human rights. Also, China's future attitude towards Taiwan, especially after the reversion of Hong Kong (1997) and Macau (1999), is viewed with critical concern and misgivings. As for the Korean Peninsula, both North and South Korea joined the United Nations in 1991, as did both East and West Germany in 1973. However, German reunification has now taken place, whereas Korea is still divided. The current reality of the Asia-Pacific seems to present itself as 'detente with *de facto* legitimatisation' while nations with different political systems coexist, that is, the European-type *détente* of the 1970s. The Cold War does not seem to be over in the Asia-Pacific region.

It seems easier to explain Russo-Japanese relations in the regional context of the Asia-Pacific region. In the same way as with other spots of conflict in the region, settlement of the San Francisco System has not yet been made. Viewing Yeltsin's Tokyo visit in this regional international relations context, it took place in the *détente* period of the Cold War, and the relations between Japan and Russia have not advanced to the post-Cold War stage. This is evidenced by the fact that the peace treaty that was not signed in San Francisco in 1951 has still not been signed. At the end of the previous chapter I said that 'considering that the territorial problem was created largely as a by-product of the Cold War, the foundation of post-war impediments to bilateral talks were removed both domestically and in a global sense'. However, it has not necessarily been the case in the regional sense of the Asia-Pacific. The Cold War foundation has not been completely removed from the region yet.

# The 'Northern Territories' problem

Yeltsin's visit took place in the period of transition where 'continuities' were mixed with new 'changes'. Explaining this from the global international relations context, the international environment of the Asia-Pacific is 'continuity', and together with the other by-products of the San Francisco System, the territorial dispute between Japan and Russia still remains. In contrast, the 'change' was the new international movement in the Euro-Atlantic region. The important 'change' with regard to the Russo-Japanese territorial dispute is the domestic affairs of the former USSR. While the collapse of the Soviet Union and the so-called 'end of the Cold War' have lessened old negative factors and begun to provide a new positive environment, a reverse movement began to be seen on the other hand. The collapse of the Soviet Union provided the Russo-Japanese territorial dispute with new international factors, i.e., the new 'near abroad'. The former Soviet republics except the Baltic republics formed the Commonwealth of Independent States (CIS), but each republic has become a sovereign state. Then, new border problems emerged. Also within the Russian Federation, there are still precincts desiring to become additional 'near abroad'. In particular, the Chechen problem has escalated to military conflict. While conflicts between centre and periphery surface over various political and economic policies, there is a fear of the potential for disintegration of Russia itself. Any validity in the 'Pandora's box' or 'domino' theory could only be seen in boundary demarcation disputes within or between Russia and other CIS members or with the Baltic states.

Viewed in the context of the 'end of the Cold War in Euro-Atlantic' and 'detente in Asia-Pacific', the global affairs surrounding Russia and Japan can be explained. This can clearly be applied to the difference in the attitudes of G-7 countries towards financial assistance to Russia. One Japanese policy agenda item carried over from the Gorbachev era was the 'internationalisation of the Northern Territories problem'. Although this approach appeared successful and seemed to be working until the Houston Summit (1990) and the London Summit (1991), Japan was not able to gain stable or reliable international support. Its unwilling attitude towards economic assistance to the Soviet Union before political and economic breakdown and to Russia after it, invited international recriminations and put it in a difficult position. The US and UK, in accord with Japan in taking a cautious attitude at the London Summit of 1991, had changed to support large-scale economic assistance to Russia at the Munich Summit of 1992, in accord with Germany and France. Japan, the only non-Euro-Atlantic G-7 member therefore ended up receiving criticism for being negative towards assistance to Russia, and came to stand on the verge of isolation, though it managed to have some references to the 'Northern Territories' included in the Munich G-7 political statement. At the 1993 G-7 Summit, though held in Tokyo, it was decided not to include the 'Northern Territories' in the Summit agenda. Furthermore, when total assistance to Russia of $43.4 billion was decided, Japan was made to promise $1.82 billion. Prior to this, in March 1993, one of the major criticisms of Japan had come from former US President Nixon, who, in an article in the *New York Times* of 5 March 1993, condemned Japan for 'conditioning aid on Russia's return of four tiny northern islands'. Nixon's condemnation well exemplified the traditionally pragmatic US attitude towards this territorial dispute. Historically speaking, Nixon himself had had much to do with this issue. As Vice-President he witnessed the linkage of the Kuriles' disposal with US Okinawa policy in the 1950s, was President when Okinawa was returned to Japan in 1972, and attentively observed the course of the Japanese–Soviet negotiations in 1973. From the Russian point of view the United States in fact handled the issue most positively among the G-7 nations in 1993, presenting assistance to Russia as 'investment', and multiplying its share by adding bilateral assistance and a proposed new foundation to promote privatisation in Russia, whereas the European nations' willingness seemed to be receding due to their worsening domestic economic situations.[4]

In hindsight international support for the Japanese 'Northern Territories' claim was obtainable due to the Cold War. This was natural, considering how the problem was created in the international context. However, the 'end of the Cold War' removed this foundation of support. This awakens us to the fact of how pragmatic the involvement of foreign nations in the territorial problem was.

Japan nevertheless has continued to show itself unwilling to launch large-scale support for Russia in a bilateral framework due to the territorial dispute. While urging Japan to become the centre pole for Russian support, the United States continues to support in principle the Japanese position in the territorial dispute. Prior to the Tokyo G-7 Summit, when a US–Russia Summit was held in Vancouver in April 1993, US President Clinton told Yeltsin that Japanese Premier Miyazawa was determined to play a constructive role in promoting assistance to Russia through the G-7 process, which Japan hosted in the same month to coordinate G-7 aid to Russia, while retaining the US support for the Japanese territorial claim. Upon the end of the US–USSR Cold War, the American attitude seems to present some potential to play a mediatory role between Japan and Russia.

## THE 'NATION-STATE' PERSPECTIVE: JAPAN

## Yeltsin's visit to Japan

### *Hosokawa regime: Japan in transition*

The Japanese Prime Minister greeting President Yeltsin in Tokyo in October 1993 was Morihiro Hosokawa, who had just formed his cabinet two months previously. In the 15 months since establishment of his party, he had come to centre-stage in Japanese politics. In order to exclude the LDP, which had lost its absolute majority but was still the largest party in the Diet, Hosokawa had formed a coalition government including all non-LDP parties in the House of Representatives except the Communists. Following the collapse of LDP domination, i.e., of the 1955 system, a fundamental transformation had just begun. Japanese party politics had entered a period of transition. The 'Cold War' and the '1955 system'; the 'end of the Cold War' and the 'end of the 1955 system' – the structural correlations between the systems of international and domestic politics became visible from time to time. It appears, and has generally been considered, that both domestically and internationally the Cold War was over. However, it does not necessarily follow that the end of the 1955 system means a new period has arrived for Japanese diplomacy. Has the Cold War between Japan and Russia come to an end?

### *Signs for changes in diplomacy: review of the history*

The new Hosokawa regime tried to differentiate itself clearly from the LDP regime period. With regard to diplomacy, clues to a policy change were observed in the beginnings of a review of past history, crucial parts of which had been left equivocal or ambiguous in the process of creating the San Francisco System. On 10 August, at his first press conference as prime minister, Hosokawa remarked regarding the Pacific War, beginning with the Sino-Japanese War, 'I personally perceive that it was an invasive war, a wrong war.' Furthermore, at the National Memorial Ceremony for War Victims on 15 August, he expressed 'condolence (*aitō no i*) beyond the national borders to war victims and their bereaved families of the whole world including Asian neighbour nations.[5] Initiation of a governmental review of its war responsibility, as seen in the issue of the 'comfort women', appeared to indicate that clearance of old Cold War thinking was beginning.[6]

It should also be noted that this movement did not necessarily begin with the Hosokawa government's inauguration, but was also observed in the last days of the LDP period. On 4 August, shortly before its resignation, the LDP Mizayawa government announced the result of a government investigation of the comfort women issue, and admitted that there was compulsion in their recruitment and transfers.[7] However, it is certainly true that neither a statement of war guilt nor a review of the comfort women issue was seen in the middle of the Cold War period, when the LDP was dominant. Looking back, a similar tendency was observed in the last days of the Soviet regime, noticeably including its policies towards Japan. That is, the Soviet government had started reviewing its policy towards Japan before its collapse, reversed the long-held position that the 'territorial problem has been solved in a series of international negotiations', and similarly changed its attitude toward the question of treatment of Japanese POWs in Siberia. However, as far as policy toward Russia was concerned, the same kind of shift had not yet been observed in the Japanese government's attitude.

## *Diplomacy of continuity towards Russia*

The domestic Cold War system of Japan, the 1955 system, ended in 1993. However, no change from the Cold War era has been observed in the policy decision-making system towards Russia. Like his predecessors at the time of the Soviet–Japanese summits, Hosokawa was a popular prime minister,[8] but like Kaifu, prime minister in the closing days of LDP dominance, Hosokawa did not have a strong political base, and could not take the initiative in policy making in general. It is often pointed out that the political change of 1993 ended the long period of LDP one-party domination, but replaced it with distinct bureaucratic dominance.[9] As Inoguchi wrote, when the political regime is weak, as when the government is a coalition or minority in the parliament, bureaucracies see through it, and politicians become almost powerless. Due to its organisational continuity, the bureaucracy in the long run tends to predominate over politicians as individuals.[10] Hosokawa's diplomacy was no exception. However, since the initiative in policy making towards the USSR and Russia was always taken by the *Gaimushō*, there was actually no change. As far as foreign policies were concerned, Hosokawa in fact had no intention of attempting radical changes or challenges. The newly inaugurated coalition government was to succeed to foreign and defence policies of the previous regime.[11]

Yeltsin's visit to Japan was indeed the diplomatic agenda that the Hosokawa cabinet inherited from the LDP Miyazawa cabinet. Though the scheduled summit of September 1992 had been cancelled at the last minute, breaching normal diplomatic practice, most of the preparations for the summit had already been made.[12] There was no indication that Hosokawa took the initiative in preparing for the 1993 summit. His remarks at the summit diverged little from the 'response manual' (*ōtō yōkō*) prepared by the *Gaimushō*.[13] Another reason for strong continuity was that the core of the coalition regime comprised politicians who had formerly led the biggest (*Keiseikai*) faction of the LDP, and the LDP itself retained a firm influence on policy making as the strongest opposition party in Japanese history.

### A bilateral summit with lowest expectations?

The atmosphere greeting Yeltsin to Japan in October 1993 was cool. The Japanese had an unfavourable image of him for his bloody suppression of his parliamentary opponents immediately before his visit, as well as for his two previous cancellations in September 1992 and May 1993. In the LDP's Foreign Affairs Committee, there was deep-rooted animosity towards treating as a state guest a Russian president who had taken guns to the parliament, saying: 'it is reminiscent Hitler's burning of the Reichstag', or 'dissolving parliament and censoring newspapers – where did democratisation go?' However, since the invitation had actually been issued by an LDP government, and not wanting to drive Yeltsin into a complex situation or another cancellation, the LDP behaved scrupulously.[14]

The business community was also prudent about developing economic relations with Russia. Little progress had been made in large-scale private-enterprise investment. Even two years after nominal transformation to a market economy, delay was a key feature of economic system improvement. Infrastructure and systems for securing foreign currencies were inadequate. Import debts from the Soviet period were not being paid. Many joint ventures initiated on account of Russia's vast resources had been terminated or were stagnating due to confusion in the Russian system.[15]

As well as stabilisation of the Russian domestic situation, there were strong voices in the business community advocating improvement and stabilisation of Russo-Japanese political relations. Due to uncertainty about Russia's ability to pay, large-scale Russo-Japanese trade could not be negotiated without government endorsement such as trade insurance.[16] Among business leaders who attended a luncheon meeting during Yeltsin's visit were such as Susumu Yamaji, the chairman of Japan Airlines, who said that 'Once Japan and Russia sign a peace treaty, enterprises can undertake investment and economic cooperation with a clear conscience.'[17]

### The 'Northern Territories' problem

In the Tokyo Declaration, the expression of the territorial problem indirectly confirms the validity of the 1956 Joint Declaration, which was not the case at the previous summit with Gorbachev. The declaration contains the clause 'all treaties and other international agreements between Japan and the Soviet Union continue to be applied between Japan and the Russian Federation'. At the press conference held after signing the Declaration Yeltsin acknowledged that the 'international agreements' included the 1956 Joint Declaration, which specified the transfer of Shikotan and the Habomais.[18]

## The Japanese 'Four Islands' claim

As I have already said, where the decision-making system and consequently approaches toward Russia are concerned, there have been no changes since the period of the 1955 system. The Japanese territorial claim was for 'four islands' return, the government's basic policy principles were 'non-separation of politics and economics' (*seikei fukabun*) and 'balanced equilibrium' (*kakudai hinkō*). After Gorbachev's visit, the Japanese attitude toward the Soviet Union appeared to be softening. Since the failure of the coup attempt, the focus of Japanese policy toward the USSR and Russia seemed to be shifting toward cooperation in assisting democratisation and conversion to a market economy. In the light of a series of progressive proposals or ideas regarding the territorial question, the Japanese government appeared to view the problem in the broader context of building a constructive relationship with Russia. To this end, Japan initiated programmes of humanitarian assistance through both public and private channels.

However, at the January 1992 Co-ordinating Conference on Assistance to the New Independent States, where Japan announced its plan to provide about $50 million in food and medical assistance, Foreign Minister Michio Watanabe reminded the international community of the Japanese policy principles for full-scale financial assistance to Russia – 'a shift to a market economy, further progress of democratisation and the conduct of diplomacy on the basis of law and justice'.[19] The last principle indicates the return of the 'Northern Territories.' He also said, 'immediate assistance for the CIS should be limited to humanitarian purposes'. This seems to retreat from the post-August 1991 Japanese position. Fearing a 'blank period' in the territorial negotiations due to political chaos in Russia, the Japanese government advanced its concerns at this time. Thus, while offering some assistance to Russia, based on the understanding that over-all improvement in relations would make an eventual solution of the territorial issue more likely, Japan nevertheless adhered to its principle that the solution of the 'Northern Territories' problem is a prerequisite to full economic assistance.

Incidentally, the Japanese government in 1992 said that it had made 'an important policy shift' with regard to the territorial problem. In an interview in the *Ekonomisuto* (15 September 1992), Director-General of the *Gaimushō*'s Asia and European Department Nagao Hyōdō said,

> When the Foreign Minister Watanabe visited Moscow in May this year, he directly notified President Yeltsin of the important policy shift of the Japanese Government. The policy shift is that, if the Japanese sovereignty over the four islands is recognised, we are ready to be flexible with the time, way and accommodation of the later return. However, it is immutable that even a slight equivocation is not allowed in the point of requesting the four islands return.[20]

This may be compared to the *Nihon Keizai Shimbun* article reporting Prime Minister Tanaka's remark at the 1973 Moscow Summit that I refered to in Chapter 3.[21] However, there was no one, even among Soviet/Russian specialists, who noticed *Gaimushō*'s old negotiation strategy at this time. Thus, without being pointed out, this 'important policy shift' again came to be used as if it had been a new concession by the Japanese Government, after the lapse of 19 years.

Another point to be made on this position of not changing the basic claim to the territories but showing flexibility in other respects providing sovereignty were confirmed, is that it somewhat resembles the position of the Soviet conservatives supporting zero island return among the diversified opinions seen prior to Gorbachev's visit. That is, there were positions proposing no change of sovereignty but offering other options such as joint management or leasing of the islands. However, even not mentioning the newspaper article of 19 years ago, compared to the drastic changes in positions of the Soviet and Russian leaderships, including those of Yeltsin himself, since the Gorbachev period, this 'important shift' by the *Gaimushō* was perceived as 'no change'. Watanabe visited Moscow again from 29 August to 4 September, and it is said that it was his rigid adherence to the 'four islands return' and the *seikei fukabun* policy that caused Yeltsin to cancel his visit.[22]

One of the basic Japanese policy principles, *seikei fukabun*, was abandoned under foreign pressure or *gaiatsu*. At the Tokyo Summit in July 1993, Japan formally promised assistance of $1.82 billion to Russia. A *Gaimushō* senior official explained that this was done to maintain cohesion within the G-7 framework, especially due to pre-summit requests from the USA, France and Germany, but that Japan had no intention of changing *seikei fukabun* in the bilateral framework, nor of shelving the territorial problem.[23] However, the limit of this *seikei fukabun* approach was evident in that the large scale assistance was nevertheless provided without certain progress in the territorial problem.

After twice experiencing a humiliating summit cancellation, Japan's attitude had softened further by the time of Yeltsin's visit. It did not press the Russian side on the question of sovereignty over the four islands, nor for confirmation of the 1956 Joint Declaration. A *Gaimushō* senior official who attended the summit reportedly said, 'it is because we reckoned that the summit could be ruined if we pressed further'. Yeltsin referred to this point in an interview, saying that the Japanese side did not thrust this (territorial) issue (in high-handed manner) as 'yes or no?' or 'islands or visits?' this time.[24]

In hindsight, the changing pattern of the Japanese attitude towards Russia leading up to the 1993 summit turned out to resemble that (towards the USSR) of the 1991 summit: the Japanese adherence to the rigid principle made it difficult to realise the bilateral summit. Then, such attitude later became, or had to be, softened. In addition to its consideration for the counterpart president's delicate domestic situation, Japan was under the apprehension that it was falling behind from the global movement or receiving foreign pressure.

## THE 'NATION-STATE' PERSPECTIVE: RUSSIA

### Yeltsin's visit to Japan

After the collapse of the USSR, Russia inherited 51 per cent of its population (148 million), 76 per cent of its territory and 61 per cent of its GNP, together with continuing political, economic and social problems. In politics, along with the collapse of the USSR, the centripetal force of the Russian government, which was maintained in order to confront Gorbachev's Soviet government, evaporated, and Yeltsin found himself in a similar position to that of Gorbachev. Despite his aspirations, Yeltsin's regime turned out to demonstrate a strong similarity to and continuity with that of the Gorbachev period. In the transitional stage of state-making for a new sovereign Russia, Yeltsin was in the centre of a political power struggle that continued until the last days before his visit to Japan in October 1993.

### *Struggle for control and policy towards Japan: cancellation of the summit*

As mentioned earlier, Yeltsin cancelled his summit visit to Japan twice. The last-minute cancellation of 9 September 1992, four days before he was due to arrive, not only especially offended the Japanese, but also surprised the world. As was later written by members of his *entourage* and the President himself in his memoirs, the major reason was Japanese rigidity on the territorial principle and its linkage with economic policy. However, it is certain that the decision also largely depended on the domestic situation.

Yeltsin's Russia had to face a mounting economic crisis and deepening social problems soon after its inauguration. During 1992 Russian production, fettered by deficiencies inherited from the former Soviet economy, decreased by some 20 per cent, while inflation reached 30 per cent a month, budget deficits increased, and trade with former Soviet republics and with the rest of the world radically declined.[25] Nationalism and depression over social and economic conditions in Russia were soon reflected in strong political opposition to Yeltsin's regime. National policies, both domestic and foreign, thus began to be used as political tools in the new power struggle in Russia.

The Russian government had formed its own Ministry of Foreign Affairs (MID) before the end of the Soviet era. Numbering fewer than 100 staff in November 1991, it expanded to more than 3,000 by absorbing the Soviet MID.[26] While the new Russian MID was established with a strong institutional basis and the confidence of its president, it came under intense attack from other powerful institutions. Such institutional players as the new parliament, opposition political parties and civil movements, and military-industrial establishments, promoted quite different foreign policies.[27] In deepening economic and social unrest, the society and politics as a whole began to show stronger nationalist tendencies. The territorial problem with Japan was not exempt from this trend.

In July 1992, the Supreme Soviet called a closed-door hearing, where the policy towards Japan prepared by the MID was exposed to severe criticism. The hearing turned into a nationalist warning from parliament to Yeltsin not to cede any of the islands to Japan.[28] It was obvious in many respects that Yeltsin viewed Gorbachev with a sense of rivalry. If there had been no movement since Gorbachev's time, it was pointless for Yeltsin to visit Japan; and after the Japanese Foreign Minister Watanabe's visit to Moscow, the Russian leadership sensed that the President's visit, scheduled to take place in few days, might produce even fewer results than had Gorbachev's.

It is safe to assume that the cancellation of the visit was decided by Yeltsin himself, based on his judgement that his political basis would be at risk. His Press Secretary announced on 9 September 1992 that after considering various situations and exchanging opinions with the leaders of his Security Council, the President had decided to postpone his official visit to Japan and the Republic of Korea.[29] The Security Council was established by the President himself and was an advisory body similar to Gorbachev's Presidential Council, so the decision to cancel was Yeltsin's.[30] If Yeltsin had made concessions to Japan, there was a strong possibility that they would not be ratified by the parliament, and he could have been isolated in Russian politics, that were becoming more nationalistic, reflecting the domestic situation.

Soon after the collapse of the USSR, due to such factors as MID personnel allocations, expectation was once heightened for 'progress' in the Russian policy towards Japan, based on the principle of 'law and justice' (*zakonnost' i spravedlivost'*) – the term Yeltsin preferred to use, rather than Gorbachev's *New Thinking*. For example, it was considered significant that in such an important post as Deputy Foreign Minister I. Rogachev, a hardliner who had termed the Japanese claims 'unwarranted', was replaced by G. Kunadze, a Japan expert who had joined the Russian MID from the Institute of World Economy and International Relations of the Soviet Academy of Sciences,[31] and who had argued that Russia should acknowledge the 1956 Japan–Soviet Joint Declaration. However, in the decision to cancel the presidential visit, the influence of MID progressives or intellectuals from the Academy of Sciences, who had been the driving force of Gorbachev's *New Thinking* diplomacy, appeared almost zero.[32]

## Suppression of parliament by force and Yeltsin's visit to Japan

Yeltsin attempted to strengthen presidential power, and made frequent use of Presidential Decrees. The Congress of the Peoples' Deputy and the Russian Supreme Soviet elected by the Congress confronted him, to the extent that a dual power situation was presented in 1993. Yeltsin then decreed suspension of the Supreme Soviet pending elections for a new parliament. Opposition centred on Vice-President Aleksandr Rutskoy and the Parliamentary Speaker Ruslan Khasbulatov, who claimed the decree was unconstitutional, and entrenched themselves with many other parliamentarians in the Supreme Soviet building. The confrontation ended only after the building was shelled by army tanks on 4 October 1993.

As this occurred immediately before the scheduled summit in October 1993, another cancellation was rumoured, but Yeltsin arrived as planned. Several reasons can be considered for this decision to carry out the visit. First, since this incident swept aside his political rivals who might be expected to lead strong opposition to the territorial negotiation, pressure on the summit talks was reduced. Second, it was then a convenient opportunity for Yeltsin himself to show confidence in his strengthened political base after gaining victory by force. Furthermore, another cancellation could worsen already deteriorating relations with Japan.

Other important factors prompting Yeltsin to carry out his visit were that there had been some signs of 'progress' in relations with Japan compared to the previous year (when he cancelled the visit) or Gorbachev period, i.e., over Japanese economic assistance and the issue of the Siberian POWs. Prior to this bilateral summit, Yeltsin had visited Tokyo in July to attend the 'G-7 plus 1' meeting which followed the G-7 Summit meeting. The Tokyo G-7 did not refer to the 'Northern Territories' problem, as had the previous summits, and regardless of Tokyo's intention, the fact was that the Japanese principle of *seikei fukabun* had collapsed in substance. At his joint press conference with Prime Minister Hosokawa on 13 October, Yeltsin himself mentioned that 'Japan has shifted its direction toward separation of economics and politics'.[33] The President's aspiration was also reflected in the political composition of the delegation he brought with him, downgrading the territorial negotiations and laying more stress on economic issues by including Yegor Gaydar, in charge of economic policy, but excluding Kunadze.[34]

As for the Japanese POWs in Siberia, Gorbachev's 'condolence' (*soboleznovanie*) became 'apology' (*izvinenie*) for 'the inhuman treatment to which Japanese prisoners of war were subjected' in the former USSR after the end of the Second World War. This was calculated to make a positive impression in Japan. Yeltsin repeated the apology several times during his stay in Japan: during his audience with the Emperor, in discussions with Prime Minister Hosokawa, and in his statement to heads of Japanese economic organisations.[35]

## The 'Northern Territories' problem

### *Yeltsin's regime and the territorial problem*

For Yeltsin, the territorial problem with Japan has been an important diplomatic agenda item and also an important political tool. Therefore he seems to have studied and familiarised himself well with the problem.[36] However his attitude toward it has not been necessarily consistent. In response to the domestic political situation he has shifted his position several times. During Gorbachev's regime, especially after his feud with Gorbachev intensified, he used it as a political tool to attack Gorbachev's government. He announced a 'five-stage-plan' (see pp. 180–1) for a solution during his visit to Japan in 1990, but then retreated and started to sound more nationalistic. At the time of Gorbachev's visit to Japan, he warned him not to make territorial concessions. Once he had disposed of Gorbachev and the USSR and taken power as national leader, he was then vulnerable to use of the same issue by his opponents as a political tool to shake his political base, just as he had used it against Gorbachev. Therefore, he could not make an incautious decision.

He wrote in his memoirs that the cancellation of the September 1992 visit was due to the territorial problem and the Japanese attitude.

> The piquancy of the situation consisted in that the Japanese had only one variant: the islands had always belonged to them and we must return them. There was no solution to the question. I then said that sincerely to the Japanese and our journalists. I had more than ten variants for solution of the problem. In the subtext this meant that not one is suitable.[37]

Yeltsin said that prior to his scheduled September visit, he had actually 14 variants for the solution of the territorial problem.[38] He said several times that he intended to reveal his decision 'on the second day' of his visit, expecting a shift in the Japanese attitude until the last minute. Depending on the Japanese response to his indication for a 'frontal breakthrough' of the settlement on the first day of the summit, he intended to place one of the 14 options on the negotiating table.[39] In this respect Yeltsin's position presented a contrast to that of Gorbachev in 1991, when he had no choice but to adhere to the Soviet position already set. However, Watanabe's Moscow visit swept such expectations away. Foreign Minister Kozyrev was said to have conveyed the Russian government's readiness to make a settlement on the basis of the 1956 Declaration, but Watanabe's response showed no sign of flexibility. On the contrary, Watanabe was said to have become more rigid in his meeting with Yeltsin, who thus did not venture to discuss the issue any further. At his Security Council they had nevertheless continued to hope for a Japanese response to Kozyrev's offer before the summit visit, but no reply had come from Japan.[40] From Watanabe's visit to Russia, they had received the impression that they could not expect any progress in negotiations while he was Foreign Minister. Sukhanov also revealed that the Russians had considered it might be wiser to negotiate with the next Japanese Foreign Minister, as they had received information that Watanabe would possibly leave the post by the end of 1992.[41]

### The Tokyo Declaration

'Russian politics is politics of the President', a senior MID official stated concisely in his interview with me in July 1994. As seen in the abrupt cancellation of the summit and forcible suppression of the parliament, Yeltsin's politics are one-man rule, somewhat resembling Khrushchev's. However, it is hard to imagine that there was such government consensus as in Khrushchev's time prior to the Tokyo summit of October 1993. Before Yeltsin's visit to Tokyo the Russian leadership indicated disunity. In the summer of 1993 Prime Minister Chernomyrdin repeatedly stated that Moscow would not negotiate on the 'Northern Territories' issue, which in his view was already resolved and therefore did not exist.[42] Deputy Economics Minister Valentin Fedorov (former Governor of Sakhalin *oblast*, which includes the disputed islands) said Chernomyrdin's statements showed he 'correctly understands that the Kurile Islands are ours'. He also said that most Russian cabinet ministers opposed returning the islands.[43] Other members of Yeltsin's *entourage* disagreed. During a visit to Tokyo, Gennadii Burbulis, head of the Strategy Centre and Adviser to the President, said that the disputed islands must be and inevitably would be returned to Japan sooner or later, and that the problem should not be left to later generations.[44] As for Chernomyrdin's statement, Yeltsin said that it was merely one of many options being considered for the President's trip to Japan.[45] Perhaps Burbulis' statement was also one of the options.

There is no specific mention of '1956' in the Tokyo Declaration of 1993. However, Yeltsin acknowledged that the phrase 'all treaties and other international agreements' in the declaration included the 1956 Joint Declaration, though he did so only orally at his joint press conference with Prime Minister Hosokawa.[46] This may be interpreted as a demonstration of his confidence in his strengthened political base after gaining victory by force over the parliament. However, it did not necessarily mean the complete disappearance of domestic opposition forces. Opposition discontent was perhaps demonstrated soon after his visit by the dumping of radioactive waste in the Sea of Japan. This practice of dumping had been revealed before the summit and in the discussions Japan had requested its immediate suspension and joint investigation of the sea area.[47] *Izvestiya* commented on 27 October that the dumping of radioactive waste in the Sea of Japan 'was an intentional, premeditated and thoroughly prepared action aimed at undermining the positive results of Boris Yeltsin's negotiations in Tokyo'. This version is said to have been supported by top-ranking officials who had prepared the president's visit. The dumping date had been postponed three times until the 'astonishingly perfect timing was achieved'.[48] The political strife did not seem to have ended for the President yet.

## THE 'BILATERAL-INTERACTION' PERSPECTIVE

If ideology was the reason for the long freeze in Soviet–Japanese relations during the Cold War, those relations should have improved when it ended, but they did not. As pointed out earlier, in various respects Russo-Japanese relations leading up to Yeltsin's visit to Japan in October 1993 presented strong continuities from, and similarities to, Soviet–Japanese relations leading up to Gorbachev's 1991 visit. The major negotiations were held equally through the official channel, i.e., both Foreign Ministries. The Soviet MID was absorbed into the Russian MID, the Soviet–Japanese Regular Foreign Ministerial Talks were succeeded by the Russo-Japanese Regular Foreign Ministerial Talks. As the Russian government had begun to participate in Soviet policy making since the concluding years of Gorbachev's era, similar staff members were still in charge of policies toward Japan. Though the name was changed, interactions between the two countries appeared to present similar pattern to those preceding Gorbachev's visit.

## *Japanese goals and Soviet goals*

The goals of both countries remained unchanged, namely political *rapprochement* by peace treaty. The other priority goals they sought from their counterparts were: for Russia, development in economic relations, especially financial assistance and economic cooperation from Japan; and for Japan, development in political negotiations, specifically achieving the long-term goal of the 'Northern Territories'. However, just as for Gorbachev, in not being able to realise these goals so easily, Yeltsin's visit itself became more like the objective. The priority of diplomacy had become the improvement of bilateral relations that kept deteriorating because of the series of cancellations of Yeltsin's visit.

## *Bargaining cards and negotiating strategies*

Continuity was clearly seen in the repetition of the basic interaction pattern between the two nations: the Japanese mixed approach of *kakudai kinkō* (balanced equilibrium) and *seikei fukabun* (no separation of economics and politics) with the territorial goal of the 'four islands' return; and the Russian position of not changing the basic territorial claim but showing 'flexibility' in other respects, providing sovereignty were confirmed was also found to be the same since the 1970s. Also, with respect to improvement of mutual perceptions and confidence between those in charge in both foreign ministries, the tendency perceived up to Gorbachev's visit to Japan, was certainly continuing or developing.

With regard to the expression of dissatisfaction, I have already pointed out, in Chapter 2 (on the 1956 summit), that 'the Soviets sometimes went beyond words, and expressed their discontent by actual and unilateral actions against Japan', raising examples of the 1956 unilateral restriction of fishing rights, the Soviets' 1960 *Aide-Mémoire*, and post-1978 military deployments in the disputed islands. Yeltsin's abrupt and unilateral cancellation of the visit was quite a psychological blow to the Japanese. Though there is no evidence to show whether he calculated that far, it is certain that this cancellation of the visit played the role of a strategic card. For the Japanese, in order to avoid the same slip and bring about a visit, took a less adamant attitude than in the past. At the Russo-Japanese Foreign Ministerial talks in New York on 5 September 1993, final discussions were held over whether or not to refer to the 1956 Joint Declaration in the statement to be released at the time of the president's visit. It has been said that it was the Japanese side which proposed to omit reference to it.[49] The cancellation of the visit indeed negatively affected bilateral relations, by worsening mutual perceptions. Furthermore, the fact that Yeltsin, after in September 1992 cancelling his visit to South Korea along with that to Japan, visited South Korea only two months later, further offended the Japanese. However, considering that many in Russia supported Yeltsin's cancellation and that the Japanese attitude eventually softened, the cancellation actually brought effects in terms of both domestic and bilateral politics.

In addition, the Japanese *seikei fukabun* policy, which was not favoured by the Russians, collapsed after the cancellation of the visit. This became clear with the large-scale economic assistance Japan agreed to provide in the G-7 arena. In retrospect it was Japan that made the territorial problem a global issue at the G-7 summit, and this G-7 card ironically came back to Japan in the form of *gaiatsu* (foreign pressure) that it should not make the bilateral issue of return of the islands a condition for assisting Russian stability, which is of global concern.

In terms of development away from the past approach, there was an issue of the treatment of Japanese POWs detained in Siberia. The shift of expressions from Gorbachev's 'condolence' to Yeltsin's 'apology' was seen as a major success and an important gesture of goodwill during the summit visit, especially because Japanese expectations of what the visit could achieve were very low.[50] The Japanese government did not in fact request compensation for the POWs. Thus, considering Japan's contribution of $1.82 billion that Yeltsin received two months later, also in Tokyo, at the G-7 summit, this was quite an advantageous development or 'advance' for the Russian side.

With respect to the improved perceptions and confidence between those who are in charge in both foreign ministries, in his volume published in 1993, Tōgō wrote,

> Seeing in retrospect the process of negotiations with the USSR and Russia that I have experienced, the first thing I feel is that mutual trust seems to have been remarkably strengthened in the relations of those who are directly in charge of the negotiations ... considering the

distrust of the Soviets we had for a long time in the past – it nevertheless seems to be an amazing change. [51]

A visible development came in a form of a specific product in the new Russo-Japanese era. That is the joint editorial project of historical materials regarding the territorial problem between both foreign ministries and the publication of the *Joint Compendium of Documents on the History of the Territorial Demarcation Between Russia and Japan* (September 1993). Publication of this Compendium was in fact proposed in 1991 by the Soviet MID during Gorbachev's era.[52] It was the initial attempt by officials of the two countries, whose territorial positions had always been contrary to each other in the past, to find common ground in their search for a mutually acceptable solution. The product of this unprecedented movement came out in visible form after the Russo-Japanese era began.

The Tokyo Declaration, the outcome of the Summit visit, differed little in content on the territorial issue from the 1991 Joint Statement. However, a significant difference or 'advance' was that a common interpretation was given. That is, Yeltsin gave verbal confirmation of the 1956 Declaration, which Gorbachev could not. Considering the factors and circumstances, it may have been natural that the Russo-Japanese relations leading up to a 1993 bilateral summit demonstrated strong continuities from the Soviet–Japanese relations leading up to the 1991 summit. However, a notable difference was added not by administrative staff nor oppositionists, but by President Yeltsin himself.

# Conclusion

Before a peace treaty could be signed to start a 'post-war' period after the Second World War, Japanese–Soviet relations became involved in the newly started 'Cold War'. The territorial dispute, or 'Northern Territories' problem, between Japan and the USSR (Russia) evolved as a by-product of the Cold War, both internationally and domestically. Even though the 'end of the Cold War' has been proclaimed, the Soviet Union has collapsed, and the LDP-dominant domestic Cold War system of Japan, the so-called '1955 system', has collapsed, this territorial problem still exists. Even after the end of the Soviet–Japanese era and the beginning of a new Russo-Japanese era, there is still no peace treaty between the two countries. During the last half-century opportunities for *rapprochement* arose, and bilateral summits took place in Moscow and Tokyo in the 1950s, 1970s and 1990s. In this study I have examined the bilateral relations, paying particular attention to the foreign-policy decision making of and between Japan and the USSR/ Russia on the occasions of the bilateral summits. I have done this by setting out the major dependent variables or issue areas – the political *rapprochement* and territorial problem – and by using the three levels of analytical framework: 'global', 'nation state' and 'bilateral interaction'. I now conclude with a summary and, with some addition of recent developments, some considerations for the future.

## The 'global international relations' perspective

The results of analysis at this level are summarised in Table 1.

Viewing Soviet–Japanese *rapprochement* opportunities from a global international relations perspective, there was always a background possibility for relaxation of the basic East–West confrontation, variously called the 'Cold War thaw', '*détente*', 'closing days of the Cold War' or 'end of the Cold War'. Also in each period there were different factors, based on regional situations or changes in their international status, that created reasons for

*Table 1* Comparison of the structure of confrontations and relaxation of tensions at the time of the Soviet (Russo)-Japanese bilateral summits

| Period / bilateral summit | Euro-Atlantic region | Asia-Pacific region |
|---|---|---|
| mid-1950s | East–West *détente* | East–West *détente* |
| Hatoyama–Khrushchev Moscow Summit (1956) | Yalta System (set in 1945) | San Francisco System (set in 1951) |
| early 1970s | East–West *détente* | East–West *détente* (Sino-Soviet conflict) |
| Tanaka–Brezhnev Moscow Summit (1973) | Yalta System (status quo legitimised) | San Francisco System |
| late 1980s– | East–West *détente* (closing days of the Cold War) ↓ | 1970s' Euro-Atlantic type *détente*? |
| Kaifu–Gorbachev Tokyo Summit (1991) Hosokawa–Yeltsin Tokyo Summit (1993) | End of the Cold War Collapse of Yalta System | San Francisco System (*status quo* partially legitimised) |

Japan and the USSR (Russia) to seek political *rapprochement*. Specifically, they were: in the 1950s UN membership and the independence movement in Asia and Africa symbolised by the Bandung spirit; in the 1970s the Sino-Soviet dispute continuing since the 1960s, resource nationalism, and also the advent of Japan as an economic power. Also, when Japan tried to re-identify its own international position during the so-called transitional periods, there were certainly movements to seek multi-directional diplomacy, or diplomacy independent of the USA. They were associated with the above-mentioned factors, and additionally with the 'Nixon Shock' of the 1970s, the US–Japan trade friction of the 1980s and also the so-called 'end of the Cold War'.

Though chances have arisen, complete *rapprochement* by signing a peace treaty has never been achieved. The biggest impediment has been the 'Northern Territories' problem. The correctness of the view that the 'Northern Territories' problem is a by-product of the Cold War seems to be verified also by those chances or expectations for its solution, that arose in parallel with the relaxation of Cold War tensions. Attempting to exploit the East–West confrontation, Japan appealed to the West, specifically the drafter-states and/or concerned states of the San Francisco Peace Treaty, during the 1955–6 Soviet–Japanese negotiations. However, the interwoven interests of those states in the Asia-Pacific region prevented their reviewing the peace treaty. Definite US support for the Japanese 'four islands' claim began during this period, but, far from aiming at resolving the 'Northern Territories' problem, it aimed to perpetuate it as an impediment to Soviet–Japanese *rapprochement*. Since then, the concerned states have almost withdrawn from direct involvement in the issue. In contrast, in the Euro-Atlantic region during the 1970s *détente*, they moved for recognition of the post-war status quo of the Yalta System, a major Soviet objective. Even in the series of 'end of the Cold War' movements since the late 1980s, neither has the territorial problem been resolved, nor political *rapprochement* achieved, between the USSR/Russia and Japan. The conclusion drawn from the international relations context is that, unlike in the Euro-Atlantic region, where the Yalta System has collapsed, the Cold War has clearly not ended in the Asia-Pacific region, and the regional Cold War structure of the 'San Francisco System' remains there to this day. The Russo-Japanese territorial dispute is after all nothing but 'one of them', i.e., one of the Cold War by-products remaining in the region. The relaxation of international tensions since the end of the 1980s has begun to resemble the 1970s Euro-Atlantic *détente* rather than the 'end of the Cold War', in the sense that it was promoted while recognising the *status quo* of the remaining Cold War structure.

## The 'nation-state' perspective: Japan

In Japan, concrete moves for political *rapprochement* with the USSR/Russia were promoted by different factors, period by period, such as pressing issues immediately post-war, economic motives, changes in political leadership, and the leadership's apprehension of falling behind global movements. As Japan's international status has changed from a defeated country to an economic power, the motives for political *rapprochement* or improving relations with its counterpart have tended to shift from direct and immediate to global but indirect factors. However, there has been little change in the factors inhibiting signature of a peace treaty, especially since the restoration of diplomatic relations. They are the territorial problem, the Japanese government's unchanging attitude towards it, and the policy decision-making system towards the USSR/Russia that has supported the unchanging government attitude, the *Gaimushō*-dominant system.

Japanese policy decision making during the 1955–6 negotiations (Chapter 2) and on the other summit occasions (Chapters 3 to 5) covers a range from pluralistic to monolithic. Decision making in the former case involved various factions with complex interactions, as Japan was then undergoing fundamental changes in its political system. The 'Northern Territories' policy then became a political bargaining tool between the two conservative parties, Liberals and Democrats, which merged into a large ruling party (the LDP), to oppose the then strengthening socialist parties. The present 'four islands claim' was founded largely as a by-product of the establishment of the Cold War system in domestic politics, i.e., the 1955 system. Since then, the 'four islands claim' has become solidified, and there have been no changes in it. Japanese policy decision making and approaches toward the USSR (Russia), seen in association with the bilateral summits of 1973, 1991 and 1993, are essentially monolithic and thorough, and still show a strong tendency to continuity, in other words absolute dominance by the administrative body, the *Gaimushō*. Japanese policy decision making towards the USSR leading up to the restoration of diplomatic relations (1956) was summarised in Chapter 2 in terms of the three groups – business (*zai*), politics (*sei*) and bureaucracy (*kan*) – generally considered the major participants in Japanese political decision making. Policy decision making towards the USSR/Russia after the restoration of diplomatic relations as described in Chapters 3–5, can be summarised under the same headings.

## *Business* (zai)

The *zaikai*, or business community, was the major promoter of improved Soviet–Japanese relations in the 1970s. However, the international circumstances of the time had weakened the voices within the *zaikai* calling for further development in economic cooperation, specifically Siberian development, by the time of the 1991 and 1993 summits. Japan had overcome the oil crisis by structural alteration of its economy, and with deepening political and economic unrest in the USSR/Russia, the *zaikai* was less positive about investing or promoting economic cooperation there. However, even when the *zaikai* was most enthusiastic, it still saw government endorsement and ultimately a peace treaty as preconditions for undertaking any large projects with the Russians; and, as in the mid-1950s, *zaikai* influence on policy making towards the USSR/Russia has generally been minimal, especially in the specific political issue area of the territories.

## *Politics* (sei)

Post-war Japanese party politics of dominance by the LDP, founded by the 1955 merger of the conservative parties, lasted until just before Yeltsin's visit to Japan in 1993. This 1955 system continued to provide an environmental or structural foundation for the Japanese 'four islands' territorial demand system, quite naturally, considering that the 1955 system itself was a reflection of the Cold War in domestic politics, and the 'Northern Territories' problem a by-product of the Cold War. But even since the collapse of the 1955 system no change has been seen in this claim, which has been advocated consistently for over 40 years, and the LDP has maintained a strong influence on policy making, first as the biggest opposition party, and later as a member of a ruling coalition.

## Bureaucracy (kan)

Regardless of the strength of the general political leadership, the initiative in specific policy making towards the USSR/Russia since restoration of diplomatic relations has consistently been taken by the *Gaimushō*. Once the 'four islands' goal had been set by political decision, the initiative in policy making was dominated by the administrative body. During the Cold War period and under the 1955 system, there was no change in this basic structure of monolithic policy decision making.

Relations between Russia and Japan are still basically those of the Cold War, not only in the global context of the Asia-Pacific region, but also at the nation-state level. Though the Cold War system of party politics has collapsed, the policy making system towards Russia remains unchanged.

In hindsight, though the main players were politicians, not bureaucrats, decision making towards the USSR during the 1955–6 negotiations showed similar features to the pattern called the Government Politics Model, Bureaucratic Politics Model, or Allison's Third Model, in that the actual policy outcome was the product, not of intellectual process nor of routine organisational procedures, but of intra-governmental bargaining, or pulling and pushing among individual players in charge of the policy decisions. The players were not necessarily guided by a consistent strategic master plan, but rather by conflicting conceptions of national and personal goals.[1] The basis of the territories policy was largely established by this process. In contrast, the policy decision pattern of the later summit occasions can be explained by the Organisation Model, Allison's Second Model, in which government policies are seen more as resulting from a routine or quasi-mechanical process based on the standard operating procedure (SOP) of large government organisations, in this case the *Gaimushō*. Top leaders tended to lack independent control of policy.[2] Since policy is made on the basis of existing SOP, it inevitably attaches importance to precedents, and tends to fall into incrementalism as a decisional pattern. That is, the decision on point 't + 1' can be anticipated by seeing what kind of decision was made on point 't'.[3] The SOP here is the principle of the territorial negotiations. The foundation of the SOP was laid during the 1955–6 negotiations. The territorial claim for 'four islands' return, the basis for which was formed in 1955, had solidified by the early 1960s, and incrementalism added the economic card in the 1970s. The Japanese negotiating strategies seen in the lead-ups to the 1973, 1991 and 1993 summits thus resembled each other.

In the series of changes in global circumstances since the late 1980s, the Japanese approach has hit the deadlock of incrementalism, presenting typical 'irrational' bargainers, as described in the revised Rational Actor Model of Glenn H. Snyder and Paul Diesing.

> The irrational bargainer is characterized by a rigid belief system that dominates his behavior. He knows from the onset of a crisis what the opponent is up to because he has studied the opponent thoroughly and understands his ultimate aims, bargaining style, preferences, and internal political problems. He also is a keen judge of men on his side, knowing whose opinions to value and whose opinions to ignore or bypass. . . . Knowing the opponent as he does, he is not going to be duped by the opponent's tricks or deceptive statements, nor is he going to lose heart at temporary setbacks, alarms, and rumors, but continues firmly on his chosen strategy through all diversions and difficulties.[4]

Japan was left behind by the global movement, by persisting in the territorial demand and *seikei fukabun* (non-separation of politics and economics) policy at the G-7 summits of the 1990s. In the end, *seikei fukabun* virtually collapsed in the G-7 arena under *gaiatsu* (foreign pressure).

## The 'nation-state' perspective: USSR/Russia

Movement towards Soviet–Japanese *rapprochement* was always initiated by a Soviet overture, with the specific approach changed on the basis of lessons Soviet leaders had learned from their predecessors' experiences. In the 1950s, Khrushchev called Stalin's failure to sign the San Francisco Peace Treaty 'a blunder', and attempted to found a basis for future policy – intended eventually to weaken US–Japan relations and expand Soviet influence – by reopening diplomatic relations with Japan. In the 1970s, in addition to its antagonism against China, the Soviet overture to Japan was supported more by economic rationalism, specifically in regard to Siberian development projects. In approaches since the late 1980s leading up to Gorbachev's and Yeltsin's Tokyo visits. ideological colour faded and disappeared, while more realistic and pragmatic motives became conspicuous, for example, seeking economic cooperation and/or financial assistance to promote their domestic reforms.

Except for its last years, post-war Soviet policy towards Japan seemed to be created by derivation from global strategies devised by the party leadership. Panov observed that the leadership had no vision regarding the concept of policy toward Japan.[5] Though there were Japan-related sections in government organisations such as MID and KGB, their roles were mostly limited to policy-output, implementing decisions coming from above, rather than making policy-input from below. As a result of Gorbachev's reforms in the late 1980s, input from below began to be taken into consideration by the top decision makers. On the one hand, as freedom of speech began to be allowed, the views of intellectuals were reflected in the policies, the territorial dispute with Japan was introduced into consideration, and various options formulated for concepts of policies toward Japan. On the other hand, the leading role of the Communist Party decreased, the political battle intensified and Soviet decision making became more pluralistic and complex. While Khrushchev decided by himself, and Brezhnev decided by himself not to decide, Gorbachev could not decide by himself. The political bases of the Soviet leaderships were stable, and policy decision making quite monolithic at the summits of the 1950s and 1970s. However, in contrast to Japanese political decision making, which was pluralistic during the 1955–6 negotiations but monolithic thereafter, the USSR's relatively monolithic decision making became pluralistic toward its end, and the trend, which continued in post-Soviet Russia, was reflected in changes of Soviet and Russian attitudes toward the territorial issue.

Soviet official positions of the 1950s and 1970s maintained that no territorial problems existed with Japan. In the 1956 Joint Declaration, they agreed to 'transfer', or 'sacrifice' the two smaller territories, 'desiring to meet the wishes of Japan and taking into consideration the interest of the Japanese State'. In the approach of the 1970s, though they unofficially again offered the two islands, the official position was still 'no territorial problem'. In Gorbachev's time *Glasnost* diversified the Soviets' opinions, Soviet visas were issued to the Japanese 'for the purpose of the territorial negotiation', and the issue for the first time began to 'exist' officially. However, it should be noted that the solid argument that led to official Soviet acknowledgment of the problem was that the territorial problem had begun to 'exist' since 1960, as the 1956 agreement for the 'two island' transfer was unilaterally conditioned by the Soviet *Aide-Mémoire*, and breached thereafter. Therefore, it was acknowledged not as a 'problem unresolved since World War II', but rather as a problem 'newly emerged in the post-war era'. Nevertheless, the Japanese claim and arguments were also introduced to the Soviets, and opinions became diversified after all. At the 1991 and 1993 summits, the names of the four islands were specified and officially admitted to be disputed territories. Yeltsin confirmed the validity of the 1956 Declaration, which Gorbachev had been unable to do. As if in reverse of the Japanese path from an unfixed position to one consistently claimed after the restoration of diplomatic relations, the Soviet/Russian position shifted from an initial 'no' to the 'yes' of Yeltsin's 14 variants.

The history of the bilateral summits suggests that the more stable the political leadership, the more flexible was Soviet/Russian policy on the territorial issue. Khrushchev and Brezhnev were most flexible when confident of their power at home, and when the domestic political landscape was relatively stable. But the positions of Gorbachev and Yeltsin were less stable. The territorial problem was a convenient tool for political battle, and public opinion began to affect the leaders' flexibility. On an officially non-existent problem, Khrushchev and Brezhnev could be flexible, but on an officially acknowledged one Gorbachev could not, and Yeltsin's flexibility was limited. *Glasnost* was a positive factor in opening up the issue and promoting discussion, but a negative factor in restricting the leaders' control.

In making policy decisions, the role and powers of the MID, the Soviet/Russian administrative body, have been limited, compared to those of its Japanese counterpart, the *Gaimushō*. Soviet and Russian decision making seems rather dependent on the basis of the political leadership, and decision making in Khrushchev's and Brezhnev's Soviet Union appeared to conform to the 'classical' Rational Actor Model – Allison's First Model. With regard either to political *rapprochement* or resolution of the territorial issue with Japan, their policies appeared more or less purposive acts of unified governments, based on logical means of achieving given objectives or 'national interests'.[6] The early Gorbachev regime's decision to make an overture for *rapprochement* to Japan was also justifiable in terms of the Rational Actor Model of calculation of the national interest. However, by the time of Gorbachev's visit in 1991, the regime's foundations had been heavily shaken and decision making had become pluralistic. Despite differences of degree, Yeltsin's regime presented the same tendency. As I indicated earlier, this showed some similarity to Japanese decision making towards the USSR during the 1955–6 negotiations, i.e., conforming to the Government Politics Model, and the similarity appears even greater because of the increased transparency imparted to the domestic political arena with the development of media independence and greater freedom of information, compared to the strictly controlled earlier periods. In this sense, it may be called decision making of the time of democracy.

## The 'bilateral interaction' perspective

With regard to documentation jointly released at the summits, the Soviet and Japanese governments interpreted references to the territorial problem differently. In the 1956 Joint Declaration, the Soviet Union interpreted the issue as closed with agreement to transfer two islands, while the Japanese claimed that a peace treaty could not be concluded because the issue of the other islands was not resolved. In 1973, interpretations differed over whether or not the 'unresolved problems' included the territorial problem.

In 1991 they differed on whether or not the 1956 Declaration was reconfirmed. Interpretations agreed for the first time at the 1993 summit, where both sides confirmed that the 1956 Declaration was included in the expression 'all treaties and other international agreements between Japan and the Soviet Union continue to be applied between Japan and the Russian Federation'. Thus, as far as the territorial problem is concerned, the 1993 Tokyo Declaration went back to the 1956 Joint Declaration. However, the biggest difference from 1956 was that in 1993 the other two islands, Kunashiri and Etorofu, were brought onto the formal negotiating table. Examination of the Japanese positions up to the early 1950s in Chapter 1 suggested that to extract even the two smaller territories would have been regarded as a success story. However, the four islands, that Japan consistently demanded against the background of the Cold War, were officially placed on the negotiating table only in the Cold War's closing days.

Review of the path of this issue during the last half century, including the origin of the dispute and the changes in positions, seems to delineate the predominant trend of the Japanese side as far as the territorial negotiations are concerned. This may possibly be explained in the context of Cold War winners and losers, as the territorial problem was a by-product of the Cold War. Another explanation may be that Japan, by retaining a comprehensive and consistent view of the USSR, succeeded in changing the position of the USSR, which did not have a comprehensive and consistent view of Japan. In other words, the thorough Japanese approach, guided by the SOP of a bureaucracy-led decision-making system prevailed over a Soviet approach which depended on the leaders' political bases, not on the techniques of those in charge of the administration.

Throughout the whole negotiations, what underlay the *Gaimushō*'s strategy, vision or SOP, may be the view that bargaining cards should be retained until the goals are achieved. In the 1955–6 negotiations, once diplomatic relations were restored, Japan would have no cards left to use to extract further concessions. In this respect, the negotiations between the war-winner (the USSR) and war-loser (Japan), ended with victory for Japan which, as a war-loser with hardly any tangible cards, achieved most of its original objectives in respect of the Japanese POWs, UN membership, and so on, by making tactical use of territorial claims and continuation of the negotiations. The USSR, on the other hand, used up its cards at an early stage of the negotiations, and though diplomatic relations were restored, was unable to achieve its original priority goal, conclusion of a peace treaty. So, by not signing a peace treaty, but having peace negotiations continue, Japan, in the *Gaimusho*'s strategic thinking, managed to retain its bargaining positions for regaining all the territories rather than just the promised Habomais and Shikotan. For the 1973 Summit, *Gaimushō* Soviet section head Koichi Arai advised Prime Minister Tanaka, 'when the Soviet Union tosses in various proposals for economic cooperation, we should not at once throw in the card of our intention to cooperate. If we throw the card in, they would only take the card, and shelve the territorial problem'.[7]

During the 1955–6 negotiations, based on the international situation and Japan's position in it, the signing of a peace treaty could be a bargaining card. However, the nature of the card did not remain unchanged. By the time of the 1991 and 1993 summits the lack of a peace treaty, instead of being a bargaining card, rather left Japan lagging behind the new global movement to end the Cold War. While it was true that Japan retained its bargaining card by not signing a treaty in 1956, it also seems true that it lost chances for later development in various areas, including for solving the 'Northern Territories' problem.

The thinking that one party's goal becomes the other's bargaining card was very effective during the so-called Cold War era. Japan could also expect an expanded effect by internationalisation. However, once the two-party confrontational system collapsed with the 'end of the Cold War', and under the new international circumstances where the interests of many nations are becoming more pluralistically interwoven, the conventional approach of the simple 't + 1' type equation seems no longer effective. A good example was seen in that the *seikei fukabun* policy could no longer be used in the G-7 framework. This illustrated a typical weakness of the Organisation Model-type decision-making approach.

## Recent developments

Since the 1993 Yeltsin–Hosokawa Summit in Tokyo there have been important developments in Japanese–Russian relations. These new key indicators must be mentioned before considering the future of the bilateral relationship.

The first is that while the political turmoil of transition continues in Japanese domestic politics, the LDP has revived as a ruling party, though, as indicated earlier, only as a member of a ruling coalition. After the Hosokawa cabinet, another non-LDP coalition cabinet was established, with Tsutomu Hata of the New Frontier Party, which had split from the LDP, as Prime Minister. But this cabinet collapsed after only two months. The LDP then came back into the mainstream of politics, forming a coalition government with *Sakigake*, another new party that had split from the LDP, and the Social-Democratic Party, which had been the LDP's biggest political rival during the 1955-system era. Tomiichi Murayama of the SDP was Prime Minister from June 1994 to January 1996, after which he was succeeded by the LDP president, Ryūtarō Hashimoto. In September 1997

Hashimoto was re-elected as LDP president, for a term expected to end in 1999.

In Russia, while Yeltsin's health problem remains a major source of political uncertainty, he has managed to maintain his regime. He has, however, announced his intention not to stand for re-election, so Russia is expected to have a new president in the year 2000.

The most important development in bilateral relations is that a deadline has been set and dialogue has accelerated toward the normalisation of relations. In addition to diplomatic dialogue, including talks at foreign-minister level, an unprecedented development has been observed in confidence-building measures, including visits to each country by the other's head of defence.[8] The movement toward *rapprochement* accelerated further in 1997, with rapid progress in top-level political dialogue.

At the G-8 Summit meeting (Russia having now officially joined the G-7) in Denver in June 1997, Yeltsin and Hashimoto agreed to open a hot-line, and to hold annual meetings. In his July 24 speech to a meeting of *Keizai dōyūkai*, the Japanese Association of Corporate Executives, Hashimoto announced a 'new diplomatic policy guideline toward Russia', enunciated a set of principles of 'mutual trust', 'mutual interest' and 'long-term perspective', and also declared his intention to aim for a breakthrough by the end of this century.[9] Furthermore, the two leaders held a 'no-necktie' bilateral summit in Krasnoyarsk in November. As it was classified 'unofficial', this summit differed in nature from the other official summits dealt with in the earlier chapters. Nevertheless, it provided an opportunity for highest-level dialogue between the two countries, and became a significant step for the future. Both leaders displayed a clear inclination toward *rapprochement*. Japan pledged to back Russia's application for membership in APEC, and Russia expressed its support for Japan's quest for a permanent seat on the UN Security Council. A wide-ranging economic cooperation programme, the 'Hashimoto–Yeltsin Plan', was also announced. The most remarkable outcome, however, was that both leaders agreed to make the utmost effort to conclude a peace treaty by 2000 based on the 1993 Tokyo Declaration.[10] On 13 December 1997 the *Gaimushō* further displayed its seriousness by announcing the opening of a local office in Yuzhnosakhalinsk from 1 January 1998.[11] This virtually constitutes Japanese recognition of Russia's sovereignty over southern Sakhalin, also seized by the USSR in 1945, reversing a long-standing position that sovereignty over it is undecided in terms of international law. Another 'no-neckties' summit is scheduled to take place when Yeltsin visits Japan in the spring of 1998.

What of the future of Russo-Japanese relations? Will a peace treaty be signed by 2000, as agreed in Krasnoyarsk? Will the territorial problem be solved? Let us now consider the possible future of the bilateral relationship.

# The future: for the settlement of the Cold War

Some futurologists argue that 'the future' has three components: (a) continuation of past and present, (b) cycles, or cyclical phenomena, and (c) emerging issues.[12] The future of Russo-Japanese relations will be discussed in terms of these three components.

## *Continuation of past and present*

This viewpoint suggests that there are some trends, continuing from the past to the present, that lead to the future. It provides the most plausible scenario for the short-term perspective, i.e., the present trend will continue. Taking account of the series of recent new developments, including the 'unofficial' 1997 Yeltsin–Hashimoto summit, the first scenario would be that this accelerated dialogue for normalising relations will continue in the near future. There have been more high-level interactions leading to the 'no-neckties' summit in Japan in the spring of 1998 and the next summit in late 1998 or 1999 in Russia, which is very likely to become an 'official' summit. After working on the 'trust' and 'mutual understanding' aspects, in accordance with the 'new diplomatic policy guideline' introduced by Hashimoto himself, a settlement with a 'long-term perspective' should be sought by the two leaders. Then what specific settlement will be possible? At a press conference on 14 November 1997, the *Gaimushō* Press Secretary said

> Now both countries have decided to widen and deepen our relationship. So under a new atmosphere, by strengthening our friendly relations, we would like to solve this difficult outstanding issue related to the signing of the peace treaty ... we should try to face the important issue, tackle the issue and solve it, rather than leave this issue unsolved for our next generation.[13]

Though it is clear that they are determined to solve this important issue, it is unclear how they will do so. Prospects for the future are considered here in terms of four possible scenarios: (1) a peace treaty with a 'four islands' settlement; (2) a peace treaty with a 'two islands' settlement; (3) a peace treaty 'shelving' the territorial dispute, i.e., a 'no islands' settlement; and (4) neither peace treaty nor territorial settlement.

The 'four islands return' scenario is the one most favoured by Japan, which has been consistent in claiming it for more than 40 years. However, stating from the conclusion first, this is an extremely difficult or rather impossible scenario. The Soviet Union was the source of both the 'Cold

War' and the 'end of the Cold War'. Since the 'Northern Territories' problem is a by-product of the Cold War, the Soviet Union's collapse provides a long-term possibility of resolving it. In various senses, such as ideology, social and economic systems, Russia has begun to step into the post-Cold War era. However, in this period of flux and instability, negative factors have also been emerging for settlement of the territorial dispute and for a peace treaty with Japan.

The final settlement will require political decisions. That is why they hold summits. In the Soviet–Japanese negotiations in the 1950s, with his leadership secure and public opinion controllable from the top, it was not necessarily impossible for Khrushchev to make the 'four island' concession, in exchange for a large concession, for example one bringing Japan close to the Communist bloc. Since the final years of the USSR, the largest concession Russia has wanted is economic assistance. Gorbachev would have had fewer domestic problems if he had achieved a settlement in 1986 or 1987, before democratisation and *Glasnost* began to take hold, putting an end to the circumstances in which the number of islands to be ceded could be decided by a small group of leaders. That lost opportunity probably doomed the 'four islands' scenario. Yeltsin acknowledged the 1956 Declaration, and agreed to having the four islands named in the Tokyo Declaration. But his action was an acknowledgment not of Japan's sovereignty over them, merely of the fact that Japan had long laid claim to them.

Then what about a referendum? The Northern Mariana Islands, which were among the Pacific islands whose sovereignty Japan renounced in the San Francisco Treaty, acceded to the USA by referendum. For residents of the disputed islands, who have become familiar with the situation in Japan through no-visa exchanges or the media, it might be a reasonable option to be joined to an economic giant such as Japan, or to receive a generous Japanese resettlement grant with which to emigrate to the Russian mainland. But the experience of Chechnya suggests that Moscow would not permit the residents alone to make a decision on the islands' future.

If the 'four islands transfer' is impossible, the next conceivable scenarios for signing a peace treaty by the year 2000 are either (2) the 'two islands transfer' or (3) 'shelving' the territorial dispute. If they aim at a settlement based on the 1993 Tokyo declaration as agreed in Krasnoyarsk, i.e., adhering to the principles of 'law and justice' and the '1956 Declaration', (2) would be the most valid settlement. This 'two islands transfer' scenario seems to depend more on Japan than on Russia. That the 'four islands return is a national wish' is a product of government indoctrination from the Cold War era. Should the 'end of the Cold War' be brought into the bilateral relations, it would be impossible to avoid reviewing Cold War thinking and its SOP. As structural alterations away from the Cold War (1955) system have been taking place in Japan's domestic political environment, some signs of such reviewing have already been observed.

The so-called 'end of the Cold War', or the arrival of the post-war half century, have provided Japan with opportunities to review its past history and diplomacy. Prime Minister Hosokawa expressed his 'condolences' (*aito no i*) at the National Memorial Ceremony for War Victims on 15 August 1993. At the same ceremony two years later, the 50th anniversary of the war's end, this became an 'apology' (*shazai*) by Prime Minister Murayama. A similar tendency was observed in the Soviet/Russian attitude towards the Japanese Prisoners of War: Gorbachev's 'condolence' (*soboleznovanie*) of 1991 had become Yeltsin's 'apology' (*izvinenie*) two years later. Despite the time lag, similar reviews of history have been taking place in both countries in transition.[14] However, in Japan's case, the review is mainly directed to its 'Asian neighbours', which do not yet seem to include Russia, despite its geographical proximity. Considering the Japanese decision making situation towards Russia, it is understandable that this is the most difficult area for the review to encompass.

One reason for the Japanese bureaucracy's predominance in decision making towards Russia is that the basic goal setting has not been changed for four decades. Thus, even leaving aside its traditional rigidity towards the Russians, it is understandable that the *Gaimushō*, a purely administrative body with no legitimate decisional right, has persisted in claiming the 'four islands return'. It has simply been pursuing since 1955 the principle then provided by the LDP's political decision. Therefore, unless and until the 'politics' part takes the lead, no drastic change of direction will occur; and even if the political leaders wish to start reviewing the legitimacy of the 'four islands' claim, they will encounter strong opposition within government against revising a claim so long-asserted. As noted earlier, in addition to the *Gaimushō*, conservative influences remain strong in Japanese politics. While the LDP has returned to the mainstream of politics, many of the new opposition parties are led by former LDP politicians. Even though the 'four islands' claim was a by-product of the 1955 system, a policy shift to the 'two islands' return would require wide-ranging reviews and drastic political decisions. Unless the political environment is right, these would be pointless. So while the potential for the 'two islands' scenario exists, making it happen by the year 2000 will be very difficult, barring some radical development within the government itself.

The third scenario, that of signing a peace treaty by 'shelving' the territorial dispute (the *Senkaku rettō* formula), is Russia's preferred option. So long as the political distance between the two countries does not diminish, and so long as Russia is occupying the territories, Moscow apparently has neither need nor intention to hasten a settlement.[15] This therefore seems the most viable political compromise.

To Japan, however, this scenario is in a sense more difficult to accept than the 'two island return'. Japan controls the *Senkaku rettō*, and from the Japanese viewpoint 'no territorial problems exist with China'.[16] Japan's basic policy regarding a peace treaty and territorial settlement remains unchanged, and contains no option based on the *Senkaku rettō* formula. For example, at the 14 November 1997 press conference, the *Gaimushō* spokesman said 'The peace treaty in fact can be signed by solving the territorial issues', and reiterated, 'So unless we solve the territorial issues, we cannot sign the peace treaty'.[17]

Against this background is the *Gaimushō*'s SOP that the peace treaty and territorial settlement are inseparable, since the peace treaty could not be signed in 1956 only because the territorial problem was not resolved. During the 1955–6 negotiations, Foreign Minister Shigemitsu saw a danger that if a peace treaty was formally accomplished without settling the territories questions, Japan would lose forever its claims for their return. That same concern exists to this day.

When Hashimoto announced the new diplomatic policy guideline, media attention was focused on the 'virtual abolition of Japan's *seikei fukabun* (non-separation of politics and economics) policy'.[18] The wide-ranging economic cooperation programme called the 'Hashimoto–Yeltsin Plan' was announced in Krasnoyarsk. It is indeed a positive factor that Japan intends to promote its economic relations with Russia in projects such as Siberian development, and not to fall behind other countries. While the short-term changes are precisely focused, however, the long-term pattern tends to be forgotten. As seen in this study, Japan has taken a mixed approach between *seikei fukabun* and *seikei bunri* (separating politics and economics) at past summits. Similar moves were observed in the 1970s around Tanaka's visit to Moscow.

The lack of a peace treaty itself, and accordingly the relatively limited interaction between the two countries, was another reason for the bureaucracy's dominance in policy making towards the USSR. A peace treaty is in a sense political insurance for peace and security, and a foundation for development of other fields between nations. Preparation of a peace treaty is the job of the Ministry of Foreign Affairs. In its relations with many (former) western nations, Japanese bureaucracy has generally tended to play smaller roles and, instead, business groups have increased their influence in national decision making. This is because once security and stability were politically secured, interaction in many other areas increased, centring on economic activity, thereby enlarging the interests of business and industry, and accordingly their influence on decision making. However, there have been no such legitimate bases for development of relations between Japan and the USSR/Russia. Thus, *seikei fukabun* after all remains, in the ultimate sense that, without a peace treaty, the business group cannot initiate large-scale investment in Russia.

The *Senkaku rettō* formula in fact does not seem a bad option, given the economics-centred development of Sino-Japanese relations over the past two decades. Once a peace treaty is signed, the *zaikai* can make a politically secured move towards large-scale investment. However, as far as the territorial policy is concerned, the worst scenario for Japan is that once a peace treaty is signed, it will not only completely lose control of the economic card, but also lose forever any possibility of regaining the territory.

In addition to the lack of a peace treaty, the reason why Japanese business groups played only a minimal role was lack of interest in the Soviet Union, in which there was no market economy. However, transition to a market economy has been in progress since the final years of the USSR, so a factor that may change the Japanese decision-making pattern has already begun to develop in Russia. There seems to be a possibility that the traditional power-balance in policy making towards Russia will collapse in Japan, as the transition to a market economy proceeds in Russia, there also increasing the potential influence of business groups on the decision-making process.

The last scenario from the viewpoint of 'continuation of past and present' is that the present situation in Russo-Japanese relations continues, with neither a peace treaty nor a solution to the territorial problem, i.e., 'continuation' considered in terms of the long-standing situation rather than of the very recent, hence still short-term, trend towards normalising relations. As was seen in the last chapter, the present state of Russo-Japanese relations can be viewed as the continuation of the 'end of the Cold War' trend initiated by Gorbachev. This view suggests that expectations of a *rapprochement* would rise towards the deadline of the 'official' summit, but that the end results would be neither a peace treaty nor a solution of the territorial problem. This scenario thus can also be included in the next category, that of cyclical phenomena.

The most likely scenario in this view is continuation of the *Gaimushō*-dominant decision-making system and its associated incrementalism in Japan. After the zigzag path and long struggle to create an atmosphere of *rapprochement*, Japan reverted at the 1991 Tokyo summit to its former ultimatum-style approach, and urged Gorbachev to make the final 'decision' or 'resolution' for 'four islands return.' If Japanese policy makers expect Yeltsin to make a brave 'decision' to adorn his retirement, as Hatoyama did with the restoration of diplomatic relations, they will probably be found guilty of wishful thinking. It was, after all, Yeltsin who cancelled the proposed 1992 summit, on realising that a 'decision' acceptable to both sides was politically impossible at that time.

An optional scenario with neither a peace treaty nor a solution of the territorial problem may be an intermediate step, the signing of a Treaty of Friendship, as was proposed by the USSR in the 1970s. This might create an impression of an 'advance' towards *rapprochement*, and preserve the face of both governments, but would not provide any fundamental solution.

### Cycles or cyclical phenomena

Both a peace 'by shelving the territorial issue' and 'neither peace nor territorial settlement' would eventually lead into the next 'cyclical phenomenon', a scenario of re-deterioration of relations. Though this study concentrates on post-1945 bilateral relations, the Russo-Japanese relationship for over a century has exhibited a repetitive pattern of deterioration and improvement, never reaching the level of sustained friendly relations. The post-war cycle of *rapprochement* arose, and summit visits took place, in the 1950s, 1970s and 1990s, suggesting that this cycle appears roughly every two decades. All these chances appeared in circumstances of global warming of international relations. In the 1950s and 1970s Japanese Prime Ministers visited Moscow, and in the 1990s Gorbachev and Yeltsin visited Tokyo. Yeltsin's visit was a continuation of the opportunity created in the Gorbachev period. If this pattern persists, the next chance will be around the year 2010.

The global analysis conducted in this study concluded that international relations in the Asia-Pacific region still retain their basic Cold War structure, the San Francisco System, and resemble those of the 1970s *détente* in the Euro-Atlantic region. The East–West confrontation, whose fundamental structure remained intact during that *détente*, re-intensified from the late 1970s, and was sometimes called the 'Second Cold War'. Similarly, confrontations in the region may intensify, including a scenario of deterioration in Russo-Japanese relations. The 'Northern Territories' problem and the other regional issues of Taiwan, the Spratlys and the Korean Peninsula all share a common nature as Cold War by-products. These remaining problems over territorial sovereignty and border demarcation have the potential to become explosive sources of international confrontation. China's attitude towards Taiwan after the reversion of Hong Kong (1997) and Macau (1999) may be determinant.

Though arguments have been put here in line with the study's conclusion of '*détente* in the Asia-Pacific', it may be possible to apply the 'end of the Cold War' as a general concept, and describe the Japanese–Russian territorial dispute and other remaining sources of regional conflict as 'legacies' of the Cold War. Even in this case, the concept of cyclical phenomena can be applied. The onset of the Cold War caused the Pacific War to be 'ended' only vaguely, without a clear settlement with many nations, and the Cold War itself appears to have 'ended' only vaguely in the Asia-Pacific region. Then it may be that, as in the past, when confrontations and complexity deepened while overlaid by the Cold War structure of the post-war international order, the region is destined to become politically more complex or 'diverse' (whether or not it retains high economic growth rates), while overlaid by some new order (or disorder?) before the Cold War really ends. A search for a new order for the 'post-Cold War' era has already begun to exhibit a growing tendency toward regionalism, centring on arrangements such as ASEAN and APEC. Then, the question is what about Russo-Japanese relations?

Global tendencies towards regionalism contain the danger of leading to exclusionism. This tendency is already becoming perceptible, though more on a national than on a regional level. Cyclical phenomena expected for Japan may be that nationalism is again reflected in policy towards Russia, irredentist movements intensify, and the government's position on the territorial problem and the peace treaty reverts to the 'traditional' rigid pattern. Since the basis of the decision-making system still remains strong, reversion to this pattern would not be difficult. As for Russia, internal trends towards regionalism and nationalism have been conspicuous. Revival of the 1960 *Aide-Mémoire* would be an extreme, but not necessarily impossible, prediction. The year 2010 scenario seems applicable, if the Russian position shifts back to Yeltsin's original five-stage plan, where 'the next generation' would resolve the question of ownership of the islands in the fifth stage.

Recurring phenomena in Japanese domestic politics and the possibility of new developments arising from them may be added to the 'cyclical' element. The present situation in Japanese domestic politics resembles that of the early- and mid-1950s, the period leading up to the first Japanese–Soviet summit, in being a period of transition to a new era, the so-called 'post-Cold War' era. But despite the global background of the new era, it presents strong continuities from the previous one. As in the 1950s, a few years after the collapse of the former Japanese imperial system, the conservatives have come back into the political mainstream; but as in the 1950s, the conservatives are nevertheless divided, some as ruling and others as opposition parties, and the scramble for power among various groups and individuals continues unabated. Therefore, there is a possibility that territorial policy will again be used as a political tool. Just as when the 'four islands return' policy was established with the 1955 system, policy could again be shaken by 'unexpected political decisions'. Cooperation among factions to secure agreement on the regime, number and fate of the islands to be claimed may become more difficult to achieve in future. However, the 'four islands' claim is currently supported by all except the Japanese Communist Party, which claims the entire Kuriles chain; so the gap between Japan and Russia seems unlikely to diminish, and the possibility for factional gain by change of policy on the islands seems low in the foreseeable future.

## Emerging issues

The most important trends of the future are said to be utterly new emerging issues, usually direct or indirect consequences of new technologies. The clearest example in the recent past would be the invention at the end of the Second World War of nuclear weapons, which changed the nature of international relations. As a result, the post-war world experienced the Cold War, a phenomenon that had not existed in the past, and the territorial problem between Japan and the USSR/Russia was largely created by it.

Unfortunately, prediction of new technology not yet in existence is impossible for this study, just as was the advent of nuclear weapons unimaginable to most people 63 years ago. In recent years, however, we have witnessed technological development, at rates inconceivable in the past, in communication, information and transportation. Exchange of information between individuals and groups is now available on a far greater scale than in the past, much easier, much faster, and much more difficult for governments to control. Just as existence of the territorial dispute eventually came to be acknowledged in Russia, so if new perspectives (including findings from this study) prevail over Cold War indoctrination, the Japanese perception of the 'Northern Territories' issue may change, or the review of history in due course be extended to cover it.

Apart from technological development, a recent new move by the *Gaimushō* is indicative of change. Its opening of a local office in Yuzhnosakhalinsk is an unprecedented move in Japanese post-war diplomacy, and may be the basis for a future breakthrough. As the 'Northern Territories' problem is a by-product of the Cold War, this contributes to creating a post-Cold War environment and an atmosphere conducive to a solution within a 'confidence-building' framework. But advocates of the 'four islands return' are likely to see this new policy as a fatal error, because it tacitly acknowledges Russian sovereignty over Southern Sakhalin, a territory over which, like the Kurile Islands, Japan relinquished sovereignty in the San Francisco Treaty, but without specifying to which country it was transferred. If this logic is followed, the Kuriles are also to belong to Russia, and Japan would then have to argue that the four disputed territories are not part of the Kuriles. But as pointed out earlier in this study, this view is a contradiction. During the 1955–6 negotiations, the territorial policies designed by the bureaucracy left their designers' hands and they lost control of them. As I indicated earlier, in the turbulence of Japanese domestic politics there is an undeniable possibility of a similar consequence's developing from this new Sakhalin policy in the future.

One final point to consider is what is there in Russo-Japanese relations that is completely new, and has never existed in past or present? The Cold War might have been a completely new movement in international relations at global level, but was not necessarily a totally new trend in their bilateral relations, which for most of their history had been cold or actively hostile. The nature of their cold relations differed before and after the Second World War; before it, their confrontation had a more 'individualistic', purely bilateral, nature, whereas after it Japan confronted the USSR under the umbrella of the United States. However, in either case, their bilateral relations were never warm, and any *détente* that appeared was only temporary. What has not existed between them in past or present is long-lasting peace with friendly relations and mutual trust. It appears essential for the issues of the peace treaty and the territorial problem (whether on a four, two or zero islands basis) to be solved for any kind of further development to produce the hitherto unprecedented long-lasting 'good-neighbourly' peace. The above scenarios were considered mainly in a purely bilateral framework, but in what follows settlement of the issues is considered within a global context.

## From bilateralism to multilateralism

In concluding this study I would like to propose a future scenario for the end of both the Pacific War and the subsequent Cold War with a clear settlement not hitherto achieved. For this, it is necessary to set the search for a settlement, as a potential option, back into the multilateral framework, including a review of the San Francisco System. In order to transcend the bilateral framework, and construct a regional order with peace and sustainable stability in security, it seems important to end the Cold War with a clear settlement of its 'legacies'. Current trends, which seem to suggest that many nations place short-term 'national' interests ahead of long-term 'global' interests, make this the most difficult scenario. But it is also the most desirable.

In Chapters 1 and 2 I indicated that the 'Northern Territories' problem may have been so formulated as to be likely to remain unresolved, so long as it remains within an exclusively bilateral framework. 'Internationalisation' or 're-internationalisation' of the problem may therefore be indispensable for its eventual solution. However, Japanese approaches of the recent past, although aimed at a kind of 'internationalisation', may have been missing the point. The final settlement will indeed require political decisions. However, international support based, as in the past, on the Cold War, will tend to become less reliable and less stable, nor is there any guarantee that the temporary support that can be mobilised by economic power can be made to last. Instead, it is more important to appeal to the 'nations concerned' with solid arguments as to why the problem has to be 'internationalised' again. The international community is already deeply involved in the problem, because of historical considerations, and responsibility for seeking a solution is widely shared.

Among recent studies there have been a couple of projects advocating trilateral cooperation, involving the USA with Russia and Japan with regard to the 'Northern Territories' problem. However, for the last four decades no proposal has advocated resolution of the issue within a multilateral framework, including a review of the San Francisco arrangement. Japan tried, but failed, to 'internationalise', or 'multilateralise' the territorial question during its peace talks with the USSR in the mid-1950s. The complicated international situation at the time, especially in the Asia-Pacific region, where the interests of different nations were interwoven into the basic structure of the East–West confrontation, made the 'concerned states' unwilling to internationalise the 'Northern Territories' problem. During the last 40 years, however, the international situation has changed greatly. For example, the USA long ago ceased to differ from the UK in its China policy. Okinawa, which was linked to the disposition of the Kuriles in the 1950s, was long ago returned to Japan. The Spratlys did not become a critical problem until their oil potential was discovered in the late 1970s. These problems thus tended to be perceived as separate issues, and their common origin was probably forgotten. While the US–USSR confrontation was continuing, the solution of other issues by political compromise did not seem to be welcomed by some concerned parties in the conflicts. After the end of the US–USSR Cold War, the US and Russia now present themselves as 'partners', and perceive no need to maintain tension in Russo–Japanese or North–South Korean relations, and the UK has withdrawn from Hong Kong, its last foothold in China (PRC).

The new prerequisites for bringing on the 'end of the Cold War' in the region are taking shape. Now that there is official acknowledgment that a territorial dispute exists between Japan and Russia, they could even seek to resolve it by legitimately 'internationalising' the issue at the International Court. But that may not appeal to Japan as a preferable option, especially after it has for so long contended that the four disputed territories are not part of the Kuriles, which it renounced at San Francisco. As I pointed out earlier, this view is a contradiction.

For the Japanese position there may be a counter-argument that the islands proposed for an international conference in the 1950s were the Northern Kuriles and Southern Sakhalin, whose return is not demanded, but not the Southern Kuriles (or 'four islands'). It is true that the 'four islands demand' has been consistently maintained for the last four decades. However, in resolutions passed by the Diet up to the end of 1997, the latest of them being in June 1995, the 'Northern Territories' that Japan is to demand have been 'Habomai, Shikotan, Kunashiri, Etorofu *and so on (tō)*'.[19] The expression seems to range over a wider definition of the 'Northern Territories' to include all former Japanese territories now under Russian occupation, including those unquestionably renounced at San Francisco. The 1955 system indeed provided the political base for the 'four islands demand'. However, once that system collapsed and the LDP was no longer the single dominant ruling party, the 'four islands demand' does not necessarily retain its validity as the government's fundamental claim for the 'Northern Territories'. If so, the definition of what is or is not part of the Kuriles chain would no longer matter in internationalising the territorial dispute.

Other options beside the International Court may be sought within a multilateral framework. As feared by the UK during the Soviet–Japanese negotiations in the 1950s, a review of the San Francisco arrangements may open up other issues derived from the treaty, i.e., the other regional conflicts that have continued to exist in the Cold War system of the region, namely the San Francisco System. However, as mentioned above, the international and regional situations are now very different from those for which the San Francisco System was devised. Thus, it may be worth reviewing these problems together, since their resolution will not only benefit the nations directly involved in the present disputes, but also serve the stability and interests of the whole region. The USA seems to have the potential to serve as a mediator for resolution of these conflicts, on the basis of its historical involvement, current influence and interest in the region. A potential framework for multilateral cooperation may be found in global and regional organisations such as the UN, APEC or ASEAN Regional Forum. With a generally recognised 'One China' policy in the region, and the Beijing regime seen as the legitimate government of China since the 1970s, the PRC may be able to play a key role in the future. Yet the different positions of the states involved in those disputes appear at least partially determined by domestic political considerations. It is beyond the scope of this study to review their individual positions here, but it should be noted that, as in the cases of Japan and the USSR/Russia, their positions and arguments are of Cold War origin, and tend to reflect short-term and myopic 'national interests'.

The above thoughts from the viewpoints of (a) continuation, (b) cycles and (c) emerging issues, are not necessarily separate scenarios. Scenario (a) is the most plausible in the short term, namely that the present trend will continue. Although I considered the possibilities of several scenarios of peace and territorial accommodation, none of them seems likely to lead to a complete or fundamental settlement in the near future. In (b), from the past cycles of certain global and bilateral phenomena, the next chance for *rapprochement* is postulated to arrive around the year 2010. While the recurring pattern of Japanese domestic politics may provide potential for a new development, a complete settlement does not seem plausible in the immediate future. In (c), newly emerged phenomena of the recent past – technological development in communication media, and Japan's policy change on Sakhalin – suggest another scenario to settle the issues of a peace treaty and the territorial problem. That was an unprecedented proposal for the most difficult but preferable scenario of a Russo-Japanese settlement as part of the total 'end of the Cold War' in the Asia-Pacific region, inspired by the conclusions of the global analysis in the study. It may have potential as both a continuation of the opportunity existing since the Gorbachev era, and a scenario for the next cycle of opportunity (around 2010?). Judging from the current international and domestic situations the latter seems more plausible, i.e., the environment will by then seem more favourable, in that China would be more motivated for a breakthrough following the reversion of Hong Kong and Macao, the domestic political situations in both Russia and Japan are expected to have stabilised, and as the market economy should have prevailed in Russia by 2010, Japan would be more motivated to settle. Furthermore, as suggested by G. Jukes' study, the strategic importance of the disputed islands will have been much reduced by then.

The key to settlement is 'post-Cold War', i.e., the global dynamism surrounding the two countries' 'end of the Cold War', 'collapse of the USSR', and 'collapse of the 1955 System'. Thus, the general and basic barriers have been removed, but the Cold War remains in the regional and domestic systems, i.e., the Asia-Pacific region and the Japanese decisional unit. Regimes in both Russia and Japan are in flux, but whether within a bilateral or multilateral framework, it will be difficult or impossible to achieve a settlement unless both political regimes can take a policy initiative. Therefore the short-run determinant is stabilisation of the political regimes in both countries.

The territorial problem, which for almost half a century has prevented the two nations from signing a peace treaty, has been an invisible wall between them, making them 'distant neighbours'. It was created by the intertwining of a number of factors at different levels and in complex ways. I sincerely hope that this study will provide a key to understanding the complex nature of the problem, and make even the slightest contribution to achievement of this 'difficult peace' some time in the future.

# Appendix 1

## Chronological chart of the 1955–6 Soviet–Japanese negotiations (key events)

**1954**

| | |
|---|---|
| 12 October | Sino-Soviet Communiqué regarding normalising relations with Japan. |
| 9 December | Establishment of the Hatoyama Cabinet. |

**1955**

| | |
|---|---|
| 25 January | Delivery of the 'Domnitsky Letter' to Hatoyama (the Soviet overture of normalising relations with Japan). |
| 14 February | (Japanese) Cabinet resolution to initiate negotiations for normalising relations with the USSR. |
| 1 June–23 September | Soviet–Japanese negotiations in London (first London negotiations). |
| 9 August | Soviet's indirect offer of the two islands upon signing a peace treaty. |
| 28 August | A new set of instructions to Matsumoto from Tokyo (unconditional return of the four islands, international conference for the Northern Kuriles and Southern Sakhalin). |
| 15 November | Merger of the conservative parties (LDP establishment). |

**1956**

| | |
|---|---|
| 17 January–20 March | Soviet–Japanese negotiations in London (second London negotiations). |
| 21 March | The Soviet government's announcement of restrictions on fishing in the North Pacific. |
| 29 April–14 May | Soviet–Japanese fishery negotiation in Moscow. |
| 14 May | Fishery Convention (with condition of resuming the peace negotiations no later than 31 July). |
| 31 July–14 August | Soviet–Japanese negotiations in Moscow (first Moscow negotiations). |
| 19 August | 'Dulles' Warning' (London Conference on 'Suez' issue). |
| 11, 13 September | Hatoyama–Bulganin exchange of letters. |
| 20 September | LDP *ad hoc* general meeting. |
| 29 September | Matsumoto–Gromyko Letters. |
| 2 October | Cabinet approval of Hatoyama's visit to Moscow. |
| 15–19 October | Hatoyama's visit to Moscow (second Moscow negotiations/Moscow Summit). The Soviet–Japanese Joint Declaration. |

# Appendix 2

## Japanese trade with the USSR and Russia

| Year | Total exports (US$000s) | Percentage increase/year | Total imports (US$000s) | Percentage increase/year |
|------|------------------------|--------------------------|--------------------------|--------------------------|
| 1958 | 18,103 | | 22,164 | |
| 1959 | 23,027 | 127.20 | 39,485 | 178.149 |
| 1960 | 59,976 | 260.46 | 87,020 | 220.39 |
| 1961 | 65,380 | 109.01 | 145,019 | 166.65 |
| 1962 | 149,390 | 228.49 | 147,276 | 101.56 |
| 1963 | 158,136 | 105.85 | 161,940 | 109.96 |
| 1964 | 181,811 | 114.97 | 226,729 | 140.00 |
| 1965 | 168,358 | 92.60 | 240,198 | 105.94 |
| 1966 | 214,024 | 127.12 | 300,361 | 125.05 |
| 1967 | 157,688 | 73.68 | 453,918 | 151.12 |
| 1968 | 179,018 | 113.53 | 463,512 | 102.11 |
| 1969 | 268,247 | 149.84 | 461,563 | 99.58 |
| 1970 | 340,932 | 127.10 | 481,038 | 104.22 |
| 1971 | 377,267 | 110.66 | 495,880 | 103.09 |
| 1972 | 504,180 | 133.64 | 593,906 | 119.77 |
| 1973 | 484,210 | 96.04 | 1,077,701 | 181.46 |
| 1974 | 1,095,642 | 226.27 | 1,418,143 | 131.59 |
| 1975 | 1,626,200 | 148.42 | 1,169,618 | 82.48 |
| 1976 | 2,251,894 | 138.48 | 1,167,441 | 99.81 |
| 1977 | 1,913,877 | 84.99 | 1,421,875 | 121.79 |
| 1978 | 2,502,195 | 130.77 | 1,441,723 | 101.40 |
| 1979 | 2,462,464 | 98.41 | 1,910,681 | 132.53 |
| 1980 | 2,778,233 | 112.82 | 1,859,866 | 97.34 |
| 1981 | 3,259,415 | 117.32 | 2,020,706 | 108.65 |
| 1982 | 3,898,841 | 119.62 | 1,682,017 | 83.23 |
| 1983 | 2,821,249 | 72.36 | 1,456,001 | 86.56 |
| 1984 | 2,518,314 | 89.26 | 1,393,987 | 95.74 |
| 1985 | 2,750,583 | 109.22 | 1,429,255 | 102.53 |
| 1986 | 3,149,547 | 114.50 | 1,972,033 | 137.98 |
| 1987 | 2,563,284 | 81.39 | 2,351,854 | 119.26 |
| 1988 | 3,129,901 | 122.11 | 2,765,759 | 117.60 |
| 1989 | 3,081,676 | 98.46 | 3,304,527 | 119.48 |
| 1990 | 2,562,831 | 83.16 | 3,350,971 | 101.41 |

| 1991 | | 2,113,711 | 82.48 | | 3,316,831 | 98.98 |
|------|----|-----------|--------|----|-----------|--------|
| 1992 | * | 1,076,743 | 50.94 | * | 2,402,972 | 72.45 |
| | [† | 1,191,835 | 90.76] | [† | 2,503,679 | 75.48] |
| 1993 | * | 1,500,792 | 139.38 | * | 2,769,226 | 115.24 |
| | [† | 1,661,876 | 139.44] | [† | 2,979,363 | 119.00] |
| 1994 | * | 1,174,387 | 78.25 | * | 3,414,689 | 123.31 |
| 1995 | | 1,153,516 | 98.22 | | 4,589,735 | 134.41 |

* Russia; † Former USSR.

*Sources:*
1958–70: Japan Ministry of International Trade and Industry (MITI), *Sengo nihon no bōeki nijūnen shi*, Tokyo, 1967, pp. 442–3; *Tsūshō Hakusho–kakuron* [The White Paper on International Trade], cited in Savitri Vishwanathan, *Normalization of Japanese–Soviet Relations 1945–1970*, Tallahassee, Fl.: The Diplomatic Press, 1973, p. 168.
1971–93: MITI, *Tsūshō Hakusho – kakuron*; Japan External Trade Organization, *White Paper on International Trade Japan.*
1994–95: Department for Economic and Social Information and Policy Analysis, Statistics Division, *International Trade Statistics Yearbook, Volume 1, Trade by Country 1995*, United Nations, 1996.

# Notes

## Introduction

1 Other than Hatoyama and Tanaka, three Prime Ministers visited Moscow as incumbent leaders of Japan, but the objectives of the trips were not for a bilateral summit. Zenkō Suzuki and Yasuhiro Nakasone visited Moscow in 1982 and 1985 to attend the funerals of Brezhnev and Chernenko respectively. Ryūtarō Hashimoto visited Moscow in 1996 to attend the Nuclear Safety and Security Summit. In 1993, Boris Yeltsin visited Japan twice as the incumbent Russian President, but the first visit in July was to attend the 'G-7 plus 1' meeting to discuss multilateral issues. In his October visit, the official bilateral summit finally took place, after previously being cancelled twice. In 1997 Hashimoto and Yeltsin held an 'unofficial' bilateral summit in Krasnoyarsk of Russian Far East. Another 'unofficial' summit between them is scheduled for Spring 1998 in Japan.

2 They are the Joint Declaration (1956), the Joint Communiqué (1973), the Joint Statement (1991), and the Tokyo Declaration (1993).

3 'In any area of scholarly inquiry, there are always several ways in which the phenomena under study may be sorted and arranged for purpose of systemic analysis. . . . Whether the micro- or macro-level of analysis is selected is ostensibly a mere matter of methodological or conceptual convenience.' David Singer, 'The level-of-analysis problem in international relations', in Klaus Knorr and Sidney Verba, eds., *The International System: Theoretical essays*, Princeton, NJ: Princeton University Press 1961, p. 77, also in James N. Rosenau, ed., *International Politics and Foreign Policy: A reader in research and theory*, New York: Free Press; London: Collier-Macmillan, 1969, rev. ed. p. 20.

4 As becomes evident with concrete cases in the text, classifications of those levels are not necessarily clear. Depending on viewpoints, certain factors or approaches can overlap different levels. Nevertheless, having a certain analytical framework helps sort multiple information, ideas or concepts.

5 Graham Allison, *Essence of Decision: Explaining the Cuban Missile Crisis*, Boston: Little, Brown, 1971.

6 Chalmers Johnson, *MITI and the Japanese Miracle: The growth of industrial policy, 1925–1975*, Stanford CA: Stanford University Press, 1982.

7 For example, see Kent E. Calder, 'Japanese foreign economic policy formulation: explaining the reactive state', *World Politics*, Vol. 40, No. 4, July 1988; Gerald L. Curtis, *The Japanese Way of Politics*, New York: Columbia University Press, 1988; Takashi Inoguchi and Tomoaki Iwai, *Gendai kokusai seiji to nippon, pāru hābā*

*gojū-nen no nihon gaikō*, Tokyo: Chikuma-shobō, 1991; also T. Inoguchi, 'The ideas and structures of foreign policy: Looking ahead with caution' in Takashi Inoguchi and Daniel I. Okimoto, eds, *The Political Economy of Japan, Vol. 2, The Changing International Context*, Stanford, CA: Stanford University Press, 1988; T.J. Pempel, *Policy and Politics in Japan: Creative conservatism*, Philadelphia: Temple University Press, 1982; John Quansheng Zhao, 'Informal Pluralism and Japanese Politics: Sino-Japanese *rapprochement* revisited', *Journal of Northeast Asian Studies*, Vol. VIII, No. 2, Summer, 1989; also 'Formation of Japanese Foreign Economic Policy', in *Chūgoku kenkyū [China Studies]*, Tokyo: Institute of China Studies, February 1988; Ezra Vogel, ed., *Modern Japanese Organization and Decision Making*, Berkeley, CA: University of California Press, 1975.

8   For example, see David Lane, *Politics and Society in the USSR*, New York: New York University Press, 1978 (2nd edn); Zbigniew K. Brzezinski, *Ideology and Power in Soviet Politics*, New York: Praeger, 1967; Adam B. Ulam, *Expansion and Coexistence: The history of Soviet foreign policy, 1917–73*, New York: Praeger, 1974 (2nd edn); Adam B. Ulam, *Dangerous Relations: The Soviet Union in world politics, 1970–1982*, Oxford: Oxford University Press, 1983; William Zimmerman, *Soviet Perspectives on International Relations, 1956–1967*, Princeton, NJ: Princeton University Press, 1969. For comprehensive texts on Soviet Foreign Policy, see Joseph L. Nogee and Robert H. Donaldson, *Soviet Foreign Policy since World War II*, New York: Pergamon Press, 1992 (4th edn); Jonathan R. Adelman and Deborah Anne Palmieri, *The Dynamics of Soviet Foreign Policy*, New York: Harper & Row, 1989. Selections of comprehensive analyses of the subject are compiled in such volumes as; Seweryn Bialer, ed., *The Domestic Context of Soviet Foreign Policy*, Boulder, CO: Westview Press, 1981; Alexander Dallin, *Soviet Conduct in World Affairs*, New York: Greenwood Press, 1975 (2nd edn); Erik P. Hoffmann, and Frederic J. Fleron, Jr., eds, *The Conduct of Soviet Foreign Policy*, New York: Aldine, 1980 (2nd edn).

9   One of the few detailed studies related to the subject is Robertson's volume, covering the 1970s and 1980s. See Myles L. C. Robertson, *Soviet Policy towards Japan: An analysis of trends in the 1970s and 1980s*, Cambridge and New York: Cambridge University Press, 1988. Kimura's volumes on Soviet politics and foreign policy towards Japan compile valuable analyses on the subject especially since Gorbachev's era. See Hiroshi Kimura *Kuremurin no seiji rikigaku*, Tokyo: Adoa Shuppan, 1991; *Sōkessan Gorubachofu no gaikō*, Tokyo: Kōbun-dō, 1992.

10   For example, the record of the 1956 Moscow summit was published in the June 1996 issue of a monthly bulletin, *Istochnik*, to mark the occasion of the 40th anniversary of the USSR–Japan diplomatic restoration.

11   John J. Stephan, *The Kuril Islands: Russo-Japanese frontier in the Pacific*, Oxford: Clarendon Press, 1974; Savitri Vishwanathan, *Normalization of Japanese–Soviet Relations, 1945–1970*, Tallahassee, FL:, Diplomatic Press, 1973; Young C. Kim, *Japanese–Soviet Relations: Interaction of politics, economics and national security*, Beverly Hills: Sage Publications, 1974.

12   Hiroshi Kimura, *Hoppō ryōdo: kiseki to henkan eno josō*, Tokyo: Jijitsūshin-sha, 1989; Horoshi Kimura, *Nichiro kokkyō kōshō-shi: ryōdo mondai ni ikani torikumuka*, Tokyo: Chūōkōron-sha, 1993; Haruki Wada, *Hoppō ryōdo mondai o kangaeru*, Tokyo: Iwanami-shoten, 1990.

13   Graham Allison, Hiroshi Kimura and Konstantin Sarkisov, eds, *Nichi-bei-ro shinjidai eno shinario: Hoppō ryōdo jirenma kara no dasshutsu*, Tokyo: Daiyamondo-sha, 1993; *Beyond Cold War to Trilateral Cooperation in the Asia-Pacific Region: Scenarios for new relationships between Japan, Russia, and the United States*, Harvard University; Ot

*kholodnoi voini k trekhstoronnemu sotrudnichestvu v aziatsko-tikhookeanskom regione: Stsenarii razvitiya novikh otnoshenii mezhdu Yaponiei, Rossiei i Soedinennimi Shtatami,* Moskva: Nauka, 1993.

14  Vladimir I. Ivanov, James E. Goodby and Nobuo Shimotomai, eds, under the auspices of the United States Institute of Peace, *Northern Territories and Beyond: Russian, Japanese, and American perspectives,* Westport, Conn.: Praeger, 1995.

15  Under the Australian Archives Act 1983, governments records over 30 years old are principally made available to public scrutiny in Australia. This so-called 'Thirty Year Rule' has been adopted in other countries with legal assurance such as in the USA (1966) and UK (1967). Though the government of Japan generally opens its records after the passage of 30 years, there is no legal basis for it in Japan. On 15 October 1989, the Japanese government opened its diplomatic records up to 1959. However, materials related to the Soviet–Japanese negotiations were all excluded from those files.

# 1 The key issue

1  The term 'Northern Territories' is roughly defined in two senses in Japan. The 'Northern Territories' in the narrow sense means the four island groups of Kunashiri, Etorofu, Shikotan and the Habomais. The 'Northern Territories' in a wider sense includes all the pre-war Japanese territories under Russian control, i.e., Southern Sakhalin and all the islands between Hokkaido and Kamchatka Peninsula including the above island groups. In this book, unless annotated, the term 'Northern Territories' will be used in the narrow sense, and the commonly accepted term 'four islands' (or 'two islands' for Shikotan and the Habomais only) will also be used as a synonym for the 'Northern Territories'.

2  For example, see Gaimushō (Ministry of Foreign Affairs, Japan), *Japan's Northern Territories,* 1996, pp. 8–10, 1987, p. 3; Gaimushō daijinkanbō kokunai kōhō-ka, *Warera no hoppō ryōdo,* 1993, p. 12.

3  Marshal Yazov, then Soviet Defence Minister, in interview with the *Mainichi Shimbun,* 10 April 1991.

4  For an analysis of the strategic importance of the 'Northern Territories', see Geoffrey Jukes, 'Russia's military and the Northern Territories issue', Working Paper No. 277, Strategic & Defence Studies Centre, Australian National University, 1993.

5  For example, see Gregory Clark, 'Hoppō ryōdo mondai – warui nowa amerika da', *Bungei Shunjū,* June 1991, pp. 138–48.

6  Note of 18 March 1870 from Charles E. DeLong, US Minister in Tokyo, to Japanese Foreign Minister Sawa, in *Minor Islands Adjacent to Japan Proper: Part 1. The Kurile Islands, the Habomais and Shikotan,* Foreign Office, Japanese Government, November 1946, p. 5, Australian Archives (ACT): A1838/2; 515/4.

7  James Byrnes released this secret agreement at a press conference on 29 January, 1946. Adding that he personally did not know of the agreement until a few days after the Japanese surrender, but that the agreement for US support for Russia's claims to the Kurile islands was reached 'with full knowledge of the American military leaders' [*Sydney Morning Herald,* 31/1/46, Australian Archives (ACT): A1838/2;515/4].

8  John Russell Dean, *The Strange Alliance: The story of our efforts at war time cooperation with Russia,* New York: Viking, 1947, p. 25.

9 The Japan–Soviet Neutrality Pact was signed on 13 April 1941. It stipulated maintenance of peaceful and friendly relations, mutual respect of territorial integrity and inviolability between the two states, and neutrality of one party if the other party became the object of hostilities by a third party(ies). It was to remain valid for 5 years from the date of ratification. 'Should neither of the contracting parties denounce the pact one year before expiration', it was automatically to be prolonged for the following five years. (Hiroshi Shigeta and Shoji Suezawa, eds, *Nisso kihon bunsho shiryō-shū: 1855-nen–1988-nen*, Tokyo: Sekainougoki-sha, 1990, p. 34; George A. Lensen, *The Strange Neutrality*, Tallahassee, FL: Diplomatic Press, 1972, pp. 277–8.

10 Andrei Gromyko, *Memories*, (trans. Harold Shukman), London, Sydney, Auckland, Johannesburg: Hutchinson, 1989, p. 89.

11 US Department of State, *Foreign Relations of the United States* [*FRUS* hereafter]: *1943, the Conference of Cairo*, 1961, pp. 448–9.

12 *FRUS: 1945, Vol. II, Conference of Berlin (Potsdam)*, 1960, p. 1281.

13 W. Averell Harriman and Elie Abel, *Special Envoy to Churchill and Stalin, 1941– 1946*, New York: Random House, 1975, p. 492.

14 Ibid.

15 The Japanese Premier, Admiral Baron Kantarō Suzuki, responded to the ultimatum that he found nothing new in the joint proclamation, adding (in the translation of the Foreign Broadcast Intelligence Service in Washington) that 'there is not other recourse but to ignore it entirely and resolutely fight for the successful conclusion of this war'. Scholars, diplomats and journalists have debated ever since whether Suzuki in fact had intended to reject the ultimatum, or to stall for time while the Japanese General Tōgō kept trying to interest the reluctant Russians in mediating more favourable terms (Harriman: 1975, p. 493).

16 Boris N. Slavinsky, *Muchi no daishō - soren no tainichi seisaku*, Ningen no kagaku-sha, 1991, p. 39.

17 *Yomiuri Shimbun*, 5 August 1992, p. 4.

18 For the details of the occupation of the Kuriles, refer to Boris N. Slavinsky, *Sovetskaya okkupatsiya kuril'skikh ostrovov (avgust-sentyabr' 1945 goda)*, *Dokumental'noe Issledovanie*, (The Soviet Occupation of the Kurile Islands, August–September 1945. Documentary Research) published at author's own expense, Moscow 1993a; also Slavinsky, *Chishima Senryō - 1945 Natsu*, Tokyo: Kyōdō Tsūshin-sha, 1993b, a distinguished study conducted with abundant classified materials from Soviet Naval Archives. (The author was banned from archival access after publication of the volume.)

19 No. 363, from Stalin to Truman (dated 16 August 1945), *Perepiska predsedatelia Soveta ministrov SSSR s prezidentami SShA i prem'er-ministrami Velikobritanii vo vremia Velikoi Otechestvennoi voiny 1941–1945 gg.*, Moskva, Tom 2, 1957, pp. 263–4; Wada (1990) p. 379; Slavinsky (1991), p. 41; also Slavinsky (1993b), p. 65.

20 No. 364, from Truman to Stalin (received 18 August 1945), *Perepiska . . .*, 1957 p. 264; Wada (1990) p. 380; Slavinsky (1991), p. 66; also Slavinsky (1993b), pp. 41–2; Shigeta and Suezawa, eds (1990), pp. 53–4.

21 Shigeta and Suezawa, eds (1990), p. 55.

22 No. 367, from Stalin to Truman (dated 30 August 1945), *Perepiska . . .* (1957), pp. 266–7, Slavinsky (1991), p. 67, Slavinsky (1993b), pp. 42–3.

23 Slavinsky (1993b), p. 67.

24 Clarification of the Central Command of the Red Army on the Surrender of

Japan, August 16 1945, in Graham Allison, Hiroshi Kimura and Konstantin Sarkisov, *Beyond Cold War to Trilateral Cooperation in the Asia-Pacific Region*, Harvard University, 1993, p. 92.

25  *FRUS: 1945, Vol. VI, The British Commonwealth and The Far East*, 1969, p. 658.

26  Slavinsky (1993b), pp. 153–4.

27  This date (15 August) is the date for commemorating the end of the war in the official Japanese calendar to this day.

28  *Sydney Morning Herald*, 28 January 1946, Australian Archives (ACT): A1838/2,515/4.

29  The discussion of the 'Northern Territories' problem and Micronesia was inspired by a discussion with Ms Toneko Hirai, and her paper, 'BELAU ER KID', unpublished paper submitted to the University of Hawaii, Spring 1990.

30  James F. Byrnes, *Speaking Frankly*, London: Heinemann 1947, pp. 220–1. Confirmation of the above account of the US attitude may be found in a newspaper article of the time, which reported that at a UN Mandate Committee meeting, the American delegate Dulles obliquely demanded the Soviets transfer the Kuriles to US Mandate. Dulles did not specifically name the Kuriles, but at a press conference following the meeting, he said that he had them in mind when he spoke. (Tokio, Kyodo News in Japanese Morse, 14 October, 1947, Australian Archives (ACT): A1838/2, 515/4.)

31  Slavinsky (1991), p. 252.

32  *New York Times*, 13 July 1951.

33  Gromyko, (1989) p. 254.

34  'Excerpts from the Statement of the First Deputy Minister of Foreign Affairs of the USSR, A.A. Gromyko, at the Conference in San Francisco, September 5, 1951', Ministry of Foreign Affairs of the Russian Federation, Ministry of Foreign Affairs of Japan, *Joint Compendium of Documents on the History of the Territorial Demarcation between Russia and Japan* [*Joint Compendium* hereafter], as translated by the Strengthening Democratic Institutions Project, p. 31 (Japanese), p. 36 (Russian).

35  *New York Times*, 6 September 1951.

36  *Treaty of Peace with Japan*, Australian Treaty Series, Dept. of External Affairs, Canberra, 1952 No. 1, p. 3.

37  Ibid., pp. 3–4.

38  In the *Aide-Mémoire* sent to the British Embassy, in March 1951 during the preparation for the San Francisco Treaty, the following clauses are found 'With respect to the carrying out of the Yalta Agreement the United States agrees that Japan should be prepared to cede South Sakhalin and the Kuriles to the Union of Soviet Socialist Republics, provided it becomes a party of the peace treaty, but believes that the precise definition of the extent of the Kurile Islands should be a matter for bilateral agreement between the Japanese and Soviet Government or for judicial determination by the International Court of Justice'. (*FRUS: 1951 – Vol. VI, Asia and the Pacific*, 1977, p. 922).

39  Departmental despatch No.10/1951, dated 2nd March 1951, From W.R. Hodgson, Head of Australian Mission in Japan, Australian Archives (ACT): A1838/2;515/4.

40  'Revised United States–United Kingdom Draft of a Japanese Peace Treaty, June 14, 1951', *FRUS:1951, Vol. 6, Asia and the Pacific*, 1977, p. 1120.

41  *Treaty of Peace with Japan*, Australia Treaty Series, 1952 No. 1, p. 14.
42  Ibid.
43  This will be dealt with in the next chapter.
44  Japan signed the San Francisco Peace Treaty and renounced the ownership of the Kurile Islands.
45  Message No. 145, To Secretary, Dept. of Ex. Affairs, from Ralph Harry, Australian Archive (ACT): A1838/2;515/4.
46  This section (before revision), together with some portion of Chapter 2, has already been published as Working Paper No. 1995/1, Department of International Relations, Australian National University, Canberra May, 1995. It has also been reprinted in *Japan Forum*, Spring 1996. Following the publication of the Working Paper, the discovery of this archival material was introduced in a Japanese newspaper *Asahi Shimbun* on July 12 1995.
47  Wada, 1990, p. 101.
48  Kumao Nishimura, *Nihon gaikō-shi 27: Sanfuranshisuko heiwa jōyaku*, Tokyo: Kajima kenkyū-shuppan-kai, 1971, p. 24.
49  Cablegram from Australian Mission, Tokyo, sent on 30 May,1947, Australian Archives (ACT): A1838/2; 515/4. Asakai Kōichirō was the chief of General Affairs Department, the Central Administration Division of Contacts regarding Termination of War (*Shūsen renraku jimu-kyoku sōmu-bu buchō*).
50  The Ministry of Foreign Affairs is very insistent on this point. For example, in Australia in December 1994 a First Secretary of the Japanese Embassy said 'the Japanese government had always maintained that the four islands, Etorofu, Kunashiri, Shikotan and Habomai are not included in the term "Kuriles"' (*Observer*, December 1994, p. 5), whereas only Shikotan and Habomai had been named in the journal of the previous month.
51  Ministry of Foreign Affairs, Japan, *Japan's Northern Territories*, 1996, pp. 5, 6.
52  Foreign Office Japanese Government, *Minor Islands Adjacent to Japan Proper: Part I. The Kurile Islands, the Habomais and Shikotan*, November 1946, p. 1, Australian Archives (ACT): A1838/2; 515/4.
53  Ibid. p. 8.
54  Ibid. p. 9.
55  W. Macmahon Ball, *Japan Enemy or Ally?*, London and Sydney: Cassell, 1948, p. 108.
56  Departmental dispatch dated March 2, 1951, No.10/1951, From W.R. Hodgson, Head of Australian Mission in Japan, Australian Archives (ACT): A1838/2; 515/4.
57  *Nippon Times*, March 9, 1951, Australian Archives (ACT): A1838/2; 515/4.
58  Memorandum dated March 8,1951, No.183/1951, For Secretary, Department of External Affairs, Canberra, From T.W. Eckersley, Head of Mission, Australian Archives (ACT): A1838/2; 515/4.
59  *FRUS: 1955–57, Vol. XXIII*, 1991, pp. 208–9.
60  Memorandum dated December 27, 1951, from R. McIntyre for The Australian Mission, Tokyo, Australian Archives (ACT): A1838/2; 515/4.
61  Departmental Dispatch dated March 2, 1951, No.10/1951, from W.R. Hodgson, Head of Australian Mission in Japan, Australian Archives (ACT): A1838/2; 515/4.
62  The argument of 'Kunashiri Etorofu Non-Kurile Theory', that not only the islands of Habomai and Shikotan but also Kunashiri and Etorofu are not included in the Kuriles, appeared in the official record as early as 6 October

1947, in the form of a petition at the Lower House Foreign Affairs Committee (originally addressed to General MacArthur by a Lower House member from Hokkaido). The Japanese Government's response at that time was, however, not positive. [Kokuritsu kokkai toshokan chōsa rippō kōsa-kyoku (prepared by Takashi Tsukamoto, Gaikō bōei-ka), 'Hoppō ryōdo mondai no keii (dai 3-pan)', *Chōsa to jōhō – Issue Brief Number 227 (Sept. 28, 1993)*, p. 6.]

63  For example, Shichirō Murakami, *kuriru shotō no bunkengaku-teki kenkyū*, Tokyo: San'ichi-Shobō, 1987; Wada, Tokyo: 1990; Yūichi Takano, 'Hoppō ryōdo no hōri' in Kokusai hōgaku-kai, ed., *Hoppō ryōdo no chii – chishima karafuto o meguru shomondai*, Nanpō dōhō engo kai, 1962; Kimura, 1993; Takamine Sugihara, 'Kokusaihō kara mita hoppō ryōdo' in Kimura, ed., *Hoppō ryōdo o kangaeru*, Hokkaido shimbun-sha, 1981.

## 2  Hatoyama's visit to Moscow, 1956

1  A chronological chart is provided in Appendix 1 for reference.

2  'Joint Declaration by the Union of Soviet Socialist Republics and Japan, Signed at Moscow, on 29 October 1956' (extract), *United Nations, Treaty Series: Treaties and International Agreements Registered or Filed and Recorded with the Secretariat of the United Nations*, No. 3768, Vol. 263, 1957, p. 114.

3  Kimura, 1993, p. 107.

4  For this point, please see the section on 'Nation State' perspectives: Soviet Union, especially, pp. 84–5.

5  Japan's obligation under Article 26 was to expire on April 28, 1955 (*FRUS: 1955–57, Vol. XXIII, Part I, Japan*, 1991, p. 12).

6  Shigeta and Suezawa, 1990, p. 115.

7  Shun'ichi Matsumoto, *Mosukuwa ni kakeru niji – nisso kokkō kaifuku hiroku*, Tokyo Asahi Shimbun-sha, 1966, pp. 114–17; Masaaki Kubota, *Kuremurin eno shisetsu: hoppō ryōdo kōshō 1955–1983*, Bungei Shunjū, Tokyo 1983, pp. 133–7; 'Memorandum of a Conversation between Secretary of State Dulles and Foreign Minister Shigemitsu, (Ambassador Aldrich's Residence, London, August 19, 1956)', *FRUS: 1955–57, Vol. XXIII, Part I, Japan*, 1991, pp. 202–3.

8  'Memorandum of Discussion at the 244th Meeting of the National Security Council, Washington, April 7, 1955' (Source: Eisenhower Library, Whitman File, NSC Records. Top Secret. Drafted by Gleason on April 8) in *FRUS: 1955–57, Vol. XXIII, Part 1, Japan*, 1991, p. 41.

9  From Tokyo to Secretary of State, No: 67, July 11, [1956] 794.00/7–1156, Record of the Department of State, International Affairs: Japan 1955–59, National Archive, Washington D.C. (N.A. hereafter).

10  For the rumours of the communist money contribution to the Japanese Socialist and other organisations, see *Nihon Keizai Shimbun* of 4 July 1956, *Hua Hsin Wen* (Chinese newspaper) dated 7 July 1956, 794.00/7–2056, N.A.

11  Egypt was increasing its voice among Asia-African countries after the revolution of 1952. In July 1956, after the US and UK refused, and the Soviet Union offered, financial assistance for construction of the Aswan High Dam, Egypt nationalised the Suez Canal. In October of the same year, this led to a military clash between Egypt on the one hand and UK, France and Israel on the other.

12 For this point, please see, The Moscow negotiations: Shigemitsu's decision, pp. 70–3.

13 Memorandum of discussion by Gleason, March 11: Eisenhower Library, Whitman File, NSC Records, in Editorial Note, *FRUS: 1955–57, Vol. XXIII*, 1991, p. 29.

14 Memorandum of discussion at the 244th Meeting of the National Security Council, Washington, April 7, 1955 (Source: Eisenhower Library, Whitman File, NSC Records. Top Secret. Drafted by Gleason on April 8), *FRUS: 1955–57, Vol. XXIII*, 1991, p. 43.

15 Ibid.

16 *Treaty of Peace with Japan*, Australia Treaty Series, 1952, No. 1, p. 14.

17 As for the details, see 'Memorandum of Conversation Between Secretary of State Dulles and Foreign Minister Shigemitsu, Ambassador Aldrich's Residence, London, August 19, 1956, 6 pm'. *FRUS: 1955–1957, Vol. XXIII, Part I, Japan*, 1991, pp. 202–4.

18 Department of State for the Press: August 28, 1956, No. 450, Secretary Dulles' News Conference of August 28, 1956, FO371/121040, XC10742, Public Record Office, London (P.R.O. hereafter), also *FRUS: 1955–57, Vol. XXIII* (1991), p. 211.

19 Letter from A.J. de la Mare, British Embassy, Washington DC, to C.T. Crowe, Esq., C.M.G., Far Eastern Department, Foreign Office, London, May 29, 1956, FO371/121039, XC10742, P.R.O.

20 *FRUS 1955–57, Vol. XXIII* (1991), p. 221.

21 FO371/121041, XC10742, P.R.O.

22 Ibid., also 661.941/8–356, N.A.

23 Refer to the section on Post-war dealing over the Pacific in Chapter 1 (pp. 19–20).

24 Takahiko Tanaka, *Nisso kokkō kaifuku no shiteki kenkyū*, Tokyo: Yūhikaku, 1993.

25 From Bill Dening to W. Denis Allen, August 18, 1955, FO371/115234, XC10742, P.R.O.

26 *The Japan News*, 13 February 1953, Kyodo-UP, London, 12 February 1953, Australian Archives (ACT): A1838/2; 515/4.

27 Ibid.

28 Ibid.

29 He was issuing instructions that the 7th Fleet 'no longer be employed to shield communist China' (*Current Notes on International Affairs, Vol. 26*, 1955, Dept. of External Affairs, Canberra, p. 164).

30 *The Japan News*, 13 February 1953, in Australian Archives (ACT): A1838/2; 515/4.

31 From A. L. Mayall, Foreign Office, to R .T. Ledward, Esq., Tokyo, 11 July, 1955, FO371/115233, XC10742, P.R.O.

32 From Bill Dening to W.D. Allen, July 27, 1955. FO371/1152, XC10742, P.R.O.

33 Matsumoto, 1966, po. 41–4.

34 Ibid., p. 49.

35 From Bill Dening (British Embassy Tokyo) to W.D. Allen (Esquire, C.B., C.M.G., Foreign Office, S.W.I), August 18, 1955, FO371/115234, XC10742, P.R.O.

36 Ibid.

37 From Allen to Dening, September 13, 1955, FO371/115234, XC10742, P.R.O.

38 Ibid.

39 From Dening to Allen, August 18, 1955, FO371/115234, XC10742, P.R.O.

40 Ibid.

41 From Washington to the Foreign Office, dated September 13, 1956, FO371/121040, XC10742, P.R.O.

42 Both the US and Japan supported the British position.

43 From A.J. de la Mare, British Embassy, Washington D.C., to C.T. Crowe, Esq., C.M.G., Far Eastern Department, Foreign Office, London, S.W.1., Air Bag Confidential 10638/2/59/56, FO371/121041, XC10742, P.R.O.

44 Telegram From the Secretary of State to the Department of State. (Department of State, Central Files, 661.941/8–22. Secret; Priority; Limit Distribution.), *FRUS: 1955–1957, Vol. XXIII*, p. 204.

45 'Memorandum of Conversation Between Secretary of State Dulles and Foreign Minister Shigemitsu, Ambassador Aldrich's Residence, London, August 19, 1956, 6 pm'. (Source: Department of State, Conference Files: Lot 62 D 181, CF745. Secret. Drafted by Arthur Ringwalt.) *FRUS: 1955–57, Vol. XXXIII*, p. 203.

46 Telegram From the Secretary of State to the Department of State. (Department of State, Central Files, 661.941/8–2256. Secret; Priority; Limit Distribution.), *FRUS: 1955–57, Vol. XXIII*, p. 205.

47 Ibid., pp.122–3.

48 Memorandum of Conversation, Confidential, Department of State, October 30, 1956, 661.941/10–3056, N.A.

49 To Mr. Plimsoll, From U.J. Percival, East Asia Section, re. 'United Press Questions Concerning Territorial Provisions of the Japanese Peace Treaty', Confidential, 5 September, 1956, Australian Archives(Can): A1838/2;515/4.

50 Ibid.

51 Ibid.

52 Matsumoto, 1966; Ichirō Hatoyama, *Hatoyama Ichirō kaikoroku*, Tokyo: Bungeishunjū-sha, 1957.

53 Takezō Shimoda, *Sengo nihon gaikō no shōgen*, Tokyo: Gyōsei mondai kenkyū-jo, 1974, Takashi Itō and Yukio Watanabe, ed., *Zoku Shigemitsu Mamoru shuki*, Tokyo: Chūōkōron-sha, 1988.

54 Akira Shigemitsu, '*Hoppō ryōdo' to soren gaikō*, Tokyo: Jiji tsūshin-sha, 1983; Kubota 1983.

55 Donald Hellmann, *Japanese Domestic Politics and Foreign Policy: The peace agreement with the Soviet Union*, Berkeley, CA: University of California Press, 1969; Savitri Vishwanathan, *Normalization of Japanese–Soviet Relations 1945–1970*, Tallahassee, FL: Diplomatic Press, 1973; Young C. Kim, *Japanese–Soviet relations: Interaction of politics, economics and national security*, Beverly Hills: Sage, 1974.

56 Wada, 1990; 'Hoppō ryōdo mondai o saikō suru', *Sekai*, February, 1992, pp. 219–32; Wada, 'Rekishi no hansei to keizai no ronri', *Gendai nihon shakai 7. kokusai-ka*, Tokyo daigaku shuppan-kai, 1992, especially pp. 297–308; Tanaka, 1993; Tanaka, 'Nisso kokkō kaifuku kōshō (1955–56) to Shigemitsu gaikō', *Kokusai seiji*, Vol. 99, March 1992, pp. 149–67.

57 As seen in that Hellmann (1969) and others dedicated entire volumes, Japanese decision making during the period of the peace negotiaitons with the USSR in the mid-1950s was extremely complicated. Those volumes may be referred to for detailed and diverse pictures during the negotiations; my study limits its focus to the above two specific issue areas.

58 For example, Junnosuke Masumi and Robert Scalapino, *Gendai nihon no seitō to seiji*, Tokyo: Iwanami shinsho, 1979; Junnosuke Masumi, *Sengo seiji*, Tokyo: Tokyo daigaku shuppan-kai, 1983, Junnosuke Masumi, *Gendai seiji*, Tokyo: Tokyo daigaku shuppan-kai, 1985; Chalmers Johnson, *MITI and the Japanese Miracle: The*

*growth of industrial policy, 1925–1975*, Stanford CA: Stanford University Press, 1982; Stanford CA: Takashi Inoguchi and Tomoaki Iwai, *Zokugiin no kenkyū*, Tokyo: Nihon Keizai Shimbun-sha, 1987; Takashi Inoguchi, *Gendai kokusai seiji to nihon: pāru hābā gojū-nen no nihon gaikō*, Tokyo: Chikuma-shobō, 1991; John Quansheng Zhao, *Japanese Policymaking: the politics behind politics: Informal mechanisms and the making of China policy*, Westport, CN: Praeger, 1993; Masaharu, Gotōda *sei to kan*, Tokyo: Kōdan-sha, 1994.

59  Hellmann, 1969, pp. 13–14.

60  See Nobutoshi Nagano, *Nihon gaikō no subete* (2nd edn), Tokyo: Gyōsei mondai kenkyū-jo, 1989, pp. 337–8.

61  Hiroshi Kimura, 'Japanese–Soviet relations: On the frontier', in Gregory Flynn *et al.*, eds, *The West and the Soviet Union*, New York: St. Martin's, 1990, p. 185.

62  According to opinion survey by *Asahi Shimbun*, the poll reflected 40 per cent approval rating and 8 per cent disapproval rating for the Hatoyama Cabinet in January 1955, while *Asahi Shimbun*'s survey on the preceding Yoshida Cabinet in May 1954 showed 23 per cent approval rating and 48 per cent disapproval rating. [Source: Kokuritsu kokkai toshokan chōsa rippō kōsa–kyoku (prepared by Makoto Tanaka, Seiji gikai-ka), 'Naikaku seitō shijiritsu no suii – shōwa 21-nen ikō', *Chōsa to jōhō – Issue Brief Number 180* (Mar. 31, 1992), p. 12.]

63  Vishwanathan, 1973, p. 70.

64  Hatoyama, 1957, pp. 111.

65  Memorandum of Conversation (participants: Shigenobu Shima, Minister, Embassy, Robert O. Blake, EE), Department of State, 661.94/2–156, N.A.

66  John Welfield, *An Empire in Eclipse*, London: Athlone, 1988, p. 131.

67  Ichirō Kōno, *Nihon no shōrai*, Tokyo: Kōbun-sha, 1965, p.26; Welfield, 1988, pp. 131–3.

68  Interview with a former MID senior official in August, 1994.

69  Foreign Service Despatch From AmEmbassy, Stockholm to the Department of State, Washington, June 7, 1956, 661.941/6–756, N.A.

70  For example, *Asahi Nenkan*, 1957, pp. 234–5, *Yomiuri Nenkan*, 1957, p. 279.

71  N. Adyrkhayev, 'The secret of the meeting between Kōno and Bulganin', *Far Eastern Affairs*, 2, 1990, p. 160–1; Kimura, (1993), p. 131.

72  Vishwanathan, 1973, pp. 114–20; Hellman, 1969, pp. 176–9.

73  Hatoyama, 1957, cited in Matsumoto, 1966, p. 160.

74  *Asahi Shimbun*, 11 August 1956.

75  Junnosuke Masumi, *Sengo seiji: 1945–55 nen*, Vol. 2, Tokyo daigaku shuppan-kai, 1983, p. 460.

76  *Joint Compendium*, pp. 36–7 (Japanese), pp. 41–2 (Russian).

77  Kubota, 1983, p. 32.

78  Hellmann, 1969, p. 34; Shimoda, 1974, p. 142; Kubota, 1983, pp. 32–4, 74; Matsumoto, 1966, p. 31; Wada, 'Hoppō ryōdo mondai o saikō suru', *Sekai*, February 1992, pp. 223–4.

79  Shimoda, 1974, vol. 1, p. 142.

80  Wada, 1992, p. 224.

81  Matsumoto, 1966, p. 43.

82  Ibid., p. 49; *Asahi Shimbun*, 20 October 1956.

83  Akira Shigemitsu is a nephew of the Foreign Minister Mamoru Shigemitsu. He accompanied the plenipotentiaries and served also as an interpreter during the Japanese–Soviet negotiations. He became an ambassador to the Soviet Union at a later period.

84  Shigemitsu, 1983, p. 52.
85  Matsumoto, 1966, pp. 44–46; Hatoyama, 1957, p. 177.
86  *Asahi Nenkan*, 1957, p. 230.
87  Shigemitsu, 1983, p. 76.
88  Masumi, 1985, pp. 447–8.
89  Ibid., p. 3.
90  Prior to this, on 22 October, the Liberal Party's Foreign Policy Deliberation Committee announced almost the same account of the territorial negotiation policy. However, on 25 October Hatoyama said that return of Kunashiri and Etorofu might be unrealisable. Matsumoto also expressed the same concern on 26 October. (*Bōei Nenkan* 1956, p. 136, *Asahi Shimbun* 22, 25 and 26 October)
91  Wada, 1992, p. 304.
92  Memorandum of Conversation, February 1, 1956, Department of State, 661.94/2–156 CSBM, National Archive in Washington DC. (See pp. 101–2.)
93  Shigemitsu, 1983, p. 139.
94  Hellmann, 1969, p. 37.
95  Tanaka, 1992, pp. 164–5.
96  *Nihon Keizai Shimbun*, 12 August 1956; *Asahi Shimbun*, 13 August 1956; Matsumoto, 1966, pp. 113–15.
97  Incoming Telegram, Department of State, From Tokyo to Secretary of State, July 19, 1956, 661.941/7–1956, N.A.
98  Tanaka, 1992, p.165.
99  Ibid.
100  From Tokyo to Secretary of State, February 8, 1955, Confidential, 661.94/2–855, N.A.
101  *Asahi Shimbun*, 31 May 1956.
102  The third meeting of 6 August 1956; *Asahi Shimbun*, 10 August 1956.
103  *Asahi Shimbun*, 1 August 1956.
104  *Nihon Keizai Shimbun*, 12 August 1956; *Asahi Shimbun*, 13 August 1956; Matsumoto, 1966, pp. 113–15.
105  Hellmann, 1969, p. 37.
106  Wada, 1990, p. 209.
107  From Allison (Tokyo) to Secretary of State, 6 September, 1956, 794,00/9–656, N.A.
108  Ibid.
109  Shigeta and Suezawa, eds, 1990, pp. 148–9.
110  Ibid., pp. 149–50.
111  Matsumoto, 1966, p. 140.
112  Ibid., pp. 139–42.
113  Ibid., p. 144.
114  Ibid.
115  Memorandum of conversation 29 October 1956, Department of State, 661.941/10–2956, N.A.
116  This point will be discussed on p. 102.
117  *Asahi Shimbun*, 29 May 1956.
118  *Yomiuri Nenkan 1957*, p. 245.
119  For details see Hellmann, 1969, pp. 131–40.
120  From A.J. de la Mare, British Embassy, Washington D.C., to C.T. Crowe, Esq., C.M.G., Far Eastern Department, Foreign Office, London, S.W.1, September 7, 1956, FO371/121040, FO371/121041, XC10742, P.R.O.

121 For example, Kimura, 1989; Kimura, 1993.
122 Trans. and ed. Jerrold L. Schecter with Vyacheslav V. Luchkov, Boston: Little, Brown, 1990.
123 The wording of the article was revised at the Supreme Soviet of August 1953, in accordance with the new rule adopted at the Nineteenth Party Congress of October 1952.
124 Joseph L. Nogee and Robert H. Donaldson, *Soviet Foreign Policy since World War II*, New York: Pergamon, 1988 (3rd edn), pp. 48–9.
125 Edward L. Warner, III, *The Military in Contemporary Soviet Politics: An Institutional Analysis*, New York: Praeger, 1977, pp. 44–5; Nogee and Donaldson, 1988, pp. 49–51.
126 Nogee and Donaldson, 1988, pp. 52–61.
127 Archie Brown, ed., *The Soviet Union Biographical Dictionary*, London: Weidenfeld and Nicholson, 1990, pp. 131, 163.
128 Nogee and Donaldson, 1988, p. 27.
129 The text of Khruschev's speech is in *The Sino-Soviet Dispute*, Documented and analysed by G.F. Hudson, Richard Lowenthal and Roderick MacFarquhar, New York: Frederick A.Praeger, 1961, pp. 43–4, cited in Nogee and Donaldson, 1988, pp. 28–9.
130 Jukes, 1973, p. 5.
131 For details, see V.I. Lenin, 'The Socialist Revolution and the Right of Nations to Self-Determination', in *The National-Liberation Movement in the East*, Moscow, 1957, p. 109, also Lenin, *Collected Works*, Vol. 22, p. 187 cited in Jukes, (1973), p. 5.
132 Nogee and Donaldson, 1988, p. 151.
133 Coal was yielding world-wide its primacy as an energy source to oil. Large new oil discoveries made in the Soviet Union were beginning to provide exportable surpluses by the mid-1950s, and Stalin-period resource policies with uncertain technological and economic prospects (such as underground gasification of coal) were being terminated. The Soviet Union began to adopt a policy of providing oil to developing countries. Some of the recipients of Soviet aid in the Middle East and South East Asia, also were associated with the fact of the abundant oil reserve, as well as the national liberation movement, in the region. (Hidetaka Miyazaki, 'Soren no shigen seisaku', in Fumio Nishimura and Seijiro Nakazawa, eds, *Gendai soren no seiji to gaikō*, Tokyo: Nihon kokusai mondai kenkyū-jo, 1986, p. 332–5.)
134 *Sovieto Nenpō 1955*, p. 665, cited in Vishwanathan, 1973, p. 66.
135 Ibid., pp. 668–70, in Vishwanathan, 1973, p. 66.
136 *Mainichi Shimbun*, 17 December 1954.
137 *Khrushchev Remembers: The Glasnost Tapes*, trans. and ed. Jerrold L. Schechter with Vyacheslav V. Luchkov, Boston: Little, Brown, 1990, p. 83.
138 Ibid., pp. 83–4.
139 Ibid., p. 85.
140 Ibid., p. 86.
141 Ibid., p. 86.
142 Robert A. Scalapino and Junnosuke Masumi, *Parties and Politics in Contemporary Japan*, Berkeley, CA: University of California Press, 1962, pp. 23–53: Vishwanathan, 1973, pp. 24–5.
143 *Khrushchev Remembers*, p. 85.
144 Ibid., p. 86.

145   Ibid., p. 85.
146   Ibid., p. 88.
147   Ibid.
148   Ibid.
149   Ibid.
150   Aleksander N. Panov, *Fusin kara sinrai e*, Tokyo: Simul Press, 1992, p. 3.
151   From interview with Kapitsa on 6 July 1994.
152   Interview conducted on 11 July 1994.
153   From interview with Kapitsa on 6 July 1994.
154   *Daiichirui dai yon-go, Shūgiin Gaimuinkai giroku daiichigō*, 30 November 1955, p. 3.
155   Vishwanathan, 1973, p. 75.
156   Matsumoto, 1966, Appendix 6, pp. 183–6.
157   *Kruschev Remembers*, p. 89
158   Ibid.
159   From interview with Kapitsa on 6 July 1994.
160   *Khrushchev Remembers*, p. 89.
161   Jukes, 1993, p. 2.
162   Jukes's study elucidates that the importance of the Kuriles changed over the years. Khrushchev was quite right at the time he wrote. The entire Kurile chain was so unimportant strategically that there were no military garrisons on any of the islands from 1963 to 1978. But the situation then changed radically for reasons such as development of new military technology and the accordingly modified strategy of the USSR, and, he argues, will change back only with implementation of START-2. For details, see Jukes, 1993.
163   Memorandum for The Secretary, Department of Defence, Melbourne, 19 March, 1950, Australian Archives (Can): A1838/2;515/4.
164   Memorandum for The Secretary, Department of External Affairs, Canberra, ACT, by W.R. Hodgson, Australian Mission in Japan Tokyo, Memo. No. 252, File 1314/4, Australian Archives (Can): A1838/2; 515/4.
165   *Nippon Times*, 21 March 1950, Australian Archives (Can): A1838/2;515/4.
166   Memorandum from Embassy Moscow for the Secretary, Canberra, Department of External Affairs, 31st March 1950, Canberra, Australian Archives (Can): A1838/2;515/4.
167   Ibid.
168   *Khrushchev Remembers*, pp. 88–9.
169   John J. Stephan, *The Kuril Islands: Russo-Japanese Frontier in the Pacific*, Oxford: Clarendon Press, 1974, p. 216.
170   Ibid., p. 90.
171   Matsumoto, 1966, p. 36.
172   Ibid. p. 38.
173   *New York Times*, 27 May 1955 (emphasis added).
174   For the list, see Shigemitsu, 1983, p. 53.
175   The Soviet government announced neither total nor partial numbers of Japanese detainees taken to its own territories. The numbers were revealed recently for the first time in Russia. According to archival data of the Ministry of Internal Affairs of the USSR, disclosed recently by Aleksei Alekseevich Kirichenko, Institute of Oriental Studies Russian Academy of Sciences, 639,635 Japanese were made Prisoners of War in August 1945. Apart from those released (65,245) or transferred to Mongolia (more than 12,000), 546,086

were taken to prison camps or labour battalions in the USSR. Aleksei
Kirichenko 'Sledi Oborvalis' v Taishete: Iaponskie Voennoplennie v GULAGe'
(The Tracks were broken in Taishet: Japanese Prisoners of War in the
GULAG), Moscow, *Shpion*, 1/1993, pp. 59–61.

176 Shigemitsu, 1983, p. 69.
177 *Proekt, Mirnyi dogovor mezhdu soyuzom sovetskikh sotsialisticheskikh respublik i iaponiei*
(Draft, Peace Treaty between the Union of Soviet Socialist Republics and
Japan), stamped *Gokuhi* (Strictly Confidential) in Japanese, attached to correspondence from A.L. Mayall (Foreign Office, London) to R.T. Ledward,
Esq., (British Embassy, Tokyo), 11 July 1955, FO371/115233, XC10742,
P.R.O.
178 Ibid.
179 Shigemitsu, 1983, p. 58.
180 For an interesting and detail analysis of this point, see Wada, 1990, pp. 166–71.
181 Memorandum of Conversation, February 1, 1956, Department of State,
661.94/2–156 CSBM, N.A.
182 Memorandum of conversation, 29 October 1956, Department of State,
661.941/10–2956, N.A.
183 From Mr. Robertson To the Acting Secretary, June 2, 1955, 661–94/6–255,
N.A.
184 *Asahi Shimbun*, 20 October 1956.
185 From: A.J. de la Mare, British Embassy, Washington, D.C., September 7, 1956,
To: C.T. Crowe, Esq., C.M.G., Far Eastern Department, Foreign Office,
London, S.W.1, FO371/121040, XC10742, P.R.O.
186 From: A.J. de la Mare, British Embassy, Washington, D.C., September 15,
1956, To: C.T. Crowe, Esq., C.M.G., Far Eastern Department, Foreign Office,
London, S.W.1, FO371/121041, XC10742, P.R.O.
187 *Bōei Nenkan*, 1956, p. 134.
188 *Khrushchev Remembers*, p. 90.
189 Hoppō ryōdo mondai taisaku kyōai (Northern Territories Issue Association),
*Japan's Northern Territories*, 1974, Tokyo, p. 39.
190 Kyodo (Sapporo, July 3) in Memo No. 729, 9 July 1958, To The Secretary,
Dept. of External Affairs Canberra From 1st Secretary, Australian Embassy,
Tokyo, Australian Archives (Can): A1838/2;515/4.
191 *Kyoto Shimbun*, 2 March 1993.
192 *Joint Compendium*, p. 39 (Japanese), p. 45 (Russian).
193 *Khrushchev Remembers*, p. 89.

# 3 Tanaka's Visit to Moscow, 1973

1 'The Soviet–Japanese Joint Communiqué, October 10, 1973', (excerpts) *Joint
Compendium*, p. 41 ( Japanese), p. 48 (Russian).
2 Joseph L. Nogee and Robert H. Donaldson, *Soviet Foreign Policy since Second World
War*, New York: Pergamon Press, 1981, (1st edn), p. 242.
3 Henry A. Kissinger, *White House Years*, Boston: Little, Brown, 1979, pp. 191–4.
4 *Asahi Nenkan* 74, p. 84.
5 For comprehensive collection of Kissinger's essays and public statements on US
foreign policy, see Henry A. Kissinger, *American Foreign Policy, Expanded Edition*,
New York: W.W. Norton, 1974.

6　Ibid., p. 165.

7　The original idea of the Soviet campaign for an all-European conference goes back to V. Molotov's proposal for an All-European Treaty on Collective Security at the Berlin conference of foreign ministers in 1954. For a comprehensive review of the background to the conference on security and cooperation in Europe, see Robert H. Donaldson, 'Global power relationships in the seventies: The view from Kremlin', in Paul Cocks, Robert V. Daniels and Nancy Whittier Heer, eds, *The Dynamics of Soviet Politics*, Cambridge, MA.: Harvard University Press, 1976, pp. 329–33.

8　Dmitri B. Petrov, *Yaponia v mirovoi politike*, Moscow: Mezhdunarodnye otnoshenie, 1973, p. 94.

9　Young C. Kim, *Kuremurin no tainichi seisaku – nichi bei chu so yonkyoku kōzō no naka de*, Tokyo: T.B.S. Buritanika, 1983, pp. 135–6.

10　Ibid.

11　*Asahi Nenkan 1973*, p. 360.

12　Kim, 1974. pp. 67–8.

13　For example, Gaimushō, ed., *Gaikō Seisho: Waga gaikō no kinkyō, Vol.1, shōwa49-nendoban (no. 18)*, 1974, p. 20.

14　Kim, 1983, p. 127. Author's interviews with former Soviet senior officials conducted in July 1994.

15　Vice President under President Eisenhower. For 1955–6 Soviet–Japanese negotiations and US involvement, please see Chapter 2, especially pp. 42–6.

16　*New York Times*, 8 August 1957; Douglas H. Mendel, *The Japanese People and Foreign Policy: A study of public opinion in post-treaty Japan*, Berkeley, CA: University of California Press, 1961, p. 212.

17　*Asahi Shimbun*, 4 July 1968.

18　*Ashahi Shimbun*, 2–4 July, 1968.

19　*New York Times*, 5–7 July 1968.

20　*New York Times*, 5 December 1950.

21　Senkaku rettō is located in the East China Sea about 190 km northeast of Taiwan, 300 km southwest of Okinawa and 350 km east of mainland China. It consists of five uninhabited coral islands and three sunken rocks.

22　*Asahi Shimbun*, 14 July 1964; *Asahi Nenkan* 1965, p. 259; Stephan, 1974, pp. 221–2.

23　*Nihon Keizai Shimbun*, 8 October 1973; *Asahi Shimbun*, 3 December 1972; Stephan, 1974, p. 223.

24　Anti-Japanese feeling in Asia was, for example, strongly demonstrated upon Prime Minister Tanaka's visit to South East Asia in January 1974, when he visited five ASEAN countries of the Philippines, Thailand, Singapore, Malaysia and Indonesia. Except in the Philippines under the marshal law, in other capitals, especially Bangkok in Thailand and Jakarta in Indonesia, Tanaka was greeted with historically unprecedented anti-Japanese demonstrations. While the 'anti-Japanese' movement contained 'anti-regime' elements in those countries, consisting of forces for democratisation emerging from civil society and concerned to end the Vietnam War, the increasing level of Japanese investment was perceived there as 'Japanese Economic Imperialism'. After his visits, Prime Minister Tanaka candidly reviewed the Japanese lack of understanding of the situation in South East Asian countries, and announced increased economic aid and establishment of an international cooperation agency.

25　According to opinion survey by *Asahi Shimbun*, the poll reflected 62 per cent approval rating and 10 per cent disapproval rating for the Tanaka Cabinet in September 1972, while *Asahi Shimbun*'s last survey on the preceding Sato Cabinet in December 1971 showed 24 per cent approval rating and 58 per cent disapproval rating. [Source: Kokuritsu kokkai toshokan chōsa rippō kōsakyoku (prepared by Makoto Tanaka, Seji gikai-ka), 'Naikaku seitō shijiritsu no suii – shōwa 21-nen ikō', *Chōsa to jōhō – Issue Brief Number 180 (Mar. 31, 1992)*, p. 13.]

26 Shigezō Hayasaka, *Seijika Tanaka Kakuei*, Tokyo: Chūōkōron-sha, 1987, pp. 327–8.

27 Ibid., p. 328

28 Ibid.

29 Sōichirō Tawara, 'Amerika no tora no o o funda Tanaka Kakuei', *Chūōkōron*, July 1976.

30 Keisuke Suzuki, *Nisso keizai kyōryoku*, Tokyo: Nihon kokusai mondai kenkyū-jo, 1974, p. 122.

31 Takashi Inoguchi and Tomoaki Iwai, *Zokugiin no kenkyū*, Tokyo: Nihon Keizai Shimbun-sha, 1987, p. 24.

32 Chalmers Johnson, 'MITI and Japanese International Economic Policy', in Robert A. Scalapino, ed., *The Foreign Policy of Japan*, Berkeley, CA: University of California Press, 1977, p. 278.

33 *Asahi Shimbun*, 27 January 1973 (evening edition).

34 *Asahi Shimbun*, 4 January 1973 (evening edition).

35 Kokkai (Diet), 'Dai ichirui dai yon-go, *Shūgiin Gaimuiinkai giroku*, showa 48-nen 3-gatu 7-ka (7 March, 1973)', *71kokkai Shūgiin iinkai kaigi-roku, 6, gaimu 1972–73*, p. 11.

36 Kinya Niizeki, *Nisso kōshō no butaiura – aru gaikōkan no kiroku*, Tokyo: Nihon hōsō shuppan kyōkai 1989, p. 169: *Asahi Shimbun*, 7 March 1973.

37 Gaimushō, *Gaikō Seisho: Waga gaikō no kinkyō*, Vol.1, *shōwa49-nendoban (no. 18)*, 1974, p. 20.

38 E.M. Zhukov, et al., *Soren no asia seisaku*, Vol. II, Tokyo: Simul Press, 1981, p. 428.

39 Ikeda was also one of those LDP Yoshida faction members who was absent from the Diet at the time of ratification of the Joint Declaration of 1956.

40 An *Aide-Mémoire* to Japan, dated 7 September 1956.

41 For example, see 'Ikeda sōri hatsu furushichofu shusō ate shokan' (15 November 1961), in Shigeta and Suezawa eds, *Nisso kihon bunsho/shiryo-shu*, Tokyo: Sekainougoki-sha, 1990, pp. 178–81.

42 Foreign Office, Japanese Government, *Minor Islands Adjacent to Japan Proper: Part 1. The Kurile Islands, the Habomais and Shikotan*, November 1946 [Australian Archives (ACT): A1838/2:515/4]; see also Chapter 1, especially pp. 24–30.

43 See Chapter 1, pp. 24–33.

44 The First Peace Treaty Negotiation (after the diplomatic restoration of 1956) was held upon Foreign Minister Ōhira's visit to Moscow, 21–4 October 1972; see p. 133.

45 *Asahi Shimbun*, 25 October 1972 (evening edition).

46 Toshima Odagiriri, *Soren gaikō seisaku no hensen*, Tokyo: Tokyo Kansho Fukyu Inc., 1978, p. 424; L.I. Brezhnev, *Leninskim kursom, rechi i stat'i*, tom 4, Moskva: Izdatel'-stvo Politicheskoi Literaturi, 1974. c.80.

47 Kubota, 1983, p. 234.

48 Minoru Hirano, *Gaikō kisha nikki – Ōhira gaikō no ninen*, vol. 2, Tokyo: Gyōsei tsūshin-sha, 1978, p. 145.

49  Ibid., p. 125.

50  Hiroshi Kimura's article, 'Soviet studies in Japan' in the journal *Soviet Studies*, October 1987, offers a thorough overview on the shortcomings of the field in Japan.

51  Gilbert Rozman, 'Japan's Soviet-watchers in the first years of the Gorbachev era: The search for a worldview for the Japanese superpower', *The Pacific Review*, vol. 1, No. 4, 1988a, pp. 420–1.

52  Interview conducted on 29 August 1994.

53  John J. Stephan, 'On the Soviet–Japanese Historiographical Frontier', *Siberica*, Winter, 1990–91, Vol.1, n2, p. 184–94, North Pacific Studies Center Oregon Historical Society, Portland Oregon USA.

54  Tatsunori Ueji, *Hoppō ryodō*, Tokyo: Kyōiku-sha, 1978, pp. 115–24. For difference of positions among parties, see Young C. Kim, 1974, pp. 47–8.

55  The Japan Communist Party (JCP) at first adapted its view on the territorial issue to that of Moscow. In a position statement of 28 January 1950, the party openly supported Soviet claims to all the Kuriles. But during the next two decades it reviewed and changed its positions.

56  Gaimushō daijinkanbō kokunai kōhō-ka, *Warera no hoppō ryōdo*, 1993, p. 36.

57  *Dai 71 Kokkai, Shūgin giroku dai 60-go*.

58  *Nihon Keizai Shimbun* (evening edition), 6 October 1973.

59  *Asahi Shimbun*, 24 March, 1972; Panov, 1992, p. 73.

60  Interview conducted in August 1994.

61  *Asahi Shimbun* (evening edition), 8 October 1973.

62  *Nihon Keizai Shimbun*, October 10 1973.

63  Ibid.

64  Ibid.

65  On 15 May, 1972, having been under the US occupation since 1945, Okinawa was returned to Japan (though the US military bases and facilities were retained). In the late 1960s, the reversion movement became intensified and the US agreed its early reversion. The formal agreement over the reversion was signed on 17 June, 1971 (and came into effect 15 May 1972).

66  Kim, 1974, pp. 40–2.

67  Hayasaka, 1987, p. 214.

68  Personal communication with *Gaimushō* officials.

69  See the Testimony of Herbert S. Levine before the Senate Foreign Relations Committee in *Detente*, Hearings before the Senate Foreign Relations Committee, US Senate, 93 Congress, 2nd session, August 15, 20, 21, September 10, 12, 18, 19, 24, 25, October 1, 8, 1974, Washington: U.S. Government Printing Office, 1975, pp. 19–30; Nogee and Donaldson, (3rd edn), p. 257.

70  Kim, 1974, pp. 56–7.

71  Niizeki, 1989, p. 223, also see Vishwanathan, 1973, pp. 91–112 for details.

72  Interview with former MID senior officials, July 1994.

73  Interview with a former Central Committee (CPSU) senior official, July 1994.

74  Brown, 1990, p. 50.

75  Ibid., pp. 50–1.

76  Hiroshi Kimura, *Soren to roshiajin – sono hassō to kōdō no yomikata*, Ōfū-sha, p. 122.

77  Eiichi Sato, 'Chapter 5: Ajia shūdan anzen hoshō kōsō no tenkai', in Fumio Nishimura and Seijiro Nakazawa, eds, *Gendai soren no seiji to gaikō*, 3rd edn, Tokyo: Nihon kokusai mondai kenkyū-jo, 1986, pp. 413–14.

78  Kimura, 1989, pp. 130–1.

79 Arkady N. Shevchenko, *Breaking with Moscow*, New York: Alfred A. Knopf, 1985, p. 210.
80 Interview with former MID officials, July 1994.
81 Ibid.
82 Ibid.
83 For example, John J. Stephan, 'Asia in the Soviet Conception', in Donald S. Zagoria, ed., *Soviet Policy in East Asia*, Yale University Press, 1982, p. 31; Kimura, 1989, pp. 123–9.
84 Interview conducted in July 1994.
85 D.V. Petrov, 'SSHA-Yaponiya: Novaya Faza', S*SHA*, 1972, No. 2, p. 25.
86 Yuri Polsky, *Soviet Research Institutes and the Formation of Foreign Policy: The Institute of World Economy and International Relations IMEMO*, Falls Church, VA: Delphic Associates, Inc., 1987, p. 18, in Hiroshi Kimura 'Gorubachofu no tainichi seisaku – henka to mondai', *Soren kenkyū* (*Soviet Studies*), No. 12, April 1991, p. 58.
87 Vernon V. Aspaturian, *Process and Power in Soviet Foreign Policy*, Boston: Little, Brown, 1971, p. 640.
88 Nogee and Donaldson, 1988 (3rd edn), p. 56.
89 Gromyko, 1989, p. 257.
90 Ibid., p. 235.
91 Interview with former MID officials, July 1994.
92 Ibid.
93 Brezhnev, 1974. c.80.
94 Letter to Prime Minister Ikeda from Khrushchev (gist) dated 8 February, 1961; Shigeta and Suezawa, eds, 1988, 1990, pp. 181–6.
95 In answering a question by Mr Orita, chief editor of *Chūbu Shimbun* in 1962, Khrushchev said clearly that the territorial problem was already resolved. See, for example, in Shigeta and Suezawa, 1990, p. 456.
96 Kimura, 1993, pp. 148–9.
97 Panov, 1992, p. 67.
98 Interview conducted in July 1994.
99 Kokkai (Diet), *Sangiin Gaimuiinkai giroku dai 20-go*, 17 July 1973, p. 14.
100 Kim, 1974, p. 34.
101 Interview conducted in July 1994.
102 Interview with scholars at IVAN and IDV in July 1994; Boris N. Slavinsky, *Chishima senryo 1945-nen natsu*, Tokyo: Kyōdō tsūshin-sha, 1993, p. 31.
103 N. Slavinsky, 'Na puti k sovetsko-Japonskomu mirnomu dogovoru', *Problemi Dal'nego Vostoka*, 3/1989, p. 142.
104 Interview conducted in July 1994.
105 Boris N. Slavinsky, *Muchi no daishō – soren no tainichi seisaku*, Tokyo: Ningen no kagaku-sha, 1991, pp. 14–15.
106 In 1978 the SLBM were deployed in the Sea of Okhotsk, from where they could attack the US mainland, additionally the bastion concept was developed to protect the sea area as sanctuary for them. Thus, the preparations for deployment must have begun much earlier. The first delta-class submarines with a 4200-km missile range had entered service in 1972, construction of facilities for them at Petropavlovsk-Kamchatskii must have begun about then if they were to be ready by 1978, and development of the longer-range missiles needed to reach the USA from the sea of Okhotsk must also have begun. Thus, it must have been clear by 1972 that the Sea of Okhotsk would cease to be

strategically unimportant by the end of the decade because of decisions already taken to deploy submarines there. For details, see Jukes, 1973.

107  Panov, 1992, p. 68.
108  Interview conducted in July 1994.
109  Interview conducted in July 1994.
110  After 24 September, preceding Tanaka's departure, with an initiative of the Soviet side, office-level sessions to prepare for the Joint Statement were held four times between the Japanese *Gaimushō* and the Soviet Embassy in Tokyo. The draft had several blank spots, especially with a big one on the territorial issue, for which the difference in the positions of the two nations became very clear. (Minoru Hirano, 1978, pp. 139.)
111  Hirano, 1978, p. 139.
112  Kunio Yanagida, *Nihon wa moeteiruka*, Tokyo: Kōdan-sha, 1983, p. 415.
113  Ibid.
114  *Izvestiya*, 13 November 1970; Kim, 1974, p. 44.
115  See Chapter 2, p. 102.
116  Kim, 1974, pp. 39–44.
117  Kazuyuki Kinbara, 'Japan and the Development of Siberia', in Kinya Niizeki, ed., *The Soviet Union in Transition*, Boulder, CO: Westview Press, 1987, pp. 200–15.
118  According to an opinion survey by *Asahi Shimbun*, approval rating for the Tanaka Cabinet in December 1974 went down to 12 per cent while disapproval rating jumped up to 69 per cent [Source: Kokuritsu kokkai toshokan chōsa rippō kōsa-kyoku 'Naikaku setō shijiritsu no suii – shōwa 21-nen ikō', *Chōsa to jōhō – Issue Brief Number 180 (Mar. 31, 1992)*, p. 13.]
119  Refer to Gaimushō daijinkanbō kokunai kōhō-ka, *Warera no hoppo ryodo 1993*, p. 24.
120  In January 1981 on the basis of resolutions adopted in the previous year, Japan's Cabinet designated 7 February – the date of the signing of the Russo-Japanese Treaty of Commerce, Navigation and Delimitation (Treaty of Shimoda) in 1855 – as 'Northern Territories Day'.

# 4  Gorbachev's visit to Tokyo, 1991

1  The Soviet–Japanese Joint Statement, April 18 1991 (excerpts), *Joint Compendium*, pp. 42–3 (Japanese), pp. 49–50 (Russian).
2  Panov, 1992; Kazuhiko Tōgō, *Nichiro shinjidai eno josō*, Tokyo: Simul Press, 1993.
3  START-1 was signed on 31 July 1991.
4  Robert Gilpin, *The Political Economy of International Relations*, Princeton, NJ: Princeton University Press, 1987, p. 347.
5  Gaimushō, *Gaikō Seisho: waga gaikō no kinkyō*, 1991, p. 12.
6  Gilpin, 1987, p. 398.
7  'Speech by Mikail Gorbachev in at a ceremonial meeting devoted to the presentation of the order of Lenin to the City of Vladivostok', *Far Eastern Affairs*, 1, 1987, pp. 13–14.
8  John Stephan, 'Historical Perspective', in M.J. Valencia, ed., *The Russian Far East and the North Pacific Region: Emerging issues in international relations, selected papers from a conference held at East–West Center*, Honolulu, Hawaii, 1992, p. 3.
9  Gilbert Rozman, 'Moscow's Japan-watchers in the first years of the Gorbachev era: The struggle for realism and respect in foreign affairs' in *The Pacific Review*, Vol. 1, No. 3, 1988b, pp. 264–5.

10  *Asahi Shimbun, Yomiuri Shimbun,* 4 May 1989.
11  *Yomiuri Shimbun,* 21 June, 1988; *Japan Times,* 23 July 1988.
12  Gaimushō daijinkanbō kokunai kōhō-ka, *Warera no hoppō ryōdo 1993-nenban,* p. 80; *Japan Times,* 12 July 1990.
13  Gaimushō, 1991, p. 5.
14  Ibid., p. 6.
15  Ibid.; *Japan Times,* 12 July 1990.
16  Ibid.
17  *Nihon Keizai Shimbun,* 11 July 1990.
18  *Yomiuri Shimbun,* 3 April 1991.
19  Ibid.
20  Kimura, 1989, p. 142.
21  *Nihon Keizai Shimbun,* 12 July 1990.
22  Kimura, 1989, p. 244.
23  According to an opinion survey by *Asahi Shimbun,* the poll reflected a 56 per cent approval rating and 25 percent disapproval rating for the Kaifu Cabinet in July 1990, ['Naikaku seitō shijiritsu no suii – shōwa 21-nen ikō,' *Chōsa to jōhō – Issue Brief Number 180 (Mar. 31, 1992),* p. 15.]
24  Hatoyama's premiership was two years (December 1954 to December 1956) and Tanaka's was two years and four months (July 1972 to November 1974).
25  Gilbert Rozman conducted a stimulating analysis of Soviet and Japanese perceptions toward each other in the first five years of the Gorbachev era, attempting interesting observation and categorization of diversified opinions and thoughts among influential opinion leaders, politicians, bureaucrats and academics both in Japan and the USSR: Rozman, 1988b, pp. 257–75; Rozman, 1988a, pp. 412–28. As for Japanese perceptions and policies toward the Soviet Union, Hasegawa's analysis based on opinion surveys is also noteworthy: Tsuyoshi Hasegawa, 'Japanese perceptions and policies toward the Soviet Union: changes and prospects under the Gorbachev era', in Pushpa Thambipillai and Daniel C. Matuszewski (eds), *The Soviet Union and the Asia Pacific Region: Views from the region,* New York: Praeger, 1989, pp. 23–37.
26  Rozman 1988a, p. 415.
27  Ibid., p. 413.
28  Interviews with Gaimushō senior officials in June and July 1994.
29  Panov, 1992, p. 34.
30  Gaimushō daijinkanbō kokunai kōhō-ka, *Warera no hoppō ryōdo 1993-nenban,* p. 27.
31  Prime Minister Toshiki Kaifu in an interview with *Literaturnaya gazeta* (carried in the 16 January 1991 issue).
32  See Lonny E. Carlile 'The Changing Political Economy of Japan's Economic Relations with Russia: the Rise and Fall of Seikei Fukabun', *Pacific Affairs,* Fall 1994, Vol. 67. No. 3, pp. 411–32.
33  Tōgō, 1993, p. 35.
34  *Asahi Nenkan 1991,* p. 75.
35  Panov, 1992, pp. 108–110.
36  Ibid., p. 108.
37  See Chapter 3, p. 130.
38  Ichirō Suetsugu, 'Gorbachofu no rainichi o oete', *Go daitoryo rainichi to kongo no nisso kankei,* Tokyo: Shinju-kai, 1991, p. 4.
39  Gaimushō daijinkanbō kokunai kōhō-ka, *Warera no hoppō ryōdo 1993-nenban,* p. 32.
40  Ibid., p. 36.

41 Kazushige Hirasawa, 'Japan's emerging foreign policy', *Foreign Affairs*, Vol. 54. No. 1, October 1975, pp. 155–72.

42 Haruki Wada, 'Chishima rettō no han'i ni tsuite', *Sekai*, May 1986; Wada, 1990, Shichirō Murayama, *Kuriru shotō no bunkengakuteki kenkyū*, Tokyo: San'ichi-shobō, 1987.

43 *Sankei Shimbun*, 10 April 1990.

44 *Asahi Nenkan* 1991, p. 75.

45 Ibid.

46 Tetsu Ueda, 'Jo ni kaete', *Hoppō ryōdo-shi shiryō-hen*, Tokyo: SBB shuppan-kai, 1991, p. 14.

47 *Asahi Jānaru*, 26 April 1991.

48 *Asahi Shimbun*, 16 April 1991.

49 Panov, 1992, p. 111.

50 Tōgō, 1993, p. 158.

51 For example, see *Warera no hoppō ryōdo 1993-nenban*, pp. 86–7.

52 Tōgō, 1993, p. 158.

53 Ibid., p. 159.

54 Ibid., p. 163.

55 In addition to the dispute with the USSR/Russia, Japan has two other unresolved boundary problems that affect its territorial sovereignty. They are uninhabited territories called Senkaku rettō (Diaoyū in Chinese) and Takeshima (Tok-dō in Korean), respectively with China and South Korea. With respect to Senkaku, located in the East China Sea about 190 km northeast of Taiwan, Japan and China agreed to freeze the status quo and entrust resolution of the issue to the next generation. This policy stance is based on the broad perspective that the territorial issue should not be an impediment to the development of friendly relations between the two countries. Through the adoption of this policy, the territorial question was put aside when normal relations were established in 1972, and when the Japan–China Treaty of Peace and Friendship was signed in 1978. The islands are also claimed by Taiwan, which Japan does not recognize as a negotiation partner. As for the ownership of Takeshima, Japan and South Korea did not reach any agreement when their relations were normalized in 1965. At the tenth annual cabinet meeting between the two nations in 1978, it was jointly decided to continue negotiations regarding ownership, but the dispute has not been settled yet.

56 Rozman, 1988a, p. 415.

57 Kokkai (Diet), *Sangiin Gaimuiinkai giroku* (12 April, 1991), p. 23.

58 For example, upon his visit to the USSR in January 1991, the Foreign Minister Nakayama demanded the Soviet 'political decision' (*seijiteki ketsudan*) and expected 'resolution' (*eidan*) on the 'Northern Territories' issue at his meetings with the Soviet Foreign Minster Bessmertnykh and President Gorbachev respectively. The 'political decision' was also demanded upon the Soviet Foreign Minster Bessmertnykh's visit to Japan in March. No concrete answer for the solution of the territorial problem was however received. [Gaimushō, *Gaikō Seisho*, 1991, pp. 318–9].

59 *Asian Financial Review*, 2 February 1995.

60 *Gaikō Seisho*, 1991, p. 320.

61 *Asahi Nenkan* 1992, p. 75.

62 Tōgō, 1993, p. 161.

63 See Chapter 2, pp. 83–4.

64 For the economic background to *Perestroika*, refer to Robert F. Miller, 'The Soviet economy: Problems and solutions in the Gorbachev view', in R.F. Miller, J.H. Miller and T.H. Rigby, eds, *Gorbachev at the Helm: A new era in Soviet politics?*, London: Croom Helm, *1987* pp. 109–35; Hiroshi Kimura, *Sōkessan-Gorubachofu no gaikō*, Tokyo: Kōbun-do, 1992, pp. 61–5.

65 Kimura, 1992, p. 33.

66 'Soren kittenno nihontsū shokugyō gaikōkan – Nikorai Sorobiyofu', *Sekai Shūhō*, 20 May 1986, p. 29.

67 Kimura, 1992, p. 32.

68 Geoffrey Jukes, 'Foreign policy and defence', in R.F. Miller, J.H. Miller and T.H. Rigby, eds, 1987, pp. 189–213; Mikhail Gorbachev, *Perestroika: New Thinking for our Country and the World*, New updated edition, New York, Harper & Row, 1988, pp. 121–46.

69 *Pravda*, 15 March 1985, cited in Panov, 1992, p. 26.

70 Panov, 1992, pp. 26–7.

71 Rozman, 1988b, p. 260.

72 'Speech by Mikail Gorbachev in at a ceremonial meeting devoted to the presentation of the order of Lenin to the City of Vladivostok', *Far Eastern Affairs*, 1, 1987, pp. 13–14.

73 Panov, 1992, pp. 28–9.

74 Kapitsa was then appointed to the director of the Institute of Oriental Studies of the Soviet Academy of Science.

75 Kimura, 1992, pp. 127–9.

76 Interview with a *Gaimushō* senior official in July 1994.

77 Ibid.

78 For example, see I. Kovalenko 'The rout of Japanese militarism and the national liberation revolution', *Far Eastern Affairs*, No. 3, 1985, p. 34.; 'The fight of the communist party of Japan against Peking's great power interference', *Far Eastern Affairs*, No. 1, 1981, pp. 14–27.

79 Kimura, 1992, p. 31.

80 For example, Hasegawa, 1989, p. 29.

81 Kimura, 1992, p. 16.

82 See Chapter 3, p. 138.

83 Brown 1990, p. 483.

84 Ibid, p. 484.

85 In most cases directly for the Supreme Soviet, for it was left to the republics themselves to decided whether they wished to have a republican Congress of People's Deputies.

86 Brown, 1990, p. 484.

87 Kimura, 1992, p. 79.

88 Yanaev, who was formerly a deputy chairman of the trade union movement and was elected from the trade unions to the Congress of People's Deputies of the USSR in 1989, was making rapid promotion in 1990 – prior to the appointment to those posts in the texts, he was appointed to a Politburo member and a Secretary of the Central Committee.

89 Panov, 1992, p. 23.

90 For example, the Japanese Ambassador Noriaki Muto's explanation about the Japanese position of the territorial dispute was introduced without modified tranlation. as before (*Asahi Shimbun, Sankei Shimbun*, 30 April 1988). Article by Stanislav Kondrashev in *Izvestiya*, 23 September 1988.

91  Panov, 1992, pp. 69–70.
92  For example, Igor Rogachev, 'Pretenzii, lishennye osnovanii', *Izvestia*, 24 April 1989; I. Latishev, 'Kadrovyi defitsit', *Pravda*, 16 March 1989.
93  *Nihon Keizai Shimbun*, 19–20 September, 1988.
94  For example, See Ovchinnikov, 'Perevernut' stranistu', *Pravda*, 15 December 1988; E. Primakov, then the director of IMEMO, also refered to *Senkaku rettō* formula between Japan and China at his interview with *Yomiuri Shimbun (Yomiuri Shimbun*, 1 February 1988).
95  Valentin P. Fyodorov, 'Preobrazovaniya na Saakhaline', *Sovetsky Sakhalin*, 29 August 1990, translated into Japanese by Hiroshi Kimura, 'Saharin chiji ga uttaeru, hoppō ryōdo mondai no "dai 4 no michi",' *Asahi Jānaru*, Vol. 32, No. 42, 19 October 1990, pp. 27–8
96  Panov, 1992, p. 74.
97  *Pravda*, 9 July 1990, cited in Panov, 1992, p. 77.
98  Panov, 1992, p. 74.
99  For example, see discussion by V. Lukin (People's Deputy of Russia, historian), G. Kunadze (IMEMO), K. Sarkisov (IVAN), Tyshetskii (MID Diplomatic Academy), *Ogonyok*, No. 20, May 1990.
100  For example, B. Slavinsky, 'Towards Soviet–Japanese Peace Treaty', *Far Eastern Affairs*, Vol. 4, 1989, pp. 106–20.
101  Panov, 1992, p. 73.
102  *Japan Times, Asahi Shimbun*, 13 October 1991.
103  Atsushi Kojima, *Soren chishikijin peresutoroika o kataru*, Yomiuri Shimbun-sha, 1990, pp. 78–9. *Asahi Shimbun*, 5 November 1989.
104  *Asahi Shimbun*, 27 October 1989.
105  Panov, 1992, p. 73.
106  Alexei V. Zagorsky, 'Naze hoppō yontō henkan o shijisuru noka – nisso kankei seijō-ka saitan no michi', *Sekai Shūhō*, 20 November, 1990, pp. 58–61; also see Hiroshi Kimura, 'Gorubachofu no tainichi seisaku – henka to mondai', *Soren Kenkyū*, No. 12, April 1991, p. 70.
107  Panov, 1992, pp. 75–6.
108  Kimura, 1993, p. 187.
109  Ueda, 1991, p. 80.
110  Ibid.
111  Panov, 1992, pp. 75–6.
112  Kimura, 1992, p. 236.
113  Jukes analyses Russian military writers' arguments on strategic importance of the disputed islands and throws questions on their validity. For details see Geoffrey Jukes, *Russia's Military and the Northern Territories Issue*, Working Paper No. 277, Strategic & Defense Studies Centre, Australian National University, 1993.
114  Panov, 1992, p. 82.
115  Ibid., pp. 82–3.
116  Ibid., pp. 98–102.
117  Ibid., p. 101.
118  *Asahi Nenkan* 1992, p. 75.
119  Ibid.
120  Gaimushō daijin kanbō kokunai kōhō-ka, *Warera no hoppō ryōdo 1993-nenban*, p. 28.
121  Ibid, p. 117–23.

122 Panov, 1992, p. 42.
123 Ibid., p. 30.
124 Ibid, pp. 33–4.
125 *Pravda*, 4 May 1989.
126 *Pravda*, 6 May 1989
127 Panov, 1992, p. 33.
128 *Sankei Shimbun*, 28 September 1990.
129 Panov, 1992, p. 149.
130 *Asahi Nenkan 1992-nenban*, p. 76.

## 5  Yeltsin's visit to Tokyo, 1993

1 'Tokyo declaration on Japan–Russia Relations (provisional translation), 13 October 1993'. *Japan Times*, 14 October 1993.
2 In January 1994, the US and Russia held a summit meeting and announced the 'Moscow Declaration' to confirm their bilateral partnership.
3 Gaimushō, *Gaikō seisho: yori anzende ningentekina sekai o motomete (1)*, 1993, p. 28.
4 *Nihon Keizai Shimbun*, 15 April 1993.
5 *Asahi Nenkan: Data book 1994*, Asahi Shimbun-sha, p. 123.
6 Though specific numbers are not known, thousands of women are said to have been forced to work as 'comfort women' (*jūgun ianfu*) at sexual-service facilities, for the comfort of Japanese occupation forces during the Pacific War. Many of them were mobilized without their consent in northeast and southeast Asia. Among them, Koreans are believed to have been the majority.
7 *Asahi Nenkan: Data book 1994*, Asahi Shimbunsha, p. 123.
8 The Hosokawa cabinet registered 71 per cent approval rating in September 1993.
9 Takashi Inoguchi, 'Shin zokugiin taibō-ron,' *Chūōkoron*, March 1994, p. 104.
10 Ibid., p. 108.
11 *Asahi Nenkan 1994*, Asahi Shimbun-sha, p. 123.
12 Interview conducted in July 1994.
13 *Asahi Shimbun*, 14 October 1993.
14 *Asahi Shimbun*, 9 October 1993.
15 Ibid., 13 October 1993.
16 *Nihon Keizai Shimbun*, 15 April 1993.
17 *Asahi Shimbun*, 13 October 1993.
18 *Yomiuri Shimbun*, 14 October 1993.
19 *Japan Times*, 24 January 1992.
20 *Ekonomisuto*, 15 September 1992.
21 See Chapter 3, pp. 132–3, also p. 147.
22 Lev Sukhanov, *Bosu to shiteno Yeltsin*, Tokyo; Dōbunshoin International, 1993, p. 259–63.
23 Interview conducted in June 1994.
24 *Asahi Shimbun*, 13 October 1993.
25 John M. Thompson, *Russia and the Soviet Union: An historical introduction from the Kievan state to the present*, Boulder, CO: Westview Press, 1994, p. 293.
26 As with all the other institutions, non-Russian employees were given the choice of staying and working in accustomed conditions, or returning their native capitals, in which many had not resided. Most chose to stay in Moscow. (Karen

Dawisha and Bruce Parrot, *Russia and the New States of Eurasia: The politics of upheaval*, Cambridge: Cambridge University Press, 1994, p. 202.)

27  Dawisha and Parrot, 1994, p. 204.

28  Interviews in July 1994.

29  Sukhanov, 1993, p. 265; *Asahi Shimbun*, 10 September 1992.

30  Sukhanov, 1993, p. 265.

31  After the Gorbachev's visit to Japan, the Bureau of the Pacific and Southeast Asian countries was reorganised as the Asia-Pacific Bureau in the Soviet MID. The Bureau was subsequently headed by A. Panov. The position was then replaced by the former Ambassador, to Japan, N. Soloviev, while Panov was appointed to the Ambassador to South Korea in May.

32  Among those, who suffered most from the political change and domestic turmoil, were the intellectuals in such institutions as IMEMO and IVAN, that used to play important roles as the Gorbachev's think-tanks. Since early 1992, soon after the collapse of the Soviet Union, the government funding to those institutions was suspended. The financial difficulties have been continuing since then. These institutions barely manage to support themselves by supplementing the funding by leasing some of the office space to private companies, and many of the researchers seem to have started other part-time jobs that pay more. The relative decline in the quality of the research may also be attributed to the lack of resources, for the institutions cannot afford even purchase of foreign journals. Many young researchers have left the institutions for other opportunities. For example, some have joined the Russian MID following G. Kunadze, and others have learned about political change while being abroad and do not seem to be interested in going home for a while. (From interviews and personal conversations with Russian academics, July 1994.)

33  *Asahi Shimbun*, 14 October 1993.

34  *Yomiuri Shimbun*, 11 October, 1993 (it had been decided that G. Kunaze would be the Ambassador to South Korea and his position as Deputy Foreign Minister be replaced by A. Panov, in return).

35  Shinju-kai, *Nisso hatsu no shunō kaidan, eritsin daitōryō no rainichi to sono sōkatsu*, Shinju-kai series No. 21, 1993.

36  Interview with K. Sarkisov in July 1994.

37  Boris El'stin, *Zapiski prezidenta*, Moskva: Izdatel'stvo 'Ogonek', 1994, p. 185.

38  Ibid.

39  Sukhanov, 1993, p. 259.

40  Ibid., pp. 260–1.

41  Ibid., p. 262.

42  *Japan Times*, 18 August 1993.

43  *Japan Times*, 29 August 1993.

44  *Izvestiya*, 11 September 1993, p. 3; *FBIS* Sov, 93/176, 14 Sep. 1994, pp. 13–14.

45  *Japan Times*, 20 August 1993.

46  *Nihon Keizai Shimbun*, 13 October 1993 (evening edition), *Asahi Shimbun*, 14 October 1993.

47  Gaimushō, *Gaikō Seisho 1993: yori anzen de ningenteki na sekai o motomete*, p. 75.

48  *Japan Times*, 1 November 1993.

49  *Asahi Shimbun*, 27 September 1993.

50  *Izvestiya*, 13 October 1993, 1.3, *FBIS* Sov, 13 Oct. 1993, 17–18.

51  Tōgō, 1993, pp. 226–7.

52  Panov, 1992, p. 44.

# Conclusion

1 Graham T. Allison, *Essence of Decision: Explaining the Cuban Missile Crisis*, Boston: Little, Brown, 1971, pp. 5–6.

2 Hideo Satō, *Taigai Sisaku*, Tokyo: Tokyo daigaku shuppan-kai, 1989, pp. 38–9.

3 Ibid., pp. 39–40.

4 Glenn H. Snyder and Paul Diesing, *Conflict Among Nations: Bargaining decision-making and system structure in international crisis*, Princeton, NJ: Princeton University Press, 1977, p. 337.

5 Panov, 1992, p. 5.

6 James E. Dougherty and Robert L. Pfaltzgraff, Jr., *Contending Theories of International Relations: A comprehensive survey*, *New York: Harper & Row*, 3rd edn, 1990, p. 476.

7 Kunio Yanagina, *Nithon wa moeteiruka*, Tokyo: Kōdan-sha, 1983, p. 415.

8 For example, in April 1996 Hideo Usui visited Russia for the first time as Director-General of the Japanese Defense Agency, and the Russian Minister of Defense, Army General Igor Nikolayevich Rodionov, in return visited Japan for the first time in May 1997. ('Saikin no nichiro kankei', The Ministry of Foreign Affairs of Japan, 1997, http://www.mofa.go.jp/mofaj/gaiko/gaikos/russia97/Kankei.html).

9 *Yomiuri Shimbun; Asahi Shimbun*, 25 July 1997.

10 *Asahi Shimbun*, 3 November 1997.

11 *Asahi Shimbun*, 14 December 1997.

12 James A. Dator and Sharon J. Rodgers, *Alternative Futures for the States Courts of 2020*, American Judicature Society, 1991, p. 80.

13 'Press Conference by the Press Secretary November 14, 1997', The Ministry of Foreign Affairs of Japan, 1997, http://www2.nttca.com:8010/infomofa/press/1997/11/1117.html.

14 Most recently, during British Prime Minister Tony Blair's visit to Japan, Prime Minister Ryūtarō Hashimoto extended Japan's 1995 apology to British POWs mistreated by the Japanese Imperial Army during the Second World War II. (*Asahi Shimbun*, 13 January 1998).

15 Yeltsin reportedly signalled that the Kremlin is no hurry to settle the Kuriles dispute, and instead believes that conflict will be best eased by strengthening economic cooperation and interdependence. (*Los Angeles Times*, 2 November 1997).

16 Personal interview with *Gaimushō* officials conducted 7 January 1998.

17 'Press Conference by Press Secretary, November 14, 1997', The Ministry of Foreign Affairs of Japan, 1997.

18 *Asahi Shimbun*, 25 July 1997.

19 "'Hoppō ryōdo no kaiketsu sokusin ni kansuru ken' no ketsugi", *Dai 132-kai kokkai shūgiin okinawa oyobi hoppō ryōdo mondai ni kansuru tokubetsu kokkai giroku dai 7-gō*, 7 June, 1995, p. 1. Also, "'Hoppō ryōdo no kaiketsu sokusin ni kansuru ken' no ketsugi", *Dai 132-kai kokkai sangiin okinawa oyobi hoppō ryōdo mondai ni kansuru tokubetsu kokkai giroku dai 7-gō*, 7 June, 1995, p. 1.

# Bibliography

## Books and monographs

Adelman, Jonathan R. and Deborah Anne Palmieri, *The Dynamics of Soviet Foreign Policy*, New York: Harper & Row, 1989.

Allison, Graham, *Essence of Decision: Explaining the Cuban Missile Crisis*, Boston: Little, Brown, 1971.

Allison, Graham, Hiroshi Kimura and Konstantin Sarkisov, eds, *Beyond Cold War to Trilateral Cooperation in the Asia-Pacific Region: Scenarios for new relationships between Japan, Russia, and the United States*, Cambridge, MA: Harvard University; *Nichi-Bei-Ro shinjidai eno shinario: Hoppō ryōdo jirenma kara no dasshutsu*, Tokyo: Daiyamondo-sha, 1993; *Ot kholodnoi voini k trekhstoronnemu sotrudnichestvu v aziatsko-tikhookeanskom regione: Stsenarii razvitiya novikh otnoshenii mezhdu Yaponiei, Rossiei i Soedinennimi Shtatami*, Moskva: Nauka, 1993.

Aspaturian, Vernon V., *Process and Power in Soviet Foreign Policy*, Boston: Little, Brown, 1971.

Ball, W. Macmahon, *Japan Enemy or Ally?*, London and Sydney: Cassell, 1948.

Bialer, Seweryn, ed., *The Domestic context of Soviet Foreign Policy*, Boulder, CO: Westview Press, 1981.

Brezhnev, L.I., *Leninskim Kursom, Rechi i Stat'i*, tom 4, Moskva: Izdater'stvo Polichicheskoi Literaturi, 1974.

Brown, Archie, ed., *The Soviet Union: A biographical dictionary*, London: Weidenfeld and Nicolson, 1990.

Brzezinski, Zbigniew K., *Ideology and Power in Soviet Politics*, New York: Praeger, 1967.

Byrnes, James F., *Speaking Frankly*, London: Heinemann, 1947.

Curtis, Gerald L., *The Japanese Way of Politics*, New York: Columbia University Press, 1988.

Dator, James A. and Sharon J. Rodgers, *Alternative Futures for the States Courts of 2020*, Chicago, IL: American Judicature Society, 1991.

Dallin, Alexander, *Soviet Conduct in World Affairs*, New York: Greenwood Press, 1960 (1st edn), 1975 (2nd edn).

Dawisha, Karen and Bruce Parrot, *Russia and the New States of Eurasia: The politics of upheaval*, Cambridge: Cambridge University Press, 1994.

Dean, John Russell, *The Strange Alliance: The story of our efforts at war time cooperation with Russia*, New York: Viking Press, 1947.

Dougherty, James E., and Robert L. Pfaltzgraff, Jr., *Contending Theories of International Relations: A comprhensive survey*, New York: Harper & Row, 1990.

El'stin, Boris, *Zapiski prezidenta*, Moskva: Izdatel'stvo 'Ogonek,' 1994.

Gilpin, Robert, *The Political Economy of International Relations*, Princeton, NJ: Princeton University Press, 1987.

Gorbachev, Mikhail, *Perestroika: New thinking for our country and the world*, new, updated edn, New York: Harper & Row, 1988.

Gotōda, Masaharu, *Sei to Kan*, Tokyo: Kōdan-sha, 1994.

Gromyko, Andrei, *Memories*, trans. Harold Shukman, London, Sydney, Auckland, Johannesburg: Hutchinson, 1989.

Harriman, W. Averell and Elie Abel, *Special Envoy to Churchill and Stalin, 1941–1946*, New York: Random House, 1975.

Hatoyama, Ichiro, *Hatoyama Ichiro kaikoroku*, Tokyo: Bungeishunjū-sha, 1957.

Hayasaka, Shigezo, *Seijika Tanaka Kakuei*, Tokyo: Chūōkōron-sha, 1987.

Hellmann, Donald C., *Japanese Domestic Politics and Foreign Policy: The peace agreement with the Soviet Union*, Berkeley: University of California Press, 1969.

Hirano, Minoru, *Gaikō kisha nikki – Ōhira gaikō no ninen*, vol. 2, Tokyo: Gyōsei tsūshin-sha, 1978.

Hoffmann, Erik P. and Frederic J. Fleron, Jr., ed., *The Conduct of Soviet Foreign Policy*, New York: Aldine, 1971 (1st edn), 1980 (2nd edn).

Inoguchi, Takashi and Tomoaki Iwai, *Zokugiin no kenkyū*, Tokyo: Nihon Keizai Shimbun-sha, 1987.

—— *Gendai kokusai seiji to nippon, pāru hābā gōju-nen no nihon gaikō*, Tokyo: Chikuma-shobō, 1991.

Ito, Takashi and Yukio Watanabe, eds, *Zoku Shigemitsu Mamoru Shuki*, Tokyo: Chūōkōron-sha, 1988.

Ivanov, Vladimir I. (principal ed), James E. Goodby and Robert A. Scalapino (Co-eds), *Japan, Russia, and the United States Prospects for Cooperative Relations in the New Era*, A Conference Report, Washington DC: United States Institute of Peace, July 1993.

Ivanov, Vladimir I., James E. Goodby and Nobuo Shimotomai, eds, under the auspices of the United States Institute of Peace, *Northern Territories and Beyond: Russian, Japanese, and American perspectives*, Westport, CN: Praeger, 1995.

Johnson, Chalmers, *MITI and the Japanese Miracle: The growth of industrial policy, 1925–1975*, Stanford, CA: Stanford University Press, 1982.

Jukes, Geoffrey, *The Soviet Union in Asia*, Sydney: Angus and Robertson, 1973.

*Khrushchev Remembers: The Glasnost tapes*, Translated and Edited by Jerrold L. Schecter with Vyacheslav V. Luchkov, Boston: Little, Brown, 1990.

Kim, Young C., *Japanese–Soviet Relations: Interaction of politics, economics and national security*, Washington Papers, Vol. II, 21, Washington DC: Georgetown University, Center for Strategic and International Studies: Beverley Hills and London: Sage, 1974.

—— *Kuremurin no tainichi seisaku – Nichi bei chu so yonkyoku kōzō no naka de*, Tokyo: T.B.S Buritanika, 1983.

Kimura, Hiroshi, *Soren to roshiajin – sono hassō to kōdō no yomikata*, Tokyo: Ōfu-sha, 1981.

—— ed., *Hoppō ryōdo o kangaeru*, Sapporo, Hakkaido shimbun-sha, 1981.

—— *Hoppō ryōdo: kiseki to henkan eno joso*, Tokyo: Jijitsūshin-sha, 1989.

—— *Kuremurin no seiji rikigaku*, Tokyo: Adoa Shuppan, 1991.

—— *Sōkessan Gorubachofu no gaikō*, Tokyo: Kobun-do, 1992.

—— *Nichiro kokkyō koshō-shi: ryōdo mondai ni ikani torikumuka*, Tokyo: Chūōkāron-sha, 1993.

Kissinger, Henry A., *White House Years*, Boston: Little, Brown, 1979.

—— *American Foreign Policy, Expanded Edition*, New York: W.W. Norton, 1974.

Kojima, Atsushi, *Soren chishikijin peresutoroika o kataru*, Tokyo: Yomiuri Shimbun-sha, 1990.

Kōno, Ichiro, *Nihon no shōrai*, Tokyo: Kōbun-sha, 1965.

Kubota, Masaaki, *Kuremurin eno shisetsu: hoppō ryōdo kōshō 1955–1983*, Tokyo: Bungei Shunjū-sha, 1983.

Lane, David, *Politics and Soviet in the USSR*, New York: New York University Press, 1971 (1st edn), 1978 (2nd edn).

Lensen, George A., *The Strange Neutrality: Soviet–Japanese relations, 1941–45*, Tallahassee, FL: Diplomatic Press, 1972.

Masumi, Junnosuke, *Sengo seiji: 1945–55 nen*, vol. 2, Tokyo: Tokyo daigaku shuppan-kai, 1983.

—— *Gendai seiji: 1955 nen igo*, Tokyo: Tokyo daigaku shuppaniai, 1985.

Masumi, Junnosuke and Robert Scalapino, *Parties and Politics in Contemporary Japan*, Berkeley CA: University of California Press, 1962.

—— *Gendai nihon no seito to seiji*, Tokyo: Iwanami shinsho, 1962.

Matsumoto, Shun'ichi, *Mosukuwa ni kakeru niji – nisso kokko kaifuku hiroku*, Tokyo: Asahi Shimbun-sha, 1966.

Mendel, Douglas Heusted, *The Japanese People and Foreign Policy: A study of public opinion in post-treaty Japan*, Berkeley, CA: University of California press, 1961.

Murayami, Shichirō, *Kuriru shotō no bunkengaku-teki kenkyū*, Tokyo: San'ichi-shobō, 1987.

Nagano, Nobutoshi, *Gaimushō kenkyū: Nihon gaikō shittai jittai to jisseki bunseki*, Tokyo: Simul Press, 1975.

—— *Nihon gaikō no subete*, 2nd edn, Tokyo: Gyōsei mondai kenkyū-jo, 1989.

Nakajima, Mineo, *Kokusai kankeiron*, Tokyo: Chūōkōron-sha, 1993.

Niizeki, Kinya, *Nisso kōshō no butaiura – aru gaikōkan no kiroku*, Tokyo: Nihon hōsō shuppan kyōkai, 1989.

Nishimura, Kumao, *Nihon gaikō-shi 27: Sanfuranshisuko heiwa jōyaku*, Tokyo: Kajima kenkyū-jo shuppan-kai, 1971.

Nogee, Joseph L. and Robert H. Donaldson, *Soviet Foreign Policy since World War II*, New York: Pergamon, 1981 (1st edn), 1984 (2nd edn), 1988 (3rd edn), 1992 (4th edn).

Odagiriri, Toshima, *Soren gaikō seisaku no hensen*, Tokyo: Tokyo Kansho fukyu, 1978.

Panov, Alexander N., *Fusin kara shinrai e*, Tokyo: Simul Press, 1992.

Pempel, T.J., *Policy and Politics in Japan: Creative conservatism*, Philadelphia, PA: Temple University Press, 1982.

Petrov, Dmitri B., *Yaponia v mirovoi politike*, Moskva: Mezhdunarodnye otnosheniya, 1973.

Polsky, Yuri, *Soviet Research Institutes and the Formation of Foreign Policy: The Institute of World Economy and International Relations IMEMO*, Falls Church, VA: Delphic Associates, 1987.

Robertson, Myles L. C., *Soviet Policy towards Japan: An analysis of trends in the 1970s and 1980s*, Cambridge and New York: Cambridge University Press, 1988.

Russet, Bruce and Harvey Starr, *World Politics: The menu for choice*, New York: W.H. Freeman and Company, 1981.

Satō, Hideo, *Taigai seisaku*, Tokyo: Tokyo Daigaku Shippan-kai, 1989.

Scalapino, Robert A., ed., *The Foreign Policy of Japan*, Berkeley, CA: University of California Press, 1977.

Scalapino, Robert A. and Junnosuke Masumi, *Parties and Politics in Contemporary Japan*, Berkeley, CA: University of California Press, 1962.

Shevchenko, Arkady N., *Breaking with Moscow*, New York: Alfred A. Knopf, 1985.

Shigemitsu, Akira, *'Hoppō ryōdo' to soren gaikō*, Tokyo: Juji tsūshin-sha, 1983.

Shigeta, Hiroshi and Shoji Suezawa, eds, *Nisso kihon bunsho shiryō-shū: 1855-nen–1988-nen*, Tokyo: Sekainougoki-sha, 1988, 1990.

Shimoda, Takezo, *Sengo nihon gaikō no shōgen*, Tokyo: Gyōsei mondai kenkyū-jo, 1974.

Slavinsky, Boris N., *Muchi no daishō – soren no tainichi seisaku*, Tokyo; Ningen no kagaku-sha, 1991.

—— *Sovetskaya okkupatsiya kuril'skikh ostrovov (avgust-sentyabr' 1945 goda), Dokumental'noe Issledovanie*, Moskva: published at author's own expense, 1993a.

—— *Chishima Senryo – 1945 Natsu*, Tokyo: Kyōdō tsūshin-sha, 1993b.

Snyder, Glenn H. and Paul Diesing, *Conflict Among Nations: Bargaining decision-making and system structure in international crisis*, Princeton, NJ: Princeton University Press, 1977.

Stephan, John J., *The Kuril Islands: Russo-Japanese frontier in the Pacific*, Oxford: Clarendon Press, 1974.

Sukhanov, Lev, *Bosu to shiteno Yeltsin*, Tokyo: Dōbunshoin International, 1993.

Tanaka, Takahiko, *Nisso kokkō kaifuku no shiteki kenkyū*, Tokyo: Yūhikaku, 1993.

Thompson, John M., *Russia and the Soviet Union: An historical introduction from the Kievan state to the present*, Boulder, CO: Westview Press, 1994.

Tōgō, Kazuhiko, *Nichiro shinjidai eno josō*, Tokyo: Simul Press, 1993.

Ueda, Tetsu, ed., *Hoppō ryōdo-shi shiryō-hen* Tokyo: SBB shuppan-kai, 1991.

Ueji, Tatsunori, *Hoppō ryōdo*, Tokyo: Kyōiku-sha, 1978.

Ulam, Adam B., *Expansion and Coexistence: The history of Soviet foreign policy*, 1917–73, 2nd edn, New York: Praeger, 1974.

—— *Dangerous Relations: The Soviet Union in world politics, 1970–1982*, Oxford: Oxford University Press, 1983.

Vishwanathan, Savitri, *Normalization of Japanese–Soviet Relations, 1945–1970*, Tallahassee, FL: Diplomatic Press, 1973.

Vogel, Ezra, ed., *Modern Japanese Organization and Decision Making*, Berkeley, CA: University of California Press, 1975.

Wada, Haruki, *Hoppō ryōdo mondai o kangaeru*, Tokyo: Iwanami-shoten, 1990.

Warner, Edward L. III, *The Military in Contemporary Soviet Politics: An institutional analysis*, New York: Praeger, 1977.

Watanabe, Yukio, ed., *Zoku Shigemitsu Mamoru shuki*, Tokyo: Chūōkōron-sha, 1988.

Welfield, John, *An Empire in Eclipse*, London: Athlone Press, 1988.

Yanagida, Kunio, *Nihon wa moeteiruka*, Tokyo: Kōdan-sha, 1983.

Zhukov, E.M., M.I. Sladkovsky, G.V. Astafiev and M.S. Kapitsa, eds, *Soren no asia seisaku*, vol. II, Tokyo: Simul Press, 1981.

Zimmerman, William, *Soviet Perspectives on International Relations, 1956–1967*, Princeton, NJ: Princeton University Press, 1969.

Zhao, John Quansheng, *Japanese policymaking: The politics behind politics: informal mechanisms and the making of China policy*, New York: Praeger, 1993.

## Articles

Adyrkhayev, N., 'The secret of the meeting between Kōno and Bulganin', *Far Eastern Affairs*, 2, 1990.

Calder, Kent E., 'Japanese foreign economic policy formulation: Explaining the reactive state', *World Politics*, Vol. 40, No. 4, July 1988.

Carlie, Lonny E., 'The changing political economy of Japan's economic relations with Russia: The rise and fall of seikei fukabun', *Pacific Affairs*, Vol. 67, No. 3, Fall 1994.

Clark, Gregory, 'Hoppō ryōdo mondai – warui nowa amerika da', *Bungei Shunjū*, June 1991.

Donaldson, Robert H. 'Global power relationships in the seventies: The view from Kremlin', in Paul Cocks, Robert V. Daniels and Nancy Whitter Heer, eds, *The Dynamics of Soviet Politics*, Cambridge, MA: Harvard University Press, 1976.

Fyodrov, V.P., 'Proobrazovaniya na Sakhaline', trans. into Japanese by Hiroshi Kimura, 'Saharin chiji ga uttaeru, hoppō ryōdo mondai no "dai 4 no michi"', *Asahi Jānaru*, Vol. 32, No. 42, 19 October 1990.

Gorbachev, Mikail, 'Speech delivered at a ceremonial meeting devoted to the presentation of the order of Lenin to the City of Vladivostok', *Far Eastern Affairs*, 1, 1987.

Hasegawa, Tsuyoshi, 'Japanese perceptions and policies toward the Soviet Union: Changes and prospects under the Gorbachev era', in Pushpa Thambipillai and Daniel C. Matuszewski eds, *The Soviet Union and the Asia-Pacific Region: Views from the region*, New York: Praeger, 1989.

Hirasawa, Kazushige, 'Japan's Emerging Foreign Policy', *Foreign Affairs*, Vol. 54. No. 1, October 1975.

Inoguchi, Takashi, 'Shin zokugiin taibō-ron,' *Chūōkoron*, March 1994.

—— 'The ideas and structures of foreign policy: Looking ahead with caution', in Takashi Inoguchi and Daniel I. Okimoto (eds), *The Political Economy of Japan, Vol. 2, The Changing International Context*, Stanford, CA: Stanford University Press, 1988.

Jukes, Geoffrey, 'Foreign policy and defence', in R.F. Miller and J.H. Miller, eds, *Gorbachev at the Helm: A new era in Soviet politics?*, London: Croom Helm, 1987, pp. 189–213.

——— *Russia's Military and the Northern Territories Issue*, Working paper No.277, Strategic & Defence Studies Centre, Australian National University, 1993.

Kimura, Hiroshi, 'Soviet studies in Japan', *Soviet Studies*, October 1987.

——— 'Japanese–Soviet relations: On the frontier', in Gregory Flynn *et al.*, eds, *The West and the Soviet Union*, New York: St Martin's Press, 1990.

——— 'Gorubachofu no tainichi seisaku – henka to mondai', *Soren Kenkyū (Soviet Studies)*, No. 12, April 1991.

Kinbara, Kazuyuki, 'Japan and the development of Siberia', in Kinya Niizeki, ed, *The Soviet Union in Transition* Boulder, CO: Westview, 1987.

Kirichenko, Aleksei, 'Sledi Oborvalis' v Taishete: Iaponskie Voennoplennie v GULAGe', *Shpion*, January 1993.

Koguchi, Motoichi, 'Nisso bōeki shiharai kyōtei no teiketsu', *Bōeki Seisaku*, No. 144, June 1971.

Kovalenko, I. 'The fight of the Communist Party of Japan against Peking's great power interference', *Far Eastern Affairs*, No. 1, 1981.

——— 'The rout of Japanese militarism and the national liberation revolution', *Far Eastern Affairs*, No. 3, 1985.

Lenin, V.I., 'The Socialist Revolution and the right of nations to self-determination', in *The National-Liberation Movement in the East*, Moscow, 1957.

McClelland, Charles A., 'International relations: Wisdom or Science', in James N. Rosenau, ed., *International Politics and Foreign Policy: A reader in research and theory*, New York: Free Press, 1969.

Miller, Robert F., 'The Soviet economy: Problems and solutions in the Gorbachev view', in R.F. Miller and T.H. Rigby, eds, *Gorbachev at the Helm: A new era in Soviet politics?*, London: Croom Helm, 1987, pp. 109–35.

Miller, R.F. and T.H. Rigby, 'Domestic determinants of Soviet external policies: Prospects for change in the 1990s', in Ross Babbage, ed., *The Soviet in the Pacific in the 1990s*, Rushcutters Bay, NSW: Brassey's Australia, 1989.

Miyazaki, Hidetaka, 'Soren no shigen seisaku', in Fumio Nishimura and Seijiro Nakazawa eds, *Gendai soren no seiji to gaikō*, Tokyo: Nihon kokusai mondai kenkyū-jo, 1986.

Moul, William B., 'The level of analysis problem revisited', *Canadian Journal of Political Science* 6, 1973.

Petrov, D.V., 'SSHA-Yaponiya: Novaya Faza', *SSHA*, 1972, No 2.

Rozman, Gilbert, 'Japan's Soviet-watchers in the first years of the Gorbachev era: The search for a worldview for the Japanese superpower', *The Pacific Review*, Vol. 1, No. 4, 1988a.

——— 'Moscow's Japan-watchers in the first years of the Gorbachev era: The struggle for realism and respect in foreign affairs', *The Pacific Review*, Vol. 1, No. 3, 1988b.

Sato, Eiichi, 'Chapter 5: Ajia shūdan anzen hoshō kōsō no tenkai', in Fumio Nishimura and Seijiro Nakazawa, eds, *Gendai soren no seiji to gaikō*, 3rd edn, Tokyo: Nihon kokusai mondai kenkyū-jo, 1986.

Singer, David, 'The level-of-analysis problem in international relations', in Klaus Knorr and Sidney Verba, eds, *The International System: Theoretical Essays*, Princeton,

NJ: Princeton University Press, 1961; also in James N. Rosenau, ed., *International Politics and Foreign Policy: A reader in research and theory*, New York: Free Press; London: Collier-Macmillan, London, rev. edn, 1969.

Slavinsky, Boris N., 'Towards Soviet–Japanese peace treaty', *Far Eastern Affairs*, Vol. 4, 1989.

—— 'Na puti k sovetsko-japonskomu mirnomu dogovoru', *Problemi Dal'nego Vostoka*, *March 1989*.

Stephan, John J., 'On the Soviet–Japanese historiographical frontier', *Siberica*, Winter, 1990–1, Vol. 1, No. 2, Portland, OR: North Pacific Studies Center of the Oregon Historical Society.

—— 'Asia in the Soviet conception', in Donald S. Zagoria, ed., *Soviet Policy in East Asia*, New Haven, CT: Yale University Press, 1982.

—— 'Historical perspective', in M.J. Valencia, ed., *The Russian Far East and the North Pacific Region: Emerging issues in international relations, selected papers from a conference held at East–West Center*, Honolulu, HI: 1992.

Suetsugu, Ichirō, 'Gorbachofu no rainichi o oete', *Go daitoryo rainichi to kongo no nisso kankei*, Tokyo: Shinju-kai, 1991.

Sugihara, Takamine, 'Kokusaihō kara mita hoppō ryōldo' in Hiroshi Kimura, ed., *Hoppō ryōdo o kangaeru*, Sapporo: Hokkaido Shimbun-sha, 1981.

Suzuki, Keisuke, *Nisso keizai kyoryoku*, Tokyo: Nihon kokusai mondai kenkyū-jo, 1974.

Takano, Yūichi, 'Hoppō ryōdo no hōri', in Kokusai hōgaku – kai, ed., *Hoppō ryōdo no chii – chishima karafuto o meguru shomondai*, Tokyo: Nanpō dohō engo kai, 1962.

Tanaka, Takahiko, 'Nisso Kokkō kaifuku kōshō (1955–56) to Shigemitsu gaikō', *Kokusai seiji*, vol. 99, March 1992.

Tawara, Sōichirō, 'Amerika no tora no o o funda Tanaka Kakuei', Tokyo: *Chūōkōron*, July 1976.

Ueda, Satoru, 'Jo ni kaete', *Hoppō ryōdo-shi shiryō-hen*, Tokyo: SBB shuppan-kai, 1991.

Wada, Haruki, 'Hoppō ryōdo mondai o saikō suru', *Sekai*, February 1992.

—— 'Rekishi no hansei to Keizai no ronri', *Gendai nihon shakai*, 7. Kokusai-ka, Tokyo daigaku shuppan-kai, 1992.

—— 'Chishima rettō no han'i ni tsuite', *Sekai*, May 1986.

Zagorsky, Alexei V., 'Naze hoppō yontō henkan o shijisuru noka – nisso kankei seijō-ka saitan no michi,' *Sekai Shūhō*, 20 November, 1990.

Zhao, John Quansheng, 'Informal pluralism and Japanese politics: Sino-Japanese rapprochement revisited', *Journal of Northeast Asian Studies*, Vol. VIII, No. 2, Summer 1989.

—— 'Formation of Japanese Foreign Economic Policy,' in *Chugoku Kenkyū [China Studies]*, Tokyo: Institute of China Studies, February 1988; also in Ezra Vogel, ed., *Modern Japanese Organization and Decision Making*, Berkeley, CA: University of California Press, 1975.

## Newspapers and periodicals

*Asahi Jānaru*
*Asahi Nenkan*

*Asahi Shimbun*
*Asian Financial Review*
*Asian Survey*
*Bungei Shunjū*
*Chūōkōron*
*Ekonomisuto*
*Far Eastern Afairs*
*Far Eastern Economic Review*
*Foreign Affairs*
*Foreign Broadcast Information Service (FBIS): USSR Daily Report*
*International Organization*
*Izvestia*
*The Japan Times*
*Journal of Asian Studies*
*Journal of Northeast Asian Studies*
*Kyoto Shimbun*
*Literaturnaya Gazeta*
*Mainichi Shimbun*
*The Military Balance*
*Moscow News*
*New York Times*
*Nihon Keizai Shimbun*
*Ogonyok*
*Pacific Affairs*
*Pacific Review*
*Pravda*
*Sankei Shimbun*
*Sekai*
*Sekai Shūhō*
*Soren Kenkyū*
*The Times*
*Washington Post*
*World Politics*
*Yomiuri Nenkan*
*Yomiuri Shimbun*

## Government documents: archive sources

### *Australia*

Australian Archives (ACT), Department of External Affairs [II], Central Office, 1947–1970: CA 18.

**USA**

Records of the US Department of State (Central Files: 1955–1959) in the custody of the National Archives of the United States, Washington DC.

**UK**

Great Britain, Archives of Her Majesty's Foreign Office, Public Record Office, Kew, London.

## Government documents: printed sources

*Australia*

Department of External Affairs, *Treaty of Peace with Japan*, Australian Treaty Series, Canberra, 1952.
—— *Current Notes on International Affairs, Vol. 26*, Canberra, 1955, onwards.

*Japan*

Bōeichō (Ministry of Defense), *Bōei Nenkan (Defense Almanac)* 1956.
—— *Bōei Hakusho (White Paper of Defense)*: 1978 onwards.
Foreign Office, Japanese Government, *Minor Islands Adjacent to Japan Proper: Part 1. The Kurile Islands, the Habomais and Shikotan*, November 1946 (Australian Archives (ACT): A1838/2:515/4).
—— Gaimushō, (Ministry of Foreign Affairs) *Gaikō Seisho: Waga gaikō no kinkyō*, 1958–1991.
—— *Gaikō Seisho: yori anzen de ningentekina sekai o motomete* (1), 1993.
Gaimushō daijinkanbō kokunai kōhō-ka, *Warera no hoppō ryōdo*, 1989, 1993.
—— *Japan's Northern Territories*, 1987, 1992, 1996.
—— *Severnie Territorii Yaponii*, 1992.
—— *Japan–Soviet Relations: Current State and Future Prospects – Experts from interviews with Japanese prime ministers published in the Soviet press*, 1991
Kokkai (Diet), *Sangiin kaigi-roku*, 1955 onwards.
—— *Shūgiin kaigi-roku*, 1955 onwards.
—— *Sangiin Gaimuiinkai giroku*, 1955 onwards.
—— *Shūgiin Gaimuiinkai giroku*, 1955 onwards.
Kokuritsu kokkai toshokan chōsa rippō kō-kyoku (National Diet Library), (prepared by Makoto Tanaka, Seji gikai-ka), 'Naikaku seitō shijiritsu no suii – shōwa 21-nen ikō' *Chōsa to jōhō – Issue Brief Number 180 (31 March 1992)*.
—— 'Hoppō ryōdo mondai no keii (dai 3-pan)' (prepared by Takashi Tsukamoto, Gaikō bōei-ka), *Chōsa to jōhō – Issue Brief Number 227* (28 September 1993).
MITI (Ministry of International Trade and Industry), Sengo Nihon no bōeki nijūnen shi, Tokyo, 1967, pp. 442–3.
—— *Tsushō Hakusho-kakuron*, 1958–1993.

### Japan and Russia

Ministry of Foreign Affairs of Japan, Ministry of Foreign Affairs of the Russian Federation, *Nichiro-kan ryōdo mondai no rekishi ni kansuru kyōdo sakusei shiryō-shū, Sovmestnii sbornik dokumentov po istorii territorial'nogo razmezhevaniya mezhdu Rossiei i Yaponiei, (Joint Compendium of Documents on the History of the Territorial Demarcation Between Russia and Japan*, as translated by the Strengthening Democratic Institutions Project), 1992.

### United Nations

Department for Economic and Social Information and Policy Analysis, Statistics Division, *International Trade Statistics Yearbook, Volume 1, Trade by Country 1995*, United Nation, 1996.
*United Nations, Treaty Series: Treaties and international agreements registered or filed and recorded with the Secretariat of the United Nations*, No. 3768, Vol. 263, 1957.

### USSR

Ministerstvo Inostrannikh Del (MID) SSSR, (Ministry of Foreign Affairs), *Perepiska predsedatelia Soveta ministrov SSSR s prezidentami SShA i prem'er-ministrami Velikobritanii vo vremia Velikoi Otechestvennoi voiny 1941–1945 gg.*, Moskva, tom 2, 1957.

### USA

US Department of State, *Foreign Relations of the United States, Washington D.C.: The Conference at Cairo and Teheran 1943*, 1961; *The Conference of Berlin (Potsdam) 1945*, 1960; *The British Commonwealth and The Far East 1945*, 1969; *Asia and the Pacific 1951*, 1977; *Vol. XXIII, Part I – Japan 1955–57*, 1991.
—— *Occupation of Japan: Policy and Progress*, Publication 267/Far Eastern Series 17.
Committee Print/Printed for the use of the Committee on Foreign Affaris, 83rd Congress 1st Session, *Second World War International Agreements and Understandings: Entered into during secret conferences concerning other peoples*, March 12 1953.

## Other printed sources by interest groups

### Japan

Anzen hoshō mondai kenkyū-kai, *Anzen hoshō mondai kenkyū-kai ni tsuite*, 1989.
Hoppō ryōdo mondai taisaku kyōkai (Northern Territories Issue Association), *Japan's Northern Territories*, 1974.
—— *Hoppō ryōdo mondai taisaku kyōkai no gaiyō*.
Nampō Dōhō Engo-kai, *Hoppō ryōdo mondai shiryō-shu*, 1966.
National Movements Liaison Council for Demanding Return of the Northern Territories, *Why there is no peace treaty between Japan and the Soviet Union*, 1987.

Nichiro yūkō giin renmei jimukyoku, *Nichiro gi sokuhō*, No. 52, 1994.8.
Nihon keizai kyōiku sentā, *Watashitachi no hoppō ryōdo*, 1990.
Shinju-kai, *Nisso hatsu no shunō kaidan, eritsin daitōryō no rainichi to sono sōkatsu*, Shinju-kai series No. 21, 1993.

## Internet sources

'Press Conference by the Press Secretary November 14, 1997', The Ministry of Foreign Affairs of Japan,
http://www2.nttca.com:8010/infomofa/press/1997/11/1117.html.
'Saikin no nichiro kankei', The Ministry of Foreign Affairs of Japan, 1997,
http://www.mofa.go.jp/mofaj/gaiko/gaikos/russia97/Kankei.html.

# Index

Note: Page numbers in bold type refer to figures; page numbers in italic type refer to tables.